COLERIDGE'S CAREER

Coleridge's Career

Graham Davidson

St. Martin's Press   New York

First published in the United States of America in 1990

Printed in Hong Kong

Library of Congress Cataloging-in-Publication Data

Davidson, Graham, 1947–
Coleridge's Career/ Graham Davidson
p. cm.
Bibliography: p.
ISBN 0–312–03683–3
1. Coleridge, Samuel Taylor, 1772–1834—Criticism and
interpretation. I. Title.
PR4484.D38. 1990
821'. 7—dc20   89–10714
                              CIP

Contents

Preface

Dicaeopolis:
   Well, the very Spartans even, I've my doubts and scruples whether
They've been totally to blame, in ev'ry instance, altogether.
Chorus:
   Not to blame in every instance! Villain, vagabond, how dare ye
Talk treason to our faces, to suppose that we should spare ye.
Dicaeopolis:
   Not so totally to blame; and I would show that, here and there,
The treatment they received from us has not been absolutely fair.
Chorus:
   What a scandal! What an insult! what an outrage on the state!
Are ye come to plead before us as the Spartan's advocate?
   The Archanians, Aristophanes, trans. J. Hookham Frere.

Very rarely can one say that a 'hunger-bitten and idea-less philosophy'[1] has led directly to the loss of human life. But the attempt of our current 'jargon of materialism'[2] to interpret a word that represents a feature of our humanity was, in 1982, the main cause of just such a catastrophe. Freedom is a word which speaks to us of a quality we cannot separate from our conception of what makes us human. But nonetheless, because freedom is only a word, it may be used, at worst, to exculpate those passions which degrade our humanity, or, at best, to begin that process by which we realize what is at first only potential in us. The word itself, detached from modes of thought and codes of conduct, has no power and no significance: consequently, there is nothing more dangerous than a passionate prejudice, hardly conscious of what it is, masquerading under the cloak of a right principle; than a blind, but deeply-seated energy, which proclaims its origin and its justification in a word of which none can doubt the propriety. And this danger is not one from which those who have made the distinction between

viii

principle and prejudice can safely stand aloof and declaim in other people, but a natural tendency never quite defeated in any one of us, and which only bold, honest and vigorous thought can control.

When the Commons gathered on Saturday morning, 3 April 1982, 'the first Saturday session of Parliament since Suez',[3] it was the absolute want of this kind of thought that made that day one of the saddest in recent British political history. That the Prime Minister and those of like mind sought no other language than the jargon of materialism with which to discuss the crisis, either then or later, was, however regrettable, no more than to be expected. And I suppose it was not much less inevitable that the Conservatives of Christian persuasion, who interpret their religion by means of their politics, and not their politics by means of their religion, showed no signs of tempering their hopes of righteous revenge with conciliatory diplomatic moves. [Hansard VI 21 643.] From those two corners not 'state-policy, only state-craft',[4] not self-effacing principle, but the rash reactions of hurt pride and bruised prejudice was all that could be expected. But where was the tradition of thought that Coleridge found in 'spiritual platonic old England',[5] and which implied a method of approaching political problems that he did much to develop? Was there no-one in our Parliament who felt themselves the heir to this tradition?

When Michael Foot rose, many people in this country hoped to hear a tempering of the tabloid belligerence of the Government benches with a strongly worded realization that the countering of force with force was likely to lead to the loss of many human lives. And upon this ground we expected a plea that the Government would respond to the Argentinian provocation with all the diplomatic skill of a mature democracy dealing with an unsteady, dangerous and irrational regime. The first principle of ordinary human as well as sensible diplomatic behaviour must be to treat other people's claims with the respect they themselves ask for them, however little we feel they are justified. The Government's failure to act according to this principle, coupled with an apparent lowering of its defence profile in the South Atlantic, were factors that had contributed to the Argentinian invasion. But Mr Foot did not speak after this fashion. He did not suggest how the Government might now act in the light of principles they had earlier ignored. In so far as he proposed any course of action, his remarks fell absolutely in line with the fiercest calls for revenge from the opposing benches. He described the invasion as 'an act of naked, unqualified aggression, carried out in the most shameful and disreputable circumstances' and asserted that any 'guarantee from this invading force is utterly worthless',[6] thus forgetting that first and foremost the invasion was a *national* movement, and only secondly a piece of political manipulation; the remark also inferred that any diplomatic negotiations were pointless – with the inevitable corollary that force would provide the only satisfactory solution. And at the end of his speech he provoked the Commons along the path they were too ready to take by saying, 'The Government must now prove by deeds – they will never be able to do it by words – that they are not responsible for the betrayal [of the Islanders' right to protection] and cannot be faced with that charge', and confirmed his position with the comment that 'there is the longer-term interest to ensure that foul and brutal aggression does not succeed in our world'.[7]

This was not the speech of a 'peace-monger', but of a man who had lost his way, who had lost sight of the guiding principles that might have informed his politics, the speech of a man who had no real answer to those willing to confuse and conflate terms such as 'freedom', 'sovereignty' and 'possession', who had no power to rise above the cries of 'defeatism' and 'appeasement' that greeted the sensible speeches of Raymond Whitney and George Foulkes, no power to force the House to think about the real meanings and consequences of the emotive words it used with such vicarious relish. And I put Michael Foot's failure down to his choice of heroes, to his allegiance to the English empiricists, to men as various as John Locke, Thomas Paine, and Bertrand Russell, to the tradition which has usurped the platonic old England of Spenser, Sidney, Shakespeare, Donne, Milton, Taylor and Hampden; and finally Mr Foot's failure is specifically attributable to his celebration of Hazlitt in contrast to Coleridge.

Coleridge and Hazlitt had much in common. They were probably the two contemporary minds best fitted to understand each other, the two minds most at ease with the metaphysics that so many Englishmen even then scoffed at. Coleridge was the only man Hazlitt had ever met who corresponded to his idea of genius. Coleridge and Wordsworth opened up to him a world he never thought to know, and in his later, bitter, years he regarded Coleridge as a kind of lost saviour, inveighing against the apparent obscurity of his writings whilst, at the same time begging him to 'Shake off the heavy honey-dew of thy soul' and 'shake the pillared rotteness of the world!'[8] But in fact Coleridge never did give up the struggle to understand the 'rotteness of the world' and to provide a remedy. Hazlitt mocked *The Statesman's Manual* without apparently ever having read it, but it is a profound attempt to define the corruption of English thought and the resulting effect on English politics. Coleridge saw 'rotteness' as the responsibility of individuals to comprehend and extirpate from themselves, and only by this process – which would inevitably lead to different kinds of political action – could the rotteness of the state be removed. Hazlitt, I suspect, believed that radical political action was what was required, and that individual morality had no significant part to play. Coleridge struggled most of his adult life to overcome the infirmities of his will, but Hazlitt seems rather to have indulged his, and to have made little effort to come to terms with his fellow men. In an unpublished notebook Coleridge wrote his private obituary of Hazlitt:

> Beneath this stone doth William Hazlitt lie,
> Thankless for all that God or Man could give,
> He lived like one who never thought to die,
> He died like one who dared not hope to live.

However alike of mind the two men may have been, they are utterly unlike in the quality of their lives. And when one chooses heroes, one chooses the life as well as the work. Coleridge's work may be difficult to assimilate (though not as difficult as many imagine), but his refusal to turn aside from what he believed to be the truths of human life, his undying hope, his final humility and gladness in ordinary human relations, his constant intellectual development, all give us reason to believe that there is a substance in his work. Hazlitt, I think, had no such grandeur or graciousness of spirit in him, and therefore he does not dignify the minds who lend him their allegiance. What finally attracts Michael Foot to him is not an undying intellectual quest, a subsumption of the person in the truth, but an endless animosity which sacrifices the person to personality – 'It was not that he had become complacent or withdrawn from the battle. He was still in the thick of it, giving blow for blow, whenever the opportunity occured.[9] This pugnacious energy, coupled to a belief that radical policies are the basis of good government, is the ground of Mr Foot's admiration of Hazlitt. For Coleridge the basis of good government is good governors, and this goodness is based on profound thought, compared to which personal qualities are ephemeral. Coleridge quoted Berkeley in *The Friend* to the effect that *'whatever the world may opine, he who hath not much meditated upon God, the Human Mind, and the Summum Bonum, may possibly make a thriving Earth-worm, but will most indubitably make a blundering Patriot and a sorry statesman'*.[10] That Saturday morning it was Hazlitt's pugnacity that went to inform Mr Foot's speech, all such truths as he may have found in the work of those personalities about whom he writes so anecdotally and so well, forgotten, unheeded, buried in the welter of personal presence.

To propose a course of action which may lead directly to the loss of human life is an awful responsibility. 'Freedom', 'self-determination', 'sovereignty', 'British territory' and 'British possessions' were words, their significance taken too much for granted, then acting like adrenalin in the veins of most of the Members. It is easy enough for those sitting on the Commons benches, or in the Cabinet room, or us sitting at home, to proclaim a simple principle such as 'no act of aggression must be allowed to succeed', or 'the Islanders' allegiance to the Crown means that their rights must be defended', and so to precipitate those events which will end in our giving human lives away. That kind of thoughtless, superficially high-minded and right-principled action is easy enough for those who will not go out to fight: but it is the duty of all people contemplating such a series of events, or even using the words which will permit those events, to ensure that the words they use are at one with their substance. Do the words which we have so easily used to send men out to die, seem such a sound justification and consolation when we contemplate our own extinction?

That you can persuade men to die fighting for a word is no great marvel – the vigorous current of popular feeling during a clash with another nation, the rhetorical repetition of emotional phrases, the chance to put their training to the test, these combined are a potent force in the minds and hearts of young, energetic men who have chosen a military career. But what when the war or the battle is over, and for perhaps the first time in their lives, those still living meet their own mortality in the deaths of their friends and comrades, their husbands, brothers, sons and uncles? What when we must face that sudden, shocking and absolute absence of those whom we had presumed would be always with us, who were part of our consciousness, without whom the sun hardly shines, and all the joy we had believed to be in life, and may have in some measure found, is suddenly taken away, and every previous pleasure makes the heart ache, and we feel nothing but a sickness at the very source of our being? Then ask the veterans, as now indeed they are, whether the euphoria which waved them away from the docks returns to comfort them in their distress, whether, with the hindsight of experience, they would go to that war again for the unconsidered word which originally sent them out.

A nation ill-at-ease with the hiatus between belief and experience exerts a tacit censorship over discomforting evidence: the relatives of those who died may have found some comfort in the belief 'that the cause was worthy, and denial of the value of the cause seems a denial of the worth of the sacrifice so many made. If it is hard to accept someone's death, it is harder still to accept that they died in a cause of questionable value, and it is out of courtesy to the bereaved that few are willing to assert the futility of that particular war. But some reports indicate that many men came home profoundly disturbed, not comforted and not convinced by the rightness of the war, finding it hard to re-establish themselves in the habits and interests which had once been the substance of their lives. The veil of permanence with which we shroud our lives had for many been blown away, and they were in search of something more substantial.

But, and this is the second string of the tragedy, what have we to offer them? Nothing but the fallacious platitudes of a society dedicated to 'the getting and spending' by which 'we lay waste our lives', a society whose leaders, inculcating this ethos on the one hand, have the impudence to inveigh against the moral decline of the nation on the other – as if their very proclamations were not both cause and evidence of the sickness we suffer. 'Put money in your purse', they cry, epitomising their willingness to betray our humanity, and equating that *ingnis fatuus*, the standard of living, with life, *human* life. And there is nothing wrong with making money, they add, as if some kraken in the depths of their conscience stirred for a moment, and they had to quell what they could not understand. What, nothing wrong in every adult member of society dedicating their intellect, their time, their hopes and even their emotions to what thus becomes an ultimate end, nothing other than the whole purpose of our lives, and which dominates the minds, hearts and imaginations even of our children? Nothing wrong with making an end of what, at very best, is only a means; but which considered as an end, obscures and darkens the real goodness of our humanity? Nothing wrong with all this? Anyone who says so, tells a lie. Having met with death, those who came back from the Falklands, and the friends and relatives of those who did not, were to be comforted with this, a handful of dust, the bitten apple turned to ashes, by a people bent on proving that Mammon and God are one. Yet subsumed in the real name of God are such truths as may comfort those who have seen the reality of their lives taken away. These are truths difficult to propound, however, and our dedication to the engendering of wealth stops up the faculties that are required to make them an active part of our lives. And the silence of the Church in countering the lies of the State, its failure to find a language which will make these truths live, a language appropriate to the experience of those who have seen the futility of much of what the State advocates, is a silence and a failure which goes hard with those who think that the Church may still be the prime guardian of human values.

But wrong as it is to misuse the words which send men out to war, for it is to ask them to die for no good cause, it is equally wrong to cast these words aside because their misuse has made them appear empty and meaningless. There are conditions in which a nation need have no reservation about sending men out to fight in the knowledge that a proportion of them will die. In essence, those conditions arise when the survival of the nation is threatened, or the principles by which it maintains its nationhood are under attack, and without which we would cease to be what we are. This permits us both to defend ourselves and those nations founded upon similar principles. And the principles upon which a nation is founded are closely related to the principles which constitute our humanity. If we die defending right principles rightly interpreted, we die in defence of our own humanity, and in some measure such an act is the fulfillment of our being. If someone dies in attempting to rescue others from a burning house, or a capsized ship, or from any other equally dangerous situation, we believe that they have died in the exercise of their specifically human nature, often overcoming the powerful instinct of self-preservation in order to carry out the task. The willingness to put our life at risk in order to save the life of another is one of the marks of our humanity.

Because, as Coleridge puts it, our being is defined within 'the hedge-girdle of the state',[11] it is likewise a mark of our humanity that we are willing to die for our country. But it is no longer an entirely voluntary decision made at the moment of crisis; the act is now circumscribed by a duty incurred when joining those services designed to defend the country. And it is the reciprocal duty of the country to ensure that it does not ask men to die unless either the nation or the principles that constitute its foundation are under threat. And so the question is, Was the nation, or were its founding principles, under attack, when the Argentinians invaded the Falkland Islands? The cry that went up in the Commons inferred that the loss of liberty suffered by the islanders (incarceration on the one hand, and subjection to a government not of their choice on the other) struck directly at the idea of freedom enshrined in our national constitution. Therefore, the tacit argument ran, it is right that we should send men out to regain this lost freedom; and because it is an attack upon one of the principles that constitute our national life, it is right, if need be, to ask those men to lay down their lives.

But there are presumptions in this argument which ultimately invalidate it. Firstly it is presumed that the material freedom of the individual is at one with, and the final purpose of, the existence of the nation. The nation thus conceived is no more than the numerical sum of individuals claiming and receiving citizenship, and so is conflated with what might properly be called the State. Coleridge constantly reminds us, in his essay *On the Constitution of the Church and State*, that such a conception of a nation is profoundly mistaken (logically, if not actually, such an entity can have no *history*, for at every birth and death it will become a different thing); and nothing called forth his scorn more than the confusion of the nation with 'that multitudinous Sand Desart of Selves – the People'. [N.53 f.16; CS 19.] He believes rather that a nation only ever exists as an idea, but as an idea beheld by all, and working in all, it is able to unite the past with the present, the dead with the living, making a vast variety of individuals and societies dispersed through time into one entity. As an idea, the nation is independent, at any given moment, of the composition of the State. It is a free and original energy, equivalent to the conscience in the individual, by which the State should seek to regulate its domestic and foreign policies, just as the individual seeks to govern his own thought and conduct by reference to his conscience. And to say that the nation is an

idea is not to say that it has no temporal or local forms: the most
obvious corollary of nationhood is geographical location, a country
in which the idea develops in a way peculiar to that nation. But
again, it is an error to conflate the idea with the country, or even
the countryside, as we all do at times. Hebraic history should
remind us that it is perfectly possible for a nation, during some
part of its life, to exist independently of a particular location.

Secondly, it is presumed, in conjunction with the notion of
sovereignty, that the individual's material freedom is an absolute
freedom – that is, any incursion into the territory where he exercises this freedom, or a limitation upon his freedom by an alien
government within that territory, is regarded as an incursion into
the body of the nation itself. But this is a closed and circular
argument: having determined what the nation is by reference to
the individual, the individual's rights then become the arbiters of
national freedom. The main consequence of such an argument is
that the defence of the nation may be invoked when actually at
stake are only the material rights and freedoms of a few people.
Such rights never have been and never can be synonymous with
the life of the nation: they are benefits relative to it, and the
degree to which they can be exercised depends upon the political
circumstances of the State. But to equate the defence of the nation
with the defence of material freedoms is, in Coleridge's language,
a fearful hysteron proteron, a frightening inversion of values,
which will have tragic consequences.

All agree that to be asked to lay down one's life in defence of
one's nation is a just request, particularly of those who have
committed themselves to serving in the armed forces. But if this
request is in fact made only to ensure the right of certain people
to follow a way of life in a certain place, the complete abolition of
which will involve neither loss of human life nor threat to the
nation (considered as the place where the idea has been chiefly
fostered), then those who lay down their lives in defence of that
right have made an irreversible and absolute sacrifice for a good
which is only minor, temporary and relative. They have died not
so that a few can continue in the life of the nation (which as an
idea once established may be beheld by those outside the fostering
country); no, they have died so that these few can continue in
nothing more than a way of life, constituted from the circumstances which first brought British people to the Falklands, and
without which particular means to subsistence the inhabitants can

survive, and survive as British people, with little more upheaval than most of us endure in moving house or changing jobs. The confusion of way of life with national life is simply another example of the false thinking that arises from identifying a nation with that 'Sand Desart of Selves – the People.' And to consider the Falklanders as a separate *people* is merely to compound the error of assigning sovereignty to the people with the error of equating material and economic separation with a cultural difference. To use an analogy more accurate than our blundering patriots and sorry statesmen will ever admit, the current jargon of materialism has so reduced our humanity that, evicting squatters from our garden shed, we would believe it right for the police to risk their lives.

And this approach to life (too indisciplined to be called thinking, or a philosophy) raises what Coleridge called 'the vile Phantom of Absolute Property' [N.55 f5], or the conflation of the nation with the territory under its control. That it is right that the country where the idea of the nation is undergoing its particular development should be defended by force of arms, no-one, least of all Coleridge, disagrees. But that every piece of land over which the country exercises control should be defended on the same basis is to forget that the nation is essentially an idea, and therefore may be distinguished from the place in which the idea is developed. One place once established for the purpose of the growth and incorporation of the idea, all other places related to the life of this nation are secondary and only of relative importance. But if the nation is regarded as including all these secondary lands then clearly an attack upon any one of them becomes an attack upon the nation. It was evident in 1982 that the Argentinians intended to possess the land, not remove or destroy the people, but so confused is our understanding of the term 'nation' that leading Parliamentarians shamelessly made British possessions a synonym of the nation. Thus Edward Du Cann made several statements which illustrate this dehumanizing state of mind, and which are at the same time infringements of common sense: 'The rule should surely be that the defence of our realm begins wherever British people are' [Op.cit.642.] A perfect example of the confusion of the nation with the people on the one hand, and sheer non-sense on the other: consider all those ex-patriots living in Argentina itself, and in every other part of the world. When the state properly seeks to protect their rights, it is not engaged in a defence of the realm, but merely upholding the human rights of those of its citizens who have chosen to live under the discipline of another government – and who of course are not necessarily less British for doing so. Not much further on in his speech Du Cann said, '. . . let us declare and resolve that our duty is now to repossess our possessions and to rescue our own people. Our right to the Falkland Isles is undoubted. Our sovereignty is unimpeachable'. The first sentence puts possessions before and equates them with people: Coleridge's 'sacred distinction' between persons and things, 'upon which all State-wisdom depends' is clearly entirely foreign to Du Cann's mind. The last two sentences beg the question that all admit is valid – to what extent may we reasonably call the Falkland Isles 'ours'? And his last and final statement is equally foolish: 'We have nothing to lose now, except our honour' [Op.cit.643.] No, nothing, except an unforeseeable number of human lives, many of which will be British.

There is probably only one absolute freedom, and that is the freedom of conscience. And from this freedom the individual can be alienated only by his own will. Thus even facing a lifetime's unjust imprisonment, or confronting immediate death, the conscience still has the power of distinguishing good from evil, God from no god, faith and dignity from doubt and despair, and so to choose the one and not the other. All other freedoms are relative, and depend upon the political, social and economic circumstances firstly of the state and secondly of the individual within that state. Our right to life is relative to the life of the nation, for it is through the existence of the nation that we come to know both to what ends our humanity may be directed, and how we may contribute to its development. But if the right to life is not the absolute right of a citizen, it is *only* not absolute in respect of the life of the nation: only if national life seems to be at risk has the state the right to ask its citizens to lay down their lives. Thus when we are discussing a form of freedom, it is essential that we ask, Relative to what other freedoms are we proposing to inhibit or enable this freedom? We must then make sure that if we intend to sacrifice one freedom to another, that the freedom sacrificed is of a lower order than that for which the sacrifice is to be made. The Argentinians didn't even appear to want to dispossess the inhabitants of the land, nor to prevent them from making a living on it. And it is utter nonsense to suppose that transferring the title of the land also transposes the nationality of those who own it or work it, as if the very earth were conscious of, and could confer, a distinct nationality upon its inhabitants: does an Englishman become a Frenchman by farming in France? Remaining British is an act of the individual will, not a condition imposed by the title of the land. The tragedy of the Falklands conflict was that a higher good, human life, was sacrificed for a lower good, the right to call a piece of land 'ours'.

However, had that land seen the origin and been the centre of national life, then the argument would have been reversed, and the sacrifice of individual lives would have been for a higher good, the continuance of that life into which all lives are finally subsumed. As it is, persons were sacrificed to things, people to possessions, a perversion of the proper order, masked by the term 'sovereignty'. That in respect of the nation, not even the people are sovereign, Coleridge reminds us:

> What, Talleyrand! between Legitimacy, the deformity and Brute Idolon of a Truth, and the Sovereignty of the People, the frightful Falsehood, is there no Third? No *Principle*? Is all else Faction? God forbid!'

In the stead of Talleyrand's 'scheme of Despair', Coleridge places the first four verses of St John's Gospel, upon which he comments,

> This living and personal Being of the Co-eternal Son of God, that he is the Truth, and that Truth *is* in him . . . the submission of every individual Will to which is the condition of all Salvation . . . this the alone rightful *Sovereignty*, of which all Kings, Presidents, Legislatures are but the Shrines and Symbols – this, I say, is the Answer. [N.50, f.19v]

If the ultimate end of our lives is to submit our will to that of God, a process which the existence of the nation enables, then we should remember that this is not achieved in abstraction from our daily lives; it is done among our family and our friends – and though we may rarely see the process at work in each other, we often feel when it is going right and when it is going wrong; and much of our happiness depends on knowing that all is well with those whom we love. The Falklands campaign is a painful scar in the body of the nation, for by allowing the blundering patriots in our Parliament to interpret right principles by the jargon of materialism, we have condemned to death, to permanent disability or to life-long bereavement, thousands of people who can now no longer work out the business of their lives in the company and through the power of those whom they love. To all those people, I cannot offer this book as a thing of comfort, but only as a reminder that Coleridge inherited and re-invigorated a tradition of thought which, had it been integrated into our system of education, might have enabled us to prevent a tragedy which has been presented as a triumph.

Debts of Gratitude

The writing of a book may be a solitary occupation, but finding sufficient time, free from service to the god Pecunia, or enslavement to the fiend-hag Anxiety, depends upon the good offices of many people: my parents first and foremost, who have supported an aging son in all the ways that most parents would have gladly resigned years ago – and all the while (and it has been a long while) suspending their disbelief as they saw the chance of my having a career fade the more I propounded that of Coleridge.

And then all those who have encouraged me in the task and further enabled my existence: my sister Fiona and her husband Robert, from whom I received my one and only grant, and who had me tying up raspberry canes in the frost – though not quite till midnight; Jamie and Catriona Mill, who first introduced me to such skills as may yet enable me to earn my living, and were most generous to their apprentice during hours as well as after hours; Alan and Jenny Privett, who took on the job of completing this training, doing so with equal generosity, but reversing the work ethic from 'get it right' to 'get it done'. My uncle Ted, the only other member of the family with an active interest in poetry, and famed for his 'edition' of *Samson Agonistes* – running to no more than ten pages; my aunt Natalie, whose allegiance is to Spinoza, but who makes a never-failing annuity to Coleridge studies; Jonathan Coram and his wife Anne (1941–85), who first housed me when I moved to Bristol; and his mother, Mrs Anne Coram, who provided me with a flat in which I lived very comfortably for longer than I have ever lived anywhere else.

My intellectual debts are, of course, chiefly to those scholars upon whose work I have drawn, often wittingly, sometimes unwittingly, and whose contributions I have in part acknowledged in the notes and bibliography. But these do not tell the whole story. For instance, Stephen Prickett's work hardly features in my text, but his two books on Coleridge, particularly *Religion and Romanti-*

cism, gave me the impetus to begin the task of reading through Coleridge's work for myself (and to the novice, the sheer mass of material, the apparent impossibility of distinguishing the important from the unimportant, and the seeming lack of order and arrangement in it all, makes that a daunting prospect). Therefore my gratitude to his work, and to many others unmentioned, is much greater than a reading of this book will reveal.

I refer to John Beer's scholarship throughout my discussion of the poetry, often, though not only, quoting his work to highlight a difference of opinion. However, my interpretation of the poems probably depends on matters of fact and pieces of interpretation silently purloined from his large store of learning. For this I owe him my apologies, as well as my thanks. But also as the first publisher's reader of this work, he looked sufficiently kindly upon it to give it further life. After two other readings and some revisions, Frances Arnold (then of Macmillan's), keeping faith with her original judgement, asked John Beer to give a final adjudication. This entailed his third time of going through the typescript – even so he was meticulous in his reading and positive in his opinion. Were it not for John Beer, therefore, it is unlikely that the book would have been published: that is a debt which I gratefully record, but which I doubt that I can repay.

And there will, I hope, be debts of the future – the gratitude I may yet feel for those people who find in Coleridge the kind of person and the kind of greatness that has fostered my research. One such is Anya Taylor, whose *Coleridge's Defense of the Human* I came across too late to incorporate into this book, but who sees the idea of person as central to his thinking.

And lastly there are two people without whom my life, and its endeavours, would seem so much dust: my sister Lindsay (1948–86), whom I cannot distinguish from the idea of life; and my wife, Perdita, the only person I have ever met to whom no thought of mine is entirely strange, and who would prefer that we should live in perfect poverty than that I should give up the pursuit of literature.

Abbreviations

AR	*Aids to Reflection* (Bohn's Standard Library, unless otherwise indicated)
AP	*Anima Poetae*
BL	*Biographia Literaria*, ed, J. Shawcross
BLC	*Biographia Literaria*, ed. James Engell and W. Jackson Bate
BM	The British Museum
CC	*The Collected Works of Samuel Taylor Coleridge*, general eds Kathleen Coburn and Bart Winer
CL	*Collected Letters of Samuel Taylor Coleridge*, ed. E. L. Griggs
CN	*The Notebooks of Samuel Taylor Coleridge*, ed. Kathleen Coburn
CPI	*Coleridge's Poetic Intelligence*, John Beer
CPT	*Coleridge and the Pantheist Tradition*, Thomas McFarland
CS	*On the Constitution of the Church and State*
C.Vis	*Coleridge the Visionary*, John Beer
EOT	*Essays on His Times*
F	*The Friend*
FQ	*The Faerie Queene*, Edmund Spenser
HH	*Coleridge: The Clark Lectures 1951–52*, Humphrey House
HCR	*The Diary of Henry Crabb Robinson*
JEGP	*Journal of English and Germanic Philology*
IS	*Inquiring Spirit*
LL	*Lectures 1808–1819: on Literature*
LPR	*Lectures 1795: on Politics and Religion*
LR	*The Literary Remains of Samuel Taylor Coleridge*
LS	*Lay Sermons*
MC	*Miscellaneous Criticism*
N	Unpublished Notebooks of S. T. Coleridge
Op.M.	The 'Opus Magnum' mss.
PL	*The Philosophical Lectures of Samuel Taylor Coleridge*
PMLA	*Publications of the Modern Language Association*

PW	*The Complete Poetical Works of Samuel Taylor Coleridge*, ed. E. H. Coleridge
PWC	*The Poetical Works of Samuel Taylor Coleridge*, ed. J. D. Campbell
RFR	*Romanticism and the Forms of Ruin*, Thomas McFarland
RX	*The Road to Xanadu*, J. L. Lowes
SC	*Coleridge's Shakespeare Criticism* (Raysor by vol. and page; Ashe by page)
SM	*The Statesman's Manual* in *Lay Sermons*
Shedd	*The Complete Works of Samuel Taylor Coleridge*, ed. W. G. T. Shedd
TL	The *Theory of Life*, ed. Seth B. Watson
TT	*Table Talk and Omniana*
VCL	Victoria College Library, Toronto
WPW	*The Poetical Works of William Wordsworth*

Coleridge was one of those unhappy persons . . . of whom one might say, that if they had not been poets, they might have made something of their lives, might even have had a career . . .

T. S. Eliot, *The Use of Poetry and the Use of Criticism*, 1933

Introduction

There are two things that this book is not. It is not an analysis of Coleridge's work in the light of one particular intellectual discipline: therefore it is a study of Coleridge not as literary critic, nor as theologian, nor as philosopher, nor as historian, nor as a political or a social thinker. Chameleon-like, he put on the colours of all these in the course of his career, but his contribution to English life and thought cannot be defined within any one of these terms. I have begun with one presumption, one hostage to intellectual fortune, which nonetheless I take to be a matter of faith first and then experience to those who write on Coleridge – that his work is in principle an entity with a developing vision and life of its own, that his poetic, critical, philosophical, political, and theological writings are related as parts to a whole. Coleridge's powers of synthesis did not cease with his production of poetry, and his originality lies more in synthesizing a whole out of established parts, less in his particular contributions to the disciplines he employed. So this book is an attempt at construction, not deconstruction. But the pitfalls of choosing a method at odds with accepted practice are obvious, and I can only hope I have avoided tumbling into the deepest and the darkest.

And just as it is the development of this body of work that is the focus of my interest, and not Coleridge's contribution to, or conformation with, distinct forms of intellectual practice, so this book is not a description of Coleridge's return to Christian orthodoxy. He *always* proclaimed himself a Christian, and it is as foolish to pretend that Christianity has no positive influence on his development as it is to suppose that it alone provides a method of interpreting his canon. But Christian orthodoxy is a tag too often used to dismiss those aspects of Coleridge's thought that modern readers either believe they understand, or think of as dull and irrelevant. And it is sometimes coupled to a charge of Coleridge collapsing through a drug-induced fatigue into a snug intel-

1

lectual cocoon. Nothing could be farther from the truth: that Coleridge sought the metaphysical significance of the major Christian
doctrines is a matter of fact, but what is interesting about his
theology is that it always seeks a ground in human experience,
and never presumes that a doctrine is a self-sufficient statement
of an *a priori* truth. He sees doctrine as representing living powers
in the form of real ideas, as a description of our humanity, and
therefore as a method of enlivening rather than fossilizing the
intellect. There were no truths, however revered, that Coleridge
allowed to lie bed-ridden in the dormitory of his soul.

It is harder to say what this book is, than what it is not. Uppermost in my mind was the integrity of Coleridge's achievement –
that far from being, say, a poet who lost his muse in metaphysics,
or a Christian platonist who took refuge in orthodoxy, he was a
man struggling to unite the various forms of thought into one
living and life-giving whole. I began with the conviction that Coleridge's mature thinking had its origins in a poetic method distinct
from and opposed to that of Wordsworth. In the latter's best
poetry we remain happily uncertain of the relative priority of
nature and the mind, but in his description of the bland and
unconvincing redemptive processes undergone, say, by Peter Bell
and the Solitary, he revealed that he was content to think that
nature was more acting than acted upon, that the mind was more
easily conceived as a thing made than a thing making. I believe
that Coleridge, in his poems of the supernatural, did quite the
opposite: beginning with the truths of our inward nature, those
truths not subject to time and place, he sought to create a sensible
world, permitting the reader to see that the mind orders the senses
and not the senses the mind.

However, throughout their lives Wordsworth and Coleridge
shared the belief that the laws or principles of nature are at one
with the ideas that constitute our humanity. But as the investigation of nature developed quickly in the century, the distinction
between the appearances and the laws of nature became more and
more significant. This distinction hardly worried Wordsworth at
all, for from his youth his heart had been intimately bound up in
certain great *appearances* of nature, and to these he clung as to the
raft of his inspiration. But Coleridge became increasingly frustrated
by the difficulty of discerning how the laws of nature are co-
ordinate with the truths or ideas of mind; and though he never
abandoned a belief from which arose some of his most remarkable

meditations on the relations between the two, I believe he tacitly ceased to hope that he could demonstrate that nature was an object of knowledge adequate to his conception of our humanity. From the 'wily old Witch', he turned to the more pliable muse of History, and there, especially in his study of Hebraic history, found an object which, with considerable refinement, was able to express his complex understanding of the subject, the humanity of man. His study of Vico, who denied the knowabilty of Nature and asserted that of History, may well have assisted him to achieve more in this field than he laid claim to, and much more than anyone else has since attributed to him.

To chart the progress of this development was my original intention. But what soon attracted my attention was Coleridge's frequent assertions as only being conscious of himself in his relations with and love of other people: these occur with the greatest frequency in the notebooks of the Malta period, when he was separated from the Wordsworths, Sara Hutchinson and his children. It seemed to me that as Coleridge approached nature in his mature thinking, beginning with the idea and seeking to arrive at sense, so he found that the substance of an individual lay not in their presence, but in their inward and invisible being. By contrast, Wordsworth rarely conceived of people in separation from what he was able to observe of them and their situation; it is no accident that the characters of Wordsworth's contributions to the *Lyrical Ballads* are largely 'taken from life', and that those of Coleridge originate as figures of his imagination: his sense of a person was often most sure when they were absent from him, when he was able to distinguish their inward nature from their outward appearance.

With these thoughts in mind, I turned back to the poetry again, for up to this point I had mostly been concerned with making a distinction between those poems in which Coleridge seems to think of nature as mind-making, and others in which it seems predominantly mind-made; and of course what I found was that almost all his poetry is filled with expressions of his need for and love of other people. In those poems in which he seemed to believe that nature was mind-making, such expressions are in contrast or in conflict with the actions of nature, and the twin motions of Coleridge's heart and mind at first appear irreconcilable. But his willingness to put another person at the centre of experience, and always a person more or less ideally conceived and deeply loved, provide a method of reconciliation. In this conventional analysis of Coleridge's poetry, I have attempted a methodological distinction between the Conversation and the Supernatural poems, a distinction which I believe is resolved in 'Kubla Khan' and 'Dejection.' These chapters are therefore both a schematic rehearsal of the current understanding of Coleridge's poetry, and a laying of the foundations for his intellectual development.

My purpose then became to show how Coleridge's development of the idea of a person enabled him to find in history rather than nature the adequate and correlative object. Although his supernatural poems offer some evidence that he was willing to conceive of the reality of human nature as independent of time and space, there is less evidence that this tenet had ever been tempered in the fire of personal experience. However, during the long and crucial period from about 1801 to 1814, this became the dominant theme of his thought. His love for Sara Hutchinson was then his greatest reality, and because he considered his marriage indissoluble, he struggled to see how Asra, as he coded her name in his notebooks, could exist for him and be loved by him in separation from the forms of temporal and corporal experience. Out of this heroic if not always glorious struggle, Coleridge emerged profoundly conscious of the inter-relations of love, human consciousness and personal immortality – aware, one might say, that the ground of all human life had its ineffable and unalterable existence in God alone. It is the achievements of these years that I regard as crucial to Coleridge's career, and it is the idea of person that I believe provides the unifying force in Coleridge's intellectual development.

Coleridge sought explanation of and expression for his private experience within the tradition of Christianity. Because he refused to dissociate his experience from his belief, he sought to re-think, re-explain and render properly metaphysical doctrines which had become petrified in the material language of Paley and the mechanists. To follow this aspect of Coleridge's development is the business of Chapter 6. The presence of God in us Coleridge called Reason, but it exists for us as God exists, a matter of faith and not of fact, and is therefore dependent upon an act of will. The possibility of experience depends upon the Understanding, which provides the forms by which we order the sensations derived from phenomena. This faculty may of course exist independently of Reason, as it does in most of us most of the time, but because the

Reason would speak of that which is not of time and space, which is invisible and incorporeal, it is dependent upon the Understanding for its expression. Because Reason is the groundwork of our distinct humanity, and the Understanding the basis of our being in time, their conjunction or union will create a person – and this incarnational relationship was, Coleridge thought, uniquely perfected in Christ.

It is our duty to our humanity to effect this union of Reason and Understanding within ourselves, for only in this way is the person fully realized. The power that enables this union Coleridge categorized as the imagination, which has its basis in an act of will. In its primary form this power neither begins with sense-presented material nor produces an object for the senses: what it does produce is an object for the mind, or a series of objects expressed as symbols which are part and parcel of the ideas that constitute our humanity. It is through this primary act of the imagination that we find our proper and divinely human being.

One significant aspect of these symbols is that not only are they the life of the 'infant Christ' in our souls, but that they also represent the progress of his unique and historical life; that is they have an 'outness', and therefore where we find life, we do not find it in abstraction from experience, but as its foundation. The function of the secondary imagination is to reconcile the revealed life within us with the world we find without us, a reconciliation which, *prima facie*, is more easily realized in respect of history than of nature.

It may seem an anomaly to outline the structure of the primary and secondary imaginations without first considering the source of that famous distinction and definition. I have done so because I believe that, philosophically, the *Biographia* is an aberration in Coleridge's thinking. It seems to me that every form of personal mediation which, first appearing in the Supernatural poems, had become central to his thinking, is abandoned, and nature made a direct or primary object, when it has only ever been an indirect or secondary object – the primary object having always been a *person* in the form of constitutive ideas. This has consequences in his criticism, and I try to trace them, but my main reservation about this work does not concern its value as literary criticism: it is the belief that not only did Coleridge, unable to draw on his most intimate and 'forbidden' experiences, put himself off his

proper thought, but he also succeeded in putting off nearly all his
subsequent commentators.

The last two chapters deal with the 'outness' of a person in
what might be called vertical and horizontal ways respectively.
We arrive at the idea of a person through the union of Reason
and Understanding. Coleridge thought of history as a gradual
process in which the Hebraic and Hellenic cultures came together
in the person of Jesus Christ, subsequently enabling the evolution
of Christianity. The Hebrews held to their Reason in the form of
a living and personal God, and the stages of their history were
stages in the revelation of his being, and stages through which
every subsequent and faithful Israelite lived. If the Hebrews
matured their Reason by maintaining the idea of a living God free
of the images of sense, the Greeks matured their Understanding
by reflection on the forms of sense, but in the light of the higher
power. Just as in the individual the union of Reason and the
Understanding by means of the imagination creates the living and
personal ideas of our humanity, so historically Christianity came
into being because of the providential union of Hebraic and Hellenic culture under the aegis of the Roman Empire.

It was Coleridge's belief that the two major institutions of a
nation, the Church and the State, bear a relationship between
them which is an analogy of the constitution of the individual. And
just as the humanity of an individual will decay if he abandons the
dictates of his conscience, his Reason activated by his will, so a
nation will decay if its leaders permit the State to usurp the functions of the Church, or if the Church embodies no higher principles than those which may be deduced from the Understanding.
The ultimate being of a nation is founded in the idea of a person,
of whom it is the symbol.

I hope that this brief outline of what I conceive to be my progress
and Coleridge's career will serve as a map – to which reference
may be made if it appears that one or other of us has lost our
way.

Part I
Two Kinds Of Poetry

We . . . seem to be driven to an unscientific distinction between the feelings aroused in the poet by external objects or events, and the feelings that arise spontaneously from his own musings, from self-communion and meditation. [Herbert Read, 'Two Kinds of Poetry', p. 38]

Coleridge contains within himself two poets, and only one of them has been properly recognized. [Graham Hough, *Selected Essays*, p. 83]

1
The Poetry of Nature

When Wordsworth and Coleridge, accompanied by Dorothy, set out for the Valley of Stones late one November afternoon in 1797, they were already well-acquainted with one another's idea of poetry. Having been neighbours since July of that year, they had visited each other daily and enjoyed 'the most unreserved intercourse'.[1] Their conversations, Coleridge records, 'had turned frequently on the two cardinal points of poetry, the power of exciting the sympathies of the reader by a faithful adherence to the truth of nature, and the power of giving the interest of novelty by the modifying colours of the imagination'. [BLC II 5.] Coleridge is seeking to illustrate this process more precisely when he suggests that these two 'cardinal points' might be co-ordinated in one image: 'The sudden charm, which accidents of light and shade, which moon-light or sun-set diffused over a known and familiar landscape, appeared to represent the practicability of combining both'. In this analogy, the 'accidents of light and shade' signify the imagination at work, 'modifying' the familiar landscape – which is not only, of course, natural scenery, but also objects or events present to the senses – Westminster Bridge at dawn, a beggar on Cumberland roads, a girl reaping by herself in the Highlands. Yet the model Coleridge has devised is almost a symbol, not only for Wordsworth's contribution to the *Lyrical Ballads*, but also for his mature poetry, as we may see if we turn for a moment to the climax of *The Prelude* – the ascent of Snowdon. Although this was Wordsworth's first time on the mountain, he treats it with the familiarity accorded to known and unconsidered things: the landscape has no significance for him until, stepping above the clouds into the clear moonlight, he looks down and sees the mountain-tops made islands by an ocean of mist; then under the influence of these 'accidents of light and shade', his heart breaks free from 'commerce with his private thoughts,' and reflecting on this experience years later he finds in the remembered details 'The perfect

image of a mighty mind'. Just as before this sight and others of
its kind, lesser minds 'cannot chuse but feel', so it is an image

> a genuine counterpart
> And brother of the glorious faculty
> Which higher minds bear with them as their own.
> This is the very spirit in which they deal
> With all the objects of the universe:
> They from their native selves can send abroad
> Like transformation . . . [1805 XII 88–94]

In this belief of the power of the imagination to 'send abroad',
to transform a landscape which, through our own 'selfish solicitude', has lost the power to excite us, we can see the consistency
of Wordsworth's best poetry with ideal aims he and Coleridge had
shared in 1797: in the description of his experience on Snowdon,
Wordsworth has both remained faithful to the appearances of
nature, and at the same time, by use of imaginative powers exactly
analogous to the accidents of light and shade he found up there,
has transformed these appearances into what was for him an
image of the way in which, at best, the human mind works.
'These', added Coleridge, referring to his two cardinal points as
unified in the imagination-transformed landscape, 'are the poetry
of nature' [BLC II 5].

And writing of 1798 in 1815, Coleridge thought of the poetry of
nature as the foundation of the *Lyrical Ballads*.[2] Though indeed
there were to be two kinds of ballads, the natural and the supernatural, the authors of both were to observe these two cardinal
points in the manner outlined in the model.[3] At the time so close
a correspondence did these two derivatives seem to have with
their original, that Coleridge cannot remember whether he or
Wordsworth suggested this distinction. And in his development of
these two forms, Coleridge continues to adduce parallels between
them. Thus the poetry of the natural was to be made of subjects
'chosen from ordinary life: the characters were to be such, as will
be found in every village and its vicinity, where there is a meditative and feeling mind to seek after them, or to notice them, when
they present themselves' [BL II 6]. The 'landscapes' of these poems
are events and incidents in the lives of ordinary people, rescued
from the flood of time by the poet's 'meditative and feeling' mind
– the moonlight or sunset casting shadows of wonder and strange-

ness upon whatever it is impressed by. The supernatural was to deal not with ordinary people, but with 'persons and characters supernatural, or at least romantic', who were to be acted on by 'incidents and agents . . . in part, at least, supernatural'. It is worth noting that Coleridge uses the word 'supernatural' both of the characters and of the incidents which are to act upon them – and of both without complete conviction. It seems that his use of the word is ambivalent: it refers both to cause and effect, to the incident or event, and to the specifically human emotion it revives or renews in the character. Whatever doubt Coleridge had as to whether the focus of a supernatural poem is the extraordinary incident, or the character created in the light of such pressures – and in different degrees both 'The Ancient Mariner' and 'Christabel' bear evidence of this dual pressure – seems resolved in favour of the character by two other passages: 'And the excellence aimed at was to consist in the interesting of the affections by the dramatic truth of such emotions, as would naturally accompany such situations supposing them real. And real in *this* sense they have been to every human being who, from whatever source of delusion, has at any time believed himself under supernatural agency'. The world in which the character moves may be a delusion, but the effect it has on him or her is real enough, and it is the effect on the character's humanity that it is the poet's task to convey. But in attempting this he is not granted the freedom to make of man whatever he chooses: that it is his duty to disclose truths we may all recognize as belonging to our humanity is brought out firmly in the well-known passage a few lines later: the writer of supernatural poems was 'to transfer from our inward nature a human interest and a semblance of truth sufficient to procure for these shadows of imagination that willing suspension of disbelief for the moment, which constitutes poetic faith' [BLC II 5]. The character created may be supernatural or romantic, but, no meaningless marvel, he or she is rather the bearer of our humanity. If this was to be the drive of Coleridge's contribution, Wordsworth's ran in harness with it: for his poems would aim 'to give the charm of novelty to things of everyday, and to excite a feeling analogous to the supernatural, by awakening the mind's attention from the lethargy of custom and directing it to the loveliness and the wonders of the world before us' [BLC II 7]. This act, 'by which ordinary things should appear presented to the mind in an unusual aspect', and which appears less likely to involve ideas of our humanity, was in fact another method of achieving the same end, for Wordsworth intended 'to make these incidents and situations interesting by tracing in them . . . the primary laws of our nature'.[4]

Ideally, therefore, both types of poetry inspire the reader with a sense 'Of something far more deeply interfused', of worlds not his, yet alive within him. John Beer has pointed out that in 1815 Coleridge identified supernature with 'natura naturans' – 'which it is the poet's task to imitate. In this view the supernatural was not separate from the natural, but the inner essence of it' [C.Vis.143]. We may conclude that the poetry of nature is theoretically inseparable from experience of the supernatural, and is to be identified with the groundwork of our humanity.

Although Coleridge and Wordsworth agreed to write upon the 'supernatural' and the 'natural' respectively, there are good reasons why we should not think that these categories enable us to identify distinct proclivities in the two men. Of Coleridge's contribution to the *Lyrical Ballads*, only 'The Ancient Mariner' is assuredly a supernatural poem. 'The Dungeon' and the 'Foster-Mother's Tale', both taken from his tragedy, *Osorio*, describe two different effects that 'nature's lore' may have upon the individual. In 'The Nightingale' the poet attempts to break up habitual association in the effort to re-awaken feeling, according to the method prescribed for the 'natural' poems. On the other hand, the emotions most often found in conjunction with the supernatural – the consequences of sin and a striving for some kind of release – were quite as significant for Wordsworth at the time as they were for Coleridge.[5] Wordsworth's *The Borderers* has a theme – one suffering man forcing another to perform acts comparable to those which caused that suffering, in order to create a bond of understanding between them – similar to the joint production of 'The Three Graves'; and both are comparable to that true incident that went to form 'Goody Blake and Harry Gill', poems in the 'natural' category. Nor is such a theme irrelevant to the relationship that develops between the ancient Mariner and the Wedding Guest.[6] If then a distinction is to be made between the poetry of the natural and the supernatural, it is found reflected neither in the discrete interests of the two men, nor in the different ends of their planned contributions – for all were designed to bring the reader to awareness of the supernatural and so to the truths of human nature. Nonetheless, the method by which Coleridge distinguished between natural and supernatural – chiefly as to whether the characters were taken from ordinary or extraordinary life – hardly supplies us with sufficient criteria to describe the differences between the two types of poetry which were actually produced – the differences evident, say, between 'The Ancient Mariner' and 'Peter Bell'. But I believe that we will find adequate grounds for these differences if we attempt to discern the different methods of composition that each poet employed as a consequence of selecting one or other of the two kinds of character with which to begin.

Wordsworth's subjects, whether taken from the everyday life of human beings, or from the appearances of nature, are always observed, always taken from sense impression immediate or remembered; these images are clearly distinguished from the mind of the observer, and it is the relationship between these two that constitutes the life of the poem.[7] The object or image has its life renewed by the stimulated imagination of the observer: at its highest, of course, these two entities are seen to participate in one common life, as Wordsworth felt on Snowdon. To the degree that the mind is excited by what it sees, to that degree it enters into a relation with the external world, and it lives in the world, and the world in it. If the observed is merely scenic nature, then we may say that it is possible for the mind to be the life of nature, and for nature to give substance to the forms of the mind. But clearly, as far as human beings go, they have an inward life distinct from that of the observer, whatever he may feel as a result of witnessing aspects of their outward lives. Because of Wordsworth's method of composition, little sense of this independent and invisible exist-ence is permitted. This is a deficiency that modern editors of the *Lyrical Ballads* have noted: 'His *personae* are never allowed a dra-matic life of their own and exist only in so far as they represent their creator's point of vision'.[8] And Brett and Jones go on to point out that the one poem where this does not hold true, 'The Thorn', 'fails at just those points . . . where the persona threatens to take on an independent dramatic existence'. And characters in other poems of the same kind – such as the mother of the idiot boy – raise doubts in our minds concerning their dramatic propriety that never even occur, let alone call upon the willing suspension of our disbelief, during a reading of 'The Ancient Mariner' of 'Christabel'. Human beings are but a special kind of object to Wordsworth. Although the scenes of human lives may affect different parts of his intellectual and emotional constitution, yet they are all imported into his poems by the same process.

Is this the process employed by Coleridge in the composition of his supernatural poems? There are reasons to think not: firstly, because these romantic or supernatural characters do not have an actual existence in the immediate world, are, indeed no more than 'shadows of the imagination', they cannot be observed in the same way as Wordsworth observed his characters. They cannot impress the receptive mind with definite sensations. Even after their creation, the Mariner or Christabel do not evoke one easily characterized emotional response, as do Simon Lee or the tearful shepherd in 'The Last of the Flock'; much less did they do so while they were still shadows in the author's mind. Because the characters of the supernatural have no original existence in a world external to us, they have no distinct and independent form for the imagination to convert into something rich and strange. Secondly, as a consequence of this vagueness of form, these shadows somehow have to be made substantial in order to be made credible; Coleridge sought to achieve this by transferring 'from our inward nature a human interest . . .' This statement presumes pre-existing self-knowledge of some kind, originating from a source other than the object contemplated: this is not a feature of Coleridge's declared model and the method of 'natural' poetry – which begins with sensation.

Coleridge began with no specific impression, no localized and limited set of circumstances, no distinct emotion to be evoked, but with vague figures, and one or two essential actions often fortuitously hit upon; and in order to realize his characters had to invest them not with emotions their formal being had inspired in him, but rather with emotions and ideas that originated within himself, yet which he would suppose had arisen in the character as a result of the circumstances in which they had been placed. The result is that the character thus created does not appear to be merely observed, but rather to live according to the laws of his inward nature, and, paradoxically, to act independently of his creator. Wordsworth observes the outward, Coleridge describes the inward life of human beings. Kathleen Coburn, comparing 'Peter Bell' with 'The Ancient Mariner' does so with this distinction in mind:

It is clear that however much Wordsworth *explains* and

describes the fear and guilt elements in his Potter's behaviour, and he does so at length, with some 'anxiety of explanation', his is a poem of behaviour – acts – events on the little rapid river Swale. Coleridge's is, without explanation, a poem of the inner life . . . The one is a poem of imagination, the other, at best, a thing of 'fixities and definites', a poem of the fancy. In poems like 'Peter Bell', Wordsworth has his eye on the object, is the spectator *ab extra* as Coleridge described him.[9]

But if we are tempted to condemn 'Peter Bell' outright, we risk condemning too the assumptions behind much of Wordsworth's best poetry: for the forces which he describes as operating on Peter Bell as he attempts to steal the ass are very similar generally to those which he describes as nature exerting on himself throughout *The Prelude*, and might be specifically compared to the occasion when he 'stole' a boat for a midnight row. Wordsworth too easily assumes that what worked for himself in relation to nature will enable him to create living characters; but Peter Bell and other of his personae have no inwardness, no life they can call their own. The Mariner and Christabel, coming into existence as a transference from Coleridge's inner nature, appear to move freely, uncertain of the end to which they are impelled, because unfettered by the kind of puppet strings that tie Peter Bell to his maker's intellect.[10]

The fundamental distinction between Wordsworth's 'natural' method and Coleridge's 'supernatural' method may then be that of observation and meditation which Coleridge makes on several occasions in his lectures on Shakespeare.[11] In Chapter XVIII of the *Biographia*, having previously scotched Wordsworth's theory that he has imitated the language of men in low and rustic life, Coleridge implicitly criticises Wordsworth's assertion of the primacy of sense impression as evident in the following and typical statement of the older poet: 'The powers requisite for the production of poetry are: first those of Observation and Description – i.e. the ability to observe with accuracy things as they are in themselves . . .' [WPW 954] Coleridge asks:

By what *rule* . . . is the [poet] to distinguish between the language suitable to *suppressed*, and the language which is characteristic of *indulged*, anger? Or between that of rage and jealousy?. Is it obtained by wandering about in search of angry or jealous people in uncultivated society, in order to copy their words? Or not far rather by the power of imagination proceeding upon the *all in each* of human nature? By *meditation*, rather than by *observation?* And by the latter only in consequence of the former?' [BLC II 82–83][12]

Although the difference between the two poets might at first seem only one of degree – concerning the relative primacy of sense impression and imaginative organization – we soon see, that for Coleridge at least, it has become an absolute matter: observation is only of value in so far as it is grounded in a preceding meditation which reflects on our essential humanity, and does not begin in sense.

Coleridge's account of the genesis of the *Lyrical Ballads* indicates that he thought poems natural and supernatural were but two species of one genus – the poetry of nature. I have attempted to show that in practice there is reason to doubt this, and that 'The Ancient Mariner' is different in kind both from his other contributions, and from those of Wordsworth. In each kind of poetry the imagination is employed in a different way: the basis of 'natural' poetry is sense impression, and the poet attempts to elevate that impression into a truth of mind; the basis of supernatural poetry is the truth of our inward nature, and the poet attempts to render these external by describing credible human emotions in what may be a very fanciful and wholly invented world: instead of the given world stimulating the imagination to the perception or re-perception of the laws of human nature, these are presumed, undefined perhaps, but nonetheless pre-established, and the poet invents a relationship between circumstance and emotion which may incorporate these laws: our belief in the emotion is only sustained, our incredulity of the physical and possibly delusory circumstances only suspended, while these two entities are seen to co-operate in embodying the truths of our human nature.

But what further complicates the issue is the fact that one facet of Coleridge's early creativity was not in the least at odds with the model for the poetry of nature he had constructed. Although there is a prima facie case for regarding 'The Ancient Mariner' and 'Christabel' as composed by a method for which the model is not adequate, yet many of his early poems may be seen as an attempt to describe the direct interaction of nature, of the sense-perceived world, with the imagination. Coleridge, even before he met him, was no stranger to Wordsworth's hope that nature, by stimulating the imagination to irradiate the object with the peculiar glow of our humanity, would thereby reveal the essential humanity in us all. In the next two chapters it is my intention to probe the apparent discontinuity between that kind of poetry which originates in some distinctly felt impression from the sensible world, and that which begins in a conception or a plan, and seeks to invest the bare bones with credible human life. This is not, as we have seen, to deal with a simple distinction between natural and supernatural, for both types of poetry claim to be concerned with the fundamental laws of human nature, and both are designed to excite a sense of the spiritual in the reader. It is rather to understand how two modes of composition were derived from, and tended to, opposing conceptions of the relation of the mind to an external world.

2
The Conversation Poems

And he, with many feelings, many thoughts,
Made up a meditative joy, and found
Religious meanings in the forms of Nature! [PW I 257]

RELIGIOUS MEANINGS AND THE UNITY OF LIFE

When Descartes asserted the utter distinction of mind and matter, he determined the mould of philosophical thought upon which the Romantic effort turned; as David Pym has said: 'In part the Romantic revolt against the 18th Century was against the dualistic outlook induced by the tradition of Descartes which set up an unbridgeable chasm between God and man, mind and matter, subject and object'.[1] The division granted, there seem but two possible ways of recovering the union: to show that mind has the properties of matter, or that matter has the properties of mind. And in this way we may largely distinguish the philosophical efforts of Descartes' successors. For Coleridge, the various modes of these two kinds of thinking were subsumed in the separate philosophies of two men: Benedict Spinoza and Immanuel Kant. In 1810 he wrote in a notebook:

> Only two systems of Philosophy – (sibi consistentia) possible 1. Spinoza 2. Kant, i.e. the absolute and the relative, the [according to what really exists] and the [according to man], or 1 the ontoso-phical, 2 the anthropological. [CN III 3756][2]

Coleridge's admiration for both men was profound, but by 1812 his preference was decided. Crabb Robinson records that although Coleridge declared that Spinoza was a gospel to him, he added, 'his philosophy is nevertheless false. Spinoza's system has been demonstrated to be false, but only by that philosophy which has

demonstrated the falsehood of all other philosophies. Did philosophy commence with an *it is*, instead of an *I am*, Spinoza would
be altogether true'.[3] It is upon what he believes in fact to be an
unresolved division of attraction to these two systems, the objective and the subjective, beginning with the material world and the
perceiving mind respectively, that Thomas McFarland has based
the principal argument of his book, *Coleridge and the Pantheist Tradition*. He believes that it is Coleridge's peculiar tragedy to recognize the attractions of each kind of philosophy, but to be unable to
reconcile them. We see that a reconciliation will be very hard to
effect because the weakness of one system is the strength of the
other: those philosophies beginning from the 'it is' position, (and
giving rise to 'natural' poetry) will tend to merge the distinct
qualities of the human mind, that which gives us our essential
humanity, with the material universe; and those beginning from
the 'I am' (and giving rise to supernatural poetry) will tend to
deny the independent reality of the external world. It was, McFarland thinks, Coleridge's grandeur to have both a hugely developed
sense of outer reality and an equally well developed sense of inner
reality, and to let neither dominate the other: the result – a tragedy
typifying the epistemological lot of the twentieth century.[4] In later
life Coleridge recorded these early struggles:

> In youth and early Manhood the Mind and Nature are, as it
> were, two rival Artists, both potent Magicians, and engaged,
> like the King's Daughter and the rebel Genie in the Arabian
> Nights' Entertainments, in sharp conflict of conjuration – each
> having for its object to turn the other into a Canvas to paint on,
> Clay to mould or Cabinet to contain. [CL V 496][5]

And though Coleridge was to act otherwise, at the time of
the *Lyrical Ballads* both poets believed that the object, whether
landscape or human event, must first impress the mind for there
to be a going forth of the imagination; the organization of the
material world precedes our realization of how our intellectual or
spiritual nature is ordered; and this theory Wordsworth had found
the practical truth of in his moonlit ascent of Snowdon.[6]
Between 1795 and 1798 Coleridge wrote a number of poems in
which the objects of immediate sense or experience are largely
responsible for each work's final form, and which are known
collectively as the Conversation Poems.[7] These works – 'The Eolian

Harp', 'Reflections on Having Left a Place of Retirement', This Lime-Tree Bower my Prison', 'Frost at Midnight' and 'The Nightingale' – have become an established group in critical discussion of Coleridge's poetry: in my study I shall also include 'Pity', the lines supposedly written while ascending Brockley Coomb, 'Fears in Solitude' and Passages from 'Religious Musings' and 'The Destiny of Nations'.[8] Except for the last two all these poems originate in a specific time and place, as their titles often indicate, and depend upon events and objects occurring independently of any imaginative organization by the poet. But his imagination is stimulated by these various objects and he seeks to discover a unity in what is at first the mere collocation of discrete phenomena.[9]

To find the ground upon which all things may be united, to know how the many may also be the one, was perhaps the dominant quest of Coleridge's career and, as he wrote later, marks the appearance of Reason in man.[10] Coleridge specifically associates this quest with Spinoza, and thus with that mode of philosophy which he calls absolute, and which deals with the concrete and visible world that the imagination seeks to transform into an image, first of itself, and finally of God. That where Coleridge finds a sense of unity in diverse phenomena, he also senses the presence of the divine spirit will become increasingly evident as we study the poems in detail. But it is an additional reason for our believing the influence Spinoza had on his thinking at this time: for though it was with disapproval that he later noted in Crabb Robinson's copy the philosopher's mistake of beginning with God as an object, rather than an act,[11] it is not difficult to imagine what an immense effect the adamantine chain of logic would have had on a young mind unhindered by objections to this premise, on a mind that had devised a model of poetry in which the concrete and immediately beheld is the proper object of the imagination, and which sought to behold all things partaking of one, divine, life. [Cf. TT 23 July 1827].

How is the desire to find a unity in immediate sense perception represented in these early poems? Mostly, by a catalogue of the actual impressions that the poet has received, and often given in the order, or the apparent order, that he felt them. So in his lines on Brockley Coomb, the description follows the pattern of the ascent:

>   With many a pause and oft reverted eye
>   I climb the coomb's ascent: sweet songsters near

Warble in shade their wild-wood melody:
Far off the unvarying Cuckoo soothes my ear.
. . . .
Where broad smooth stones jut out in mossy seats
I rest: and now have gain'd the topmost site.
Ah! what a luxury of landscape meets
My gaze . . . [PW I 94]

The description is rich and delightful, but the question that arises
is whether the reader is either able to discern from these lines the
emotion infused in the collected images, or a unity of idea. Is
anything conveyed by or in these lines that unifies the separate
perceptions? Do we know what to think or to feel as a result of
their collocation? Only in the last two lines does the poet let us
into the feeling arising in him as he rests on the hill-top:

> Deep sighs my lonely heart: I drop the tear:
> Enchanting spot! O were my Sara here!

These act as a kind of counterpoint to the loveliness of the foregoing images, for without them the poem would have no discernible
significance. But this emotion, this longing for someone else with
whom to share his delight, is not one necessarily arising out of
the preceding lines: as we ascend, following Coleridge's description, we are in no way made ready for this conclusion; even with
the benefit of hindsight we can find nothing in the lines that looks
forward to that state of mind. Though I hope to show later that
this longing is characteristic of Coleridge's experience of natural
beauty, here it is a feeling arising from nothing we can discern in
the lines themselves. Once we are aware of that emotion the lines
have their place, but are not infused with a secondary or deeper
significance. Brockley Coomb, we might think, was in no sense
Coleridge's Snowdon, for nature has not wrought the mind into
an idea of herself, nor revealed the essential unity of the poet's
separate perceptions.

The difficulty of revealing the idea in the image is further apparent in 'The Eolian Harp'. The first ten lines are a paradisaical
description, but Coleridge comes very close to performing the trick
for which he condemned Bowles' second volume of poems – that
of being unable to look upon the forms of nature without moraliz-

ing them, so proving the poet's faintness of impression.[12] Thus he writes

>   most soothing sweet it is
> To sit beside our Cot, our Cot o'ergrown
> With white-flower'd Jasmin, and the broad-leav'd Myrtle
> (Meet emblems they of Innocence and Love!)
> And watch the clouds, that late were rich with light,
> Slow saddening round, and mark the star of eve
> Serenely brilliant, (Such should Wisdom be)
> Shine opposite! [PW I 100][13]

These remnants of eighteenth century personification may not seem a very serious intrusion into the picture that Coleridge is drawing for us. But they testify to the more profound difficulty of giving particular significance to the selected images or details of the scene. Coleridge seems to have been aware that their presence was not entirely fitting: Paul Magnuson has pointed out that the 'parenthetical figuration of jasmin and myrtle bothered Coleridge. He left it out of the 1802 text and reinserted it later in 1817. It conspires with the emblem of the evening star to transform the natural landscape into a literary backdrop'.[14] If the reader is, however, entranced by the opening 12 lines, the peacefulness of which is summed up in the line and a half, 'The stilly murmur of the distant Sea/Tells us of silence,' then the subsequent lines return him to a rush of varied sensation, and the direction they are taking is not apparent; a first-time reader might well be excused for wondering, by line 25, what the poet is trying to convey. It is not explicit in anything that those 25 lines contain.[15] His purpose is of course declared in the subsequent passage, which asserts the existence of 'the one Life within us and abroad', in the 1828 and subsequent texts; but in 1803 Coleridge omitted lines 21–33, testifying to his uncertainty about the imagery of elfins and fairy-land, and the text then read:

> Such a soft floating witchery of sound –
> Methinks, it should have been impossible
> Not to love all things in a World like this,
> Where e'en the Breezes, and the simple Air,
> Possess the power and Spirit of Melody!
>   [PW I 101; Cf. N.37 f.28ᵛ]

The philosophy of the later text is more distinct, but the earlier is substantially the same in intention.[16] The method by which Coleridge hopes to help the reader to a realization of the harmony of all life is comparable to that by which he sought to give significance to the myrtle, jasmin and evening star of the first ten lines – by providing a commentary on the text. This is a perfectly acceptable method, if the commentary illuminates the passage with a life hidden within it – if, in contrast to Bowles' sonnets, the revealed life is integral with the apparent or natural life. Having read the 'one life' lines, do we find that there is a significance breathed into the first part of the poem previously unavailable to us? Do we suddenly see order, and thus unity, where we saw mere aggregation?[17] Not in my opinion: the parts remain parts, gaining no further significance in relation to each other, as a result of the poet's commentary, which itself lacks any distinct idea. By comparison we might take the opening section of 'The Dry Salvages', which is ostensibly the description of a river:

> – sullen, untamed and intractable,
> Patient to some degree, at first recognized as a frontier;
> Useful, untrustworthy, as a conveyor of commerce;
> Then only a problem confronting the builder of bridges.
> The problem once solved, the brown god is almost forgotten
> By the dwellers in cities – ever, however, implacable
> Keeping his seasons and rages, destroyer, reminder
> Of what men choose to forget.[18]

And this description of the common function of rivers, we enjoy for its own sake, as we take an aesthetic pleasure in Coleridge's description. A transition passage follows in which Eliot hints at his deeper meaning, but the lines immediately afterwards begin with a simple statement of his conception:

> The river is within us, the sea is all about us.

Suddenly we realize that what we had taken largely as description, Eliot's imagination has subtly ordered so as to reveal his idea of how our spiritual lives progress. In this union of the appearance of nature with the truths of mind, we glimpse the possibility of their unity, of one order informing both what goes on within us,

and without us, in the external world. The river has taken on the
status of a symbol.

   Why is Coleridge unable to achieve this – the kind of unity he
asserts? In part, because of his receptivity to all the impressions
of nature and forms of thought, coupled with his belief that in his
own passivity he would find a harmony uniting them. He is in a
mood that Keats declared the most fitting for the creation of poetry
(and a mood he thought Coleridge did not know)[19] – when the
brain is not irritably searching after fact and reason. Thus Coleridge compares his condition to that of the lute in the breeze:

> . . . on the midway slope
> Of yonder hill I stretch my limbs at noon,
> Whilst through my half clos'd eye-lids I behold
> The sunbeams dance, like diamonds, on the main,
> And tranquil muse upon tranquility;
> Full many a thought uncall'd and undetain'd,
> And many idle flitting phantasies,
> Traverse my indolent and passive brain,
> As wild and various as the random gales
> That swell and flutter on this subject Lute! [PW I 101–2]

In his tranquility, Coleridge makes no effort to re-order his images
in the light of a distinct emotion or idea. The implicit argument is
that if all life is one Life, then all its forms should be seen to
participate in that Life, and from any given form the substantiating
idea will emerge. And this mood of 'wise passiveness'[20] is one
which we may discover in various forms in all the Conversation
poems: the mind of the poet is the Harp played upon by the wind
of sensation, producing what Coleridge hopes will be a heavenly
harmony. Thus in 'Reflections . . .' he compares the achieving of
happiness with listening to a lark:

> Oft with patient ear
> Long-listening to the viewless sky-lark's note
> (Viewless, or happly for a moment seen
> Gleaming on sunny wings) in whisper'd tones
> I've said to my Belovéd, "Such, sweet Girl!
> The inobtrusive song of Happiness,
> Unearthly minstrelsy! then only heard
> When the Soul seeks to hear; when all is hush'd
> And the Heart listens!" [PW I 106–7]

The passiveness required to hear the song of happiness is evident in the verbs and adjectives Coleridge uses: 'patient', 'long-listening', 'whisper'd'. 'inobtrusive', 'hush'd' and 'listens'. Not many lines later he makes it clear that any positive activity of the heart, any attempt to impress hopes, desires, attitudes, or ideas on the world would have been an interruption of this happiness:

No *wish* profan'd my overwhelméd heart.
Blest hour! It was a luxury, – to be![21]

Again, passive attention to the sky-lark while stretched out on the heather is the recipe in 'Fears in Solitude' by which a young man, having escaped from his youthful follies, might create within himself 'a meditative joy':

Here he might lie on fern or withered heath,
While from the singing lark (that sings unseen
The minstrelsy that solitude loves best)
And from the sun, and from the breezy air,
Sweet influences trembled o'er his frame:
And he, with many feelings, many thoughts,
Made up a meditative joy, and found
Religious meanings in the forms of Nature. [PW I 257]

The joy is to arise from the images and sensations of nature activating the mind in the manner suggested by Hartley. Coleridge hopes that as a consequence of the common ground he assumes between mind and nature, 'the one Life', the forms of nature working on his senses, will be revealed in his mind as religious meanings, or specific forms of divine life. But if this transfiguration did occur, it is not revealed in the poem: for no given form of nature is associated with a specific religious meaning.

'The Nightingale', the only Conversation poem Coleridge subtitled as such, and in the course of which he proclaims its origin in 'A different lore' from that of earlier poems on natural subjects, does little more in this respect than exchange one pathetic fallacy – that the nightingale's song is melancholy, for another – that the voices of Nature are 'always full of love/And joyaunce', the common fallacy being that there is any kind of emotion in nature at all. Coleridge asserts that a young poet, instead of 'building up the rhyme' in poems about the melancholy associations of the

nightingale, and thus succumbing to a tradition unsubstantiated
by experience, (the knowledge of which passes for thought),
would have fostered his own development much more satisfactorily had he:

> stretched his limbs
> Beside a brook in mossy forest-dell,
> By sun or moon-light, to the influxes
> Of shapes and sounds and shifting elements
> Surrendering his whole Spirit, and of his song
> And of his fame forgetful! [PW I 265]

The 'indolent and passive' brain upon which the images and sensations of nature play, like the wind on the Eolian harp, is thus a
model for what Coleridge believed to be the right means of realizing in oneself the harmony of all things, and which is thus to
share 'in Nature's immortality'. Just as his model of poetry in
chapter XIV of the *Biographia* supposed the primacy of the objective
world, so here nature is seen as making rather than being made
by the inward and spiritual life of the individual: and it is notable
that all these poems are prospective, and like a manifesto, propose
only the ideal method of poetic creativity, and are not themselves
the product of that method in practice. The very tranquility of
mind and soul, here considered as the necessary means, prevents
the operation of the imagination, that process of selection and
diffusion by which the poet seeks to harmonize the external world
with that which he finds within himself [BLC I 304].[22] The power
that Coleridge later considered the prerequisite of creativity is in
abeyance here *because* it seeks to impose an order where, were we
but sufficiently attentive, we would find order already *is*; and the
order is there, of course, because Nature, Coleridge thinks, is a
second book of Revelation, God's transcript of himself by which
we may discern the attributes of his being – a view he had established before meeting Wordsworth. That our insight into Nature
may give us an insight into specific features of Divine life was
Coleridge's litany of the mid-1790s. And in this respect, a passage
from 'The Destiny of Nations' makes clear how well-ordered the
natural world might seem to Coleridge at this stage of his career:
he is disserting on the proper use of freedom:

But chiefly this, him First, him Last to view
Through meaner powers, and secondary things
Effulgent, as through clouds that veil his blaze.
For all that meets the bodily sense I deem
Symbolical, one mighty alphabet
For infant minds . . . [PW I 132]

The ideal order is in nature, and if we attend to it closely by means
of our senses without attempting to impose upon it our own
schemes of thought, then our spiritually childish minds will learn
this alphabet properly and we will understand every aspect of
nature as part of the perfect language of God. Nor, at this time of
his life, did Coleridge baulk at finding God present in his creation
– the necessary consequence of seeking a unity of life having taken
the objective world as one's starting point:

Glory to Thee, Father of earth and heaven!
All-conscious Presence of the Universe!
Nature's vast ever-acting Energy! [PW I 146–7]

Time and again in these poems, Coleridge is tempted to such
pantheistic sentiments; and at the same time, in the same passages, we must note the dominance of sense impression over
imaginative organization, of linked images without an integral life
of their own, all depending upon a concluding assertion to give
them significance: despite the association of all the appearances
of nature with God, Coleridge tells us of no distinct powers, no
distinct offices, no definite activities; and because he fails to convey
any distinct idea of God, he also fails to convey, in these typical
passages, any discrete religious meanings. Thus in
'Reflections . . .':

Here the bleak mount,
The bare bleak mountain speckled thin with sheep;
Grey clouds, that shadowing spot the sunny fields;
And river now with bushy rocks o'er brow'd,
Now winding bright and full, with naked banks;
And seats, and lawns, the Abbey and the wood,
And cots, and hamlets and faint city-spire;
Dim coasts, and cloud-like hills, and shoreless Ocean
[PW I 107]

From this beautifully described scene it is not possible to guess what idea the poet has in mind; from the first two lines we might think that we are going to be treated to an esteecean version of Wordsworth's 'visionary dreariness'. But the sun breaks through, the river is bright and full, and our mind's eye is brought back to the habitations of men. From the pressure evident in the writing, its pleasing breathlessness, we might deduce a fulness of spirit, but more than that is impossible. What follows is of course,

> It seem'd like Omnipresence! God, methought,
> Had built him there a Temple; the whole World
> Seem'd imag'd in its vast circumference:

Michael Cooke supplies what I believe to be the most apposite comment on this passage:

> Certainly, just about everything is cited, but we may wonder whether it is proper to identify the presence of everything with Omnipresence. No explicit power of emotion or intellect is enlisted to make the 'all' into a 'whole'. We seem to have 'an immense heap of *little* things' suffering from a lack of 'something *great*' to unify them.[23]

The great belongs to the world of ideas, but in this passage all distinct or determinable ideas have been smothered in the embrace of the term 'Omnipresence'. And just as strong thought and strong feeling give rise to each other in Coleridge's experience, so we may note here that the want of a distinct idea is coupled with the want of clear or profound feeling. That the poet feels something is evident – as it is evident in his description of the ascent of Brockley Coomb – but what he feels has become no clearer by the conclusion of this passage.

A variant form of this structure, which incidentally indicates a line of his future development, is used in 'This Lime-tree Bower my Prison'. Imagining Lamb and the Wordsworths passing through the landscape he knows and loves so well, Coleridge asks Nature to intensify her appearances:

> 'Ah! slowly sink
> Behind the western ridge, thou glorious Sun!
> Shine in the slant beams of the sinking orb

> Ye purple heath flowers! richlier burn, ye clouds!
> Live in the yellow light, ye distant groves!
> And kindle, thou blue Ocean!' [PW I 179–80]

This charitable command to Nature to be more herself is not made, in contrast to the hopes expressed in other poems, because she will thus disclose certain religious meanings more clearly, or because in the arrangement of these images there is an essential order, but because any and all impressions of this kind will in some way infuse the sensitive and attentive heart of Charles Lamb with a 'deep joy', and like the poet on previous occasions, he will be overwhelmed and stand,

> Silent with swimming sense, yea gazing round
> On the wide landscape, gaze till all doth seem
> Less gross than bodily; and of such hues
> As veil the Almighty Spirit, when yet he makes
> Spirits perceive his presence.' [PW I 180]

The method Coleridge describes here is at odds with hopes, expressed in other poems, that the sense of divine presence will be revealed through the specific forms of nature. Here, for the joy to be known, for omnipresence to be experienced, the senses must swim; that is, sensation leads to an experience distinct from sensation. Although the intensity of natural appearances is responsible for the creation of joy in the heart and mind of the observer, that joy arising obliterates all distinct impression and particular sentiment, and rather than illuminating the separate aspects of the landscape, as Eliot's idea illuminates the separate features in the opening lines of 'The Dry Salvages', spreads an emotional and intellectual monochrome across them all, indifferent to their particular forms.[24]

The relationship between God and Nature, here recorded as a matter of experience rather than deliberation, is more complicated than Coleridge's scheme for poetic creation has permitted: this link has been stretched if not broken, and it is interesting that Coleridge experiences a joy comparable to that planned for Lamb and the Wordsworths, not through contemplation of his obviously delightful prison, but by thinking on the experiences he wishes for his friends: his own joy arises, at first, in distinction from his experience of nature.

If Coleridge had experienced the powers of nature vicariously in this poem, in 'Frost at Midnight' he does so through his son, by planning his ideal education; and here, if anywhere, we might expect Coleridge to give an account of what religious meanings Nature is to teach Hartley:

> But *thou*, my babe! shall wander like a breeze
> By lakes and sandy shores, beneath the crags
> Of ancient mountains, and beneath the clouds,
> Which image in their bulk both lakes and shores
> And mountain crags: so shalt thou see and hear
> The lovely shapes and sounds intelligible
> Of that eternal language, which thy God
> Utters, who from eternity doth teach
> Himself in all, and all things in himself.
> Great universal Teacher! he shall mould
> Thy spirit, and by giving make it ask. [PW I 242]

But this brings us no closer to knowing what truths the universal teacher would transmit, no more certain what religious principles nature would be able to disclose. In these 'clear Images' there are no 'distinct conceptions' [CL IV 574–76], no evidence of the 'eternal laws' to which at the beginning of 'France: An Ode', Coleridge believes that all the appearances of nature 'Yield homage'. Hartley did indeed grow up 'exquisitely wild',[25] but he was far from thinking that the forms of nature had moulded religious principles in him. A different, and much more poetically commonplace kind of chemistry is evident in his dedicatory sonnet to his father:

> I "wander'd like a breeze",
> By mountain brooks and solitary meres,
> And gather'd there the shapes and fantasies
> Which, mixt with passions of my sadder years,
> Compose this book.[26]

He has not found his passions or ideas in nature, but only 'the shapes and fantasies' to express them.

Coleridge's poetic and imaginative impulse had required him to see the world not as a mass of little things, but as a whole – to perceive how the many can also be the one. He made his first efforts to portray this unity by beginning with 'what really is', with the details of the sense-presented world, and simultaneously, quite logically, sought to surrender his whole being, or that of others, to the influences of the natural world, and repress as alien all other hopes and desires.

This effort had very definite effects on the form of his poems and gave rise to a distinct kind of poetry. Firstly, the subject matter is always rooted in an experience of one particular time and place; and though this may give the poem an attractive concreteness, it prevents the poet from dissolving, diffusing and dissipating the immediate world in order to re-create it in the mould of his self-consciousness: the corollary to which is that the substance of consciousness is not adequately defined in these poems. Secondly, and closely associated with this inhibition, because the natural world is made by God, is at the very least, a temple built by and for Himself, and because 'nature itself would give us the impression of a work of art, if we could see the thought which is present at once in the whole and in every part',[27] the selection of images is not necessary to perceive the unity and design, to perceive God's presence; indeed, it might even be regarded as wilful interference with the providential order by our 'meddling intellect'. Therefore Coleridge feels justified in making lists of what is evident to the senses at any one time in order to convey the harmony of life, or God's all-pervading presence. And because these lists have no apparent unity in themselves, over this unpointed and perhaps unmortared brickwork he smears the render of asserted unity; but the poem gains no architectural strength from the exercise. Consequently, though Coleridge believes that it is possible to find religious meanings in the forms of nature, he never associates one specific form with one specific meaning, and is content to describe joy, or the sense of God's omnipresence, as the one emotion or idea which will issue from the co-presence of a multitude of forms acting on the individual. That a more precise association is possible we know from the poetry of Wordsworth – and Hopkins and Eliot can supply us with further examples. But it would seem that Coleridge's determination to feel the wholeness of the separate aspects of creation prevented him from making any concentrated effort to perceive distinct relations between the parts. The unity spoken of in these poems is therefore not a unity in multeity: when God's omnipresence is actually experienced, it is so at the expense of the originating impressions of nature: the delight aris-

ing from the separate details finally overwhelms the senses, and
in the soft-focus joy resulting, Coleridge experiences the presence
of a God of no distinct offices and making no distinct claims upon
him.

THE RETURN[28]

But in respect of the structure of these poems, equally important
as his vision of nature is Coleridge's awareness of his social
relations. If Wordsworth tended to see people as objects, separate
from his observing mind, Coleridge sees them as aspects of his
own life.

'The Eolian Harp' opens with the contented, if pensive, couple
sitting outside their cottage, with Coleridge conscious of the peace
Sara has brought him. No wish nor desire profanes this peaceful
contentment, and his mind is thus relaxed and prepared for the
'one Life' experience with its accompanying love for 'all things in
a world so fill'd' [PW I 101]. Meditating on this experience, he
then imagines himself transposed to a nearby hill-top, where he
is accustomed to entertain his reveries undisturbed; there, in a
flight of mind, and comparing the wind on the harp to the 'idle
flitting phantasies' darting across his brain, he extends his analogy
to see all aspects of animated nature as examples of the harp, and
the wind as the divine soul inspiriting each separately, yet itself
undivided.

Up to this point the poem has been more or less well received;
but the last passage, which is I think a 'return' of the kind that
G. M. Harper has found in 'Reflections . . .' and 'Fears . . .',
and involves a descent from the mount of vision to the vale of life,[29]
has been censored or condemned by most critics as a flaw in the
poem's structure. Sara reappears, ostensibly ticking Coleridge off
for his unorthodox propositions, and he kow-tows. George
Watson sees her as a 'nuisance', spoiling, by her governessy insistence on orthodoxy, the aesthetic unity of the poem.[30] Kelvin Everest risks making a heretical mountain out of a heterodox molehill
when he says that 'Coleridge rejects speculations of the poem on
obviously fabricated grounds of Christian piety that are foreign to
the whole cast of his mind'.[31] Although his opinion of the cast of
Coleridge's mind is strange, he is right, I think, to assume that it
is Coleridge himself who rejects his speculations, and not his
uxorious nature forcing him to kow-tow to Sara's conventional

expressions – Yarlott's opinion.[32] Of the many critics who might be cited as antagonistic to this passage, by contrast I have met only one sympathetic to it – Basil Willey, who thinks that Sara's calling Coleridge back to Christ foreshadows much of his future development.[33]

That Sara should reappear at the end of the poem is of course aesthetically satisfying, for she was largely responsible for the contentment that allowed the central vision: it is her apparently narrow piety that has upset so many critics. But it seems to me that in fact she promotes a second kind of return – from God seen as the omnipresent life of his creation to God the saviour of mankind, from an impersonal deity to Christ the personal redeemer, from a God without distinct offices to God in definitive human form, and from the Incomprehensible, and therefore that about which nothing can be said, to the knowable, or that which is the object of discourse.[34] From having been aware of God's presence in all things, the poet reminds himself that he is, or was, a sinful man requiring salvation; and it is in Sara and his domestic life that he feels that his salvation has been realized: he speaks of Christ as having,

> with his saving mercies healéd me,
> A sinful and most miserable man
> Wilder'd and dark, and gave me to possess
> Peace, and this cot, and thee, heart-honour'd Maid.
>
> [PW I 102]

Thus the two forms of return are co-ordinated in one image: on the wings of his mind he descends from the 'midway slope' to the cottage, the scene of his social and domestic life: where, by recognizing Sara's role, he also recognizes that of Christ. He returns from visions of God's omnipresence in nature to the realization of Christ as the substance of society. It is, of course, difficult to read these lines without remembering Southey's cruel mockery and the facts of Coleridge's future life.[35] But had the kind of thinking evident here, and in other Conversation poems, been dependent on his relationship with his wife, and not representative of something integral to Coleridge's thinking, he could have withdrawn or altered them. He never did so, and for some time regarded this as his favourite poem. I think we will see his descent from the visionary mount where he experienced God's omnipresence, to the social world where Christ acted, as marking a definite direction of his thought. Coleridge felt that his prospective marriage would enlarge his social sympathies and inspire him with a Christian compassion: he has seen an old man, shivering with cold, and he imagines how he shall help him:

> I'll melt these frozen dews
> That hang from thy white beard, and numb thy breast.
> My Sara too shall tend thee, like a child:
> And thou shalt talk, in our fireside's recess
> Of Purple Pride, that scowls on Wretchedness –
> He did not so, the Galilean mild,
> Who met the Lazars turn'd from rich men's doors
> And call'd them Friends, and heal'd their noisome sores!
> [PW I 93]

Entitled 'Pity', this poem indicates how, in his prospective happiness, Coleridge saw his turning towards human kind as an imitation of Christ's behaviour. His ideal love would not set him apart on a 'mount sublime', but rather enable him to lighten the burden of other people's suffering by bringing them into community with his family, so rescuing them from the ills otherwise inflicted on man by man.[36]

Because Coleridge believed that exclusive attachment was the basis of society,[37] his marriage no doubt had some influence on his emerging social and political ideas. 'Religious Musings', written between 1794 and 1796, so bridging his bachelor and his happily married days, is much concerned with the state of society. Coleridge imagines a 'younger angel' looking down on humanity,

> . . . and behold!
> A sea of blood bestrewed with wrecks, where mad
> Embattling interests on each other rush
> With unhelmed rage! [PW I 113]

This is a gory image for what we now regard as the quite normal battle of commercial life – the stock-jobbers, merchant bankers and monied interests of all kinds be-thinging themselves in the pursuit of profit, from whom the weak and sick and old will need to be rescued. But if this fact of the Understanding has no life in Reason, in what is essentially human, what is the proper end of human relations?

> Tis the sublime of man,
> Our noontide Majesty, to know ourselves
> Parts and proportions of one wondrous whole!
> This fraternizes man, this constitutes
> Our charities and bearings. But 'tis God
> Diffused through all, that doth make one whole; [PW I 113–14]

Here we have a social version of the 'one Life' vision, with the added difference that were the vision realized we would also realize 'Our noontide Majesty' – our essentially *human* nature: to this vision Coleridge remained faithful all his life. This notion is never present in the isolated individual's sublime experiences of nature, in separation from society. In the light of this ideal Coleridge then examines the institutions maintained by nominal Christians, and discovers that they all – most notably the slave trade – pervert this proper end.[38] The consequences to individual members of society are far-reaching, for everyone is at the mercy of

> spells that film the eye of Faith,
> Hiding the present God; whose presence lost,
> The moral world's cohesion, we become
> An Anarchy of Spirits! Toy-bewitched,
> Made blind by lusts, disherited of soul,
> No common centre Man, no common sire
> Knoweth! A sordid solitary thing,
> Mid countless brethren with a lonely heart
> Through courts and cities the smooth savage roams
> Feeling himself, his own low self the whole; [PW I 114–15]

As Coleridge sees it organized, society prevents its individual members from realizing their humanity; for only by the kind of 'sacred sympathy' that he himself had hoped to extend in 'Pity', by making personal relations free of selfish interests, will the individual become integral with the whole, and the whole become one Self. Having established this as his end, Coleridge declares the means:

> Self, that no alien knows!
> Self, far diffused as Fancy's wing can travel!

Self, spreading still! Oblivious of its own,
Yet all of all possessing! This is Faith!
This the Messiah's destined victory! [PW I 115]

So the principle of the 'one Life', of 'God/Diffused through all',
may be realized in our social life by Christ, our 'common sire', a
man epitomizing our haminty.[39] Unlike Coleridge's vision of God's
omnipresence in nature, there is a workable relationship between
God the life and unity of the nation and Christ the redeemer of
individuals: God and Christ are in proper opposition, are not mere
contraries as they are when God is proposed as the unity of the
life of nature. Christ is the model that Coleridge, in his prospective
happiness, felt he was following when his heart went out towards
the wretched and the suffering, wishing to heal them from the
fountain of his own blessing; and this love universalized in the
crucifixion will eventually restore mankind to its proper humanity,
when each individual will see himself as a part and a proportion
of 'one wondrous whole' – each individual's true Self; the integrity
of which is God.
    A similar pattern, rooted in a strong sense of social responsi-
bility, and which contains a realization of the disjunction between
God's omnipresence in nature, and Christ's action in society, is
evident in 'Reflections . . .' The poet remembers climbing from
the 'low Dell', 'a Blessed Place', 'up the stony Mount' on which,
surveying the goodly scene, he experiences God's omnipresence.
That moment described in its full perfection, the poet then reflects
on his subsequent actions: 'Ah! quiet Dell! dear Cot, and Mount
sublime!/I was constrained to quit you . . .' [PW I 107]. The pressure he felt came from his realization that the charity and compassion of the world was cold and hypocritical – conventional
Christians involved in very un-Christ-like actions.[40] He feels he
must do differently:

I therefore go, and join head, heart and hand,
Active and firm, to fight the bloodless fight
Of Science, Freedom, and the Truth in Christ. [PW I 108]

These lines have sometimes been criticized as bombast, because
all that Coleridge actually did was to move to Bristol to be nearer
a library.[41] Such criticisms betoken a failure of imagination: the
manner in which one chooses to fight 'the Truth in Christ' must

be in accord with one's talents; one may accuse Coleridge of many things, but not of mistaking where his abilities lay. On the other hand it is not surprising that a young man should want to see an immediate and practical fulfillment of his beliefs, and that he should find it hard to accept the hiatus between profound thought and political action: this is the sentiment that substantiates lines 43–59, to which the three lines quoted form the fitting conclusion. Although there is a definite disjunction in this poem between the 'one Life' vision and the return to fight the truth in Christ, the poem does not end with this battle cry. Rather the happiness he has known in his cottage and dell, and which he thinks has enabled him to climb the stony mount of knowledge, to an experience of God's omnipresence, as it had in 'The Eolian Harp', is the happiness he seeks for all, the end for which he goes to fight on Christ's behalf:

> . . . sweet Abode!
> Ah! – had none greater! And that all had such!
> It might be so – but the time is not yet.
> Speed it, O Father! Let thy Kingdom come!' [PW I 108]

The truth in Christ will realize the kingdom of the Father, and then a state of society will exist in which all may be as blessed as he has been. The 'redemption' he had experienced in 'The Eolian Harp' is here seen as the ideal redemption for every member of society – but it is seen as a gift rather than a process, the implications of which Coleridge has yet to discover.

'Fears in Solitude' has a structure comparable to that of 'Reflections . . .' while echoing in its much greater length many of the sentiments found in 'Religious Musings'. The poem begins with a description of a 'small and silent dell' 'amid the hills', where the poet lies down to let the 'sweet influences of nature' tremble 'o'er his frame'. Although this is part of the process by which he hopes he will find 'Religious meanings in the forms of nature', yet, as is fitting in 1798, the year of the supernatural poems, this process is immediately interrupted and instead of his senses being so impressed as to rise through joy to a vision of omnipresence, they are 'gradually wrapt /In a half sleep'. [PW I 257]. Freed from the immediate, he begins, not to dream 'of better worlds', but to meditate on the state of English society and its relation to his own hopes. Although he would, he cannot 'preserve/His soul in

calmness' by holding himself at a remove from society, typified
by his isolation in the 'green and silent spot', because he 'perforce
must feel/For all his human brethren'. In his dream-like meditation, he has already escaped his philosophic solitude and is
beginning to suffer with those whom he fears are suffering an
imagined invasion of England by France. Napoleon, however, is
but the instrument of God's wrathful visitations upon the sinful
English:

> We have drunk up, demure as at a grace,
> Pollutions from the brimming cup of wealth;
> Contemptuous of all honourable rule,
> Yet bartering freedom and the poor man's life
> For gold, as at a market. The sweet words
> Of Christian promise, words that even yet
> Might stem destruction, were they wisely preached,
> Are mutter'd o'er by men, whose tones proclaim
> How flat and wearisome they feel their trade:
> Rank scoffers some, but most too indolent
> To deem them falsehoods or to know their truth. [PW I 258]

These and other sentiments befitting an angry young unitarian
radical occupy lines 29–175. But lines 176–97 are a tribute to Britain
– to her natural landscape it seems, rather than to her history or
to the men that have made her. Britain has indeed sustained those
whom he loves most, and in whom he finds his being as 'a son,
a brother and a friend/A husband, and a father!'; but Coleridge
still seems to place his emphasis on the British landscape's enrich-
ment of his intellectual life:

> O my Mother Isle!
> How shouldst thou prove aught else but dear and holy
> To me, who from thy lakes and mountain-hills,
> Thy clouds, thy quiet dales, thy rocks and seas,
> Have drunk in all my intellectual life,
> All sweet sensations, all ennobling thoughts,
> All adoration of the God in nature,
> All lovely and all honourable things,
> Whatever makes this mortal spirit feel
> The joy and greatness of its future being?
> There lives nor form nor feeling in my soul
> Unborrowed from my country! [PW I 262]

Although Coleridge was later to repudiate the notion that one's attachment to one's country was to its turf, and only a year later in the lines written from the Harz Forest [PW I 315] he asserts that landscape can mean nothing if not associated with the love of those in whom one finds one's being, this paean reminds us that Coleridge began this poem by believing that the influences of nature would make up a meditative joy in him and so reveal 'the God in nature'. That he here asserts that these forms belong to his country seems preparatory to that change of mind he was to undergo, stimulated, probably by the experience of homesickness in Germany. Certainly, the notion that people are the main object of his attachment is evident at the end of the poem; for as he leaves his dell, Coleridge comes to the brow of the hill, and sees just that landscape that in other poems has stimulated the sense of God's omnipresence. Here the image before his mind is not seen as revelatory of God's being, but as an anology of society:

> I find myself upon the brow, and pause
> Startled! . . .
> This burst of prospect, here the shadowy main,
> Dim-tinted, there the mighty majesty
> Of that huge amphitheatre of rich
> And elmy fields, seem like society –
> Conversing with the mind, and giving it
> A livelier impulse and a dance of thought!

He then spots the church-tower of Nether-Stowey, and descending the hill with 'quickened footsteps', makes his way home, his mind full of 'the thoughts that yearn for human kind'. Coleridge is clearly beginning to realize that he will find his joy where he finds his being – in his attachment to those whom he loves as son, brother, husband, father and friend – and which will give him the power to love and benefit 'all his human brethren'.

We have discovered that it is characteristic of the poems so far considered that the 'return' involves an explicit or implicit recantation of those passages which either are or approach a vision of the 'one Life' of nature; co-ordinate with this we may distinguish between a God-ordered nature and a Christ-ordered society, with the poet moving uneasily between the two. In the one he finds a means of realizing his visions of unity, and in the other a place for his being and his human hopes. Although there are some hints

that the two worlds may be reconciled – for instance, when God's
kingdom comes on earth, and all will possess such a spirit-healing
nook as the poet has possessed, or in the notion that God diffused
through all is both the life of nature and society (and we will see
that Coleridge did indeed come to think of the Word as the informing power of nature) yet these poems present a structural 'fault'
between the vision of the unity of the life of nature, and the
poet's felt obligations towards society – in its nuclear form as his
immediate family and close friends, or in its extended form as the
State. But Coleridge's descent from the 'mount sublime' and
visions of omnipresence, his return to his wife, child and cottage,
and the mansion of his friend, was more than a poetic device: as
his belief in the sensational powers of nature to mould the spirit
declined, so his 'thoughts that yearn for human kind' grew, and
as they grew they became increasingly organized not by the God,
but by the Christ, of Christianity.

TWO POEMS OF FRIENDSHIP[42]

It is a feature of the development of some poets that what we
learn to see as central to their mature work appears early, but
between the blossom and the fruit there is a long interval during
which the process of maturation either goes on hidden from our
sight or, and this I think is the case with Coleridge, actually takes
a course apparently inimical to that development. In his sonnet
on the ascent of Brockley Coomb, we saw that the quality of the
landscape inspired in him a longing for another person, in the
love of whom the poet would be able to unify the disparate images
of his perception. The notion that we 'see' nature through our
love of another is crucial to Coleridge's later thinking, and though
it is a subsidiary and often subliminal theme in several poems,
including 'Dejection . . .', it is not self-evident, and inscribed in
the notebooks, until some years later. But then, as is characteristic
of Coleridge, he finds himself in his own past productions: in
Notebook 47 he thinks of this sonnet as expressing 'the universal
feelings of minds loving or even disposed to Love' [N.47 p.75].
    However, two of the Conversation poems, 'This Lime-tree
Bower my Prison' and 'Frost at Midnight', hint at one mode of
feeling, and consequent poetic method, that was to enable this
development. In contrast to the other Conversation poems, these

two do not have the poet but a close friend or relation experience the powers of nature.[43] Thus in 'This Lime-tree Bower . . .' Coleridge has been prevented from going on what we now see as a typical excursion from his cottage, and up the hill towards a vision of omnipresence, because 'Dear Sara' (is there any irony in that endearment?) had poured a skillet of boiling milk over his foot.[44] Instead his imagination follows the adventures of Charles Lamb and the Wordsworths, who take a route the poet knows; Coleridge, unable to share, imagines their gladness, especially that of Charles:

> . . . but thou, methinks, most glad,
> My gentle-hearted Charles, for thou hast pined
> And hunger'd after Nature, many a year,
> In the great City pent, winning thy way
> With sad yet patient soul [PW I 179]

and a line or two later follows that great apostrophe to Nature to appear to Lamb with unusual intensity. Then Charles will stand 'Struck with deep joy . . .' in the presence of the Almighty Spirit. And as he contemplates 'With lively joys the joy he cannot share' so Coleridge's regret vanishes and

> A delight
> Comes sudden on my heart, and I am glad
> As I myself were there!

This imaginative reconstruction of an experience not his own (though in fact probably rather more his than Lamb's[45]) may be thought of as a process which socializes the 'one Life' vision: for when the vision is to the poet alone, it always requires some degree of separation from his social environment: here the vision comes vicariously upon him whilst he remains in his place of being, amongst his family, but simultaneously keeps in mind his pure and gentle-hearted friend. It is very much a harbinger of the method he will employ in the verse-letter to Sara Hutchinson.[46]

'Frost at Midnight' is a variety of this experience: the poet is more securely lodged at home on account of the conditions of time and clime explicit in the title, and the world of nature makes no visionary impression upon his mind. At first, the excursion of his imagination follows no close friend or relation: inspired by the

cradled and sleeping child beside him, and the fluttering film of
soot, a 'companionable form' presaging the arrival of some absent
friend, Coleridge remembers his days at Christ's Hospital, 'In
the great city, pent 'mid cloisters dim', when, the same stranger
flickering in the school's fire-grate, he dreamt of Stowey, the
church bells, and 'the hot Fair-day':

> And so I brooded all the following morn,
> Awed by the stern preceptor's face, mine eye
> Fixed with mock study on my swimming book:
> Save if the door half-opened, and I snatched
> A hasty glance, and still my heart leaped up,
> For still I hoped to see the *stranger's* face,
> Townsman, or aunt, or sister more beloved,
> My play-mate when we both were clothed alike! [PW I 241–42]

The stranger's face that Coleridge hopes to see is in fact no stranger
at all, and this hope of the appearance of someone whom he
loves to redeem his solitude or to realize his vision of beauty
is characteristic, and carries over from the poet's youth into his
adulthood. But as a young father, this longing is partly satisfied
by the sleeping presence of his 'babe so beautiful'. His heart moves
out to Hartley as a prospective companion, whom the poet will
seek to give the advantages of a childhood in the grand images of
nature that he had been denied. And as Coleridge imagines
Hartley's delight, we meet the elements that would make up a
'one Life' vision, a vision that he believes will come to his son
because the forms of nature are

> The lovely shapes and sounds intelligible
> Of that eternal language, which thy God
> Utters, who from eternity doth teach
> Himself in all, and all things in himself.

The only irony is that whereas 'in the great city, pent', Coleridge's
heart has 'leaped up' at the hope of being visited by someone he
loves, this very hope which influences the structure not only of
this poem, but other of the Conversation poems, and is crucial to
a proper reading of 'Dejection . . .', appears to have no place in
the scheme of Hartley's education. His heart, Coleridge hopes,

will, like Wordsworth's, leap up at the beauties of nature. It is as
if Coleridge has yet to realize the significance of his own memories.
The vision the poet has on Hartley's behalf is prospective, and
as Coleridge has this hope or vision in his domestic surroundings,
the only hint of a 'return' is in the imagery derived from the
immediate circumstances. The poem ends by looking forward to
the time when Hartley shall enjoy all the seasons, and the poet
hoping that his son will be blessed as he himself has not been:

> Therefore all seasons shall be sweet to thee,
> Whether the summer clothe the general earth
> With greeness, or the redbreast sit and sing
> Betwixt the tufts of snow on the bare branch
> Of mossy apple-tree, while the nigh thatch
> Smokes in the sun-thaw; whether the eave-drops fall,
> Heard only in the trances of the blast,
> Or if the secret ministry of frost
> Shall hang them up in silent icicles,
> Quietly shining to the quiet moon.

As Coleridge had established a possible community of spirit with
Lamb, and had potentially integrated his vision of nature with his
social existence by finding his joy in the joy of another, so here
nature lives for him not in its immediate impression, but in the
effect he believes it will have upon the development of his son.[47]

In all the Conversation poems, Coleridge's starting point was
experience of the concrete and sensible world; of this world he
desired two things: to see there the forms of nature existing as
truths of intellect, and simultaneously to understand how all sep-
rately existing things participate in one life. His constant temp-
ation at this time was to think and feel that the life of nature was
also the life of God: to describe this one life in poetry then becomes
little more than listing what may be observed under the influence
of this feeling: but the unity of life is not apparent in the resulting
heap of broken images'. It has to be asserted subsequently. As a
consequence, these, the distinct forms of nature, carry no particular meaning, are not bound to any definite truths of intellect, or
religious ideas. The desire to see the life of nature as revealing the
spiritual life of man is thus thwarted by the desire to see all forms
of life as one life.

But nature was not the only influence on Coleridge at this stage
of his development. His long search for a 'sheet-anchor'[48] made
him acutely conscious of his social and political responsibilities.
His search for a unity in society, ideally ordered in Christ, is
almost as strong a force in him as his hopes of finding a unity in
nature ordered by an impersonal God. In some respects, these
appear as opposing hopes: in earlier Conversation poems the
'return' to the dell of society seems to exclude the vision of God's
omnipresence on the 'mount sublime'. But we have seen there is
at least a partial reconciliation in 'This Lime-tree Bower . . .' and
'Frost at Midnight'. This is achieved by putting off immediate
sense impression and entering imaginatively into the joy of others:
his heart goes out into their lives, and through them he imagines
nature acting. This is also true, in a more diffuse way, of 'The
Nightingale', in which his pleasure is shared directly with the
Wordsworths, with 'a most gentle Maid', and with his son. This
willingness to place another person at the centre of his vision is
near the heart of Coleridge's development: only in the binding of
our being to that of another, only in religion in the profoundest
sense of the term, can the tendency of Reason to seek a whole be
adequately expressed through the particular and the individual,
and the one not be lost in the many, nor the many lost in the one.
And, of course, Coleridge's tendency to make another mind the
centre of experience was entirely conducive to the writing of the
supernatural poems.

3

The Supernatural Poems

All made out of the carver's brain. [PW I 222]

The best part of human language, properly so called, is derived from reflection on the acts of the mind itself.[BLC II 54]

Poetry . . . is purely human; for all its materials are from the mind, and all its products are for the mind. [BL II 254]

THE METHOD OF THE SUPERNATURAL POEMS

In the first chapter I suggested that although Coleridge asserted that poems of the supernatural were but a branch of the poetry of nature, yet his description of them as involving characters no more than 'shadows' until invested with the human interest of our inward nature fitted badly into the model of poetry he had adduced to describe the *Lyrical Ballads*. To produce the supernatural the imagination is not working or re-working sense-presented material; it begins with an act and not, Spinoza-like, with a thing or sensation. It first of all dreams up a Cain, an ancient Mariner or a Christabel, and then seeks to give life to this creature by discovering for it quintessential human truths. The immediate plays no part in the construction of these poems, and in the struggle between Mind and Nature, Mind has been given the upper hand: to invert an old illustration, Nature is now the *tabula rasa*, to be written on and not to do the writing.[1] That this freedom from material and immediate circumstance was, in Coleridge's opinion, proper to a certain kind of poetry is evident in his comments on *The Faery Queene*:

You will take especial note of the marvellous independence and true imaginative absence of all particular space or time in the

45

Faery Queene. It is in the domains neither of history or geography; it is ignorant of all artificial boundary, all material obstacles; it is truly in the land of Faery, that is, of mental space. The poet has placed you in a dream, a charmed sleep, and you neither wish, nor have the power, to inquire where you are, or how you got there.

[MC 36–7/LR I 94–5; cf. SC II 85, CN III 4501 f.136v]

Such a description cannot but remind us of 'The Ancient Mariner', the ocean upon which the drama occurs emphasizing the poem's freedom from 'all artificial boundary'. And Coleridge's self-reported reply to Mrs Barbauld is not only a repudiation of the fitness of moral intentions in a poem of imagination, but also an assertion of such a poem's freedom from the normal patterns of cause and effect in society:

> It ought to have had no more moral than the Arabian Nights' tale of the merchant's sitting down to eat dates by the side of a well, and throwing the shells aside, and lo! a genie starts up, and says he must kill the aforesaid merchant *because* one of the date shells had, it seems, put out the eye of the genie's son.
>
> [TT 31 May 1830]

Of course, as Humphry House has pointed out, the story that follows is highly moral: inconsequence is not piled upon inconsequence.[HH 90–91]. What Coleridge is arguing for is not a freedom from moral regulation, not the pursuance of any kind of behaviour under any circumstances, or rapid transitions between kinds of behaviour, but the freedom to invent origins and causes, to penetrate behind the limited conventions of quotidian society, the freedom to reveal states of mind and truths of our inward nature that would necessarily be curtailed by, or inexpressible in, our actual lives. This comes out quite clearly in his review of M. G. Lewis's *The Monk*:

> . . . in a few weeks after his first frailty, the man who had been described as possessing much general humanity, a keen and vigorous understanding, with the habits of the most exalted piety, degenerates into an uglier fiend than the gloomy imagination of Dante would have ventured to picture. Again the monk is described as feeling and acting under the influence of an

emotion which could not co-exist with his other emotions. The romance-writer possesses an unlimited power over situations but he must scrupulously make his characters act in congruity with them. Let him work physical wonders only, and we will be content to *dream* with him for a while; but the first moral miracle which he attempts, he disgusts and awakens us.

[MC 370–71]

The business of the supernatural or romance writer is not to play magician with our humanity, which long before he expressed it as grounded in the Reason which is God, Coleridge regarded as a datum, and the poet's business to disclose rather than to create. When the poet is able to invent the world of his poem, and is not imposed upon by the conventions and limitations of his own age or making, he is best able to reveal his understanding of our humanity. And it is Spenser again who provides Coleridge with an image for the ideal conduct of this kind of poem:

> As pilot well expert in perilous wave,
> That to a stedfast starre his course hath bent,
> When foggy mistes or cloudy tempests have
> The faithful light of that faire lampe yblent,
> And cover'd Heaven with hideous dreriment;
> Upon his card and compas firmes his eye,
> The maysters of his long experiment,
> And to them does the steddy helme apply,
> Bidding his winged vessel fairely forward fly.'

[Ibid; FQ II vii 1]

The relation of pilot to ship is that of poet to poem; the external world is entirely obscured, and no bearings may be had from it to enable the guiding of the poem or vessel. In fixing his eye upon his card and compass, 'The maysters of his long experiment', Coleridge is, I think, supposing that the poet is ceasing to look outward on the world, and requiring his imagination to depend on the mind's own resources. [Cf. CN III 4501 f.136]. Whatever external world then comes into existence will be of the poet's creating, just as the true course of the ship will be dependent on the mariner's use of his compass. The boy who found his Hellespont in the Strand has become the man sailing to the South Pole in Nether Stowey [Gillman 17].

Yarlott has identified this means of composing poetry as Addis-
on's 'faery way of writing', and thus thinks that Coleridge was
rooted 'in the fecund loam of English folk-lore'.[2] But though Yarlott
associates this kind of writing with the unshackling of 'the creative
imagination from the fetters of neo-classicism', and though he
adduces a passage from Young as 'an almost perfect defence of
the poetry of Coleridge, Blake and Shelley yet to come',[3] he still
finds proper evidence of 'the faery way' only in 'The Eolian Harp',
'Religious Musings' and 'The Songs of the Pixies', where the literal
appearance of the faery world marks the mode of composition.
But, as we have seen, the real significance for Coleridge of this
method is not just the right to bring on the little men, but as in
The Faery Queene or *The Arabian Nights* the right of the poet to
emancipate himself entirely from the stimuli of the immediate
world, and in its stead to create a world imagined. It is the power
to reject immediate sense impression that I think is the source of
the distinction between the Conversation and the Supernatural
poems; it is also the ground of his differences with Wordsworth,
who would have thought that separated from nature, man hardly
has any other means to self-knowledge.[4]

The power of dismissing the immediate world is cognate with
the power of dreaming – a power that Coleridge thought that
Wordsworth did not take sufficient account of. Hazlitt relates that
Coleridge criticized his friend as not being 'prone enough to
believe in the traditional superstitions of the place, and that there
was something corporeal, a *matter of factness*, a clinging to the
palpable, or often to the petty, in his poetry in consequence'.[5] We
may see in this criticism (which was of his *Lyrical Ballads* and not
of his philosophical poetry) Coleridge's thinking that the palpable
and the corporeal were, in one kind of poetry, hindrances to the
poet's proper use of his imagination.[6] In 1800, and at Wordsworth's instance – who was perhaps responding in kind to this type
of criticism, Coleridge's one completed supernatural ballad was
subtitled, 'A Poet's Reverie'. Of course, from Wordsworth's point
of view, this was an implicit criticism of the poem, and marked
its difference in kind from his own contributions which were set
so firmly in a world of space and time external to that of both poet
and reader. Lamb took this bait when he wrote to Wordsworth to
challenge the disingenuous note in which the poet had outlined
his notions of the poem's defects. He begins by declaring 'I am
sorry that Coleridge has christened his Ancient Mariner "a poet's

Reverie" . . . what new idea is gained by this Title, but one subversive of all credit, which the tale should force upon us, of its truth?'[7] Lamb means that the journey ought to be conceived as having taken place objectively, in the same way as the episodes upon which Wordsworth drew had taken place. He is not willing that the dreaming mind should produce its own perceptions, and so create what seems to be an external world. He speaks in a very Wordsworthian vein when he says, 'After first reading it, I was totally possessed with it for many days – I dislike all the miraculous part of it, but the feelings of the man under the operation of such scenery dragged me along like Tom Piper's magic whistle' [Ibid.]. It is by no means certain that the scenery does operate on the Mariner: were Lamb correct in his assumptions, the poem would be more easily established as of a kind with the rest of the *Lyrical Ballads*.[8]

What neither Wordsworth nor Lamb will allow the mind to do is to dismiss the immediate world altogether and dream of another. But this is the ground of the comment upon the poem by the everperceptive Hazlitt: '. . . his most remarkable performance . . . and in it he seems to "conceive of poetry but as a drunken dream, reckless, careless, and heedless of past, present and to come" '.[9] Not a flattering appreciation, but despite its implied references to Coleridge's addictions, quite in accord with the poet's own concept that the writer of romances not only may but must emancipate himself from 'past, present, and to come'. And De Quincey speaks of Coleridge as having been occupied the previous summer with the writing of a poem on 'delirium, confounding its own dream scenery with external things, and connected with the images of high latitudes'.[10] Finally, upon the modern mind, this poetry makes a similar mark: 'There is a strange, dream-like quality, in his greatest poetry, a combination of vivid impression and fluid movement, which stamps them as products of the imagination at its purest and most untramelled'.[11]

This freedom granted, and the brain purged of the mist of immediate impressions, we should hardly be surprised at the fortuitous origins of many of the narrative elements of this new poetry. Novel circumstances could encourage the poet to disclose latent but nonetheless essential truths of his inward life.[12] But equally, the plot could thus be invented without any certain knowledge of the truths it was to embody.[13] Coleridge always claimed, for example, that the whole conception of the tale of

'Christabel' was present to his mind from the beginning. Beer's comment on Gillman's record of this plot is very interesting: '. . . it represents the plot of the poem, without telling us how the symbolic structure of the poem would have been developed and finally resolved.' [C.Vis. 188]. This division between the story and the human truths it was to embody is echoed in Coleridge's account of why the poem remained unfinished:

> The reason of my not finishing Christabel is not that I don't know how to do it – for I have, as I always had, the whole plan entire from beginning to end in my mind; but I fear I could not carry on with equal success the execution of the idea, an extremely difficult and subtle one.[14]

Some commentators, I think, do not pay sufficient attention to this distinction between plan and idea; for whereas the material of the story, the supernatural events, may be the work of fancy, the human and inward truths which will make up the character are the work of the imagination; having understood the plot we are not necessarily any closer to understanding the poem.

Coleridge himself discovered the depth of this distinction, or division as it finally proved to be, when having outlined the plot of 'The Wanderings of Cain' he asked Wordsworth to produce the first canto. Coleridge wrote the second 'at full finger speed', but found that Wordsworth had written almost nothing in the same time. [PW I 286]. The plot was presumably comprehensible to Wordsworth, or he wouldn't have sat down pen in hand; but he was unable to dream Coleridge's dream, to find within himself, unstimulated by sense impression, those truths with which to invest the characters and the action. This failure, however, did not prevent the two men from immediately planning 'The Ancient Mariner' instead, and it is clear from the accounts of its origin that it began, as did both 'Cain' and 'Christabel', with an invented world, a world of 'mental space', which freed the poet from all the contingencies of the real world. Thus, inevitably, it was Coleridge's poetic genius that was liberated by this method of composition; Wordsworth's seems to have been stifled, for he withdrew from the enterprise, feeling that he could 'only have been a clog upon it' [PWC 594] and having only contributed three or four lines.

THE METHOD OF 'THE ANCIENT MARINER'

But many critics attempt to read 'The Ancient Mariner' as if it had been composed according to the method that is the model for the *Lyrical Ballads,* and which informs the Conversation poems. It is generally supposed, for instance, that the blessing of the watersnakes signifies that the Mariner has had a version of the 'one Life' vision, and that this has enabled him to begin his 'return' in the form of penance, to the vale of society. Even John Beer, from whose work I have drawn so much support for my argument, and who is ever alert to the differences between Coleridge's two kinds of poetry [C.Vis.136], writes apropos the essay of Robert Penn Warren:

> The basic theme of the poem, he declares, is the 'one Life' . . . This is so: . . . If there is one common thread in Coleridge's spiritual quest, it is his conviction that by meditating on the material universe, man will come to understand the realm of the spiritual . . .[15]

The assumption that our contemplation of nature may also realize the spiritual life in us underlies Humphry House's remarks:

> . . . in the poem the method of relating nature to the moral world is not by 'dim analogies' nor 'in the shape of formal similes' . . . but by the poet's heart and intellect being intimately *combined* and unified with the great appearances of nature . . .
> The function of the elements is not merely to *image* the Mariner's spiritual states (though indeed they do this), but also to provide in the narrative structure of the poem the link between the Mariner as the ordinary man, and the Mariner as one acquainted with the invisible world, which has its own sets of values.' [HH 87–9]

The objectivity of the natural world is that which is presumed to provide the link between the Mariner and the reader, for it is believed to exist independently of both. But Coleridge's concept of mental space hardly allows any consideration of nature in this objective and mind-ordering capacity that House and Beer determine for it. Dreams, Coleridge wrote in his later years, had been the worst realities of his life [CL VI 767], and the outer world of a dream is entirely created by the dreamer. It is my belief that in the Conversation poems Coleridge began with sense, intending to arrive at thought, but that in the Supernatural poems he began with thought, seeking to arrive, as the dreamer does involuntarily, at sense and reality.

However, if the current opinion is true, and the Mariner does move in a material universe which provides insights into the realm of the spiritual, we need to be assured that that world exists outside him, acting on him so that he cannot choose but feel. The opening of 'The Rime . . .' leaves us very far from sure. In a first line of striking immediacy we are introduced not to the world in which the hero is to move, but to the hero himself: 'It is an ancient Mariner:' [PW I 187] and the first act of this man is to stop one of three people, all clearly dressed up with somewhere to go, and to whose mundane common sense the old Navigator seems a man possessed – a 'grey-beard loon'. The sense of possession grows upon the reader as it does upon the unfortunate Wedding-Guest:

> He holds him with his glittering eye –
> The Wedding-Guest stood still,
> . . . .
> The Wedding-Guest sat on a stone:
> He cannot choose but hear: [PW I 187]

We feel we are entranced, like the Wedding-Guest, and are entering into the Mariner's mental world; for bar the fact that the crew set off in good heart we know no other detail of the journey which might enable us to determine its objectivity and its distinction from the Mariner's consciousness.[16] It rather feels as if the venture originates in his will, just as the subsequent events prove dependent upon it.

If we can find no stable ground in the origin of the journey, we might be more successful if we look at the scenery through which the ship moves. Lamb implied that the Mariner's mind did not make, but was made by what it saw. If this is true, we should expect it to have some bearing on the central action of the poem – the shooting of the albatross. That nature may disclose to man the evil in himself, as well as the good, Wordsworth assures us:

> One impulse from a vernal wood
> May teach us more of man,

> Of moral evil and of good,
> Than all the sages can.[17]

What we must look for in the scenery of Part I is any hint of impulses coming from it which might encourage or discover the latent evil in the heart of the Mariner. Does the scenery operate on him so as to precipitate the shooting of the albatross? Does it *act* on him at all?

The five verses that describe the journey to the South Pole are all impregnated with the horrors of the voyage. And though the ship seems at first in the grip of the wind, and then in that of the ice, and moves on almost independently of the wishes of the crew, yet we receive no hint that the Mariner is in any way altered by these experiences, or that they act on him, or any other member of the crew, morally or spiritually. Whether the fear he might have experienced made him more susceptible to mistaken acts, the poem does not let us know. The appearance of the albatross even signals, in some measure, the apparent end of the troubles of the voyage. Having been hailed as a Christian soul, it seems to have a significant, if unspecified, bearing on the ship's escape from the ice-pack, enabling it to traverse the South Pole:

> It ate the food it ne'er had eat,
> And round and round it flew.
> The ice did split with a thunder fit;
> And the helmsman steered us through! [PW I 189]

The ship is moving northward again, a significant part of the journey accomplished, and the albatross is befriended by the Mariner:

> The albatross did follow,
> And every day, for food or play,
> Came to the mariner's hollo.

Nothing external to the Mariner tempts or provokes his action, just as nothing but 'the strange Lust of Murder in Man' tempted the sailors to take pot shots at a tired hawk that alighted in the rigging of the Speedwell as it rolled the constipated Coleridge on his wearisome and fickle voyage towards Malta.[18] There is no conflict, say, between a moral command and a necessity of nature, and the scenery has not acted on the Mariner so as to precipitate his deed: rather, on a rational basis, it has militated against it, for the albatross has been recognized as a 'pious bird of good omen'.[19] The criminal act has arisen spontaneously from the heart of man, independently of the world in which he moves, and in conflict with it.

What we sense, therefore, is a disconnection between the world in which the Mariner acts, and the manner of his action. The albatross is, if nothing else, a benign and innocuous being, and enters the Mariner's world without malice aforethought. As Part II demonstrates, this discontinuity remains a feature of the consciousness of the crew, who, by judging only according to their senses – by the effects of the Mariner's act, not the act itself – make themselves accomplices in the crime. But simultaneously a power we must presume latent until then is awoken in the Mariner, for it is at this point that the miraculous parts, so disliked by Lamb, begin. Whether what happens to the Mariner has the same form of externality as that of a dream, or whether it is more objective, cannot be discerned from the poem: cases may be made for both points of view. But it is important to recognize that whatever the status of the events that apparently happen to, rather than within, the Mariner, they are, in general terms, symbolic of his consciousness: they are neither literal nor metaphorical, but a combination of inner and outer by which the Mariner's *life* – the union of his typical, timeless humanity with the forms of time – is expressed. What I think does *not* happen is a making of the Mariner's consciousness by the natural and supernatural events of the poem; in principle, priority belongs to the Mariner's mind, but I would no more argue this as the basis of a coherent interpretation of the poem, than I would accept the objectivity of the events described.

In the Conversation poems, Coleridge hoped that the visible forms of nature would reveal distinct religious ideas; in the Supernatural poems he begins, if not with any distinctly conceived ideas, then with the belief that reality was to be spun out of the poet's human innards. By way of showing how these two approaches might be resolved in an image that conveys both something inward and something outward, and yet is the matter of common experience out of which a poem must be constructed so as to provide the reader with an intelligible world, we might take perhaps the two words, 'Sun' – for the idea familiar to Boehme,

Swedenborg and the Neo-platonists, and 'sun' – for the everyday image of the thing itself.[20] The effort Coleridge was making was to unite the idea and the image, to create a world neither literal nor metaphoric, but symbolic, in which all the major appearances of nature were incorporated in distinct ideas: the Sun with the sun, the Moon with the moon, the wind with 'one intellectual breeze', 'the God of all', and the sky with Heaven. Given the two series of words, there are two starting points, and those who believe that meditation on the material universe may enable man to disclose his spiritual nature tend to make the mistake of believing that in his supernatural poems Coleridge began with the sun rather than the Sun; and Wordsworth, clinging to the palpable and the matter-of-fact, to the sun and the moon, was thus prevented from understanding what Coleridge was doing, from following the Mariner as he undergoes the painful process of realizing the Sun in his mind and heart. It would certainly be very wrong to believe that every effective image communicates an idea: for the poem was composed in the ebullience of youth, when Coleridge was more possessed by ideas – often barely compatible – than possessing them; but this is a safer error than to suppose that nature breathes into the Mariner a second and spiritual breath, such as Wordsworth attempted to force into Peter Bell.

'THE WANDERINGS OF CAIN'

We may see how closely image follows idea in Coleridge's supernatural method if we turn to his canto, Canto II, of 'The Wanderings of Cain' [PW I 288–92]. The poem opens with Cain and his son, Enos, working their way through a forest, the path having become narrow, and the fir trees high above them shutting out the light of the moon. They are hoping to come to a clearing; Enos describes his chasing of the squirrels: 'I clomb a tree yesterday at noon, O my father, that I might play with them, but they leaped away from the branches . . . Why, O my father, would they not play with me?' This little story, and its question, oppresses Cain bitterly and 'he sank to the earth, and the child Enos stood beside him in the darkness'. The cause of his oppression is two-fold: he can no longer find the joy in living things that his son feels, and he knows he is responsible for Enos's disappointment because of his re-enactment of the Fall. He laments: 'The Mighty One that persecuteth me is on this side and on that; he pursueth my soul like the wind, like the sand-blast he passeth through me . . . O that I might be utterly no more! I desire to die . . .' He goes on to complain that God's persecution has dried up his being. When he and his son find the clearing and come out into the moonlight, we discover that both Cain's appearance, and the landscape in which he moves, are realizations of his moral condition: '. . . and when Cain, his father, emerged from the darkness, the child was affrighted. For the mighty limbs of Cain were wasted, as by fire; his hair was as the matted curls on the bison's forehead, and so glared his fierce and sullen eye beneath . . .' The withering of his limbs is, I think, to be directly associated with the drying up of his moral and spiritual life, and the sullen eye (not dissimilar to that of Geraldine), and the bison's hair, are an indication of his sinking towards the condition of a beast.

The clearing into which they come is no romantic lawn, no green and sunny glade: 'The scene around was desolate: the bare rocks faced each other, and left a long and wide interval of thin white sand . . . There was no spring, no summer, no autumn: and the winter's snow, that would have been lovely, fell not on these hot rocks'. That this is a symbolic landscape, and constructed to reveal Cain's inner world, and not one with primary objective status, becomes apparent when we remember that Cain has just emerged from a pine-forest where the fir branches dripped their moisture on Enos: the juxtaposing of these two types of climate could not occur in a mind seeking to give independent and consistent life to a physical world which might act on his characters; instead, the physical inconsistencies represent moral consistencies, and so fulfill Coleridge's brief for the supernatural poem.

One other feature of the poem requires some comment. It is divisible into two halves, the second of which is entirely taken up with Cain's re-establishing a relationship with Abel. Cain first sees, but does not recognize him, standing beside the rock precipitated by the fall of Adam and Eve. His back is turned and he cries out: 'Woe is me! Woe is me! I must never die again, and yet I am perishing with thirst and hunger'. This form of life in death was familiar to the Mariner. The sweetness of Abel's voice calls up half-remembered days in Enos, who creeps round the rock to come face to face with the spirit of Abel – described now as 'the Shape' by the poet; this being shrieks and turns round to face Cain, who 'stood like one who struggles in his sleep because of the exceeding terribleness of a dream'. Beer suggests that 'Abel is an apparition conjured up by Cain's own faulty consciousness' [CPI 114] – an idea which, in a modified form, is essential to my reading of the supernatural poems, and to which I shall return. Abel is certainly no 'meaningless marvel', for he becomes a guide to his brother's wanderings. His most surprising characteristic is his suffering. When Cain asks him, 'The Creator of our father, who had respect unto thee, and unto thy offering, wherefore hath he forsaken thee?', Abel's torment issues in a shriek, and the tearing of his garments. This exposes 'his naked skin [which] was like the white sands beneath their feet'. Whiteness of skin, as white as leprosy, is characteristic of Life-in-Death in 'The Ancient Mariner'. This might be a coincidence, but the parallel can be reinforced by the distinction that Abel draws between the God of the living, and the God of the dead. Cain repeats his question, and Abel replies: 'The Lord is God of the living only, the dead have another God'. Abel's torment is to remember the God of the living while having to endure, in some non-corporeal way, 'death's dream kingdom'. 'Woe is me', he says to Cain, 'For I was well beloved by the God of the living, and cruel wert thou, O my brother, who didst snatch me away from his power and his dominion.' Cain's killing of Abel was not only a bereaving of his physical life, but a disordering of his spiritual existence, and might be compared to Geraldine's disordering of Christabel's inner life. The existence of this being, 'who had power after this life, greater than Jehovah', is a revelation to Cain: 'The curse of the Lord is on me; but who is the God of the dead?', a question which inspires further shrieking on Abel's part. When Cain catches up with him again, he tells Abel that, like the ancient Mariner, who cannot pray, he is unable to mourn him because of the dryness in his heart, and asks him to lead him to this God. Abel consents and the fragment ends with the three of them setting off.[21]

'THE ANCIENT MARINER'

Part II and the beginning of Part III of 'The Ancient Mariner' may be compared in general terms to what we have of 'The Wanderings of Cain'. The commission of the crime, Part I of 'The Rime . . .' and what was to have been Canto I of 'The Wanderings . . .', is followed by a short period of motion, of Cain wandering through the forest with Enos, and the Mariner and his crew continuing to sail in a strong south wind. Then as the ship bursts upon the silent sea, and Cain and Enos come out of the forest, there follows a period of intense dryness and lack of directed motion, the period in which both Cain and the Mariner begin to realize the consequences of their crimes:

> Day after day, day after day,
> We stuck, nor breath nor motion;
> As idle as a painted ship
> Upon a painted ocean.
>
> Water, water, everywhere
> And all the boards did shrink;
> Water, water, everywhere,
> Nor any drop to drink. [PW I 190–91]

Coleridge glossed this second verse, 'And the Albatross begins to be avenged'. The dryness in Cain is spiritual, and represented in his appearance; he says to Abel, '. . . the spirit within me is withered, and burnt up with extreme agony' [PW I 292], and thus he cannot lament for his brother's sufferings. This is no doubt the Mariner's condition too but, as is characteristic of the poem, it is represented by his physical suffering:[22]

> And every tongue, through utter drought,
> Was withered at the root,
> We could not speak, no more than if
> We had been choked with soot.

In both poems the heat that is withering the protagonist's inner life is also represented as external. Cain wanders into a desert of 'hot rocks and scorching sands' and the Mariner stagnates beneath 'a hot and copper sky'.

The desiccation of body and soul in both men is also a prelude to a re-establishing of some relationship with the murdered being, and thus to motion, penitence and resolution. Cain discovers Abel in the desert, and the Mariner has the albatross, which he and the crew had hailed in God's name and as a Christian soul, slung about his neck. The next stage of the journey takes place in the company of the murdered soul: Cain and Abel, with Enos, go off

to find the God of the dead; the Mariner, burdened by the albatross, and with the crew, is confronted by Death and her shipmate,
Life-in-Death. The prose fragment ends as the trio set off, and so
we do not know what was to happen when they entered the
courts of the God of the dead.[23] But the Mariner's meeting with
Life-in-Death begins his awful realization that 'Victorious murder'
is but 'blind suicide', that his soul is dead within him: for even
though in a symbolic action, he looks to heaven, he cannot pray,
nor find the means to his salvation.

   The albatross's revenge continues, and takes several forms: after
Death has won the crew, and the soul has passed out of each
body, 'Like the whizz of my cross-bow', the Mariner suffers a
fearful solitude, a life in death:

> Alone, alone, all, all alone,
> Alone on a wide, wide sea!
> And never a saint took pity on
> My soul in agony. [PW I 196]

The dead men appear beautiful and are contrasted with what
continues to exist: 'And a thousand thousand slimy things/Lived
on; and so did I'. He feels himself to be part of the 'rotting sea',
and when he turns his eyes from that, of the 'rotting deck'. All
things about him speak to him of his crime, and appear to degenerate as a consequence of it. Because we know that the 'slimy things',
'the creatures of the calm' and the watersnakes are the same
animal despite their different modes of appearance, we can be
sure that a power in the Mariner's mind is creating his perception
of these degenerate forms.[24] We are now at the nadir of the poem,
and the Mariner remains seven nights thus cursed, unable to free
himself by prayer or action, trapped in 'loneliness and fixedness'
by the rotting calm he has caused. John Beer has remarked that in
contrast to traditional notions of the Fall in which the protagonists,
whether men or angels, move from a static state of bliss to a
dynamic state of evil, the Mariner, and Cain, discover that the
consequence of their crime is powerless and enforced inaction,
and that motion is associated with the beginning of penance.[25]
But, though prayer has proved impossible, in his 'fixedness' the
mariner notes that

> The moving Moon went up the sky
> And nowhere did abide, [PW I 197]

and the touching gloss attached to this verse makes it clear that the
Mariner's spirit goes forth, for 'he yearneth towards the journeying
Moon, and the stars that still sojourn, yet still move onward'. This
yearning for motion is an essential part of the Mariner's redemptive process. Kathleen Coburn has noted a parallel between this
gloss and Jeremy Taylor's funeral sermon on Lady Carbery. Taylor
suggests that, translating from his own Latin, ' "when the soul is
entered into her own house, into the free regions of the rest, and
the neighbourhood of heavenly joys", then its operations are more
spiritual, proper, and proportioned to its being;' [CN I 1473 n].
These words, which have their clearest echo in the gloss, indicate
that what the Mariner finds in the motion of the Moon and the
stars is a motion he seeks in himself, a spiritual motion of which
his looking to heaven was the first and thwarted instinct. The
resolution of the Mariner's condition originates in his looking to
a form of life outside himself – which in this instance is associated
with a pure soul seeking its appointed home. If his fixedness is
relieved by yearning for the motion of the moon, his loneliness is
relieved by his blessing of the watersnakes:

> O happy living things! no tongue
> Their beauty might declare:
> A spring of love gushed from my heart
> And I blessed them unaware [PW I 198]

This sudden access of love enables him to pray, and as he does
so the albatross falls from his neck into the sea. The burden of his
guilt is removed, his solitude and fixedness are ended, rain refre-
shes him, and a wind breaks the calm. His journey of repentance
has begun, and will take him back to the world whence he came,
but it is a world that he will see afresh in the new and searching
light that has awoken in his consciousness.

THE GROWTH OF THE MARINER'S CONSCIOUSNESS

At this point in the discussion it might be as well to determine
the general nature of the Mariner's new awareness.[26] I have sug-

gested that in writing this poem Coleridge's use, among other images of nature, of the sun as an idea was anterior to his conception of it as a thing. In his interpretation of the poem John Beer takes this line, and associates the word with a distinct force or power. He begins with the hierogram of the Egyptian trinity – the Sun, the Serpent and the Wings – and comments on their communion:

> If the pattern is broken, the wings will disappear, and the other components lose their glory. The sun will become unbearably hot, the serpent loathsome . . . If harmony is to be recreated, it will be done not by destroying the serpent, but by raising it up to its former glory. [C.Vis 69–70]

Much later in life, Coleridge noted that the serpent was the Egyptian symbol of the human understanding, and throughout his career we see an association of God, the Sun and Reason.[27] The separation of the human understanding from the divine Reason leads to the former's fall and corruption. The key to Beer's interpretation lies in the Mariner's destruction of this communion:

> . . . the Mariner, in killing the albatross, destroys the connection between the sun and the serpent. In consequence the two become separate, and equally alien to man. The serpent, representative of the flesh, becomes loathsome and corrupt, while the sun, now that the true inward vision is lost, is apprehended only as heat or wrath. Or in psychological terms, the Mariner is trapped between the fearful wrath of his conscience, which is all that remains of his Reason, and his consequent loathing of the flesh. Caught in this vicious circle, he is truly in Hell. [C.Vis. 157]

Broadly, I agree with this interpretation for it is very much in line with Coleridge's later thinking, and particularly with what he regarded as his all-important distinction between Reason and Understanding. But I would like to make some reservations. It is not certain that Coleridge knew of the hierogram, and we know that Wordsworth suggested the shooting of the albatross. We cannot therefore rely on the formal relations that Beer has established between the parts of this Egyptian trinity as an accurate guide to the poem. So, for instance, the serpent may represent the flesh, and the watersnakes do at one stage appear vile and corrupt, but I do not think that we may therefore assume that the Mariner suffers a loathing of the flesh: I find no traces of that Swiftian sentiment in the poem, and it is not one that is evident in any of Coleridge's other writings. And although the Mariner's world degenerates around him, yet he finds a beauty in what we would expect to fill him with most horror – the bodies of the dead sailors scattered on the deck. The Mariner's punishment is more subtle, and more distinctly Coleridgean, than a simple horror of mortality: it is to find his senses making him a world antagonistic to his true being, and which, robbed of all joy is nothing but a fearful burden: 'For the sky and the sea, and the sea and the sky/ Lay like a load on my weary eye' [PW I 197]. It is a world in which what might be seen as beautiful appears corrupt. His senses are not illuminated by Reason, and so through them he is punished for their improper use; they make him a world in which his proper being has no place.

Although it is not clear whether there is any difference of mind between Mariner and crew before the shooting of the albatross, it would be a mistake to assume that either party begins the journey with any degree of 'inward vision.' [C.Vis. 149–52]. It is more probable that they begin, like the sailors of the Speedwell who aimed to shoot a hawk resting in the rigging, in a state of non-feeling permitted by their non-thinking, in a state of ordinary unenlivened consciousness.[28] The Mariner's act opens the door to a power of which he has not previously been aware, but which by the end of the poem we see as the new basis of his conscious-ness.[29] It is a power which realizes the limitations of normal consciousness and so first makes the Mariner aware of his own Life-in-Death, and of the Death of his compatriots – rather as the weary Tiresias of *The Waste Land* looked down on the hoards streaming over London Bridge, and assigned them to a moral and spiritual limbo.[30] The crew, like the inhabitants of the unreal cities, judge by use of their senses: their assessment of the criminality of the Mariner's act is based only on its effects and not on any principle more substantial or permanent. If they are unaware of the power essential to their proper consciousness, then the Mari-ner's act involves a denial of this power – is a challenge to its actuality. The challenge is met – with a vengeance – and in this respect we may think of the Mariner's sin as behovely, for it will enable him to don his proper humanity.

THE FIGURE OF MEDIATION

As Coleridge asserted the distinction between Reason and Understanding, so did he insist on the necessity of their co-ordination in the life of the individual. The Mariner begins his journey, as do the crew, in a state of mind which we might characterize as the Understanding unenlightened by Reason, a state we could describe as day-to-day consciousness. Understanding provides us with the means of ordering the phenomena of perception so as to make sense of the material world; it is in the ideas and principles derived from Reason that we recognize our distinct but invisible humanity. Therefore Reason can only be adequately expressed through and in the forms of the Understanding, and the Understanding unenlightened by Reason is the road down to sensuality and the dereliction of one's humanity. The ideal union of these two fundamental components of our being Coleridge was to find in Christ.[31] Consequently, the Sun revealed by the shooting of the albatross is, in Beer's words, 'the angry "Typhonian" sun, unendurable because improperly apprehended' [C.Vis 162]. Beer then quotes Coleridge to the effect that 'Only in the Mediator . . . can the Holy One, of eyes too pure to behold iniquity, cease to become a consuming fire to all Corruption' [N.44 f.35]. The note continues, 'and this is the mystery and the unspeakable comfort of the Truth in Christ . . .' The mediator, epitomized in Christ, who enables the sinner to free him or herself from a burden of guilt, is of course the pivot of Christian mythology. In Coleridge's second shot at supernatural poetry, several commentators believe that this is the role that Christabel was designated to fulfill, as Enos seems likely to have become in 'The Wanderings of Cain'. Neither of them, it is noted, succeed in the task the commentators have appointed them.[32]

The idea of a mediator is, I believe, an essential one in Coleridge's thinking, but it is one that grows rather than arrives fully blown: after all, even if we do not take his flirtation with the Unitarians very seriously, Coleridge himself did, and went on arguing against what he supposed their chief tenets throughout his life.[33] If then there was a time when he believed that God might be apprehended directly, without mediation – as is further evident in the Conversation poems – we should not be surprised if the idea of mediation and the role of mediator have little more than walk on parts in the poems written at that time.

We have already seen hints of this mode of activity in Coleridge's vision of nature through the eyes of Charles Lamb and his own son, and in his short-lived belief that his wife was a 'Meek Daughter in the family of Christ' in whom he had found his redemption. In 'The Wanderings of Cain' Enos, the unfallen spirit in Cain's fallen world, does not influence the action. But a note, probably written much later in Coleridge's life, and apparently a draft of the third canto, begins: 'The Child is born, the Child must die . . . And we too all must die of Thirst/ for not a drop remains. But whither do we retire/ to Heaven or possibility of Heaven/'. The child dies, is buried and seems to be metamorphosed to a fountain, relieving the thirst of those still in the desert; this enables them to travel onto 'Heaven Gate' where 'the Child – then an angel – rushed out to receive them' [CN II 2780 & n]. If Enos is this child, his conception is more subtle than that of an innocent child of nature. His redeeming act involves his death and his ascent to heaven, which have obvious parallels with the Christian model. And it is possible to imagine, for instance, that in his sanctified state he might act as a mediator by maintaining the true idea of his father which his father had lost, rather as Cordelia acted in the light of her idea of Lear, and not according to the demands of the degenerate old man.

In 'The Ancient Mariner' no figure comes immediately to mind as fulfilling the role of innocent mediator. But at the very nadir of his desolation, when he is 'Alone, alone, all, all alone,/ Alone on a wide, wide sea', the Mariner is bitterly conscious of his need of such a figure: for in the two lines following he laments, 'And never a saint took pity on/ My soul in agony'. The Mariner knows only his solitude and powerlessness, that he has no resources to rescue his own soul, and feels that only a pure spirit from the 'upper sky' could relieve his suffering. It is easy to overlook such lines because of their conventional tone, but Coleridge seems to have some definite intention in mind: for the extended verse in which the Mariner blesses the watersnakes, and which most commentators think of as one of the two or three key moments in the poem, concludes with: 'Sure my kind saint took pity on me,/ And I blessed them unaware'. From having no guardian saint to relieve his spiritual agony, the Mariner is now able to recognize a purer being specifically assigned to the care of his soul – without whose aid, it is intimated, the spring of love could not have burst from his heart, nor could he have found it possible to pray again. That his restoration to love and prayer depends upon a will not his, yet acting within him, is evident in his repeated insistence that he blessed the watersnakes 'unaware'.

Who this kind saint is we are not told, and this I think signifies his or her relative unimportance in the action of the poem. However, beings of the upper sky continue to act on behalf of the Mariner: after finding himself able to pray and relieved of the dead albatross (and this simple piece of supernatural action shows us the justice of Beer's belief that Abel was the function of Cain's faulty consciousness[34]) the Mariner falls asleep – to recover from the long watch in the world of his sin; this sleep is 'a blessing from above':

> To Mary Queen the praise be given!
> She sent the gentle sleep from Heaven,
> That slid into my soul. [PW I 198]

And it is also be grace of the Holy Mother that the Mariner is refreshed with rain. There are few moments in this poem when we are not aware of powers 'above' or 'below' working on the Mariner as the agents and assistants of his conscience: we may think, for instance, of the Polar Spirit, and his fellow daemons, not as seeking the Mariner's destruction, but rather as furies chasing him along the road to redemption, acting on behalf of the murdered Christian soul, as Abel was to lead Cain to the God of the Dead; when his spirit is healed, then their task is finished and, as Geraldine was to have done upon the completion of her task, they disappear. The few moments when the Mariner is not aware of these powers are the moments of his greatest desolation:

> 'O Wedding-Guest! this soul hath been
> Alone on a wide wide sea:
> So lonely 'twas, that God himself
> Scarce seemed there to be. [PW I 206]

But when his saint takes pity on him, when Mary Queen of Heaven sends sleep into his soul and rain to refresh him, then it is implied, the Mariner knows the presence of God.

THE DEAD ARISE

The dead men too seem to have a life related to the state of the Mariner's conscience. It is after having seen 'The many men, so beautiful', lying dead on the rotting deck, that he first tries to pray unsuccessfully; and it is the Mariner's worst and most horrible punishment to have to endure the living curse in their eyes for seven days and seven nights. But after the blessing of the watersnakes, the dead men rise again, and the ship moves on under their guidance in the newly risen wind. The 'troops of spirits blest' that inspire the sailors' bodies are not their souls, nor 'daemons of earth or middle air' according to the gloss, but angelic spirits 'sent down by the invocation of the guardian saint'. It is likely, although it is not certain, that this guardian saint is also the 'kind saint' who took pity on the Mariner in his agony. If this is so, then it seems possible that he or she is giving the Mariner not only a vision which may offer him some consolation for the effects of his crime, but also a vision of the ideal relationship between the spirit and its divine source: for at dawn and after the re-animated bodies have done their work, they gather round the mast, as in some kind of service or hymn-singing, and the sounds they utter are material and bird-like:

> Sweet sounds rose slowly through their mouths
> And from their bodies passed.
>
> Around, around, flew each sweet sound,
> Then darted to the Sun;
> Slowly the sounds came back again,
> Now mixed, now one by one. [PW I 200]

If we accept that the Sun, 'like God's own head', is a symbol of divine power then we see here a relation established between the many individual spirits and their one, divine, source. That their relation is described through the conflation of what we think of as two distinct senses is perfectly in accord with Coleridge's ideal harmony – 'A light in sound, a sound-like power in light' [PW I 101]. The two following verses unite the bird imagery with angelic song as the skylark of the Quantocks is compared to 'an angel's song/ That makes the heavens be mute'. The platonically minded have often used the skylark as a symbol of the soul delightedly singing its own song, free of the mortal cage, and it is entirely characteristic of Coleridge's supernatural method that the idea should precede the associated image: what the Mariner sees, and remembers, is the result of the development of his conscience, and therefore consciousness, which is in some measure responsible for re-animating the mortal body, not with souls in an undetermined state of salvation, but with the pure and redeemed spirits of heaven. This act, this making of a pure being in our idea of another person, we shall find at the very core of Coleridge's theories of the redemptive process, and the groundwork of his idea of society. It is no coincidence that the Mariner should first recognize, or admit the existence of, his 'brother's son' when his body has been re-animated by one of the angelic spirits – for it is this recognition of the pure being of another that enables us to find the true person in any body. And our last glimpse of the crew is caught after the spell was snapped, when their bodies are lying flat and lifeless on the deck: but '. . . by the holy rood!/ A man all light, a seraph-man,/ On every corse there stood'. As we should expect, these spirits appear in the shape of men, for they are the true persons in all of us, escaped from the mortal and imprisoning body; and when they waved, their last act, it is to the Mariner 'a heavenly sight!'

THE HERMIT

The last person of significance in the poem, the Hermit – the central figure of Part VII – is also associated with the Mariner's new consciousness. As the representative figure of 'the kirk' he is aware of the heavenly powers that the Mariner has found within himself and which have operated on him in his isolation from society and the patterns of normal consciousness – represented in this poem not only by the sailors, but also by the Marriage Feast and the Wedding Guest. It is because of this that when he, the Pilot and the Pilot's boy are rowing out to the ship, and the Pilot is, like the Wedding Guest afraid of what he sees, that the Hermit is able to say cheerily, 'Push on, push on!' And when the ship is sunk 'by that loud and dreadful sound', and the Pilot, shrieking like Abel in the presence of Cain, falls down in a fit, and his boy becomes hysterical, the Hermit is able to remain calm though shaken. He is not a stranger to the Mariner's condition, for we

may believe that his own exile from society has enabled him to
reach a level of consciousness not known to the Pilot or boy, and
it is to him that the Mariner initially turns for the final relief from
his guilt. But although the Hermit's experience may be of the same
kind, it is much less acute, and formalized in his profession. The
question with which he intends to begin the process of shriving,
'What manner of man art thou?', is the result of his witnessing
the active power of forces which perhaps led him out of society,
but which are now dormant within him, and the effects of which
he has forgotten. This desire to know whether he is dealing with
the forces of good or evil does not inspire a simple response in
the Mariner, perhaps because he does not know himself. In order
to answer that question, he feels that he must rehearse his tale,
not to a man familiar with the general terms of his experience, but
to a man who, though at first in that state of ordinary consciousness with which the Mariner and the crew seem to have begun
their journey, is yet receptive to that development which has been
the root of his experience, and in whom it will live acutely, as it
lives acutely in the Mariner.[35] In the act of rehearsing his story,
the Mariner establishes a community between himself and his
auditor which finds its proper focus in the kirk. The kirk is closely
associated with the manner in which the ancient Mariner comes
back to his own country, both the Arguments of 1798 and 1800
ending with variations of this significant phrase [PW I 186]. As in
the Conversation poems there is a journey out, an experience and
a return, but unlike the Conversation poems, the person returning
feels compelled to relate his experience to selected individuals, as
it is an experience which has in some respects set him apart from
ordinary society. But the kirk, as well as being closely associated
with the Mariner's country, is that which enables him to put his
experience into a social context, finding the communal act of
prayer more appropriate to his altered state of consciousness than
the celebrations of the Wedding Feast. It is as if the life of the kirk
is based on the principles of Reason, and the Wedding Feast on
the notices of sense. As a result of his vicarious experience the
Wedding Guest is a wiser man, having become conscious of a
latent power within himself, but sadder because this wisdom turns
him away, as it turned the Hermit and the Mariner away, from
the simple pleasures of quotidian society.[36]

THE MORAL CONCLUSION

The many objections that have been raised against the overt morality of the poem begin with the poet himself. Mrs Barbauld thought
it had no moral, but Coleridge thought it had too much, 'and that
the only, or chief fault, if I may say so, was the obtrusion of the
moral sentiment so openly on the reader as a principle or cause
of action in a work of such pure imagination' [TT 31 May 1830].
What is curious about this anecdote is that neither Mrs Barbauld
for one reason, nor Coleridge for another, seem to have in mind
the six lines to which critical exception is usually taken:

> He prayeth well, who loveth well
> Both man and bird and beast.
>
> He prayeth best, who loveth best
> All things both great and small;
> For the dear God who loveth us,
> He made and loveth all. [PW I 209]

Mrs Barbauld cannot have doubted that this is the moral of the
tale, and only a lapse of memory or a want of attentive reading
could have allowed her to make her remark without qualification;
Coleridge's comment, on the other hand, and its continuation into
the want of moral relation between throwing date-stones, blinding
genie's sons and suffering death, indicates that his attention is on
the first part of the poem, on the albatross as the stated symbol
of a Christian soul, hailed in God's name, from the killing of which
the main action stems, as the main action of 'The Wanderings of
Cain' was to have stemmed from the killing of Abel. With hindsight, Coleridge would have been quite content to have made the
Mariner's killing of the albatross as accidental as the merchant's
blinding of the genie's son. But he queers this pitch by first of all
making the bird symbolic of God's presence, then entering the
crew, and especially the Mariner, into cordial relations with it (a
'bird that *loved* the man/ Who shot him with his bow' [PW I 202]),
and finally calling it, in the gloss, 'a pious bird of good omen'. So
instead of the thoroughly arbitrary relation between a given cause
and effect that Coleridge believed appropriate to 'a work of such
pure imagination', he has established the basis of what could
hardly be a more profound relation, that of an individual and his

recognition of God's presence in another form of being. As it is here that we find the 'principle or cause of action' of the poem, so it is here that we find an 'obtrusion of moral sentiment' on the reader.

While taking exception to the quoted lines, critics have, like Mrs Barbauld, by and large failed to recognize the moral basis of the poem. This may be because it is possible to dismiss Coleridge's references to God, Christian souls, pious omens and other religious paraphernalia as a platitudinous part of the poem's machinery. In my opinion one should hesitate to read any poet or poem in such a manner, for it is to risk letting great and general truths lie bed-ridden in the dormitory of the soul; but least of all should one thus read Coleridge: for of all English poets, he is perhaps the most aware, and even at this stage of his life, one of the best qualified to determine, the philosophical and theological implications of his words. In order to obtain a satisfactory reading of lines 612–17, I think it is important to recognize at the outset that the groundwork of the poem is ineradicably moral; that is, it is concerned first with the relationship between actions as a cause, and conditions of spirit as an effect, and subsequently between conditions of spirit as a cause and actions as the effect. There can be no separation, in Coleridge's thinking, between the moral and the spiritual, no possibility of spiritual regeneration without co-ordinate growth in the understanding of the significance of human behaviour.

If this is recognized, then I think we are on the right footing to argue for the appropriateness of lines 612–17. Firstly, as a summary always is, they may be inadequate to the whole of which they are speaking, but the idea that they convey is closely related to the moral idea that Coleridge believed was the cause of the action of the poem. Their function is not to re-present the experience we have just undergone, but to remind us of its moral basis. Secondly, despite appearances, these lines invite neither a literal nor a pru-dential response from the reader: it has been said, in a remark as erroneous as it is witty, that the only moral that may be drawn from the poem is, 'Don't shoot albatrosses'.[37] This is to take the world of the poem, a poem of the pure imagination, in none but a literal way, and therefore to be able to draw from it only a moral which assumes a fixity and definiteness about the external world, a fixity and definiteness in which the whole of the Mariner's experience ought to have taught us to disbelieve. Edward Kessler sums up his version of these two kinds of error:

> The albatross had either been viewed as a physical thing, leading to the partial truth that the poem deals with man's relationship to external nature; or it had been seen exclusively as a metaphor . . . The latter view ignored the life outside the mind and led to the absurd conclusion that the Mariner murdered a concept.[38]

In this poem, the albatross is a symbol, existing as the resolution between the literal and the metaphorical, in the same way that we might say that the world of the poem is inseparable from the Mariner's consciousness: it is both an inward and an outward world. And if one thinks that Coleridge is advocating some sort of humane sentimentalism which values equally human and animal life, that infers that to take the life of a bird is an act which in itself endangers one's own being and that of one's companions, one could not be further from the truth. Coleridge poured scorn on those who attempt to bring legislation about the rights of animals before Parliament: it was, for him, to make a blasphemous confusion between a person and a thing. Reason, the image of God within us, is the basis of our personal being – and in its absence all other forms of being are things, and may be used solely instrumentally. For the Mariner, the albatross is symbolic of God's presence, and his shooting of it is only significant in relation to this fact. Had he shot it because he and the crew were hungry, or because it was, say, siren-like tempting them into the ice-pack rather than out of it, the action would have had an entirely different significance.

It is therefore possible to see that the much criticized lines are more appropriate than is normally believed. 'He prayeth well, who loveth well' is a principle precisely deduced from the Mariner's experience at the crux of the poem; he longs to pray, but his heart is 'as dry as dust', and only when grace is given to him by his 'kind saint' is he able to feel a 'spring of love' for the watersnakes: at 'the self-same moment' he finds himself capable of praying, the act which begins his long course of penance, and eventually returns him to his point of departure. The following three lines might easily be taken as implying that it is 'man and bird and beast' in themselves that ought to be the objects of love, rather than whatever qualities inhere in them as symbolic of God's being: and it is these lines, I believe, that are chiefly responsible for the frequent mis-reading or mis-interpretation of this passage. However, the last two lines of the moral, 'For the dear God who loveth us,/ He made and loveth all', re-assert that the significance of man, bird or beast resides in their creation by God. In order to read these lines correctly, and to avoid laying stress on existence rather than on existence in God, we should remember that at this time Coleridge thought of nature as an 'eternal language' which spoke of God's presence, and that he was never to contemplate nature in seclusion from God. It is not their literal nor their metaphorical but only their symbolic existence that gives the beings of this poem any significance.

Finally, and in the context of 'Dejection . . .' we should remember that it is only the person who loves who is able to send his soul abroad, who can illuminate the natural world with his or her creative joy. It is precisely this, by grace of his guardian saint, that the Mariner did after witnessing the beauty of the watersnakes. Nature is waiting to receive this light, this luminous mist; the Mariner is indeed a god of love who tamed the chaos of his perception that had been rendered hellish by the disorder in his being. Not only, therefore, are these lines, taken symbolically, appropriate in the context of the poem, but they speak of a conjunction of feelings significant in other of Coleridge's poems, and, as we shall see, which are very much at the heart of his theology.

SUMMARY

We have seen, I think, that the 'Poet's Reverie' was one in which, by dismissing the limits of sense-based consciousness, Coleridge dreamt of a human being who acted according to a force or energy originating in the deepest recesses of the human heart; who was not acted on by the dreary impressions of the visible world,[39] but who found that the mind, having powers of its own, was sense-making and not sense-made; who learnt that the murder of another being was but a form of suicide, and who discovered that in order to work out his redemption he required the co-operation of another being to mediate between himself and the alienated powers; and whose experience finally matured his consciousness to a new realization of the relations between people as well as respect for all things having their life in God. The Mariner sees this relationship as represented by the kirk, a word sufficiently close to 'church' to share some of its significance, but sufficiently removed from 'the Church' not to disturb Coleridge's Unitarian sympathies. The Marriage Feast represents life as it is formed from sense-based consciousness, from the notions of the Understanding rather than from the principles of Reason.

THE WORLD OF 'CHRISTABEL'

If the Mariner's condition was largely revealed through his changing relationships with the various forms of nature, that of Christabel is more evident in her relationships with the various characters of the poem. For 'Christabel' is, in contrast to 'The Ancient Mariner', a network of social relationships: between Christabel and Geraldine primarily, but also between Christabel and her dead mother; between Christabel and her absent knight; between Christabel and her father, Sir Leoline; between Leoline and Geraldine, and Geraldine and Christabel's mother; between Geraldine and the absent knight. The relationships between Leoline and Bard Bracy, and between Sir Leoline and Sir Roland (Geraldine's supposed father) as children, also have small but significant roles in the poem. It is the effect that Geraldine has on the people who constitute Christabel's world from which the action of the poem springs, and she is the pivot about which all these relationships turn.

If we are unsure about the state of consciousness in which the Mariner sets sail and the poem begins, we can be certain that Christabel demonstrates her charitable nature and good faith by praying for her lover and rescuing Geraldine from the forest – even if what she soon learns of her guest's nature comes into conflict with her duties of hospitality. With what seems to be supernatural power, Geraldine is able to neutralize the protective influence of her mother in order to work a necessary spell on Christabel. Sir Leoline, who had parted from Sir Roland in their youth with 'words of high disdain', sees Geraldine as a means of restoring this broken friendship with 'his heart's best brother'; this hope, and his physical attraction to her, is in part responsible for his alienation from his daughter and the erasing of his dead wife from his memory. Bard Bracy, a poet and seer, and therefore wiser than men of sublunary sense, it also at odds with Sir Leoline because he has a vision of the trouble Geraldine has brought upon Christabel. Geraldine was to have impersonated the Knight, in whose pseudo-presence Christabel was to have felt deeply uneasy, before the vision vanished at the return of the Knight himself. Geraldine is at the heart of the poem, and is its greatest puzzle. So Nethercot in *The Road to Tryermaine*: 'It is Geraldine, and Geraldine alone, who can afford the key to the riddle'.[40]

THE CRIME

The riddle, or the identity of Geraldine, is complicated by the fact that, unlike 'The Wanderings of Cain' or 'The Ancient Mariner', there is no certain crime, committed by the eponymous hero, the expiation of which is the development of the poem. Superficially, so superficially as to be ignored by most critics, a crime has been committed against Geraldine. Without apparent cause, she was seized by five warriors and, so she says, dumped unceremoniously in the forest, ill-clad for a night in the open. Although this 'crime' against Geraldine is partly righted by Christabel's action in saving her from further exposure in the forest, and it is part of Leoline's plans to complete the process by proclaiming the infamy of her still unnamed abductors, challenging them to a tourney if they dare deny it, yet this crime, committed by persons who make no appearance in the poem itself, and who suffer no consequences because of it, remains outside the central action – Geraldine's transformation of Christabel. What readers, though none of the characters, suspect is that this 'crime' is Geraldine's method of legitimately entering into the hearts of Christabel's household, and there beginning the work which she has either chosen or been sent to do.

James Gillman records that a main purpose of the poem was to illustrate the fact that the virtuous, whom he supposes to be Christabel, saves the wicked.[41] But who would Christabel save? Geraldine, Sir Leoline and the absent Knight are the possibilities that have been canvassed. Geraldine may require salvation, but the technical problem, to dig no deeper, is that as the poem stands she proves to be the agent of evil, and not its object; there is no hint that she was to do more than induce, and partly control, the action. And what is Sir Leoline to be saved from? What crime has e committed equivalent to the murder of his brother, or the hooting of a Christian soul? It is true that in his youth he broke 1 bitterness from his closest friend, and that he now lives in a world of death. But the two facts are not apparently connected, or it is only since his wife died that the matins bell has tolled him ack to his dead world – where, like the Mariner's crew, he judges ccording to the understanding, and thus quickly falls prey to Geraldine's wiles. He may not be a good man, but he is not evil; ke the crew, his destiny is of little consequence, for his soul is n inhabitant of limbo, a rag shaken by any wind that blows. And 'hristabel's nameless lover – what of him – the candidate most requently chosen for the uncomfortable business of salvation? Although nameless, he is of significance, for Christabel dreams of im:

> She had dreams all yesternight
> Of her own betrothéd knight;
> And she in the midnight wood will pray
> For the weal of her lover that's far away. [PW I 216]

ut since the poem has a medieval setting, the Knight is probably crusader, and Christabel is therefore more likely to be conscious f his needing physical rather than moral protection: we certainly eceive no hint that he is in need of redemption, or that she has ny notion that her business is to redeem him. On the other hand, might be argued that were she conscious of her redemptive owers, she would invalidate them, and like Orpheus, aware of is action and letting it turn his head, she would send her lover ack to Hades. But were this process to happen in her subconcious, what is the nameless knight to be redeemed from, all nawares, by his beloved? From lust to love is John Beer's nswer.[42]

The establishing of a right relationship between these two owers is, I believe, the single most important theme in the poem: iews such as Beer's however, tend to have us reading a poem bout a subconscious action by an unconscious agent on an unconcious object. But this reordering does make sense if we think of in respect of Christabel, rather than her absent and nameless night. After the first two of the four lines quoted above, the first dition had:

> Dreams that made her moan and leap
> As on her bed she lay in sleep.

The outcry against the poem when it first appeared was chiefly
directed against its apparent sexuality. 'The most obscene Poem
in the English Language' declared one pamphlet vindictively, and
Coleridge took great delight in discovering, in an old book in
Coleorton, *Paradise Lost* decried on similar grounds.[43] But perhaps
he was more sensitive to these and other such criticisms than he
admitted; certainly he chose to excise these two lines from later
editions. A woman lying in bed at night, dreaming of her lover,
and moaning and 'leaping' may well make the reader wonder
whether she isn't being visited by images of 'unwonted lust'.[44] This
receives a degree of confirmation from a comment on Christabel's
dreaming after Geraldine has cast her spell on her, and Christabel's
star is about to set and Geraldine's about to rise:

> Fearfully dreaming, yet, I wis,
> Dreaming that alone, which is!
> O sorrow and shame! Can this be she,
> The lady, who knelt at the old oak tree?

This suggests, firstly, what we have come to see as the practical
basis of the supernatural poems, that truth or reality – 'that alone,
which is!' – is apprehended in the suspension of sense-based
consciousness, in dreams. Secondly, though Christabel wants no
more than 'The weal of her lover that's far away' on the level
of waking consciousness and kneeling 'at the old oak', at the
subconscious level her hope is a cause of 'sorrow and shame', a
hope, perhaps, more of eros than of agape. Two worlds and two
states of being are clearly contrasted in these lines. Christabel left
the castle in order to pray for her lover because her prayer is an
act of her conscious and charitable nature, not of her subconscious
and yet to be disclosed erotic nature. The castle is associated with
death, and as Sir Leoline shows so conclusively in his fascination
with Geraldine, with the sensual rather than the spiritual. So to
answer Johnny Wordsworth's question as to why Christabel
cannot pray at home, she leaves the castle because any prayer
uttered there for her lover (she does manage to pray to the Virgin
when her lover is not on her mind) would not reflect its real
intention.[45]

Two other pieces of evidence also point to the fact that Coleridge is seeking to order human sexuality in a relationship of love.[46] He once mentioned that lines 43–65 of Crashaw's 'Hymn to St. Teresa' 'were ever present to my mind whilst writing the second part of Christabel; if, indeed, by some subtle process of the mind they did not suggest the first thought of the whole poem'.[47] The passage Coleridge cites describes St Teresa's willingness to seek martyrdom. As a result, most critics have concentrated on discovering comparable aspects of Christabel's nature: her innocence, her desire to save and protect others, and the fact that hers has 'Christ's Name in't', have all been suggested as fitting her for a role as a martyr. But unlike St Teresa, Christabel is very far from seeking martyrdom: she is betrothed, not vowed to chastity, and has no high vision of her destiny. To see her as a martyr is thus not to heed Coleridge's warning that the relationship between the inspiring thought and the resulting poem might be a very devious one. Humphry House thinks that another aspect of Crashaw's poem may have been in Coleridge's mind – the description of charitable love in erotic terms:

> She never undertooke to know
> What death with love should have to doe
> Nor has she ere yet understood
> Why to show love shee should shed blood. [HH 130]

House comments: '. . . there seems a strong likelihood that Coleridge was hampered by problems which belong to the psychological borderland where matters of religion overlap with those of sex . . . Coleridge, of all Englishmen then living, was the one most likely to have had some understanding of this borderland . . .'[48]

The simplest and most obvious way they overlap is in the attitude of the lover to the beloved. Christabel's love of her knight depends on her *idea* of him, not on his presence, just as her mother, whom she has never seen and never will see, is also a living person to her. This belief in the reality of the person, whatever the state of their body, is the ground of the Christian's belief in the living presence of Christ. However, Christabel has not chosen the saint's way, and looks forward to her marriage, to the expression of her love through her senses. The danger is that these forms of expression may seem to the individual to have a life and rites of their own. Not so, says Coleridge, for if they seek

to usurp the life of Reason, they will usurp the idea of the beloved
who will then become a mere object of sensual gratification.[49]

There is, of course, one myth to which this 'overlap' between
religion and sex is central – the fall of Adam and Eve; and one
poem in the English language where the usurpation of Reason by
our undisciplined sexual nature, and consequent degradation of
our humanity, is seen as the profoundest consequence of the fall
– *Paradise Lost*:

> As with new Wine intoxicated both
> They swim in mirth, and fansie that they feel
> Divinitie within them breeding wings
> Wherewith to scorne the Earth: but that false fruit
> Farr other operation first displaid,
> Carnal desire enflaming, he on Eve
> Began to cast lascivious Eyes, she him
> As wantonly repaid: in Lust they burne: [Bk. IX ll.1008ff.]

We know that from 1794 Coleridge had been planning a poem on
the Origin of Evil, and that *Paradise Lost* formed as much a part of
his dreaming as his waking life.[50] He himself had experienced a
confusion of erotic and charitable impulses in the hopes he had
had of his marriage, and he would fight the battle again in his
relationship with Sara Hutchinson – indeed this may already have
begun after he met Sara in 1799, before he began to compose the
second part of Christabel.

These things, taken together with the fact that Coleridge was
exploring the truths of our inward nature, make it fitting that we
should regard 'Christabel' not only as describing this particular
inversion of our nature rightly and ideally considered, but also as
having been begun in the hope of regaining this lost paradise. By
taking Geraldine in from the forest, into her bed-chamber and
bed, Christabel in some manner accepts the precedence of her
sensual over her charitable nature, a precedence which constitutes
Coleridge's idea of the fall. This disfigures our true humanity
which perhaps explains why in a manuscript alteration, after these
lines.

> Her silken robe, and inner vest,
> Dropt to her feet, and full in view
> Behold! her bosom and half her side –

Coleridge added

It was dark and rough as the Sea-Wolf's hide.[51]

The 'crime' thus becomes an extremely subtle one. It is the conflict between what Christabel consciously wants – to love 'All things both great and small' in a selfless and charitable way – and the reality of her desire, first seen in her dreams, later forming some part of her consciousness, and which in separation from her charitable self is associated with a bestialization of her nature. She begins in a state of mind comparable to that at which the Mariner arrives – consciously wishing good to all beings – but has to learn the real power of her erotic nature which will, temporarily, usurp her conscious and charitable self.[52] The plot of the poem would then be the reordering of this extremely common, if not universal, disorder, and the establishment of the right basis of marriage, a prothalamion in which Reason first conquers and then rules sense and Understanding.

THE METHOD OF CHRISTABEL

Coleridge set himself a considerable technical problem in this poem: how is he to demonstrate this disorder, to bring it out from behind the curtain of Christabel's charitable appearance into her consciousness, and permit it to act in such a way that it is transformed, and ceases to be the governing force of her reality? Interestingly, George Eliot faces a similar problem in *The Mill on the Floss*. It is not until Maggie allows herself to be taken down the river by Stephen that she experiences the full power of her sensual nature – and having been borne along by that current she is subsequently able to prevent herself from acting under the influence of it. Hers is, though, a question of renunciation rather than transformation, of combatting her sensual nature rather than reorientating it. The technical difficulty of revealing this aspect of Maggie's nature is solved by the presence of Stephen. Coleridge has attempted to treat of the same matter at a more fundamental level: there is, first, no sense of renunciation in Christabel; her erotic nature is not to be suppressed but to form an element essential to her marriage: were her Knight-lover present, any obstacles to the marriage that the poet chose to invent would either seem to draw out the inevitable conclusion to an unnecessary distance from its beginning, or make the marriage inappropriate to the ideal characters of the protagonists: in either case the poet would hardly be able to suspend the disbelief of his readers. The disorder in Christabel's heart must therefore be worked out in separation from her future husband. Yet because she is at first presented as a charitable figure whose idea of her knight rules her sense of him, had her soul been stirred in a way that Maggie's was by Stephen, by the physical presence of another man tempting her to infidelity, then we would cease to see her as an idea, as the final and proper order of things, however well she came out of the temptation. For were she not genuinely touched by this secondary figure, there would have been no temptation, and nothing would have changed. But were she properly tempted, we would have to ask what qualities in her were attracted to this man which remained dormant in the presence or the memory of her knight. The poet would have allowed circumstance to sully his idea. So her erotic and energetic nature must be revealed to her, and to the readers of the poem, by some other means – in some way which discloses the disorder within her, but does not compromize either her relationship with her future husband, or the integrity that she outwardly presents and which, after her fall, she will realize.

If the poem is to function at the level of human relationships, then the only possibility is another woman who has herself been made aware of her erotic nature.[53] Geraldine has been abducted, and though we need not believe her story as she tells it, yet we do not doubt that she is in some way conscious of her own sexuality. She will cause the alteration in Christabel's consciousness, and such phrases as 'Thou'st had thy will' in reference to her lying down with Christabel, and the description of the latter's 'after-rest/ While in the lady's arms she lay'[PW I 230] all have a tone of sexuality that Coleridge made no effort to deny. But what happens to Christabel is not in any way connected with desire for Geraldine, as must inevitably have been the case had another man made her aware of her erotic nature: rather it is an awakening of a force within her that her conscious will would still reject, though powerless to do so.

Bracy the Bard's dream plays an important part in every interpretation of the poem; and justly, because it confirms for us the continuing innocence of Christabel and the 'evil' of Geraldine. Because this excursion of Bracy's is a dream, what he discovers is much nearer to the true nature of Geraldine, and her relationship with Christabel, than any other character, particularly Sir Leoline, has managed to discern in the presence of their guest: what he saw in his dream was a dove, Christabel, entrapped by a snake whom we know to be Geraldine:

> . . . I saw a bright green snake
> Coiled around its wings and neck.
> Green as the herbs on which it couched,
> Close by the dove's head it crouched;
> And with the dove it heaves and stirs,
> Swelling its neck as she swelled hers! [PW I 232]

The interesting feature of this image is that neither animal seems to be fighting for conquest or survival; their relationship, as the relationship of the vulture and the snake in 'The Wanderings of Cain', is static and intimate. We know that Coleridge associated snakes and serpents with the Understanding divorced from Reason, and that green is the colour the Middle Ages associated with sexual love. From this image and Christabel's later behaviour, we see that sexual love in her is holding charitable love in subjection. The sympathetic heaving of the necks in Bracy's dream finds this echo in the main narrative: on awakening, Geraldine asks Christabel whether she slept well, and Christabel observes her speech:.

> And while she spake, her looks, her air
> Such gentle thankfulness declare,
> That (so it seemed) her girded vests
> Grew tight beneath her heaving breasts.
> 'Sure I have sinn'd!' said Christabel,
> 'Now heaven be praised if all be well!' [PW I 228]

Geraldine seems to have put on a renewed femininity, and Christabel is aware of a disordering of her nature connected with Geraldine's conspicuous sexuality.

The action of the poem concludes with Bracy asking not to be sent to Sir Roland as the bearer of the good news of his daughter's safety, as he wishes 'To clear yon wood from thing unblest'; and with Christabel, having been dogged up by reptilian looks from Geraldine, falling at her father's feet and pleading, 'By my

mother's soul do I entreat/ That thou this woman send away!
This insult to his hospitality is too much for Sir Leoline, and
commanding Bracy to be off, he escorts the gorgeous Geraldine
from the hall, leaving Christabel on her knees, alone and desolate.
As the plan was to develop in Cantos III and IV, Christabel was
to have been cast out of house and home, Bracy to discover that
Sir Roland's castle had been washed away, and thus that Geraldine
was an impostor; and she was then to have transfigured herself
into the likeness or 'shape' of the absent knight. Christabel, having
returned from her 'exile', feels disturbed by 'his' presence, and
only very reluctantly prepares to go ahead with the marriage. This
would appear to indicate that Christabel's soul is now rightly
ordered (a process to have been initiated perhaps by her 'song of
desolation' [N.30, f.60v] and which might have been comparable
to the Mariner's meeting with Life-in Death or to Cain's audience
with the God of the Dead) and that she is not now judging according to the senses. That scene might be compared to the one we
have in Part II, in which living in a world of death, Sir Leoline
judges Geraldine solely by virtue of her appearance. But before
Christabel does get married to the disguised Geraldine, the true
knight enters, Geraldine disappears, her task complete, and to
symbolize that all is now well both in Christabel's soul and in her
life, the clock strikes 12 and her mother's voice is heard from
beyond the grave, as had been prophesied.[54] The marriage would
then have been of the truest kind, in which charitable love provides the foundation for erotic love.

CHRISTABEL'S REDEEMER

I have already noted my disagreement with John Beer's belief that
Christabel herself was to be the innocent who would redeem her
absent knight. Of the three works professedly supernatural, the
titles of two are eponyms of the figure to be redeemed, and not
the redeemer or mediator. It would be curious, I think, suddenly
to find this trait overthrown in the last of the three works, and to
have the focus of consciousness shifted from the figure undergoing
the main action to a figure who enables only part of that action –
as curious as if we were to retitle *King Lear* 'The Triumph of
Cordelia'. However, it is not my intention that we should see
Christabel as of a kind with Cain and the Mariner: she is not a

murderer in any sense at all. But she is the protagonist for that painful maturation of consciousness, involving both her original innocence and acquired guilt, which has parallels in the experience of both Cain and the Mariner. The 'crime' she commits is much more subtle than murder, and far closer to the crimes of conscience we all commit.[55]

But if Christabel is the protagonist, then we are still in search of a person who might be described as her redeemer or mediator. She, like the Mariner, was to have been exiled from her world as a result of her crime, before returning in an altered state of consciousness. If in his exile the Mariner had found it impossible to pray or bless without assistance from some being charged with the care of his soul, then we might reasonably expect to find Christabel cared for by a similar being.

Both Christabel and the poet on her behalf invoke two of the best-known inhabitants of heaven to her aid in moments of crisis. As she is about to come upon Geraldine in the forest, the poet prays, 'Jesu, Maria, shield her well!' [PW I 217] – a line which is repeated much later in the poem after Bracy has narrated his vision, and Geraldine has turned and looked askance at Christabel [PW I 233]. Christabel herself, when she see Geraldine for the first time, cries, 'Mary mother, save me now . . . And who art thou?' [PW I 218]. These spontaneous but conventional *cris de coeur* have little effect on the development of the action, for come hell and high water Christabel *has* to undergo a time of suffering and desolation. But they remind the reader that the poet and Christabel, like the ancient Mariner, believe that there are powers 'above' which may intervene in the action of those suffering trials on the middle earth.

The invocation of the Queen of Heaven in her role of mother may only be coincidental, but it does underline Christabel's consciousness of her own mother – who, though she was never to appear, nonetheless has a significant role even in the unfinished poem. This consciousness is of a very particular kind, for she died in giving birth to Christabel. So what Christabel knows of her is not in any way the result of experience in the world of the senses: her mother therefore is an idea to her, an act of her conscience. That, however, she is a living force in her daughter's life and her guardian spirit, Geraldine is fully aware:

> Alas! what ails poor Geraldine?
> Can she the bodiless dead espy?
> And why with hollow voice cries she,
> 'Off, woman, off! this hour is mine –
> Though thou her guardian spirit be,
> Off, woman, off! 'tis given to me.' [PW I 223]

What Christabel's mother guards seems to be the holiness of her daughter's heart, a holiness which Geraldine is set on disturbing, and so possibly enriching, as the Mariner's consciousness was enriched by his disordering. The conflict between the two women is a conflict between the unregulated life of the senses – a form of life-in-death in which Sir Leoline so willingly participates – and the life of Reason, in which idea and spirit, the proper 'supernatural', become the ground of the senses.[56]

The lines describing Christabel's sleep, after her enchantment by Geraldine, make it seem likely that Christabel's mother is also a saint in heaven, with a status analogous to that of the Mariner's 'kind saint':

> No doubt she hath a vision sweet.
> What if her guardian spirit 'twere,
> What if she knew her mother near?
> But this she knows, in joys and woes,
> That saints will aid if men will call:
> For the blue sky bends over all. [PW I 226]

The blue sky, as so often for Coleridge, is a metaphor for heaven. Two notebook entries clearly connect Christabel's vision of her mother with the act of looking up to heaven, and so to the saints:

> One lifts up one's eyes to heaven as if to seek there what one had lost on Earth/ Eyes –
>   Whose Half-beholdings thro' unsteady tears
>   Gave shape, hue, distance, to the inward Dream [CN III 3649]

Christabel has lost her mother, and it is to heaven that she looks for her: but the impetus of her looking comes from 'the inward Dream', the idea of her mother which she finds within herself and as part of herself. But it is characteristic of the human senses to seek outside the self for realization or expression of this idea, and this corresponds closely to Coleridge's method in the supernatural poems. In a note which seems preparative to his continuation of the poem, he writes:

> Christabel – My first cries mingled with my Mother's Death-groan/ – and she beheld the vision of Glory ere I the earthly Sun – when I first looked up to Heaven, consciously, it was to look up after or for my Mother . . . [CN III 3720]

Her mother was sanctified by a vision of spiritual glory before Christabel's senses had properly developed, and when through them she gained a form of consciousness, the first use she put this to was to look for her mother. John Beer thinks that the line, 'That saints will aid if men will call', an 'outcry from the primary being [which] will find an answer in the life-echoing universe' [CPI 191] but this is to forget that Christabel calls upon a *person*, the idea of whom she has found within herself as an inward dream, and who is glorified as a person because she exists free of the senses. It seems likely that Coleridge wanted the reader to think of Christabel's mother as sanctified, and therefore capable of acting as a pure and innocent mediator or redeemer.[57]

Exactly how Christabel's idea of her mother would have assisted her reorientation or redemption we cannot know for certain. But it is clear that Geraldine and her mother are in competition for aspects of Christabel's being. Perhaps then, in her desolation, the spirit of her dead mother would have returned to Christabel to enable her to re-establish the charitable and the reasonable as the guiding force of her being; perhaps by holding this idea of her mother constantly before her, an idea united with a sanctified person, Christabel could have achieved the same end. We can be certain, though, that she, like the Mariner, was powerless to expel or control a force that her better nature would reject, except through the aid of someone she conceived of as external to her: for when she begs her father, 'By my mother's soul do I entreat/ That thou this woman send away!', she is not merely attempting to prevent her father from making a fool of himself, she is also, perhaps chiefly, asking her father to do what she cannot do, and prevent that fearful disruption in her being that Geraldine has precipitated and her presence continues. In her agony she appeals to her father to remember the woman who should still act in his conscience – but who has been rendered impotent in hers.

That her mother represents an ideal order which Christabel will realize in herself and so be united with her again, is evident in the planned conclusion of the poem. Her mother's voice from 'beyond the grave' is the life of Reason or the spirit speaking through and directing the life of the senses. It is heard also by Christabel's father who, having realized Geraldine's Duessa-like nature, rediscovers the memory of his dead wife as the voice of his conscience, and so is reconciled to his daughter. Christabel's marriage is therefore symbolic of the complete reintegration of the family.

CONCLUSION

What I have attempted to show in these last two chapters is that, beginning as Wordsworth does, with distinct and definite images, Coleridge failed to disclose discrete 'religious meanings' in nature, and that as a consequence he was unable to bring into poems originating in sense impression the essential features of our humanity. This failure had two major components: the hope of seeing all aspects of natural life as participating in one life – a hope he sought to realize by supposing that a non-personalized God was the common life of all – prevented him from seeking the relations between particular ideas and particular forms; and, to realize this vision of unity, he presumed that a receptivity and passivity of mind would allow nature to act so as to disclose to us both her being and ours.

In contrast to this direct relation of the poet's mind with nature, yet occurring in the same poems, is Coleridge's developed sense of living through his family and friends. Unlike Wordsworth's, none of Coleridge's poetry seeking to find a harmony between intellect and nature is without a framework of affection for other people. In the Conversation poems this conflict between the presence of and responsibility to another human being, and the possibility of realizing our humanity from attention to sense impressions, is dramatized in the contrast between the hill-top vision and his thoughts that yearn for human kind, but is never adequately resolved. But in the supernatural poems, because Coleridge has largely dismissed immediate perceptions, freeing his imagination from the restrictions both of sense impression and particular relationships, so he is able to invest his idea or 'shadow' of a human being with what he feels are the essential forces or ideas of our humanity. The imagination is primarily, in these poems, a person-creating faculty, echoes of which we find in the means by which the protagonists conceive their redeeming agents.

What Coleridge discovered in his exploration of the idea of human nature is that it is, in at least two significantly different ways, disordered. The Mariner's shooting of the albatross is evidence of his thoughtless and uncharitable bearing towards his fellow beings; this act stimulates into life a power he had neglected and so he discovers his alienation from the world in which he moves. When he is restored, he sees that society as a whole lives in that state of consciousness which was his before his crime. Therefore, in order to explain his own alteration of consciousness, which depends upon a power invisible to the senses, he feels he must compel other selected individuals to undergo the same process vicariously. Christabel begins in that state of charity at which the Mariner arrives: her disorder is her lack of consciousness of her sensual and erotic nature, and so not to have tried and tested the strength of her life in reason. Her sin – in which the life of the senses temporarily subjugates her charitable being – also exiles her from her world, and her desolation would have presumably been as great as that of the Mariner, if of a different kind. But both these characters, and Cain as well, cannot escape from the consequences of their sin, and begin their penitential journeys, without the mediation of a purer being, associated with heaven or heavenly powers, who is also in some degree a function of their conscience. Cain's son, Christabel's mother and the Mariner's kind saint are all products of 'the inward Dream' which looks to heaven for its realization.

And if we think of the strange lust of murder as one consequence of the fall, and the inversion of our sexual and spiritual natures as another, then it is possible to see that in his two supernatural poems Coleridge has given us a profound account of his vision of human nature, and of the peculiar process by which man may be redeemed. 'The Ancient Mariner' and 'Christabel' are original attempts to justify the ways of God to Man, not by reference to any action of our predecessors, to history or mythology, but by reflection on that which every man may find existing within himself.

4

Kubla Khan and Dejection: An Ode

'a more than usual state of emotion, with more than usual order'
BL II, 12

Coleridge's two kinds of poetry have in common their interest in the redemption of the individual. We have seen that what Harper characterized as the 'return' of the Conversation poems is also the shift in perspective of a man suddenly awakened from visions of the unity of 'animated nature' to an awareness of his social relations. This shift might be called redemptive because as Coleridge reminded himself of his allegiance to people in time and place, simultaneously he saw Christ as the means by which disorders in himself had been, or those in society, could be, righted. From pantheistic visions of God's ominpresence in the life of nature, he returns to a vision of social relations ordered in the person of Christ.

The process by which this redemption is to be effected, either at an individual or a societary level, we are not told. (The gift of wife and cottage had proved a phantom salvation for the poet.) What we find in these poems is a refocussing of intention, a shift from one kind of hope to another, and not the dramatic working out of either kind itself. In separate ways, the process which enables redemption is realized in 'The Ancient Mariner' and 'Christabel'; but in order to permit this process Coleridge has had to sacrifice the reality of his natural and social worlds. The exploration of sin and redemption takes place apart from his family, friends and his immediate impressions of nature.

But if the truths that invigorate the Supernatural poems are truths that the poet finds within himself, we may reasonably expect that they will come to animate his social relations. In the Conversation poems, though the poet is conscious of familial and

88

friendly ties, and feels that he owes his allegiance to someone outside himself, there is little sense that these others are entering into the life of the poet along the lines which accord with the essential truths of human nature. We receive only the barest hints, for instance, that his wife, the once 'Meek Daughter in the family of Christ', or close friends such as the pure and gentle-hearted Charles Lamb, mediate to resolve his sin or to enable his vision of nature. If there is in Coleridge such a deep sense of dependence on and love for others that it is in part responsible for the structure of the Conversation poems, then I think we might reasonably expect these two poetic methods to fuse in some measure at one or two points in his career: in the person loved we may find the idea realized, and the world of his immediate sensation to become the world of experience and expression.

In some degree, I believe that these two opposing methods of composition are progressively synthesized in 'Kubla Khan' and 'Dejection . . .' In neither poem does the poet finally give up his own self to a character of his imagination; and at the same time he depends upon the vision of a person to re-create the world he has before him, present to his senses, so that it appears as a unified imitation of God's original creation. The narrator is no longer passive, merely attendant upon the impressions of nature, and the disordered state that characterized the course of action of the Supernatural poems, exiling the protagonists from their worlds, is now found in the poet himself, and preventing his creativity: he believes that his power will be revived or restored through his love of a more or less ideal figure, a saint from above, who plays that role we have outlined for the innocent mediator in 'The Ancient Mariner' and 'Christabel'.

KUBLA KHAN

The structure of this poem [PW I 297] is essentially simple.[1] The first 36 lines describe what the Khan built and the poet's admiration of certain parts of this creation; the last 18 lines determine under what conditions the poet might imitate the Khan's activity and how he would be received by those who saw his building.[2] In that the poem is composed of an adequate description, followed by a commentary upon that description, it is undoubtedly complete.[3] However, what the Khan's building signifies, and therefore what the poet wants to create, is a more complex matter.

Some critics have asserted that 'Kubla Khan' is a poem of veritable no meaning; and when a work has been loaded with such a weight and such a variety of meaning, the freighted critic, finding a port in the opinions of such respected men as J. L. Lowes, for whom 'the linked and interweaving images' form a 'pageant . . . as aimless as it is magnificent' [RX 412], or T. S. Eliot who thinks that the imagery is unused,[4] is tempted to unship his cargo. But I believe that we may find a general meaning by considering the structural features of the poem, and that we may determine the significance of many of the images in relation to the intention of this whole.[5]

The first 11 lines are an account of what the Khan built, where he built it, and in part, of what he enclosed by his building. He built 'A stately pleasure-dome' and in accomplishing this end he enclosed 'twice five miles of fertile ground' with walls and towers. It is important, I think, to notice that the making of the dome involves the making of a very grand park in which it may stand.[6] The 'dome' is not in any way a folly, nor, bearing in mind the dignity of the word 'pleasure' in Coleridge's theories of creativity [cf. BL II 10], is it a place where a powerful ruler might escape protocol and indulge his senses unlicensed. It is rather where the best of life may be found, for it includes not only a sacred river, 'forests ancient as the hills' and flowering incense trees, but also gardens, walls, towers and 'sunny spots of greenery'.

Order and control are characteristic of the first 11 lines of the poem, and the poet describes what he sees with ease and delight: what the Khan made seems good to the beholder. But in line 12 he turns his attention to one aspect of the Khan's creation, and it is clear from the altered mood in which the line begins, and the length of the description that follows, that the poet's attention is heightened and intensified in thinking of this aspect of the landscape:

> But oh! that deep romantic chasm which slanted
> Down the green hill athwart a cedarn cover!
> A savage place!

This section is the longest of the various sections in the poem, and it is a witness to the poet's deepened concentration.[7] What Coleridge is chiefly describing is the origin of the river:

> And from this chasm, with ceaseless turmoil seething,
> As if this earth in fast thick pants were breathing
> A mighty fountain momently was forced:
> Amid whose swift half-intermitted burst
> Huge fragments vaulted like rebounding hail,
> Or chaffy grain beneath the thresher's flail:
> And 'mid these dancing rocks, at once and ever
> It flung up momently the sacred river.

We have here a scene in direct contrast to the order, control and serenity of the opening lines of the poem. The chasm is 'deep' and 'romantic' – 'A savage place' where a woman might wail for her demon lover. From this chasm issues a fountain 'seething' 'with ceaseless turmoil'; and from amidst the dancing rocks (like ping-pong balls on water jets at the fair) the sacred river is 'flung up'. There is a very free life here, and it is to be contrasted, I think, with the confining form by which Kubla Khan has enclosed it.[8] It is from the interacting opposition of these two principles that we get what Coleridge conceived of as the near-ideal work of art:

> In Rapahael's admirable Galatea . . . the circle is perceived at first sight; but with what multiplicity of rays and chords within the area of the circular group, and with what elevations and depressions of the circumference, with what endless variety and sportive wildness in the component figure, and in the junctions of the figures, is the balance, the perfect reconciliation, effected between these two conflicting principles of the FREE LIFE, and of the confining FORM! How entirely is the stiffness that would have resulted from the obvious regularity of the latter, *fused* and (if I may hazard so bold a metaphor) almost *volatilized* by the interpenetration and electrical flashes of the former.
>
> [BL II 234–45]

The first 30 lines of 'Kubla Khan' seem to me to be directly comparable to this description of 'The Triumph of Galatea'. We are first given the circle, the enclosure of the grounds, the frame of the picture to perceive 'at first sight'; and then, as the substance of

the picture, a description of the romantic chasm and the volatile
and flashing river issuing from it. Lines 12–24 are the heart of the
poem, its life and energy, rather as the onward rushing, dolphin-
drawn shell of Galatea – of which she is only half in charge – is
the life and energy of Raphael's picture. Many critics have noticed
that Coleridge's description of the origin of the sacred river has
overtones of sexuality. But this imagery is far from specific, and
resides mostly in the kind of energy that these lines convey – an
energy associated with the 'woman wailing for her demon lover'.
Therefore the most we can reasonably say is that the energy at
the heart of the poem has erotic origins. The same observation
may be made of the 'Galatea': Pygmalion had fallen in love with
Aphrodite, who had refused him. So he made an ivory image of
her, laid it in his bed, and prayed to the goddess to have pity on
him. She did, and entering into the image, brought it to life as
Galatea – who then bore Pygmalion two sons. Clearly it is a tale
of both ideal and erotic love; and when we look at Raphael's
picture, we recognize that these two opposing states have been
reconciled.

    That Coleridge should have chosen a painting in which erotic
forces play an important part as an example of a work of art
approaching ideal perfection, is significant in relation to his own
development. We noticed that 'Christabel' was a poem in which
he was trying to establish a right relationship between the life of
reason and that of the senses. Much the same may be said of
'Kubla Khan', with these exceptions: firstly, it is not a narrative
and dramatic re-ordering of the disordered; it is rather a presentation of the idea of the rightly ordered: if the 'mighty fountain'
is a direct visitation from a disordered subliminal self [CPI 154],
then as it becomes a river it may be seen as the erotic and 'energic'
in our nature rightly ordered by the conscious will – which made
the park. 'In poetry', said Coleridge, 'it is the blending of passion
with order that constitutes perfection' [SC II 106–90]. Secondly, a
distinction is made in this poem between the ideal end and the
poet's ability to realize that end. No such distinction occurs in
'Christabel' of course. He does not present himself as having a life
separate to that of his creation, and as readers we are asked to
share Christabel's trial, as we share that of Lear, or other dramatic
heroes or heroines. But in 'Kubla Khan' the poet states the conditions in which he might imitate the hero, and we are therefore
aware of his being in the life of the poem.[9] It is significant that as

Coleridge never did realize the conditions in which he might have imitated the Khan, so he failed to finish 'Christabel'.

Thirdly, instead of conflict and reorganization, Coleridge seeks another form of synthesis between his two opposing forces. If the description of the chasm is contrasted with the acts of enclosure with which the poem opens, I think we may find a further synthesis made out of the birth and death of the river. The dome is situated at the point where the river disappears into the measureless caverns, to reappear again as the ocean within sight of Kubla's creation: and at this point, the river is not the wild uncontrolled thing which emerges from the romantic chasm, nor has it lost its fluminal identity by pouring down the measureless caverns into the sunless sea. It is moving with order and control, and in this state has fertilized the Khan's many 'gardens bright with sinuous rills'. It seems that we are looking at two opposing moments in the course of the river: that moment when it is barely a river because of its superabundant energy, and that moment when its very form and conformity are kinds of death which will permit it to run straight into the lifeless ocean. The dome is situated so as to synthesize these two moments:

> The shadow of the dome of pleasure
> Floated midway on the waves;
> Where was heard the mingled measure
> From the fountain and the caves.

In the dome a music is made which is the synthesis of the two extreme states of the river: it is therefore that place which permits the conflicting sounds, coming from the free life and the confining form, to issue as harmony.[10] Music, Coleridge suggested, is poetry in its grand sense – 'Passion and Order aton'd! Imperative Power in Obedience!' [CN II 3231]. The building of the dome thus becomes an image of the creating of a perfectly ordered work of art – in which the free life is precisely balanced against the confining form. Most critics agree that the perfection associated with the Khan's creation is paradisaical[11]; we are not only given a knowledge of a work of art ideally realized, but also a picture of the redeemed state – when the forces governing our lives are constructive rather than destructive of each other.

But since the vision of the Khan's paradise is a dynamic and not a static state, since it depends upon the continuing resolution of conflicting forces, this state, like that of Eden which depended upon man's continuing obedience, may be disturbed. But it cannot be disturbed from within, for all there is in balance and harmony. It must be disturbed from without. It is generally felt that the 'Ancestral voices prophesying war!' are forces that may eventually destroy the Khan's creation.[12] They are voices 'from far', that is, from outside the enclosing walls. But they are associated with the descending of the river into the caverns measureless to man:

> Through wood and dale the sacred river ran.
> Then reached the caverns measureless man,
> And sank in tumult to a lifeless ocean:
> And 'mid this tumult Kubla heard from far
> Ancestral voices prophesying war!

At the very least the voices are associated with loss of vitality and identity, and almost certainly with death – as one might expect of voices speaking of war.[13] One is tempted to think of Satan, far distant from Eden, swearing undying revenge and ceaseless war upon his God and His creations. But the origin of those voices will remain a mystery; all we can be sure of is that, like Hrothgar's hall which 'heatho-wylma bad/ lathan liges',[14] we are simultaneously presented with the existing glory and future destruction of the Khan's paradise – another minor reconciliation of opposites.

Of the poem's two parts, the first is not more than a description of what the Khan made. It is not until we come to the last 18 lines of the poem that the voluntary effort characteristic of, even if characteristically thwarted in, 'The Wanderings of Cain', 'The Ancient Mariner' and 'Christabel', makes its appearance. In these lines the poet delineates the conditions which would enable him to imitate the Khan. We may notice that Coleridge does not expect that his conditions will be immediately or easily realized: for he does not preface his conditions with 'when', but with the far less confident conditional tense:

> Could I revive within me
> Her symphony and song,
> To such delight 'twould win me,
> That with music loud and long
> I would build that dome in air
> That sunny dome! Those caves of ice!

The Khan's dome, by synthesizing sounds from the fountains and the caves, creates music. The poet's dome will be made out of music arising from delight discovered in his heart. This is a reversal of the process by which the original dome was made, but it demonstrates the interdependence of music and the dome: one could not, or would not, exist without the other. The dome to be made by the poet has, unlike that of the Khan in Xanadu, no geographical location. Indeed one feels that it would come into existence wherever and whenever the poet experienced a deep delight within him. Certainly his imagined audience would only *see* the dome when they *heard* his music:

> That sunny dome! those caves of ice!
> And all who heard should see them there,

The dome, the offspring of music and delight, is to be built 'in air', and this further illustrates its magical, faery nature: it is the product of a 'higher dream', won entirely from sources *within* the poet. In this respect it is of the same kind as 'Christabel' and 'The Ancient Mariner': as Kubla's semi-divine *fiat* brings into existence the dome and the gardens, so those two poems are produced almost *ex nihilo* in relation to what Coleridge called Nature. And the poet's pleasure-dome is to be produced solely out of his bliss-filled carver's brain.[15]

Finally we come to that upon which the whole remaking of the Kubla's dome depends – the vision in a dream, the Abyssinian maid. It is impossible to distinguish her from her singing, since it is this music revived in the heart of the poet that would enable him to imitate the Khan. She is singing of Mount Abora, and it is this song that Coleridge would like to issue from his heart. Much research has been done into the location and antecedents of this mountain. But the most interesting fact is that the surviving manuscript has two variant readings from the published version. Coleridge first wrote 'Amora', and then changed it to 'Amara'.[16] Only upon publication did the poem get its current reading. 'Mount Amara' is one of those places which Milton compares to God's true Paradise. It is where the Abyssinian kings lived, guarding their issue, and is 'by some suppos'd/ True Paradise'.[17] Kubla Khan might have held this belief, and, of course, it is very probable that an Abyssinian maid would have held it. Thus we may be more or less sure of what the rest of the poem has led us to believe

– that the Khan's original creation is a kind of paradise, perhaps
more Coleridgean than oriental, but nonetheless to be thought of
as a version of the archetype. As for the printed version, H. W.
Piper has pointed out that:

> From Mount Abora flowed the biblical river Chebar beside
> which Ezekiel had his visions and ate the scroll that 'that was
> as sweet in my mouth as honey.' The *Book of Ezekiel* has a
> reference to the 'land flowing with milk and honey,' (Ch. 20 v.
> 6) but in a biblical context this repetition is hardly needed to
> make the connection between honey and 'the milk of Paradise'.[18]

But what then caused the various transformations before Coleridge arrived at his final reading? Might we suppose that having
first written 'Amora' he became aware that he had made a Freu-
dian slip, and saw that he was thinking more of love than Paradise,
of the love that the Abyssinian maid represented, and less of the
ostensible subject of her song? Such a minor orthographical error
might well have come from the hand of a man whose need to love
and be loved constituted one of the strongest forces in his life –
most especially if he was beginning to be aware of the insuffici-
ences of his wife. Geoffrey Yarlott, because the name 'Mary' is
substituted for 'Lewti' in an early draft of that poem identifies the
Abyssinian maid with Mary Evans.[19] Her loss was one of the four
heart-wrenching agonies which Coleridge remembered to the end
of his life [CL V 249–51]. It is thus not in the least strange that
Coleridge should wish to prevent not only his readers associating
the damsel with love, but also to minimize the association in his
own mind. We might wonder why he was not content to change
'Amora' to 'Amara' – the place that some suppose true paradise.
I would suggest that while wishing to retain the ideas of Paradise
in the word, he wanted to rid it of all latinate overtones of love,
and of the bitterness of disappointed love; furthermore, 'Amara'
is inevitably associated with Milton's description of Paradise, and
with the bliss of Adam and Eve 'imparadis'd in one another's
arms' – a bliss so envied by Satan, and to think of which must
have been tenting Coleridge's deepening private wound. 'Abora',
on the other hand, has those kinds of association entirely compatible with the Khan's building, and with the final vision of the
inspired poet-prophet, an Ezekiel with his mind elevated to the
potential glory of his nation, unconfined by the frailties of his

personal life. Certainly it was Coleridge's life-long view that the
creation of a nation depended upon the vision of a person much
in the same way that the poet's imitation of the pleasure-dome
depends upon his vision of the Abyssinian maid.

   Although we are not told that the inner life of the poet is in any
way disordered, as those of the Mariner and Christabel more
obviously are, yet his power is in check, and dependent on his
reviving within him the music of the Abyssinian maid. If Coleridge
was occupied with the fundamental truths of our nature in the
Supernatural poems, and under the pressure of those ideas created
three very different characters, this poem is the first sign that he
is considering the same ideas in relation to his own life; for just
as the redemption of Cain, the Mariner and Christabel involved
each of them in a relationship with a purer or unfallen spirit, so
the poet-prophet here cannot call up his creative power to make
the paradisaical image of the redeemed state, until he finds within
himself the pure spirit of the Abyssinian maid.

   'Love', Coleridge confided to a notebook, 'is the Spirit of Life,
and Music the Life of the Spirit'.[20] Love was the 'vital air' that
would make in him the music which would enable the creation of
what, in being a perfect work of art, would also be an image of
Paradise, or the state of man redeemed. But this necessary love is
not in the poem, for the 'symphony and song' of the damsel's
inspiration, if we take her to be associated with Mary Evans, has
been lost to his life, his soul divorced from its proper companion.
So he cannnot speak of a delight known, and experience had, but
only of a delight desired, an experience sought.

'Kubla Khan' is a prophetic poem: what the poet would create is
a state epitomizing that which he has sought for the personae of
all his other poetry, and is analogous to the state of redemption.
The Khan is an omnipotent figure, making by his mere decree,
a garden which represents human nature ideally ordered – the
deliberate will charged with a free life, the Apollonian reconciled
with the Dionysian aspects of our nature. But the fallen poet has
none of the Khan's omnipotence: the only way he can create or
the individual redeem himself is through the love of a being who
is a function of their conscience, their 'inward Dream', but yet to
find whom the individual looks up to heaven, or towards Paradise.
Were the poet himself to know the music of the Abyssinian maid,
he would indeed have 'drunk the milk of Paradise' and become

again a mortal immortal, and so to be viewed by the inner vision
'with holy dread'. The poem is prophetic because, in Coleridge's
words, it speaks 'of what must be', of the ideal order of our
humanity, and of the method by which we must seek to reorder
what has mysteriously fallen into disorder. But it is also prophetic
in a simpler and sadder sense: Coleridge would never realize in a
completed work of art what he has planned and imagined here.
And if he is only present as an ideal figure in this poem, in the
next we are to consider he is present in all the weary particulars
of his life, yet speaking of the same ideas, and the same order of
truth, as we have found in 'Kubla Khan'.[21]

DEJECTION: AN ODE[22]

This poem is an account of the condition of a poet who has not
heard in his heart the music of a damsel with a dulcimer. Where
Coleridge had hoped for a 'deep delight' he now finds 'A grief
without a pang, void, dark, and drear', and as a consequence,
instead of finding within himself the power to 'build that dome
in air,/ That sunny dome!', his 'genial spirits fail' and he senses
the loss of his 'shaping spirit of Imagination'. What makes them
fit companions in a study of Coleridge's poetry is their common
concern with relating the creative act to the sense-perceived world
through the love of another person. We will see, I hope, that
'Dejection . . .' by and large resolves the conflicting interests of
the Supernatural and the Conversation poems according to the
creative method established in 'Kubla Khan'.

Nature and Creativity

We have seen that the world of 'The Ancient Mariner' is like that
of 'Kubla Khan' in the respect that what we call nature in each of
them is mind-made rather than mind-making: in these poems we
do not begin with the appearances of nature, but with truths or
powers of our inward being, and these control our conceptions of
the external world – even as the Mariner's altered states make
virtually different creatures out of the watersnakes. However, we
saw in the Conversation poems that Coleridge expected the features of nature to be able to make up a meditative joy in the poet's
mind – that is, to act upon his mind so as to ameliorate his spiritual
condition. But we also saw that in these poems no distinct ideas

or conceptions were enunciated in the mind by his belief in the power of nature, and that finally there was a division between what the poet hoped for and what he realized. A letter often quoted gives us a clue as to why this divided state little affected the poet's creative spirit:

> My mind feels as if it ached to behold and know something great – something *one and indivisible* – and it is only in the faith of this that rocks or water-falls, mountains or caverns give me the sense of sublimity or majesty! – But in this faith *all things* counterfeit infinity! [CL I 350]

Coleridge goes on to quote, *variatim*, lines 38–43 of 'This Lime-tree Bower My Prison', and then adds: 'It is but seldom that I raise and spiritualize my intellect to this height - '. We must note that when this letter was written he still felt able to hold this faith: joy was still dallying with him despite his distresses, and the 'seldom' probably refers to those moments of creativity which have given us the Conversation poems. But it is not the presence of the things themselves that create this mood; rather, he believes, a state of mind like that of faith, and existing logically prior to any sense impression, may order all perceived objects so that they seem to speak of infinity or omnipresence. Though elsewhere hoping that the appearances of nature would make up a joy in him, Coleridge here asserts the contrary, making a clear distinction between what he perceives, and the means by which the perceived objects come to have a significance for him.[23]

Such a distinction lies at the heart of 'Dejection . . .' The faith or joy that we have seen as an essential constituent of his ability to find sermons in stones, and a world in a grain of sand, has deserted him. Consequently nature is disordered, not in a perceptual sense, for he can see quite clearly what he thinks he ought to find beautiful, but conceptually: the appearances of nature have lost all significance because they are not perceived under the influence of that emotion (joy, faith and delight are all synonyms in this respect) which enables their ordering. The kind of sense impressions that speak of omnipresence in the Conversation poems are all present in the second stanza of the poem – and in that they are more perceived than felt, they are more precisely, even more thoughtfully, described. But these outward forms neither make life in the poet, nor have any significance to him.

And his particular observations are symbolic of his entire relations with the natural world: nothing out there can create its life in the poet. Joy, won from within, is the only remedy.

There is always the temptation to regard Coleridge's stated attitudes to nature in this poem as unrepresentative, and arising from the diseased state of mind which gave the poem its published title, and about which he is so eloquent in the original version of the poem – the verse letter to Sara Hutchinson. I do not share this opinion of course, but it is common amongst those whose ideas of how the first English Romantics responded to nature are chiefly based on Wordsworth; for, as we have seen, there is no doubt that Wordsworth believed, not only during his most creative years, but throughout his long life, that the forms and appearances of nature could stimulate insight into the structure of our minds, and that therefore what we perceive might always stir within us thoughts and feelings to which access was denied by other routes.[24] And in that some critics think of 'Dejection . . .' as a Conversation poem, they tend to suppose that that hope disappointed is the real basis of the work. But Coleridge's greatest poems show us nature not as mind-evolving but in a conceptual sense as mind-made. All the action of 'The Ancient Mariner' and 'Christabel' originates in the minds or from human relationships of the protagonists, not from their perception of, or influence by, natural forms. The attitude to nature outlined at the beginning of 'Dejection . . .' – that its forms can of themselves give us nothing, can alter nothing within us, and that only the beautiful and beauty-making power of joy issuing from us, 'This Light, this Glory, this fair luminous mist', acting on our perceptions will so diffuse, dissipate and re-organize them as to create a transfigured world – is one which is fully consistent with all we have discovered with regard to nature in the Supernatural poems: that perception is not the gate to conception, and that nature, conceptually, is a thing made, not a thing making.

Nonetheless, even if it is only in recognition of his own methodological error, and to point up its alternative with more emphasis, Coleridge begins 'Dejection . . .' with his immediate world of sense impression, apparently hoping for that kind of experience he had had on the hill-tops of the Conversation poems. He seeks at first a unity from various disparate perceptions – a new moon, a ballad, a rising wind, an Aeolian harp, the song of a thrush, a green light in the western sky, thin clouds and the emerging stars

– all present to him one April evening in his study at Keswick. He discovers that because of his joyless mood, these perceptions remain external to him, unrelated to his being, untransformed from that which is merely observed to that which becomes part of his humanity:

> I see them all, so excellently fair,
> I see, not feel, how beautiful they are! [PW I 364]

He knows that he cannot hope to win this lost joy from 'outward forms': this is the thesis of the poem, the condition in which he begins and from which he seeks relief. The question he is implicitly asking, and to which I believe he finds an answer in the course of the poem, is, What is the source of that lost faith or joy that will again make nature live for him?[25]

It is interesting, and not often enough mentioned in connection with 'Dejection . . .', that the very same disappointment in the sights and sounds of nature that informs the Ode also informs a poem written in Germany some three years before: 'Lines written in the Harz Forest'. The poet is descending from the Brocken (where he has had the sight, but seemingly not the experience of omnipresence) in a low and languid mood not unlike that of 'Dejection . . .' During his descent he notes his sense impressions, but there is no joy associated with what are, in themselves, delightful images – and the gloomy mood of the poet tells upon his choice of words:

> Heavily my way
> Downward I dragged through fir groves evermore,
> Where bright green moss heaves in sepulchral forms
> Speckled with sunshine; and, but seldom heard,
> The sweet bird's song became a hollow sound;
> [PW I 316]

Nature is unable to make up a meditative joy in the poet, and we feel a conflict between the delightful things observed and the way in which he describes them. We sense that there ought to be pleasure where there is only indifference or a numbing melancholy. Coleridge realizes this too, of course, and is quick to analyze the cause:

                              . . . I had found
That outward forms, the loftiest, still receive
Their finer influence from the Life within;
Fair cyphers else: fair, but of import vague
Or unconcerning, where the heart not finds
History or prophecy of friend, or child,
Or gentle maid, our first and early love,
Or father, or the venerable name
Of our adoréd country!

Coleridge's references to the human relations a man may have
in his life sound most general, and could be passed over as thum-
pings on the Miltonic drum; yet each may bear the name of a
person at the heart of his life: the 'friend', his 'sheet-anchor', Tom
Poole, separation from whom he always regretted; the child, his
first-born son, Hartley, who grew up so peculiarly like his father,
each having a special affection for and understanding of the other
the 'gentle maid, our first and early love', Mary Evans, whose
loss, never forgotten, might then have been becoming poignant
to him again, as his marriage failed after a brief happiness; and
the 'father', his own father, by whom the boy was especially
beloved, being the child of his old age, and whose death marked
the beginning of Coleridge's alienation from his family, and the
end of what happiness he had known in childhood. Such associations reinforce what Coleridge has presented as the method by
which nature might be made significant. In contrast to Wordsworth, the forms of nature in themselves have little or no significance for Coleridge – they are 'of import vague/ Or unconcerning'
What is permanent in Coleridge's inner world are certain very
close relationships with other human beings.[26] In the light of these
the appearances of nature gain their secondary and dependent
significance – 'Fair cyphers else'. Indeed, so strong an impression
does a memory of his 'native Land' and the relationships which
in some measure constitute his 'adoréd country' make upon his
immediate perceptions that

                        . . . all the view
From sovran Brocken, woods and woody hills,
Floated away, like a departing dream,
Feeble and dim!

The power of his imagination, once set in motion by thoughts of those he loves, actually diminishes, through want of association, his awareness of what is present to him. He presumes, in lines 18–21, that a person's friend, child, first love or father, are not merely people to whom he owes certain duties, but that they actually make up a man's inner life – they constitute the core of his being.[27] So far from the forms of nature making up a meditative joy in him, we see that, *in extremis*, their very perception depends upon the love he bears his kinsmen and his country.

The Letter to Asra

The lines written in the Harz forest were composed in May 1799. In October of that year, Coleridge first met Sara Hutchinson, on her brother's farm at Sockburn. It is clear from later notebook entries that he soon fell deeply in love with her. Sara Fricker's 'want of sensibility', her lack of 'heart-nursing sympathy', had starved Coleridge of the kind of companionship essential to his emotional well-being. In April 1802 he wrote 'A Letter to Asra' which was published in October of the same year as 'Dejection: an Ode'. There are substantial differences between these two poems: firstly, of length, as the 'Letter . . .' is 340 lines and the Ode only 139; secondly, in their focus: although 'Dejection . . .' was finally addressed, indirectly, to Sara Hutchinson as the 'Lady', it is more or less impersonal, being in the third person and having at one point been addressed to Wordsworth. The 'Letter . . .' is quite different, and most of the lines cut from it are to do with memories and hopes centred on Coleridge's relationship with Sara, and with his unhappy marriage. The two works thus have an entirely different effect upon the reader – and certain key passages, such as the storm wind to which the poet turns after it 'has long rav'd unno- tic'd', have radical differences of significance in the separate versions. It is because Coleridge's crucial relationship with Sara Hutchinson determines the structure and significance of the poem that I have chosen to study the longer, original and more personal version.[28]

In the first three stanzas of the Ode, and the first 51 lines of the Letter, there is only one notable difference – to which I shall return in a moment; but subsequently we may see the drastic results of Coleridge's revisions:

> Though I should gaze for ever
> On that green light that lingers in the west:
> I may not hope from outward forms to win
> The passion and the life, whose fountains are within
>   [PW I 365]

So concludes stanza III of the Ode: stanza IV, quite logically, goe
on to assert the necessity of a power issuing from us to give natur
her proper life, and stanza V proclaims that this power is joy. Bu
in the Letter, Coleridge turns not to what will be in effect hi
conclusion – still nearly 250 lines away – but to thoughts that Sar
might be watching the sky he is watching:

> These lifeless Shapes, around, below, Above,
>   O what can they impart?
> When even the gentle Thought, that thou, my Love!
>   Art gazing now, like me,
>   And see'st the Heaven, I see –
> Sweet thought it is – yet feebly stirs my Heart! [52–57]

This, I think, is an interesting development, quite without a para
lel in the Ode. If Coleridge began this poem ostensibly believin
that the sights and sounds of nature should be able to revive hi
genial spirits, here he deliberately denies the supposition. That h
is not abandoning all hope by doing so, derives from his consciou
ness that Sara may be watching the same night sky: it is n
accident that he is looking to 'Heaven' as she enters his consciou
ness. This thought of her has a power not found in nature, an
the 'when' at the beginning of line 54 compares her power in hi
heart with that of nature: the appearances of nature can impa
nothing to him in comparison with his thought of her. She an
what she is doing is that which, however feebly, stirs his hea
and begins the revival of his genial spirits.

   This thinking of Sara and feeling the first faint signs of li
reviving in his heart recalls an experience of his school days whic
he later connected with notions of moral purity: when either look
ing from the 'barr'd window' or lying on 'the leaded School-roof
he gazed upwards – for 'The Sky was all, I knew, of Beautiful
this platonic and heavenward gazing was associated 'With man
secret yearnings' in his soul which had to do with an idea of lov
– an idea that no man, however far down the road to perditio
could wholly obliterate within himself. Sitting or lying he gazed

And to myself would say –
There does not live the Man so stripp'd of good affections
As not to love to see a Maiden's quiet Eyes
Uprais'd, and linking on sweet Dreams by dim Connections
To Moon, or Evening Star, or glorious western Skies –
While yet a Boy, this Thought would so pursue me
That often it became a kind of Vision to me! [67–73]

For a realization of this vision, the source of his alienated joy and closely associated with the Mariner's dependence on his guardian saint and Christabel's consciousness of her mother, Coleridge yearned throughout his life. The constancy of the longing is, I think, the reason why most commentators find that Mary Evans, the Abyssinian maid, and Sara Hutchinson, are all really manifestations of one idea or person that, realized, Coleridge saw as enabling his creativity and perfecting his life.[29] It is evident that here he associates his boyhood vision with Sara, and as he recalls it we see a 'dim Connection' between the idea of love and the natural world; it is not stressed, and the proper development of this idea does not occur until the conclusion of the poem. But by having associated his boyhood vision with the woman he loves, he discovers that the faint stirrings of life within him have blossomed into a real, if partial and temporary, relief from 'the smoth'ring Weight' of his dejection:

Sweet Thought! and dear of old
To Hearts of finer Mould!
Ten thousand times by Friends and Lovers blest!
I spake with rash Despair,
And ere I was aware,
The weight was somewhat lifted from my Breast! [74–79]

What enables Coleridge to feel some relief from his burden has nothing to do with the influences of nature, and everything to do with his locating his inward dream in Sara and other close friends. No such development is evident anywhere in the Ode.

Because he has felt his 'spirit moved', and is conscious that Sara's 'dear wild Eyes' see 'Even now the Heaven, I see,' he is enabled to remember more recent and happier times spent with Sara and her sister, Mary. Coleridge does not, as we might have expected, return to 'The Green Light lingering in the West' or to

other natural phenomena, and show how, by the influence of this
revival of his genial spirits, he can now both see *and* feel how
beautiful they are. Instead, he continues to concentrate on memories of events shared with those whom he most loves, and in
conclusion, writes:

> Ah fair Remembrances, that so revive
> The Heart, and fill it with a living Power, [111–12]

Up to this point the poem, and the poet, seem to be going from
strength to strength; in his love for Sara the poet seems to have
found a remedy for his proclaimed dejection. But the development
of the relationship has inevitably been thwarted by Coleridge's
mistaken marriage: what might have been joyous and life-giving
has been shorn of all its proper forms, so that what has grown
between himself and Sara was probably most unlike the glories of
his boyhood vision.[30] One unhappy result of this stunted growth
was a 'complaining Scroll' that Coleridge had written to Sara, and
which 'even to bodily Sickness bruis'd . . .' her soul. That letter
has not survived, so we do not know what it contained or why it
had such a devastating effect upon her. But in regretting his deed
he regrets

> Whatever turns thee, Sara! from the course
> Of calm Well-being and a Heart at rest! [131–32]

Coleridge imagines that when Sara is living with the soon-to-be
married Mary and Wiliam, a household that he describes as 'the
dear *abiding* Home of All', she will have those blessings, finding
the forms of her spiritual life in the place of her being and in the
objects of her affections. He knows that he cannot share the life
of this household, but promises that, echoing the Intimations ode,

> I too will crown me with a coronal –
> Nor shall this Heart in idle Wishes roam
>   Morbidly soft!No! let me trust, that I shall wear away
> In no inglorious Toils the manly Day, [136–40]

If Sara is happy in her household, it will allow him to feel an
enabling contentment, even if they are not in the same place: 'Be
happy, and I need thee not in sight'. This happiness of hers could

e a form of permanence in him, which he would prefer to *know*
1 his heart than to *behold* with his senses, for 'To all things I prefer
1e Permanent' – a preference which decidely diminishes the sig-
ificance of temporal existence. If he were to visit Sara and the
Vordsworth household, then the transientness of the visit would
ecessarily inspire him with a sense of impermanence, of his
aving no physical place where he would find his permanent
eing:

> For Change doth trouble me with pangs untold!
> To see thee, hear thee, feel thee – then to part!
> Oh! – it weighs down the Heart! [154–56]

Ie is unable to enjoy a brief moment with his beloved in the
ousehold where she has her being because it would symbolize a
·roper consummation unachieved, his failure to locate his being
1 time and place:

> The transientness is Poison in the Wine,
> Eats out the pith of Joy, makes all Joy hollow,
> All Pleasure a dim Dream of Pain to follow! [160–62]

The argument by which he is trying to reconcile himself to his
·hysical separation from Sara runs contrary to his poetic instinct:
or joy is that which would integrate the loveliness of nature
vith his proper being, and, imitative of God's original creation, is
reative of time and place: now, in order to preserve his love of
ara, he is trying to undo the significance of time and place. It is
 fruitless task, and he finds that he cannot 'beat away the
hought' that if Sara was ill, he should not be allowed to attend
er, and he protests against the notion in lines 177–82, which are
ne most strident and least attractive in the poem. He has worked
p an enormous head of emotional steam which has no engine to
rive. All he can do is break off, and consider something other
han this dream:

> Nay, wherefore did I let it haunt my Mind
>   The dark distressful Dream!
> I turn from it, and listen to the Wind
> Which long has rav'd unnotic'd! [184–87]

The subsequent passage on the wind has a very different contex
in 'Dejection . . .' It comes after the passages on joy and abstrus
research and has no clear connection with the Lady to whom
the poem is addressed. But in the Letter Coleridge's growing
consciousness of his disordered relationship with Sara is associate
with the rising of the wind.

The poem began in a low key mood, describing the tranqu
night, the moon, the foretold storm, and the poet's 'unimpassion'
Grief': intense poetic energy, the divine afflatus, is missing, an
all the poet is capable of is summarized in his description of th
wind, which lightly touches the lute, so making

> . . . the dull sobbing Draft, that drones and rakes
> Upon the Strings of this Eolian Lute,
> Which better far were mute. [6–8]

A 'dull sobbing Draft' is an excellent pun describing the wear
complaints with which this Letter opens. The 'this' of line 7 ma
of course refer to himself: certainly the last line of the quote seem
a most pertinent summary by the poet of his need to speak, an
of his judgement that it would be better not to.[31] In the Ode h
explains his wish 'that even now the gust were swelling/ And th
slant night-shower driving loud and fast!' as the result of hi
experience that such sounds have often previously removed hi
dejection and sent his soul abroad in the Wordsworthian manner.
But no such explanation is given in the Letter: instead his desir
for a storm is addressed to Sara, the love of whom, and not an
impulse from nature, will in some measure restore the poet. N
more is heard of the wind until line 186 of the Letter.[33] When th
poet's attention is turn'd from his tortuous dreaming to the exter
nal world, he discovers that the wind 'long has rav'd unnotic'd
We might ask why, at this point in the poem, when his dreamin
about Sara has become unendurable to him, it is to the wind an
the lute that the poet's attention is turned.[34] If there is an analog
between the force of the wind on the harp, and the poet's degre
of imaginative power, then we may see this redirected attentio
as an expression of the kind of poetic power that has been woke
in him by his increased consciousness of Sara. It is certainly ver
tempting to read

What a Scream

> Of agony by Torture lenthen'd out
> That Lute sent forth! [187–89 cf. n. 35][35]

as a perfect reflection of the poet's self torturing of the previous 40 lines or so, gradually building up in vigour until it issues in that final scream of sick-bed melodrama. The consciousness of a storm growing within is perhaps reflected in the very phrase that follows the lines above, 'O thou wild Storm without!' The 'without' is redundant unless, like Robert Frost, Coleridge is attempting to portray the relation of the internal to the external, to convey or comment on the condition of the mind by reference to the natural world.[36] The analogy between wind and poet is made directly in lines 198–9:

> Thou Actor, perfect in all tragic Sounds!
> Thou mighty Poet, even to frenzy bold!

The frenzy of the wind is comparable to Coleridge's 'frenzy' at the thought of not being able to be with Sara or to nurse her in her illness. Although his love of her has revived Coleridge's power in some measure, it has also determined its limitations. The poet's task is to give the ideal and permanent a being in time and place: Coleridge has found the ideal in Sara, but has been denied the forms essential to its proper expression. So the storming wind represents this revived power uncontrolled by and invested in definite form.[37] It is as if the 'mighty fountain' of 'Kubla Khan' has not become the sacred river, but dies a redundant energy, vexing its own creation.[38]

Lines 216–25 are a prayer that Sara may not suffer now or in the future as he has suffered this evening:

> 'Tis Midnight! and small Thoughts have I of Sleep –
> Full seldom may my Friend such Vigils keep –
> O breathe She softly in her gentle Sleep!
> Cover her, gentle Sleep! with wings of Healing.
> And be this Tempest but a mountain Birth!

We cannot read so little into these lines as to think that Coleridge is only asking that this outward storm may be short lived for Sara,[39] or that her sleep in days to come may rarely be so interrupted. He is asking that the forces which are deep-rooted in him and which have gone into the making of this letter (inevitably disturbing its recipient) may be rare and of small effect in her. That they are in her, just as the storm is present to her, Coleridge is both too sane (for he remembers her reaction to his 'complaining Scroll') and too proud a lover to doubt. But he hopes that these forces wil be resolved quickly and easily in her, as perhaps comparable forces were present and to be resolved in Christabel.

If 'the wings of Healing' do their job, she will return to a state he does not expect to know:

> Healthful and light, my Darling! may'st thou rise
>   With clear and chearful Eyes –
> And of the same good Tidings to me send!
>   For oh! belovéd Friend!
> I am not the buoyant Thing I was of yore –
> When like an own Child, I to *Joy* belong'd; [223–28]

Coleridge attaches importance to Sara's sending him 'good Tidings' because her renewed joy will in some sort belong to him. Having described his own lack of that emotion and briefly outlined its cause, he again addresses her,

> . . . thou, dear Sara! (dear indeed thou art,
> My Comforter! A Heart within my Heart!) [249–50]

One might be forgiven for taking the last phrase as merely a piece of conventional love poetry; but I think it is testimony to a real process, incipient in the Supernatural poems, that love of Sara had begun to develop in Coleridge's consciousness, the profoundest implications of which are recorded in the notebooks. Here the sentiment, however lightly or seriously we take it, is sufficient to explain why Sara's joy is of importance to him: not just because he wishes for her what to a greater or lesser extent we all wish for those we know – that they should be happy, but because her happiness in some degree *constitutes* his happiness; her heart is the inner life of his, as he had recognized in respect of other people during his descent from the Brocken. If there is joy in her, he will be able to find some joy in himself.

This integration is not completed until the end of the poem, but Coleridge has partially dispersed his feeling of dejection by reflecting on his relationship with Sara. The emotion, and its corre-

sponding powerlessness, no longer dominates him entirely, and
so he has given himself adequate room to analyze its cause. He
begins by asserting that Sara and the few they love are sufficient
to make up a world of hopes and fears for him, a world he cannot
find in his own household, for his

> . . . coarse domestic Life has known
> No habits of heart-nursing Sympathy,
> No Griefs but such as dull and deaden me,
> No mutual mild Enjoyments of it's own,
> No Hopes of its own Vintage, None, O! none –
> Whence when I mourn'd for you, my Heart might borrow
> Fair forms and living Motions for it's Sorrow. [259–64]

He is saying much what the Mariner and Cain had said – that his
heart is withered within him, preventing him from praying, and
so restoring his being to his immediate world, to that world to
which it was originally consecrated. We see in these lines what a
peculiarly crushing burden his marriage was to Coleridge. It had
caused in him that division of thought and feeling, between ideal
being and its incarnation in reality, that turned him to metaphysical research. As Coleridge could derive no forms of life from his
marriage, he attempted to think in a way independent of emotion:
he ceased to think like a poet, uniting the ideal and the real, and
began to ratiocinate like a scientist or a scholar.

Because the root of Coleridge's dejection lies in his inability to
locate his being in his own home and marriage, the consequences
of that marriage, 'Those little Angel Children', create deeply
ambivalent feelings in him. They are in themselves 'a Joy, a Love/
A good Gift from above!' – words wich reflect the qualities essential
to the mediator – but simultaneously they reinforce, and remind
the poet of, the indissolubility of his marriage, turning his 'Error
to Necessity'. As part of that relationship in which Coleridge
cannot 'find' himself, because he is the prayerless sinner burdened, like the Mariner, with a 'wrong' world, his children act on
him in a way almost opposite to that we would expect of a
mediator and 'pluck out the wing-feathers' of the poet's mind.
When confronted by this knowledge, and by the thought what a
blessed lot his might have been had they not been Sara Fricker's
children, then he has occasionally 'half-wish'd, they never had
been born!' This is a life-denying wish comparable to that which

allowed the Mariner to shoot the albatross. Coleridge's awareness of this deep disorder within himself, which takes its origin in his marriage to his 'instrument of low desire', has been brought acutely into his consciousness by his loving another woman as profoundly as he was out of love with his wife [Cf. CL I 151].

But Coleridge's analysis of his dejection does not end the Letter, for it is only at this point, line 296, that he begins to describe the operation of joy, chiefly as he imagines it occurring in Sara Hutchinson – a description which came much earlier in the course of the poem, in stanzas III and IV. By contrast to himself, Sara, his heart within his heart, not stained with moral conflict and disorder, may know the nature-making power of joy: she is pure, and thought and emotion are not in conflict in her:

> Joy, innocent Sara! Joy, that ne'er was given
> Save to the Pure, and in their purest Hour,
> Joy, Sara! is the Spirit and the Power.
> That wedding Nature to us gives in Dower
>   A new Earth and a new Heaven
> Undreamt of by the Sensual and the Proud! [313–18][40]

The sensual and the proud are shut out from the vision Coleridge imagines for Sara because these passions limit their intelligence to the conceptions of this world; they are not 'pure' and constitute the 'poor loveless ever-anxious Crowd,' whose knowledge of nature is not more than can be given by sense impression – 'an inanimate cold World'. But joy unshackles the imagination to reveal the new order of nature – that which informs or makes the senses, and is not made by them. Coleridge's determination of the conditions by which Sara will be able to send forth an animating joy does not, however, begin and end with the idea of purity: the nature of her familial attachments is fully as important:

> Sister and Friend of my devoutest Choice!
> Thou being innocent and full of love,
> And nested with the Darlings of thy Love,
> And feeling in thy Soul, Heart, Lips and Arms
> Even what the conjugal and mother Dove,
> That borrows genial Warmth from those, she warms,
>   Feels in the thrill'd wings, blessedly outspread –
>   [324–30][41]

We may pause here before going on to the completion of Coleridge's statement, and examine the nature of the relations he imagines Sara entering into with the Wordsworths; it is both spiritually ordered ('Soul, Heart') and sensually ('Lips, and Arms'), and I think it is no accident either that the words were written in this order, or that Coleridge has first stressed Sara's innocence and the fullness of her love; for what he imagines of her is what he had hoped to realize for Christabel – not a denial of the sensual, but its government by the charitable; secondly, his comparison of her relations with William, Mary and Dorothy to the mother dove on her nest of younglings is designed to evoke two responses: by using the word 'conjugal' of this relation Coleridge indicates that Sara is to enter into this household in the most intimate possible way – by being 'married' to it; she will find her spiritual role in it in perfect harmony with her maternal feelings – she will be warmed by those she warms; the genial and creative warmth that Coleridge felt so lacking in himself, she will discover because, in her purity and innocence, she is able to enter into a right and harmonious relationship with her elected family, her place of being. His exclusion from such harmony in his own marriage is the chief cause of his dejection, of his inability to send forth a 'luminous cloud' from his soul to order and animate nature. And of course Coleridge's particular words in referring to the dove – 'the thrill'd wings, blessedly outspread' – cannot but remind us of Milton's use of the same image to portray the activity of the Holy Ghost:

> . . . thou from the first
> Wast present, and, with mighty wings outspread
> Dovelike satest brooding on the vast Abyss,
> And madest it pregnant: [Bk. I 19–23]

The Holy Spirit orders Chaos, creating the world we know. So Sara, in the joy derived from her properly ordered relations, will be able to animate nature, to find in it the conceptions which make up her soul:

> To thee would all Things live from Pole to Pole.
> Their life the Eddying of thy living Soul. [335–36][42]

And to this hope for the pure heart beating within the impurities

of his own, Coleridge adds a reminder of his hopes for their
domestic and practical relations:

> O dear! O Innocent! O full of Love!
> A very Friend! A Sister of my Choice –
> O dear, as Light and Impulse from above,
> Thus may'st thou ever, evermore rejoice! [337–40][43]

If Sara is willing to think of herself as the poet's sister or friend,
this will enable their day to day relations; but ideally Coleridge
thinks of Sara as a 'Light and Impulse from above', as his inward
dream or guardian saint, upon whom he calls in his agony and
desolation, and whose perfection is his one hope of salvation.

SUMMARY

In the Letter, Coleridge asserts two things: (1) that one real and
living person, separate from him, properly loved, constitutes his
inner life; (2) that only when our domestic and social relations are
ordered by such a love may we know that nature-creating joy.
Until that moment nature, though of course perceived, has no
coherency and no reality; when joy or delight springs from the
loving heart, then the whole of the living world becomes part of
one's living soul, and we create in and around us what the Khan
decreed. Although tragic in its revelations of the desperate state
to which Coleridge's marriage had brought him, the Letter is
still something of a triumph: for he has managed to bring the
uncomfortable truths that animated the Supernatural poems into
focus in his own life, and has found a means of redemption by
loving another human being conceived of as pure and and perfected. From the liberties of speculation that went to make up the
Conversation and the Supernatural poems Coleridge has forged a
way of thinking which will eventually return him to a profound
understanding of Christianity, and is about to impel him on his
longest journey.

Part II
A Metamorphosis

Conceive a spirit in hell, employed tracing out for others the road to that heaven, from which his crimes exclude him!

[CL II 511]

5

The God Within

It seems to me more than an accident of temperament or circumstance that 'Dejection . . .' marks the end of Coleridge's career as other than an occasional poet. It is something that in the first instance we might regard as a combination of historical conditions with the peculiarities of writing poetry. Although the careers of some English poets seem to represent a steady maturation of their powers, others make their major contribution early and, if they do not then go off to their graves, add nothing but quantity to their canon. It was part of the myth that the Romantics held about themselves that poets were born bright and hot, 'in joy and gladness', but soon faded into 'despondency and madness': Chatterton, 'the marvellous boy', was the prime example of this largely self-fulfilling prophecy.[1] Subsequently, poets have struggled to throw off the yoke. One poet who has in some measure succeeded has also given an indication of the nature of the problem. Eliot believed that 'anyone who would continue to be a poet beyond his twenty-fifth year' must obtain 'the historical sense, which is a sense of the timeless as well of the temporal and of the timeless and temporal together'. Only by this 'great labour' will he discover 'what makes a writer traditional' [Selected Essays 14]. Coleridge and Wordsworth planned the *Lyrical Ballads* in the light of a partial knowledge of this kind. The Preface sought in effect to justify the abandonment of custom in the pursuit of tradition. But the hastily conceived experiment was not to provide the real basis for the mature poetry of either man. I have already tried to show how Coleridge's Supernatural poems were, as Wordsworth jealously feared and Coleridge sometimes declared, beyond the pale of the agreed guidelines; but Wordsworth also included in the collection several poems 'in his own character', as Coleridge put it, and these, notably 'Tintern Abbey', are clearly more of a kind with his mature poetry than the poems designed for the 'experiment'. But though Coleridge's confidence in his poetic powers was rapidly eroded by increasing unhappiness, it is my belief that in one historically important way he squared up to a problem, inherent in the idea of tradition, from which Wordsworth had turned away defeated. Some of the finest poetry of *The Prelude* occurs in Book I when Wordsworth is confronting the problem of what story to tell. He finds none of course, and this failure casts an unforgettable shadow over the rest of the poem: the reader remains conscious of the fact that what he is being given is second best – a display of the furniture for which the house was never found.[2] Unlike Coleridge, Wordsworth never doubted his powers, and he abandoned the search for a story out of the pressing necessity of self-belief and self-expression, inspired by the confidence he had drawn off from Coleridge.

It is this problem that, not at first deliberately or consciously, but by cause of his method of thinking, I believe Coleridge set himself to tackle. Any poet has but two questions to ask himself: has he a story to tell, and has he the power to tell it? Has he, in other words, consciousness of an active inner life, and consciousness of an outward world to be made at one with that life? Wordsworth asked himself these questions, and found that he had the power, but not the kind of world that as a self-elected rival to Milton he saw was required. But he was aware of moments in his past when he seemed to 'find' himself in certain images and expressions of nature. And out of these he would forge a history of the growth of his own mind: what he was unable to do was to express that mind in a story from the stock of the literary tradition. Nor did Wordsworth feel that it was his business to investigate the grounds of the power he was conscious of, and he clung tenaciously to the first forms of its manifestation, in which it seemed that nature was acting on him, and revealing his inward being. From this principle of nature active, acting, and revelatory, Wordsworth never deviated, and we may see that it prevented him from any philosophic self inspection apart from moments of poetic perception.

How different this procedure is from that of Coleridge is, I hope, becoming clear. Not only had Coleridge, by the age of 29, decided that nature cannot act *in* the individual, but that the process must indeed be reversed – that our discovery of the order and unity of nature depends upon a power issuing *from* us, a power that nature can in no way give. Secondly, Coleridge was quite prepared to reflect upon his inner existence as an entity in itself, and not in conjunction with the object by which it gains expression; such a reflection had, in principle, formed the basis of the Supernatural poems; he expected to be able to identify and isolate those human truths that Wordsworth could only contemplate in an object. And this reflection upon his inner life was not 'the abstruse research' of 'Dejection', but a power native to Coleridge's mind which he had been exercising since first reading Iamblichus and Plotinus at the age of 15 or 16.

This investigation into the nature of human nature, was to form the first pole of Coleridge's bi-polar development of subject and object. It consists in his deepening and at first very private insights into what constitutes a person, and how we recognize this person as both self and other. Without this power of recognition, we can be neither religious – for we cannot re-bind our being to that of another, nor creative – for without the power of conceiving 'a guardian saint' we will be trapped in a world antagonistic to our being, like the Mariner, or exiled from our place of being, like Christabel, or unable to create an ideal world like the visionless poet of 'Kubla Khan'.

The other pole of Coleridge's development is of the object – the 'world' or 'story' through which the inward and invisible life of man is given a visible form. The 'world' Wordsworth used, that of nature, is superficially more nearly universal, more accessible to the past and future generations of our civilization, than any myth or story derived from history. But whether the appearances of nature are adequate to the depth and complexity of man's inward life is a question which seems to have become more and more clearly formulated in Coleridge's mind the older he became. That he was always alert to the potential union between the Logos, or the creative spirit, and the visible world is not a matter of doubt. Yet equally he saw that Nature was 'a wily old Witch', never to be at the service of Lady Mind. So he perhaps became increasingly aware of the need of a more coherent knowledge in which our humanity may be expressed. His long and painful progress towards his understanding of the constitution of a person was to culminate in the belief that the spiritual Christ was the essentially human being in every individual. What then troubled him deeply was whether there was a real union between Christ and the man Jesus: whether or not the life of Jesus was an adequate expression of the truth of Christ. His study of both Old and New Testaments might be said to have been inspired solely by his hope of verifying this relationship. His conclusion was that the history of the nation is the objectification of the lives of its members. Jesus Christ, he believed, epitomized the history of the Jews from Abraham to Malachi; in him was their history, and their history was nothing more, and nothing less, than the revelation of his being through the works of time. Coleridge had abandoned nature as a practical or working object, but he had managed to show how 'the *Objective* [might] rise up, as at a celestial Birth, in and from the universal Subject'.[3] It is this success in discerning the idea in the story, and the story in the idea, that is the mark of Coleridge's major achievement. Although his own poetic powers were at first inhibited by his unhappiness, and then withered through his lack of confidence, yet he continued to think and work in a way that would potentially enable poetry of the very highest order, a poetry in which the whole of a national history becomes the symbol of the inward life of each and every member. By giving up his life as a poet, Coleridge was able to explore the two poles of creativity, the subject and the object, and show their vital interrelation, in a way that no poet from Wordsworth to the present day has consistently managed. Coleridge's later writings are a great resource from which we have as yet only drawn one or two cupfuls; to trace how this undertaking develops out of the poetry is the business of the following chapters.

THE DISORDERED SELF

We might think of the years 1801–14 of Coleridge's life as the time of his own exile and desolation, or in the way that he later described them, as a form of crucifixion.[4] Certainly by 1812 all his mortal hopes had been shot down, for he had parted irrevocably from his wife, the Wordsworths and Sara Hutchinson, from those people in whose lives he had hoped to find his own, and whom he saw as constituting his very self. 'Alone, alone, all, all alone' cried the ancient Mariner, and in those years Coleridge knew little of the 'lone yet genial hour' of the poet, and much of the ache of unrelieved solitude. He unburdened himself in his notebooks, where we find small but significant links with his earlier and creative years: he occasionally identifies his experiences with those of the Mariner.[5] Kathleen Coburn believes that 'recollections and identifications with the Ancient Mariner . . . are evident from the

Scottish tour onwards' [CN II 1913.n]. Whether the tour itself
stimulated this identification, it is not possible to say: but we may
see from at least one notebook entry, and from Coleridge's letters
during late August and early September 1803, that Wordsworth
had ceased to be a wholly satisfactory companion: 'My words and
actions imaged on his mind, distorted and snaky as the Boatsman's
Oar reflected in the Lake' [CN I 1473]. Coleridge must have found
Wordsworth's continual misapprehension of his thoughts and
deeds, as well as the older man's incommunicative silence and
self-centredness [CL II 978], a very bitter kind of solitude, to which
actual solitude might have been preferable. After he had parted
from Dorothy and William, Coleridge claims that he found himself
happy alone: 'I am enjoying myself, having Nature with solitude
and liberty; the liberty natural and solitary, the solitude natural
and free' [CL II 979]. We can believe that he felt some relief to be
without the Wordsworths, but Coleridge never enjoyed nature
without, at the least, longing for a companion; so we should not
be deceived into thinking that Coleridge might have been happy
or recovering his genial spirits. A mere nine days later he sent
Southey that most fearful account of his inner life, 'The Pains of
Sleep', with these attached comments: '. . . but my spirits are
dreadful, owing entirely to the horrors of every night – I truly
dread to sleep/ it is no shadow with me, but substantial Misery
foot thick, that makes me sit by my bedside of a morning, and
cry'.[6] Dreams, which had played a main part in the method of
apprehending the reality of human nature in the Supernatural
poems, were indeed becoming the worst realities of his life, speaking of the same truths as those suffered by the Mariner and Christabel. The circle of domestic affections in which Coleridge had
hoped to anchor his being had never properly formed around
him, and now he sees all the objects of his love beginning to be
alienated from him. It is not surprising that the reflection on prayer
with which 'The Pains of Sleep' opens should be addressed to
'Love', nor that the heart of the poem is a 'fiendish dream' describing a love disordered, torturing the poet:

> Desire with loathing strangely mixed
> On wild or hateful objects fixed.
> Fantastic passions! maddening brawl!
> And shame and terror over all!
> Deeds to be hid which were not hid,

Which all confused I could not know
Whether I suffered, or I did:
For all seemed guilt, remorse or woe,
My own or others still the same
Life-stifling fear, soul-stifling shame. [PW I 390]

That this was no passing moment in Coleridge's life, the notebooks constantly remind us. His sleep, he recorded in May 1804, was 'a pandemonium of all the Shames and miseries of the past Life from early childhood all huddled together, and bronzed with one stormy Light of Terror and Self-torture'.[7] Coleridge is not specific, either in the note or the poem, as to the nature of his shames and miseries, but 'Desire with loathing strangely mixed' is not an inappropriate description of Christabel's inner struggle, and the 'soul-stifling shame' that the poet suffers is echoed in his description of Christabel after her 'fall': 'O sorrow and shame! can this be she,/ The lady who knelt at the old oak tree?' Coleridge's internal disorder creates fear and shame in all his relations with others, alienating him from them in his own mind, as Christabel and the Mariner were alienated from their societies.[8] On the third occasion of these nightmares, he is awakened by his 'own loud Scream' and then he 'wept as I had been a child'. These images and events have clear parallels with the verse letter. He was there awakened not from a nightmare but from a disordered day-dreaming by the harp's 'Scream/ Of agony by Torture lengthen'd out', a scream which is as much internal as external. In the letter the storm seems to speak of 'a little Child' that 'has lost its way' and in this poem Coleridge weeps like a child: both the child and the poet utter cries seeking to arouse love and affection. The storm which was representative or symbolic in the verse letter has become fully internalized in this poem, and co-ordinate with the conscious presence of sin:

Such punishments, I said, were due
To natures deepliest stained with sin,–
For aye entempesting anew
The unfathomable hell within

Coleridge has, of course, fathomed before, as he has so vividly here, in other poems and other ways, 'the unfathomable hell within', the dark and infernal side of man's nature. Cain, as a consequence of his deed, bestialized his appearance and placed himself in a barren and seasonless world. The Mariner creates a hell of isolation for himself by shooting the albatross, and Christabel was to have suffered a hell of desolation as a result of her nature being perverted by Geraldine's. These inward truths of human nature are now rising into the living consciousness of the poet (even though he is barely willing to admit that these nightmares are fit punishment for *him*) and making his life barren, desolate and bestial. It is love of a purer being which will harrow all these hells, and relieve the dreamer of his terrible dream: in some way not disclosed, the innocent Enos was to have been his father's redemption, as the innocent Asra is to be that of the dejected poet; the Mariner's stationary isolation is relieved in part by the intercession of his guardian saint, and in part by his watching the moon move up the sky, an image of the soul progressing to its appointed home in heaven[9]; Christabel was to have reorientated her fallen nature, possibly by calling upon her guardian saint, her mother. And here Coleridge says in conclusion, almost too nakedly, but nonetheless almost as a summation of his vicarious experience in his characters:

> To be beloved is all I need,
> And whom I love, I love indeed.

GUILT ACTIVE

In this poem we can see Coleridge discovering his own sense of guilt active, not merely contemplated. But nearly five years earlier, while he was still completing 'The Ancient Mariner', he had written to his brother George – ordained and orthodox, facts which may have coloured Coleridge's tone though not his essential belief–

Of GUILT I say nothing; but I believe most steadfastly in original Sin; that even from our mother's wombs our understandings are darkened; and even where our understandings are in the Light, that our organization is depraved, and our volitions imperfect; and we sometimes see the good without *wishing* to attain it, and oftener *wish* it without the energy that wills and performs it – And for this inherent depravity, I believe, that the Spirit of the Gospel is the sole cure. [CL I 396]

It is significant that this belief should have been expressed while he was composing 'The Ancient Mariner'. A sense of guilt, so apparent in 'The Pains of Sleep', is not expressed anywhere in the earlier poem and remains similarly unexpressed in this letter, Coleridge apparently not finding much evidence of the emotion in himself.[10] It might seem a little contradictory to hold a belief in original sin so firmly, and to have no concomitant sense of guilt; but this I think is the difference between having the idea in mind, and feeling that idea active in one's being. By 1803 and finding guilt working in himself, Coleridge had begun to move from one condition to the other. In October of that year he recorded a note which reveals him fully aware of the disorder at the centre of his being; he is looking out from his study window at Keswick:

A grey Day, windy – the vale like a place in Faery, with the autumnal colours . . . the light yellow, the yet lingering Green, Beeches and Birches, as they were blossoming Fire and Gold . . . and now the Rain Storm pelts against my Study Window – O Asra Asra why am I not happy! why have I not an unencumbered Heart! these beloved Books still before me, this noble Room, the very centre to which a whole world of beauty converges, the deep reservoir into which all these streams and currents of lovely Forms flow . . . O Asra! wherefore am I not happy! why for years have I not enjoyed one pure and sincere pleasure! – one full Joy! – one genuine Delight, that rings sharp to the Beat of the Finger!* – all cracked, and dull with base Alloy! Di Boni! to me it has been strength and courage, – but whether to you . . . alas! this hopeless love!' [CN I 1577]

We can see how structurally similar this note is to the 'Letter to Asra'. Both begin in tranquility, and in delighted observation of what he can see from his study window; even the very quality of the light, 'yellow, the yet lingering Green', is as he had observed it two years earlier – 'a peculiar Tint of Yellow Green'. Into this scene of the late afternoon or early evening, enter a storm, and associated with it, the poet's thoughts returning to the condition of his own mind and heart. And he feels burdened, despite the loveliness of the world and the splendid resources of his study and intellect. As in the Letter, all these potential pleasures ring false to him, because in their founding in him they have been mixed with the impurities of a 'base Alloy'. Towards the end of the note Coleridge makes this mark *, and adds a footnote:

But still to have said to the poetic Feeling when it has awak'd in the Heart – Go! – come tomorrow!'

His divided heart has dammed up the fountain of joy within him and so disabled him from finding in himself that life latent in the beauty of nature. He hopes, without much hope, that in bidding the poetic impulse to return another day, it will return to a heart that does not make the pleasures of the world ring false. His love of Sara has given him strength and courage, but he also thinks of it as hopeless, or as he has phrased it in another note – impossible [CN I 1065]. That is, it can have no being in time and place, in the forms of the world; and though it is of itself good, yet because it cannot have the expression it would seek, it operated in Coleridge's conscience as guilt operates – denying the integrity of his consciousness.

Consequently we will see that the idea of life as a process of redemption emerges in various ways in these years; but one note in particular, written some two years later in 1805 in Malta, unites this idea with echoes of 'The Ancient Mariner' and 'Dejection . . .' On the evening of 11 July he was watching the moon, which appeared

. . . like a new-moon with the old moon in her Lap, only that the silver Thread was not there, and its colour was reddish smoke-colour/ its countenance in the same shape . . . When it first struck my notice, the moon was *all* like a round of silver completely lost in egg-tarnish . . . After some time the Seaward Edge was brightened as by a laborious Scouring/ till it became a crescent as before described . . .

I awoke at 2 o'clock, Friday morning 12 July, and the full moon was in all her Purity, bright, and the Stars were bold and mighty that could abide her presence – What a picture this of a man commencing Life with a character utterly tarnished, and gradually scouring itself, and revealing little by little till it become a Shakespeare, or – [CN II 2610] and there the note ends. Coleridge later discovered that he has been watching 'a grand Eclipse', but he holds to his analogy. His discovery of a natural phenomenon as a metaphor for the main business of a man's life, the purifying of his tarnished nature, is also a metaphor for the development of his creative powers, and the two processes are inseparable. Every man who has scoured himself into moral purity might put on the mantle of Shakespeare's power. The two images of the moon enhance this picture: in 'Dejection . . .' we saw that the new moon with the old moon in her lap foretells a storm which Coleridge had hoped would awaken his creative powers; in 'The Ancient Mariner' the rising of the moon with 'A star or two beside' is a prelude to the Mariner's restoration to the right use of his senses: the gloss Coleridge added later, which contains echoes of this note, confirms for us that having begun life in the poem with a character thoroughly tarnished, the Mariner is scouring himself, or being scoured, into a moral and creative purity. The association of creativity with the process of redemption might be inferred from the Supernatural poems and from 'Kubla Khan' and 'Dejection . . .' But it would be difficult to determine how conscious the poet himself was of the association. Here, however, we may see the union of the two processes fully present to his own mind. And this union Coleridge always maintained until in the fullness of his thought we find him asserting that the very life of the nation is a process of creation in itself redemptive.

'Suffering is action' proclaimed an equally unhappy man, and as the knowledge got from his suffering grew, so Coleridge was more and more willing to see that its cause lay in him and was of him. In 1810 he wrote: '. . . Guilt is justly imputable to me prior to any given act, or assignable moment of time, in my Consciousness' [CN III 4005]. This change in some 12 years, from an unwillingness to say anything about guilt, to an assertion of it as an immediate fact of consciousness, is a measure of Coleridge's growing awareness that the ideas and motives that he had employed in the Supernatural poems had become active in himself.

THE LIFE OF NATURE

The idea that our vision of nature depends upon our interest in and love of another person continued to grow in Coleridge's consciousness: only one entry before his prose version of the 'Letter to Asra' he had copied and expanded this from a notebook of 1799:

> Print of the Darlington Ox, sprigged with Spots. – Viewed in all moods, consciously, unconsc. semiconsc. – with vacant, with swimming eyes – made a Thing of Nature by the repeated action of the Feelings. O Heaven when I think how perishable Things, how imperishable Thoughts seem to be? [CN I 1575][11]

The print of the ox, in the Hutchinson's farmhouse at Sockburn, is associated with untainted pleasurable feelings. It was during this visit that he met and fell in love with Sara, and covertly held her hand while they and the other members of the family stood up round the fire. But what does he mean when he says that the print of the ox was 'made a Thing of Nature by the repeated action of the Feelings'! It seems to me that Coleridge is recording a particular example of that process of mind by which he had hoped all Things from Pole to Pole' would receive their life from 'the Eddying' of the pure Sara's 'living Soul'. But in the note he does not begin with a thing of nature, rather with the print of such a thing. As a consequence of the image being at a remove from the particular thing itself, Coleridge is more able to consider it as an idea, and to return to it on various occasions in order to view it in all states of consciousness. Because it is not the Darlington Ox in a field, in someone's farm, or at a show, the sense impression is diminished as the idea of it is developed. Coleridge's feelings act on this idea, and in doing so make it not just a farming phenomenon, but 'a Thing of Nature', just as Sara's soul was seen as the essential life of all things of nature in the verse letter. The permanency is not the thing, but the idea of it, the thought, and this, united with human feeling, is its nature.

In several other notebook entries, Coleridge illustrates how our relationship with another person determines and is expressed by our conception of the external world. In September 1803 he records a moment when he has been watching Sara, and notes that

> Wherever her eye turned, gladness came, like spots of Sunshine
> on green Moorland Hills, creating a new field in the Waste/ –
> spots of sunshine seen thro' floating mists or thinning Showers.
> [CN I 1503]

This note speaks primarily of the joy and gladness that Sara creates
in those upon whom she turns her presence. But Coleridge's
metaphor for this effect is inescapably associated with the power
this joy has of creating order when focussed on waste and chaos:
the floating mists and thinning showers are the perceptual fog
through which the sunshine of joy pierces in order to create the
life and harmony of nature. The chaos of the senses has been
'tamed' to create a distinct and harmonious world.

But the nature of Coleridge's relationship with Sara, and their
frequent absence from each other, often denied him this ordering
power. In April 1804 he wrote:

> Why an't you here? This for ever/ I have no rooted thorough
> thro' feeling – and never exist wholly present to any Sight, to
> any Sound, to any Emotion, to any series of Thoughts received
> or produced/ always a feeling of yearning, that at time passes
> into a Sickness of Heart. [CN II 2000]

Because Sara, his source of joy, is absent, and because his own
resources are poisoned, all his experiences ring false to him. This
inability to find himself in the sensations, feelings and thoughts
of his life, inspires a deep yearning (a key word in Coleridge's
vocabulary) for the person whom he imagines able to complete
his moral being, and restore himself to himself. But still worse
than Sara's absence is her imagined death:

> Asra's death – What? submit that the streams, skies, fields,
> mountains, yea, human smiles should be changed into curses
> to my eyes? No, [if I am to be separated,] let it be in an [separate
> world.] [CN III 3374, 1808]

If Sara's absence had disabled the poet from a full participation in
his own experience, her death would make all experience a curse
upon his life. He would suffer that kind of desolation Baudelaire
spoke of when he found himself in 'un univers morne à l'horizon
plombé..un pays plus nu que la terre polaire'. And as the enciph-

ered language so graphically implies, if he is to be separated from
Sara, he may as well be separated from this world, from any hope
of giving his permanent being a place in time.

Two years later, in 1810, he summed up these experiences in
which the person he loved is felt to be the medium through whom
the natural world is made visible:

> Suppose a wide and delightful Landscape – and what the Eye
> is to the Light, and the Light is to the Eye, that interchangeably
> is the Lover to the Beloved. [CN III 4036, f.34]

And in the same note he goes on to say that were he confident
of his being loved, he would address his beloved as 'Light of mine
eye! by which alone I not only see all I see, but which makes up
more than half the objects seen'.

These are private thoughts, but they speak of feelings unknown
to few. The pity of it is that Coleridge was never able to incorporate
them into his public thinking about how man comes to see nature.
Had he done so, the shape and emphasis of certain later works,
particularly the *Biographia Literaria*, might have been very different.

LOVE AND DESIRE

Coleridge felt profoundly that Sara could set him on the path to
virtue and 'self-amendment': 'O yes, Sara! I did feel how being
with you I should be so very much a better man' [CN II 2495,
f.39v.]. But if it is love that may improve a man 'why should it be
[of] a *Woman*, and a beloved *Woman*? will the sneerers ask'. Yeats's
unlovely answer – because 'Love has pitched his mansion in/ The
place of excrement',[12] – implies the intimate union of the life of
the spirit with that of the body. Coleridge, in a heavily enciphered
note, finds cause to agree with him:

> The *painful* Disgust felt by every good mind, male or female, at
> certain things & Images [semen compared with urine] is itself a
> proof of the natural union of [love and lust – thoughts and
> sensation] being [so exceedingly . . . dissimilar from the vehicle
> – as if a beloved woman] vanishing [in our arms] should leave
> [a huge toad] – or worse. [CN III 4019]

In Kathleen Coburn's words an association of this last phrase 'with the Lamia-like figure of Geraldine in *Christabel* is inescapable'. Should love cease to be love in the act of physical consummation, and dissolve into lust, should lust gain the ascendancy over love, then the beloved will cease to be a person, and become bestialized in the act of a selfish and sensual gratification.[13] Something of this nature I suggested happened in the mind of Christabel when she took Geraldine into her bed, and she was to have become an outcast on account of it.[14] Whatever battle was going on in Christabel, and however directly conscious Coleridge was of the forces he was portraying, his love for Sara Hutchinson has brought the distinction into the centre of his thinking. But if love is not usurped by desire, if indeed love makes the pleasures of sex, and not sex the pleasures of love, Coleridge then has a wonderful vision of 'sleeping with the Belovéd' as increasing his active benevolence:

> O best reward of Virtue! to feel pleasure made more pleasurable, in legs, knees, chests, arms, cheek – all in deep quiet, a fountain with unwrinkled surface yet still the living motion at the bottom, that 'with soft and even pulse' keeps it full – and yet to know that this pleasure is making us more *good*, is preparing virtue and pleasure for many known and many unknown to us. O had Milton been thus happy! Might not . . . more than 20 million of Souls . . . have received new impulses to virtuous Love, till Vice was stared at as voluntary Torment, slow gratuitous Self mangle-murder! – O and the thousand thoughts arising in this state, only connected with it, inasmuch as Happiness is a Fountain of intellectual activity . . . [CN II 2495, f.40][15]

Coleridge combines this imagined union of love and sexuality with one of his favourite images of domestic harmony – the spring softly pulsing through a cone of sand, yet leaving the water at the surface smooth and tranquil – an image that in its context here is as erotic as the fountain in 'Kubla Khan'. The connection that Coleridge makes between sexuality, happiness and creativity again gives us an insight into his peculiar difficulties. But his thinking on love and desire, under the pressure of his difficult relationship with Sara, was more often concerned to distinguish what he considered as the two elements and to demonstrate the true place and function of each. So he reflects on a man and a girl walking together:

A fellow that puts his arm inside the Girl's and so walks cud-
dling to her, is in lust with her, – a fellow who walks with a
girl in his arms, with a face of tenderness, but without pressing
on her or perhaps looking on her, is in love perhaps – the first
is certain . . . [CN I 448]

The idea latent here is that a man who is in love is not in love
with the appearances of his belovéd, that love is in itself free of
sensation: if one's love depends upon the senses, then it is not
love, but lust. The mistaking of desire mixed with affection for
love is played upon by Coleridge in what he called 'Nonsense
Verses for the trial of a Metre':

Some sager Words two meanings tell
For instance, Love is such!
. . . cannot LOVE *too well*
And yet may *love too much*
Would we make sense of this we must
First construe Love as Love: [and lust as lust] [CN II 2224]

Loving too well is impossible because it is a spiritual activity ever
seeking a perfect end; and we can love too much, because this for
Coleridge indicates a disordered sexual appetite. Although the
distinction between the two has here only been lightly drawn, yet
ideally Coleridge will not let them be divided, as he would not
divide body and soul. A note of April 1805 makes a more profound
analysis of these two poles of human loving, while asserting their
essential communion:

Real and symbolical – Motion and Rest at the Goal. Love and the
grandeur of loving the Supreme in her – the real and symbolical
united . . . in loving her thus I love two Souls as one, as com-
pleat, as the *ever improving* Symbol of Deity to us, still growing
with the growth of our intellectual Faculties: - and so uniting
the moving impulse and the *stationary* desire. O that I may have
heart and soul to develope this Truth so important and so deeply
felt. [CN II 2530]

What in a note of January 1804 Coleridge had called 'the vital and
the personal' [CN I 1822] is here seen as the supreme in Sara, and
in his love Coleridge reverences the invisible being of his beloved,

that which is not apparent to the senses. This love enables the growth of our intellectual faculties, and proposes some perfect end for this growth; as a fountain of intellectual activity it seeks to connect until all disparate experiences are united in one whole. In absolute terms this whole cannot be other than God.[16] Thus it is not surprising that he thinks that in loving the supreme in Sara he is creating a symbol of the Deity, which will become more perfect as his intellectual faculties expand under the influence of this love. But though this love may in itself be symbolic of God, it still requires some form of visible expression in the immediate world; and this it gains by being united to stationary desire, the creature of sense and time and place.

What began as respect for another person's inward and invisible being, can be seen as progressing towards a recognition that this being finds its true identity in God. The idea that the two opposing states of love and desire, the permanent and the real on the one hand, and the visible and immediate on the other, find their resolution in a symbol, is often present in Coleridge's thinking. It appears again later in 1805 for instance, in a dream Coleridge had of his return to England and Sara:

> With all the merely bodily Feelings subservient to our Reason coming only at its call, and obeying its Behests with a gladness not without awe, like servants who work under the Eye of their Lord, we have solemnized the long marriage of our Souls by its outward Sign and natural Symbol. It is now registered in both worlds, the world of the Spirit and the world of the Senses. We therefore record our deep thankfulness to Him, from whose absolute Unity all Union derives its possibility, existence, and the meaning, subscribing our names with the blended Blood of this great Sacrament.
>
> [CN II 2600; cf.CN III 3605,f.118 and CN III 3764

This note describes a relationship between the senses and the spirit of the kind that Coleridge later asserted as essential to his thought – that between Reason and Understanding; Reason, the life of God within us, must order and control the Understanding, but cannot express itself but by means of the Understanding: the resolution of these opposing forces creates a symbol. So the marriage of souls, which must order the senses and desires, gets its outward sign from the sexual union of the two lovers – a note of the dream itself makes it clear that this is what Coleridge had dreamt of. Coleridge's imagined union with Sara is fully consistent with the teachings of the Church: marriage is regarded as a sacrament – an outward and sensible sign which participates in an inward, invisible and spiritual union – a union which itself represents the union of the invisible Christ with his visible Church, of the timeless with the forms of time.[17]

But this union was nothing but a dream, and so did not belong to the world of space and time; it was a dream from which Coleridge had to awake. Having burdened himself with an ideal union of love and desire which could have no legitimate expression in his own life, he often feared that his desire might usurp his love: consequently, many notes assert the supremacy of love over desire, and they become contrary rather than opposing forces in his life:

> Could I feel for a moment the supremacy of Love suspended in my nature, by accidents of temporary Desire; were I conscious for a moment of an interregnum in the Heart, were the Rebel to sit on the *Throne* of my Being . . . I should feel myself as much fallen and as unworthy of her Love . . . as if I had roamed, like a Hog, in the rankest Lanes of a city . . . but when Love, like a Volcano beneath a sea always burning, tho' in silence, flames up in his strength at some new accession, how can the waters but heave and roll in billows. [CN II 2984]

Much of what we have discovered in Coleridge's poetry is present here: the ideal supremacy of love over desire; the usurpation of love by desire as a form of man's fall, the idea that love progressively discloses new insights, accessions of the heart and intellect – the burning sea possibly an echo of that moment in 'The Ancient Mariner' when grace is about to break upon him and unlock his prayerless heart; the inner and invisible nature of this love, requiring the forms of sense, but these tied to a forbidden desire; and finally, so very like 'Dejection . . .', the threat of a storm or tempest when this love cannot find expression on the surface and appearances of life, thus becoming a threat to the stability of that surface.

Three notes between May 1807 and April 1808 indicate that under the pressure of this conflict Coleridge was struggling to maintain his distinction between love and desire, and to show that love might gain expression through a minimum use of sense, and wholly separate from desire. Two enciphered comments on a poem wrongly attributed to Dante take up this task:

> In the Soother of Absence introduce love singing the ordinary song of desire from beauty as for instance that of Dante . . . and then to describe myself unaffected uninfluenced till the soul within through the face and form declares a primary sympathy.
> [CN II 3017]

Dante, one feels, would have had his views on beauty best reflected in Coleridge's comments, rather than in the poem ascribed to him. The soul shining through the face or form is of course love or Reason preceding Understanding or sense; but this phraseology implies that Coleridge sees very little integration of the two: the soul would be willing to desert the body it must use. A similar non-integral relationship between the soul and the senses appears in a fragment of poetry:

> All look and likeness caught from earth
> All accident of kin and birth,
> Had passed away. There was no trace
> Of aught on that illumin'd face,
> Uprais'd beneath the rifted stone
> But of one spirit all her own;
> She, she herself, and only she
> Shone through her body visibly. [PW I 393, 18]

Coleridge feels that he has had momentary contact with Sara's essential self, with what he elsewhere calls in respect of his love for her and his children, 'a Universal personified' [CN II 2441]. This has occured by the sloughing off of all those accidental and inherited features apparent to sense – of everything by which every other person would recognize her, and which form the objects of desire. Coleridge has abandoned the normal vehicles of sense, and though he asserts the visibility of Sara's essential self, it is open to question whether anyone else at that moment could have seen what he saw: this experience is perhaps an example of supernatural perception, of the observer more than half-creating what he sees, as the Mariner had two distinct kinds of perception of the watersnakes. And in this experience of Sara's timeless self,

Coleridge has briefly realized that 'primal sympathy' for which he
longed, a marriage of true minds. And he quotes this fragment
himself in a note which describes the fatuity of fame to a man of
genius who longs for, but has been denied, this kind of contact:
to such a man:

> . . . if his nature force him to seek for a *completer* of whose
> moral nature he shall be the completion . . . if on [after] knowl-
> edge and tender affection *one look* of the eyes, one vision of the
> countenance, seen *only* by the Being, on whom it worked, and
> by him only to be seen . . . [Coleridge here quotes the lines
> above] . . . If such be the Instinct of his moral nature, and
> that Instinct called into intensest activity, and yet baffled and
> thwarted – to such a man, I say, let him have the Genius of
> Shakespeare, yet Fame must necessarily be to him, something
> like . . . the thought of tomorrow's Breakfast to one, who is
> fainting hopelessly for his today's dinner. [CN II 3291]

The imagined communion is moral and spiritual, and almost
wholly unmediated by the senses: the emphasis on the word
'vision' suggests that what is 'seen' is mystical rather than material;
certainly the communion is quite capable of existing without any
physical contact between the lovers. What Coleridge seeks of Sara
Hutchinson, and hopes she seeks of him, is that part of his nature
which cannot be whole except by its loving of another person;
but Coleridge has fully established that what he would love is
independent of those qualities bound to time and sense; thus any
contact of the senses that may or may not happen between them,
or even the desiring of any such contact, is more or less irrelevant
to their love. The true concomitant of this love is therefore not
desire but friendship:

> To promote the welfare of another equally as our own is
> Friendship/ to prefer it to our own whenever the one or the
> other must be sacrificed, is the height of Friendship – To do this
> and in addition to all this to receive all our happiness by giving
> it, is Love! . . . [and] mutual Love [is] the best Emblem and
> Foretaste of Heaven. Why then should I fear to say, I *love* you,
> love you always, and if I sometimes feel desire at the same time,
> yet Love endures when no such feeling blends with it –
>
> [CN III 3284]

Desire in this and the previous note is seen as having no function in revealing the inward and spiritual condition of the lovers. It has been relegated to the position of an occasional and unwelcome interruption which in no way need disturb the established order.

When the break with Wordsworth made the separation from Sara more or less permanent, and Coleridge found that the future could hold out no hope of their domestic communion, he reoccupied a position he had first taken in 1806, when he thought that Sara was estranging herself from him, and which may well speak most eloquently of the nature of his love for her: then he felt the inadequacy of language and of the senses in conveying the love that burned within him:

O *Beloved!* – Beloved! – ah! what are Words but air? and impulses of air? O who has deeply felt, deeply, deeply! and not fretted and grown impatient at the inadequacy of Words to Feelings, of the symbol to the Being? – Words – what are they but a subtle *matter?* and the meanness of Matter must they have, and the Soul must pine in them, even as the Lover who can press kisses only on the garment of one indeed beloved/ O bear witness my Soul! bear witness the permanence of my Being! – even such a feeling must accompany the strictest union, the nearest kiss that can be – it is still at once the Link and the Wall of separation. O what then are Words, but articulated Sighs of a Prisoner heard from his Dungeon! powerful only as they express their utter impotence! [CN II 2998]

In this note Coleridge supposes that a fully realized love cannot be adequately expressed by the senses, and that consequently such a love must always result in the separation of the lovers. In a note in verse of September 1808 Coleridge develops the Pyramus and Thisbe theme, and states clearly that want of material means of communication could ennoble and elevate the lovers' love:

The Builder left one narrow rent,
Two wedded hearts, if e'er were such,
Contented most in discontent
There cling, and try in vain to touch!
O Joy with thy own Joy at Strife,
That yearning for the Realm above

Woulds't die into intenser Life
And union absolute of Love. [CN III 3379]

It is not difficult to see this short poem as containing the kernel of Coleridge's love for Sara Hutchinson. His idealism, his Platonism, are yearnings for 'the Realm above', and tortuous and tortured though many of his notes are – the pressure of desire being a real pressure – yet they are almost always illuminated by his joy of intellectual and spiritual discovery which this love prompts him to. One cannot imagine Coleridge at ease in 'the sty of content'.

In the earlier years of his knowing Sara, on one occasion he wrote in a notebook: 'Why we two made to be a Joy to each other should for so many years constitute each other's melancholy. O! but the melancholy is Joy!' [CN I 1394]. These are not the words of a man hurrying to resolve his dilemmas. Because Coleridge's idea of love was always developing, because he was constantly in search of 'new accesses of thought and feeling', he refused to give his love definite or limited expression. It needed an object, but had this object been so material a thing as a wife or a mistress, his ideation of this love would probably have been inhibited. So Coleridge constantly refused desire, refused to fix his growing love in the forms of time and place. Only when the idea had found its proper focus in an immortal being did he begin to build a 'home' for it – in the forms of national history. And in this ample dwelling every individual and every family was to find the fully developed forms of their humanity which, by supplying an energy from their own lives and hearts, they might make into symbols of the life and course of the spirit.

PERSON, IMAGINATION AND IDEA

Because Coleridge believed that love was a separate element, he thought that love must have a life and growth of its own, and is not therefore always dependent on an intimate and sensible knowledge of its object. It is characteristic of many commentators on this aspect of Coleridge's thought to declaim as unreal a love not wholly realized in an individual, to mock with Donne those who have no mistress but their muse. The imagination, seeking to bring to life and to give substance to that which is not immediately visible, has no role to play in their concept of loving. Thus they insist that the loving of a person and the pursuit of an idea are irreconcileable and exclusive activities. So Geoffrey Yarlott thinks it of importance to redeem Coleridge from Suther's charge that he was under-sexed, and therefore mystical about matters of love: he asserts, quite rightly, that Coleridge 'was neither passionless nor under-sexed,' but quite wrongly implies that passion and sexuality are constituents of love.[19] For Yarlott, as for Suther, and as Coleridge concluded of Wordsworth in contrast to himself, love has no reality except as a combination of affection and desire. So it is not possible to read Coleridge's notes on his love for Sara Hutchinson with any sympathy or profit in such a state of mind.

But whether this love, which finds its energy chiefly in the imagination, can be of or for a particular person, Coleridge himself at first had doubts: in this note he is discussing dread, fear of pain, or shame as the cause of his lifetime's 'faulty actions':

> . . . a state of struggling with madness from an incapability of hoping that I should be able to marry Mary Evans (and this strange passion of fervent tho' wholly imaginative and imaginary Love uncombinable by my utmost efforts with any regular Hope – / possibly from deficiency of bodily feeling, of tactual ideas connected with the image) had all the effects of direct Fear . . . [CN II 2398]

Considering how well he once knew Mary Evans and her family, and how, as he said, he and Mary 'formed each other's minds,' to call his love for her 'wholly imaginative and imaginary' seems at first sight a harsh assessment of what never ceased to be a heart-ache to him. It might, in part, be an attempt to distance himself from the pain, but he gives us a more specific cause of his suffering: it is the division between his imagined love and a source of 'regular Hope' in 'tactual ideas' and 'bodily feeling'. Marriage to Mary Evans was felt to be impossible because his ideal love of her could find no elements of worldliness, bodiliness or domesticity – nothing by which the idea might be realized definitively in her and her life. This is a deep-seated conflict that Coleridge experienced all his life: the belief that a person, first represented in Mary Evans and then in Sara Hutchinson, is indivisible from the life he finds within himself, coupled to a refusal to fit this love to domestic forms.

However, we have seen that Coleridge disciplined himself to

ive up his natural hopes of Sara; and when he considered not
ʜeir material and impossible union, but the love itself, then he
ᴇgan to disclose a relationship between person and idea. In 1809
e begins a note by meditating on her absence and her possibly
ᴇrmanent separation from him, but in so doing revives in himself
is idea of her:

> So intensely do I feel your absence that sometimes the strange
> thought forces itself on the sleep of Reason, that it must be
> forever – and that you are gone – And O! still oftener, and
> always after these thoughts your Image is so before me, that it
> seems impossible that you should ever die – the idea so very
> vivid, it seems imperishable – and how should I in these trances
> disconnect the Idea of you, and you. It is truly the Idea, you:
> even as when present, it is you, the Idea. [CN III 3512]

ᐧe may take Sara's absence as a metaphor of the material and
ɴrealizable aspect of their relationship: thus when this fact is
dmitted to the Reason, it is known to be a permanent condition
ɴalterable either by her actual presence or absence, and a con-
ition which, as we have seen, Coleridge welcomes in some barely
ᴐnscious way. But as a consequence of this sense of permanent
ᴇparation – 'always after these thoughts' – he is freed to concen-
ᐧate on that idea of her which he has seen shining 'through her
ᴏdy visibly'. This re-creation of her by thought rather than sense
ᵴ notably similar to the method by which he recreated the Darling-
ᴐn Ox from the print 'sprigged with spots': though the material
ᴏbject must perish, the idea, which carries its essential life, is
ɴperishable. It therefore follows that the idea will exist prior to
ʜe object, and that at a given moment the individual holding the
ᴵea will find it realized in a particular being. Coleridge describes
ʜis 'co-adunation' of his idea and Sara's person in an image
ᴐmparable to that which he had formerly used of marriage:

> As when the Taper's white cone of Flame is seen double, till
> the eye moving brings them into one space; and there they
> become one – so did the Idea in my imagination co-adunate
> with your present Form/ soon after I first gazed on you with
> love. [CN II 2994]

ᴏ those whose love arises out of the senses, Coleridge's platonism

is not a realizing but a mysticizing of love; yet a poet who never
lost himself in mysteries speaks of love in exactly this voice:

> Twice or thrice had I lov'd thee
> Before I knew thy face or name;
> So in a voice, so in a shapeless flame,
> Angels affect us oft, and worshipp'd be:

Sara's person is a focus for Coleridge's realization of the idea of
love. And just as he has accepted, in moments when his Reason
has been forced awake, their material separation as a condition of
their relationship, and has indeed seen it as a way of realizing
their union in an absolute sense (rather as Kierkegaard renounced
marriage to his fiancée in the belief that in some way she would
be restored to him), so Coleridge had long accepted the pain
arising from this separation. In 1804 he had written that though
necessarily absent from Sara, he would never, even if it were in
his power, transmute the concomitant pain into pleasure [CN II
2058]. We may think that the pain somehow enabled him to conjure up the idea of her, and so permit a union which would be
denied to more sublunary lovers, whose soul is sense, and whose
love therefore cannot exist in their absence. This idea is wonderfully conveyed by Coleridge in a note of September 1808:

> Some philosophers have affirmed, that two bodies may be sup-
> posed to fill one space, each the whole, without a contradiction
> in reason. Whether this be true of matter I am as ignorant as
> whether matter has a being at all – but in things of Soul and
> Spirit I am sure it is true. For Love, passionate in its deepest
> tranquility, Love unutterable fills my whole Spirit, so that every
> fibre of my Heart, nay, of my whole frame seems to tremble
> under its perpetual touch and sweet pressure, like the string of
> a Lute – with a sense of vibratory Pain distinct from all other
> sensations, a Pain that seems to shiver and tremble on the
> threshold of some Joy, that cannot be entered into while I am
> embodied – a pain of yearning which all the Pleasure on earth
> could not induce me to relinquish, even were it in my power –
> and it *is* a pain, an aking that spreads even into the eyes, that
> have a look as if they were asking a what and a where even of
> Vacancy – yea, even when the Beloved is present, seeming to

look thro' her and asking for her very Self within or even beyond her apparent Form – [CN III 3370]

The joy Coleridge hopes for cannot be experienced while he is still bound into the world of time and sense, and thus inevitably he sees as insufficient and inappropriate the forms of sense given to him by marriage, or even by Sara's appearance and presence: he seeks 'a form . . . irrelative to the imprisonment of Time and Space', a form which he believes really is discernible in and as Sara's being. An 'intolerable shirt of flame' we might call this experience, but, like Eliot, Coleridge knew that Love had devised the torment, and he had the courage to put on the immortal garment.

The moments of undisturbed joy that he and Sara shared must have been few, but Coleridge records one which Sara might have felt, if not as Coleridge describes it, at least in the tranquility and serenity which lies at its heart. It is a moment which would have vanished had the lovers sought contact through their senses, a moment of communion at the deepest level Coleridge imagined possible, and which briefly realizes his hopes as expressed in the 'Letter to Asra', in which the objective and natural world lives in the joy they create in each other:

'I fear to speak, I fear to hear you speak' – So deeply do I now enjoy your presence, so totally possess you in myself, myself in you – The very sound would break the union, and separate *you-me* into you and me. We both, and this sweet Room, its books, its pictures and the Shadows on the Wall Slumbering with the low quiet fire are all *our* Thought, a harmonious Imagery of Forms distinct on the still substance of one deep Feeling, Love and Joy – A Lake – or if a stream yet flowing so softly, so unwrinkled, that its flow is *Life* not Change –/– That state, in which all the individuous nature, the distinction without Division, of a vivid Thought is united with the sense and substance of intensest Reality. [CN III 3705]

On his way to Malta, Sara was of course not with him, but nonetheless he had found that thinking of her created a real and vivid sense of her presence – particularly at moments of falling asleep, when consciousness of the external world was diminished, and in his dreams; indeed, she sometimes seemed to be their invisible substance:

> . . . they instantly lead to Sara as the first waking Thought/ no recollection giving a hint of the means, except only that in some incomprehensible manner the whole Dream seems to have been – about her? nay – perhaps, all wild – no form, no place, no incident, any way connected with her! – What then? Shall I dare say, the whole Dream seems to have been *Her-She?* [CN II 2061]

When he was with her, and if he sought her essential self shining through her apparent self, he could always think that this self or presence was not his creation, but her true being, external to him. But when mere thought or feeling could conjure up an equal sense of her presence, and this presence in *him*, was it not possible that she was nothing but a function of his imagination?

On 27 April 1804, the Speedwell was becalmed on a sunny but cloud-bespattered day. Standing on deck, and looking away from the sun, Coleridge saw 'My Shadow the Head in the center of the crater which now forms a Glory about my Head' [CN II 2052]. He had been interested in this phenomenon, the 'Brockenspectre', as early as 1796, and had no doubt climbed the Brocken in 1799 in the disappointed hope of seeing it; however, he made use of the phenomenon as late as 1825, in the *Aids to Reflection*, when he says he had seen it twice himself. In her notes to this entry Kathleen Coburn suggests that this is one of the two sightings: where the other occurred we do not know. The phenomenon also makes its appearance in two poems – 'The Three Graves' and 'Constancy to an Ideal Object'. Miss Coburn comments on the note in relation to the latter poem: '. . . there is a revealing concatenation of images associated with the observation in this entry, . . . with 'The Ancient Mariner', and with Sara Hutchinson, especially in the last ten lines of the poem'.

We have seen that in his love for Sara before and after the voyage to Malta, Coleridge had also known a reciprocal insight which prompted his intellectual and spiritual life. On the one hand loving was a process of self-discovery, but on the other to want to find the completer' of one's moral nature *outside* oneself, in the being of another person, constitutes the yearning of true love. On the way to Malta, as we have seen, the order of this relationship was reversed for Coleridge: he no longer sought the idea in the presence or memory of the person, but the idea, the thought, was almost creating the person. Out of airy nothing, Coleridge was spinning the sensation of Sara's presence: he was confronted by the possibility that his love was nothing but a projection of his own being.

If we read 'Constancy . . .' with this fact in mind, and remembering the experience he had had aboard the Speedwell, we may see that many of the difficulties it seems to present will be found to be typical of Coleridge's thinking, and the poem a stage in his development:

> Since all that beat about in Nature's range,
> Or veer or vanish; why should'st thou remain
> The only constant in a world of change,
> O yearning Thought! that liv'st but in the brain?
>
> [PW I 455]

These lines, recording for some commentators Coleridge's despair and isolation from nature,[20] state nothing we have not already discovered in the Supernatural poems and the 'Letter to Asra'. 'How perishable things, how permanent thoughts seem to be!' we have heard him exclaim. 'Thoughts' in this context are not just the products of thinking or reflecting, but representations of reality or essential being. In a note of April 1805 Coleridge considered that thought and reality are 'two distinct corresponding sounds, of which no man can say positively which is the Voice and which the Echo' [CN II 2557]. Therefore the 'Thought' of this poem, a whole composed of distinct ideas, is the one ideal object. But what significance will this object have to 'The faery people of the future day – '? None, Coleridge answers emphatically, until 'that shining swarm', 'the insect youth' (these lines seem redolent of Gray's Ode to Spring'), are subject to the idea of death, until the world of the senses dies in them: then, 'in the porch of Death', they may breathe life into Thought.[21] This platonic process is analogous to that we have seen developing in his love for Sara Hutchinson. Not until he has found a communion with her wholly independent of the senses, not until he has rid his love of all that is temporal and conditional does he feel that he has found its true, and immortal, object. Thinking on death enables us to put off the imprisoning world of the senses, and such a 'fearful meditation' is often the beginning of a properly spiritual life.

After considering the relation of thought to death, Coleridge continues:

> Yet still thou haunt'st me; and though well I see,
> She is not thou, and only thou art she,
> Still, still as though some dear embodied Good,
> Some living Love before my eyes there stood
> With answering look a ready ear to lend,

The introduction of 'She' takes the reader by surprise, and the rest of the poem asks us to consider the relations between thought and a person. And these particular lines are, I think, crucial to that consideration, for we can see Thought undergoing a metamorphosis into a person. There is a clear, if rapid, transition in Coleridge's mind from the abstraction, Thought, to its embodiment in Good (one part of the trinity, the Good, the True and the Beautiful, which represent ultimate reality in Plato's scheme) and from there to a living Love standing in person before him, ready to listen.[22] And having, Pygmalion-like, created this living being out of the statue of thought, he addresses her:

> 'Ah! loveliest friend!
> That this the meed of all my toils might be,
> To have a home, and English home, and thee!'
> Vain repetition! Home and Thou art one.

Coleridge has co-adunated his Thought with a person – the capitalization of lines 11–19 has more significance than is normally discernible in his liberal use of them. And in this union of thought and person he finds his *nomos*, or place of being. It is worth emphasizing again that Thought precedes and is the substance of the person of whom he dreams. Coleridge realizes that Sara herself is also other than his thought ('She is not thou'), and that, despite this, thought is in some respect her essential being ('and only thou art she'), but yet he insists ('Still, still . . .') that his thought takes on the lineaments of her whom he loves. And without this person who is also Thought, all his hopes of an English home are as life-denying as the world in which the Mariner found himself:

> The peacefull'st cot, the moon shall shine upon,
> Lulled by the thrush and wakened by the lark,

Without thee were but a becalméd bark,
Whose Helmsman on an ocean waste and wide
Sits mute and pale his mouldering helm beside.

)nly when his Thought is realized in a person will Coleridge feel
ıt home', finding his ideal being existing in time and place.
  The final stanza introduced a metaphor to encapsulate the inter-
ction between thought and person that has informed the progress
f the poem. This metaphor is a version of that experience of
ıe 'glory' he had had on board the Speedwell. However, as is
ppropriate in a poem, it is the images associated with the best-
nown version of the phenomenon that he uses here.[23] He begins
ıe last stanza with, 'And art thou nothing?' Although it is not
lear whether he is chiefly addressing Thought or Sara, the ques-
on is largely rhetorical: in finding such an exact analogy of his
xperience Coleridge has determined that it is something. The
roblem is that most commentators have felt that the something
ıat Coleridge discerned is to all intents equivalent to nothing in
ıat it is a projection of his own being, and merely himself writ
ırge. There is reason to admit this point of view in the immediate
ontext of the poem, because Coleridge himself seems uncertain
/hat value to place upon the experience.[24] Is he in the same state
s the rustic, worshipping what is only a projection of himself –
ossessed by an idea, but not possessing it? And if the poet is
onscious that all he sees is a form of himself, does this undermine
ıe value of the vision? What aspect of himself does the glory
epresent? Is it merely a 'shadow' of his mortal self, or is it his
ssential being stripped of the conditional and the temporal? These
re questions that the poem does not answer, but which must be
nswered before we can determine what value to put upon the
xperience. And they were questions that Coleridge seemed to be
evolving in his mind as the Speedwell rolled on towards Malta.
  It is my opinion that he soon came to think that what he had
vitnessed was not only of positive significance, but an analogy of
he very hallmark of genius. Not more than a month later he
vas thinking concertedly about Shakespeare, whom he frequently
ised when he wanted to illustrate creative genius working at its
ınest. In his Shakespearian lectures he was to say that 'One
haracter attaches to all true poets: that they write from a principle
vithin, independent of everything without' [SC II 212]. This, Col-
ridge asserted throughout his lectures, was pre-eminently true of

Shakespeare: his characters were not born of observation of the
world and its ways, but by the poet's study of his own mind; each
person he created was but a fragment of himself projected into
the forms of the world, and Coleridge uses images derived from
the phenomenon of the Brockenspectre to illustrate his claims:

> In the plays of Shakespeare everyman sees himself, without
> knowing that he does so: as in some of the phenomena of
> nature, in the mist of the mountain, the traveller beholds his
> own figure, but the glory round the head distinguishes it from
> a mere vulgar copy . . . every form is true, everything has reality
> for its foundation; we can all recognize the truth, but we see it
> decorated with such hues of beauty, and magnified to such
> proportions of grandeur, that, while we know the figure, we
> know also how much it has been refined and exalted by the
> poet. [SC II 125]

The groundwork of this theme seems to have been laid in Malta:
in May 1804 he recorded this insight:

> Poetry a rationalized Dream dealing to manifold Forms our own
> Feelings, that never perhaps were attached to our own personal
> Selves – What is Lear, the Othello, but a divine Dream, all
> Shakespeare, and nothing Shakespeare – [CN II 2086]

To dream is, as we have seen in the Supernatural poems, to find
out the essential truths of our invisible humanity. Lear and Othello
have their origin in Shakespeare's power of self-reflection, which
discovers truths or feelings that are of the poet's humanity rather
than peculiar to him as a private individual. But these inward
discoveries are perfectly projected into the forms of the world, or
the story he has chosen to retell, so that what is 'all Shakespeare'
is presented as 'nothing Shakespeare'.[25] And Coleridge had discovered that his actual dreams which were 'nothing Sara' in their
outward form, yet were 'all Sara' in their substance, and that Sara
and thought were virtual synonyms. Shakespeare, and Coleridge
at first, are like the rustic in that each hardly knew how much he
made the shadow, or external form, that he pursued in the act of
creation. Coleridge was also discovering at this time that 'The
Ancient Mariner', of which the forms and incidents seemed so
remote from his experience, had its life and origins *within* him.

That Coleridge was whole-heartedly to adopt the method of creation the realization of which had caused him such a shock on his way to Malta, is evident in the *Aids to Reflection* where he returns to the metaphor of the Brockenspectre to illustrate the power of genius:

> Pindar's fine remark respecting the different effects of Music, on different characters, holds equally true of Genius – as many as are not delighted by it are disturbed, perplexed, irritated. The beholder either recognizes it as a projected form of his own Being, that moves before him with a Glory round its head, or recoils from it as a Spectre. [AR (1825) 220, PW I 456]

Here the image is incorporated into the heart of Coleridge's thinking. Not only does the individual genius project his own being into the forms of his art, but by doing so, he realizes the essential being in us all. The glory that moves before us is not our superficial or external existence, but our essential and permanent humanity – that which those who have obeyed the heaven-descended injunction to know themselves will easily recognize and find delight in. So the thought of Sara was Sara, his idea of her, her true life and the substance of his being. The doubts evident in 'Constancy . . .' have been resolved in his mature thought.

Our perception of our essential being depends upon its externalization; we cannot see it in ourselves until we find a means of expressing it in the life of another. And when we love another person what we are doing is finding in them our inward humanity in its perfected and externalized form. Coleridge's Brockenspectre experience on board the Speedwell, though it may have at first unsettled his sense of the objectivity of his love, soon enabled new accesses of thought and feeling. In April 1805, whilst in Malta, he felt he loved the supreme in Sara 'Because I love her as being capable of being glorified by me and as the means and instrument of my own glorification' [CN II 2530]. Without Coleridge Sara's glory could not be realized, and without Sara the poet could not know his own glorification.[26] The parallel with the phenomenon of the Brockenspectre is not exact because each person is the glory of the other, each person makes visible for the other the truth of that person's being as well as of their own, but the language uses to describe this relationship is clearly derived both from his own experience and other records of the phenomenon. It is also clear that what each person loves in the other is very much the same thing; so Coleridge goes on: 'In loving her thus I love two Souls as one', and it is a small step from there to the 'human form divine'. Coleridge takes the step in the same month: 'The best, the truly lovely, in each and all is God'. This statement is immediately applied to Sara as though it were a discovery: 'Therefore the truly Beloved is the symbol of God to whomever it is truly belovéd by!' [CN II 2540]. How close the person is to an idea, or thought, may be seen in Coleridge's use of the impersonal 'it'. This manner of thinking is carried on through the note:

> The Lover worships in his Beloved that final consummation of itself which is produced in his own soul by the action of the Soul of the Beloved upon it, and that final perfection of the Soul of the Beloved, which is in part the consequence of the reaction of his (so ameliorated and regenerated) Soul upon the Soul of his Beloved/ till each contemplates the Soul of the other as involving his own, both in its givings and receivings, and thus still keeping alive its *outness*, its *self-oblivion* united with *self-warmth*, and still approximates to God!

We can see that by adoring in the beloved the idea of God – 'that final consummation of itself' – each person enables the amelioration and regeneration of the other's soul: for what is honoured is not the actual condition of the other person's being, but that which he or she inspires as a result of contact with the one who is loved. It is not so much a question of pulling oneself up by one's bootlaces, but more of each pulling the other up by the heartstrings. In discussing so minutely the action and reaction of two souls upon each other, what Coleridge is struggling to ascertain is the continuity of inness and outness, of the truly human and personal self found in the being of another.

Coleridge was always conscious that his idea of Sara was the maker of his inward life: he described how he felt her soul acted in his in a fragment of verse:

> You mould my Hopes, you fashion me within;
> And to the leading Love-throb in the Heart
> Thro' all my Being all my pulses beat
> You lie in all my many Thoughts, like Light

Like the fair Light of Dawn, or Summer Eve
On the rippling Stream, or cloud reflecting Lake. [CN II 2996]

Without light the things of nature are invisible: we have already
seen that Coleridge 'saw' nature through his love of Sara. In these
lines we see him feeling that Sara's being is the reality of his, she
is that which underlies his many thoughts, and is thus, in his use
of the word, their substance, as she had earlier been the substance
of his dreams. This thinking is very finely developed in a note
written later in 1807:

> All our Thoughts all that we abstract from our consciousness
> and so form the Phaenomenon Self is a Shadow, its whole
> Substance is the dim yet powerful sense that it is but a Shadow,
> and ought to belong to a Substance/ but this Substance can have
> no marks, no discriminating Characters, no hic est, ille non est/
> it is simply Substance – and this deepliest felt during particular
> phenomena with a consciousness that the phenomenon is in us
> but it not in the phaenomenon, for which alone we yet value
> the phaenomenon, constitutes the craving of True Love.
>
> [CN II 3026, cf.CN II 2546]

By the last 'it' of this note, I presume Coleridge means consciousness. All self-reflection, he seems to be saying, leads to a concept
of self that is phenomenal and insubstantial, but that it is the
nature of this self to seek the true substance which it cannot find
in itself; and this substance, though not differentiated into form,
is yet the essence of all form; and the hope of substantiating the
natura naturata of consciousness by the natura naturans of the
noumenal or essential self is the yearning or craving of true love.
But this necessarily involves a relation of self and other, for our
consciousness only permits us to form the phenomenal self; what
is essential is the glory of another person. So Coleridge continues
the note above: 'Love a sense of Substance/Being seeking to be
self conscious, 1. of itself in a Symbol. 2. of the Symbol as not
being itself. 3. of the Symbol as being nothing but in relation to
itself'.

The paradox is that the person loved is both the essential being
of the lover, and other than him or her; the symbol or glory of
the lover's being is only known in the beloved, and it is only in
the beloved that the lover is raised into self-consciousness – not

of their phenomenal, but of their essential or noumenal self. The sense of the inadequacy of the phenomenal self, of needing love, is most acute when witnessing natural phenomena, because it is only through a relationship with the beloved that the lover can gain that sense of the noumenal which is the *natura naturans* of consciousness giving substance to his perceptions – or in an earlier vocabulary, that joy issuing forth to order the natural world in the image of his being – thus bringing it into the realms of self-consciousness. It is only through the reciprocated love between two people – each of whom finds his or her essential being in the other – that the natural world gains that harmony and unity which originates in God.

There is little doubt that as Beatrice was Dante's so Sara Hutchinson was Coleridge's 'God-bearing' image. She was to him a 'shechinah in the heart', a 'consciousness within a consciousness' [CN II 2999]; he worshipped the supreme in her, thinking that the best and truly lovely in each and all was God – of whom their relationship became 'an ever improving symbol' [CN II 2530]. When the break with Wordsworth finally came, and with it permanent separation from Sara, we might have expected Coleridge to despair. Far from it: his thoughts on love had so penetrated his consciousness, loving had become so much a condition of his being, that he is stimulated to make a magnificent declaration of his faith: what we read is not a statement which looks to the past, but to the future; not to what has been, but to what must go on being:

My love of Asra is not so much in my Soul as my Soul in it . . . To bid me not to love you were to bid me to annihilate myself – for to love you is all I know of my Life, as far as my Life is an object of my Consciousness or my Free Will. God is our Being, but thro' his works alone doth he reveal himself– . . . I hold it therefore neither Impiety on the one hand nor Superstition on the other, that you are the God within me, even as the best and most religious men have called their Conscience the God within them. But you, tho' existing to my senses, have ever abode within me – you have been, and you alone have been, my Conscience – in what form, with what voice, under what modification can I imagine God to work upon me, in which *you* have not worked? – All evil has kept aloof – you have worked ceaselessly everywhere, at all times – and the sum of your influence and benignant Grace has been, Horror of what-

ever is base, Shame and compunction for whatever is weak and
unworthy, fervent aspirations after good, and great, honourable, and beautiful things . . . [CN III 3996].[27]

Coleridge finds his life in his love of another, not himself: the true
nature of this other is found in God alone, as he is the substance
of all being. But because we cannot behold God directly, we know
him only through the mediation of his works – and in this respect
Sara is God working in him. To love this person is therefore a
duty, for it is the only method of realizing our essential, and
divine, humanity. However, since it is clear that the object of this
love is not Sara in her phenomenal existence, but that being who is
the being of all human beings, Coleridge is soon able to distinguish
between his 'disappointed Love' and its proper object. After his
break with Wordsworth and his enforced separation from Sara,
Coleridge continued to feel the duty of loving, but detached his
power from these two people:

> Tho' I have said, that Duty is a consolation, I have not affirmed
> that the scar of the wound of disappointed Love . . . would be
> removed in *this* Life – No! it will not – nay, the very Duty must
> for ever keep alive feelings, the appropriate Objects of which
> are indeed in another World . . .

Thus he distinguishes the proper objects of his feelings from their
origin in Sara – and Wordsworth, the heavenly from the earthly,
the divine from the human; but as this object has come to us
through the imperfect medium of human love, so

> . . . our human nature cannot avoid at times the connection of
> these feelings with their *original*, or their first, tho' mistaken,
> forms and objects – and so far therefore from removing the scar,
> will often and often make the wound open and bleed afresh/-
> but still we know that the feeling is not *objectless* – that the
> counterfeit has a correspondent *Genuine* – and this is the com-
> fort. [CN III 3300]

The counterfeits of Coleridge's love were Wordsworth and Sara
Hutchinson: the Genuine is the subject of the next chapter.

6

Coleridge's Christology

The final introduction to thought takes place in the transfer of person from the senses to the invisible. The reverence of the invisible, substantiated by the feeling of love, this, which is the proper definition of religion, is the commencement of the intellectual life, of the humanity. [Op.M.II.f.79]

CONSCIENCE AND THE DUTY OF LOVE

. . . the difference explained between Will and Volition . . .
(Keats, 1819)

Two Selves

In his book, *Coleridge and the Idea of Love*, which has been a valuable aid to my study, A. J. Harding at one point asserts that 'Coleridge's concern in *Aids to Reflection* is . . . not personal salvation . . . but relationship'.[1] This is true so long as we remember that in this context 'personal' is to all intents equivalent to phenomenal: for individual salvation was Coleridge's prime concern, but it was of the noumenal and not of the phenomenal self. That we may confuse these two aspects of self, and are tempted to think that our desire for the one is aspiration to the other was, for Coleridge, nothing but an insidious fact of our nature, and a prime example of original sin at work in us. Don Juan is the archetype of all those people whose desire that others should love them is not the hope of realizing their permanent being, but the hope that love will immortalize their peculiar and phenomenal self:

. . . it is among the miseries, and abides in the dark ground-work of our nature, to crave an outward confirmation of that *something* within us, which is our *very self* . . . Love *me* and not

152

my qualities, may be a vicious and insane wish, but it is not a
wish wholly without a meaning. [BLC II 216–17]

It is a wish Coleridge struggled for many years to defeat, and it
is closely connected with his longing to be understood, the hope
of which 'always more or less disappointed, gives the *passion* to
Friendship'.[2] If the language of this passage from the *Biographia*
leaves some doubt as to what Coleridge means by 'very self' – for
it seems akin to essential or noumenal self, an entry in Notebook
46 confirms that Coleridge has something other than man's immortal soul in mind: there as an example of his dictum that 'nothing
finite can stand by itself' he asks us to

> . . . take the yearning to be beloved, the craving for sympathy,
> in persons of active and constitutional sensibility . . . and then
> watch the day dreams . . . by which the creaturely will *subjec-
> tively* realizes for itself the sense of being beloved . . . It is there-
> fore selfishness: that is, the self is not only the starting-point
> *from*, but the Goal, to – which the Soul is working during such
> moments . . . The whole procedure therefore is anti-
> redemptive . . . It has the true mark of the Hades, contradiction,
> falsehood . . . [N.46, f.21v.–22]

As we have seen Coleridge spent his middle years trying to cast
off these kinds of hope; but this long-continued effort was not his
means to denying the self, rather the necessary preliminary to its
discovery. In one notebook entry he writes of his soul as a third
person, contemplates its torment with horror, and thus discerns
his duty to this being within him:

> ..but my self in eternity, as the *object* of my contemplation,
> differs unimaginably from my present Self – Do but try to think
> of your *Soul* in misery – you will find, that you are stricken with
> horror *for* it, even as for a third person/ conceive it in hazard
> thereof, and you will feel commiseration *for* it, and pray for it
> with an anguish of sympathy very different from the outcry of
> immediate Self-suffering.
>   [CN III 4007, f.9 Cf.N.47, f.73, N.38, f.6v]

It seems to me that unless we are alert to this 'growing between
two worlds' in Coleridge, we will in some measure confuse the

two very distinct meanings that he attaches to the word 'self'. Harding quotes this, for instance, from Notebook 26, as proof that Coleridge is denying the validity of self-contemplation: 'Self-contempl, [sic] or a sinking back into the potential, a willingness to evanescence of the Personal in us, a virtual Suicide – it is truly a self-centering – we will not the will of God'.[3] For Harding, Coleridge is saying that self-contemplation turns us away from the will of God, which is alone the truly personal in us. I have examined this entry, and the word is 'self-contempt', and may be compared to a very similar entry in Notebook 44: 'O God . . . preserve me from the deadly Hensbane of self-contempt – the worst and most concentrated form of selfishness. For it is a sinking down into the mere Self, an abstraction from the redeeming God' [f.44v]. Coleridge is asserting the opposite of what Harding would have us believe: that self-contempt, the turning away from the permanent self within us, is a turning away from the will of God, and the truly personal.[4] Self-respect is vital for our recognition of the divine will, because we cannot believe anything of God that we do not first find within ourselves.[5] As a consequence of this confusion, Harding puts a false emphasis on Coleridge's efforts to escape the 'misery of the self', and believes that he sought to forget himself in his loving, and his self-consciousness in his relationships.[6] It is much more accurate to say that through his loving Coleridge sought a self and a self-consciousness that were at one with God.

Self and Will

Coleridge believed that the will was the spiritual element of our humanity, and he had associated the will with the self as early as 1803 while reading and disagreeing with Kant:

> Der Wille, says Kant, is nichtes anderes, als practisches Vernunft. This I doubt/ My will and *I* seem perfect Synonimes . . . I do not feel this perfect synonimousness in Reason and the Wille. [Cf. N.44, f.18][7]

By dissociating the Reason and the Will, Coleridge is able to make room for his recognition of the fallen and imperfect nature of man.[8] Therefore, when he associated will with self, Coleridge made a distinction between the two aspects of self, and this is concomitant with two modes of action by the will. Wordsworth's 'Ode to Duty' provides one kind of self of which Coleridge is not thinking as the object of redemption. For two years, he writes in 1805, he has felt a decline in his 'Enthusiasm for the Happiness of mankind in particular places and countries' corresponding inversely to a rise in 'my sense of Duty, my hauntings of conscience from any stain of Thought or Action!' He goes on to contrast this desire for absolute freedom from material causes (another example of the supernatural method at work in him?) with Wordsworth's desire to encumber himself with the world:

> I remember the having written a strong Letter to my most dear and honoured Wordsworth . . . in consequence of his Ode to Duty and in that letter explained this as the effect of *Selfness* in mind incapable of gross Self-interest – decrease of Hope and Joy, the Soul in its round and round flight forming narrower circles, till at every Gyre its wings beat against the *personal Self*. But let me examine this more accurately. It may be, the phaenomenon may come out more honourable to our Nature.
>
> [CN II 2531]

It does not come out much more honourable to Wordsworth's nature. His poem is the cry of a man who, suffering a want of inner direction ('Me this unchartered freedom tires') longs for the circumscription of duties imposed upon his personal or phenomenal self – of a man who would become a distributor of stamps, 'just for a handful of silver', and so earn Browning's disapprobation. He and Coleridge are men of genius, and thus unlike the merry money-makers of the world, incapable of gross self-interest, both wanting something outside their personal existence in which to 'find' themselves. But Wordsworth, because his loss of interest in the world is a result of disappointed social and political hopes with its consequent blunting of his 'Enthusiasm for the happiness of mankind,' because he has not discovered that man's real good lies elsewhere than in the individual's material condition – whether considered as freedom from poverty or as investiture in the full rights of citizenship – seeks refuge only for his material or phenomenal self. Coleridge, on the other hand, seems busy shrugging off his mortal coil, divesting himself of what is material and temporal, not in order to find a refuge for his private self, but as the means of transcending it. As his interest in the material happiness of mankind declines, so his sense of duty grows towards what he calls 'the unindividual idea, Self or Soul, when conceived apart from our present living Body and the world of the senses'.

[CN II 4007, f.7v]

Self-love, and Self that loves

The phenomenal or personal self is the mere shadow of the substantial or noumenal self. And this essential self can only be known to exist when in opposition to and outside the phenomenal self – which in seeking its substance performs the act of true love. It is the phenomenal self which wills to love, and finds its free will in whom it loves, but it is a mistake to think that this is synonymous with self-love:

> The Doctors of Self-love are misled by the wrong use of words – we love ourselves – now this impossible for a finite and created Being, in the *absolute* meaning of SELF; . . . there is a state possible even in this Life, in which we may truly say - My self loves, freely constituting its secondary or objective Love in what it *wills* to love, commands what it wills, and wills what it commands. The difference between Self-love, and Self, that loves, consists in the Objects of the former as *given* to it according to the Law of the Senses – while the latter determines it's objects according to the Law in the Spirit. [CN III 3559]

The phenomenal self, by an act of will and guided by the laws of the spirit not sense, discerns spiritual objects as the proper or secondary objects of love. The self that constitutes its objects from sense alone, because it has thus abandoned its true agency, Reason, is therefore always in some kind a fallen self:

> The voluptuary begins with a desperate error. He seeks his *Self* in that which is only the common soil of his animal Life, i.e. in his Nature . . . And having given this false meaning to the *Self*, he offends by *seeking* it, when he should [be] seeking and finding a nobler Self in the love and service of his neighbor – first his neighbors in *place* – secondly, in *time*, i.e. his own *future* self, his soul. [N.42, f.27v.–28]

Love, Coleridge had discovered, is primarily an act of the will, commanded by a sense of duty, and the means by which the phenomenal self is able to discern the noumenal. Through this act of will, the fallen self participates in the life of the redeemed self, as Christabel was to hear the voice of her mother after she had re-ordered her love. Coleridge describes the futility of the unloving self in a note of 1807: he feels he must love someone 'who is and who is not myself – not myself, and yet so much more my sense of Being . . . than myself, that myself is therefore only not a feeling for reckless Despair, because she is its object/ . . . O! what mad nonsense all this would sound to all but myself-'⁹ Not mad nonsense at all, assuredly, but the painful realization of the truth that the only permanence our being has cannot be found in the phenomenal self – which according to its state of mind may either be the subject of reckless despair, or numbing lassitude, or gratifying self-indulgence, or stoic restraint, but all equally impermanent, all in themselves forms of not being. Only in willingly loving that which is not our immediate self do we discover that which is essential and permanent, that which might be the means to our immortality. Coleridge felt these things deeply, and when his love had lost its visible object in Sara Hutchinson, he continued to affirm that the act of love was necessary to his existence:

Seven years ago . . . I wrote thus:

> O ye Hopes! that stir within me!
> Health comes with you from above!
> God is with me! God is *in* me!
> I cannot die: for Life is Love!

And now, that I am alone, and utterly hopeless for myself – yet still I *love* – and more than ever feel that Conscience, or the Duty of Love, is the Proof of continuing, as it is the Cause and Condition of existing, Consciousness. [CN III 3231, f.14v]

Faith, Love and Conscience

Coleridge formalized his thinking on the relationship between the two aspects of self and of will in the 'Essay on Faith'.¹⁰ His main effort is to show how we find the free and permanent will, and therefore our essential self, by obeying the dictates of our conscience. He begins by defining faith as 'fidelity to our own being – so far as such being is not and cannot become an object of the senses-' [LR IV 425]. With respect to himself, the one feature of this being of which he is distinctly aware is the categorical imperative within him 'commanding me to do unto others as I would they should do unto me'. This is Coleridge's one premise, and it is one that he believes distinguishes 'man from the brutes' [LR IV 426]. He therefore calls it his 'conscience', and it forms, he believes, the root of all distinctly human consciousness.[11] The dictates of conscience, if unimpeded, are the objects of free will[12] – that will which is able to disclose the ideas of Reason as the truths of Religion, and the person in each and every individual.[13]

Our conscience arises simultaneously with our sense of duty towards another – but not necessarily any particular duty in respect of any particular person – and through this act we recognize what constitutes our free and permanent will: that 'other', or the object of our conscience, is the self considered ideally, the perfected being towards which we have a duty as to our soul. In conjunction with Reason, the free and permanent will determines the ultimate ends of our lives: for it is in the conscience that Reason and free Will are united, and united to form a person – the 'inward Dream' which is his 'kind saint' for the Mariner, her mother and 'guardian spirit' for Christabel and the 'vision in a dream' for the beleaguered poet.[14] Denial or inhibition of the act of conscience amounts to an incapacitation of Reason, and so the individual cannot form the idea of a redeemer. In order to become aware of our conscience – that is, to become self-conscious in respect of the noumenal self – we begin with an act, which recognizes another as the equivalent of ourselves; without that act consciousness of our proper self is impossible, and therefore 'there can be no I without a Thou . . .', or as Coleridge puts it elsewhere, 'Distinct Self-knowledge begins with sense of Duty to my Neighbor' [N.26, f.39v]. From the notion of a Thou, there arises the concept of free will – and the ideal object of action – and so we find our free will in our recognition of a Thou, and not in recognition of our self, which has only been effected, and only continues to exist, through our sense of duty to another: 'If then I *minus* the will be the *thesis*, Thou *plus* will must be the *antithesis* . . . ' In our *conscience* we find the permanent will, and our conscience is the recognition of another as equal to ourselves: '. . . the equation of Thou with I, by means of a free act . . . is the true definition of conscience'.

Therefore we cannot have a sense of self, of I, without also having
an idea of the free and noumenal will existing in another not
ourselves.

What Coleridge formulated in the 'Essay . . .', he had discovered as the truth of his being many years before. When fearing
Wordsworth's infidelity with Sara Hutchinson at Coleorton in
1806, he had felt that to permit himself to 'believe conscientiously
and intellectually such a doubt would have been the sin against
the Holy Ghost, against my own spirit, that would have absolutely
destroyed the good principle in my conscience' [CN III 3547, f.23].
His conscience, his spirit, his belief in the third person of the
Trinity, all depend upon his continuing fidelity to another person's
being. Not to be permitted to love, to exercise his free will, was
to Coleridge virtual annihilation 'for to love you', he had written
as though to Sara Hutchinson, 'is all I know of my Life, as far as
my Life is an object of my Consciousness or my Free will' [CN III
3996]. Coleridge cannot think of his true and proper self without
thinking that it is located in someone not himself – and who is so
much more his sense of being than himself.

His conscience is thus inescapably involved with his effort to
find his true being in his love of another, and this effort required
the co-ordination of the free will and the Reason. This conjunction,
as we have seen, strives to produce not merely a set of ideas, or
of truths, but a person, in whom we will find the human being
perfected. In 1805 he had written, in a peroration against Roman
Catholic idolism, that Christ is 'the unconditional obedience of
free will to the law of pure Reason'.[15] This is a theme that appears
consistently in Coleridge's thinking once he had enunciated it: in
1810 he noted that the first Commandment required the 'Unconditional Obedience of Will to the pure Reason, or Conscience/ the
Reality of which is *God* . . .' [CN II 3293, f.15]. And in the
Essay . . .' itself he writes that 'Reason, as one with the absolute
will, (*In the beginning was the Logos, and the Logos was with God, and
the Logos was God,*) and therefore for man the certain representative
of the will of God, is above the will of man as an individual will'.[16]
For Coleridge, it is only in the unfettered act of conscience, in our
properly ordered loving, that this union occurs; and then we are
constantly finding and creating the divine, and so essentially
human aspect of our nature in another. The recognition of the
noumenal in ourself is dependent upon our recognizing Christ in
our love of another, for we cannot find this Person immediately

in ourselves. Our conscience is that which requires us to seek the perfection of our nature, our true personality, in someone not ourself, but who yet re-presents our humanity to us. 'The true love of Christ,' Coleridge wrote in a notebook, is

> a love of the highest and intensest kind, beyond the love for our dearest Friend, for the inborn Christ will be both truly Ego et Rex Meus. [N36, p.123]

The first part of the 'Essay on Faith' is wholly concerned with the relation of the act of conscience to self-consciousness, with establishing the idea of self in our idea of another. Ideally, when the laws of Reason are perfectly known, and the free will uninhibited, we find our permanent will in our sense of another as our self: what that other is constitutes the will because he or she constitutes the perfect frame of humanity. Under these conditions, our service of that being is perfect freedom, for it is perfectly co-ordinated with what we believe of ourselves. All this is in the nature of conscience, that which we arrive at prior to any particular act. But, as Coleridge points out, experience soon comes into play, and 'We learn that there are other impulses beside the dictates of conscience . . .' [LR IV 430] – the impulses of the phenomenal self, some of which as contrary to the conscience we must utterly reject, as Coleridge rejected the idea of Wordsworth's infidelity, and others which we must subordinate, as Christabel was to have learnt to subordinate sexual desire to charitable love. If faith in its primary sense is the becoming conscious of the conscience by an act of allegiance to another, then 'The preservation of our loyalty and fealty under these trials . . . constitutes the second sense of Faith' [LR IV 428]. In this second and more common sense, faith is the deliberate effort of the phenomenal self to preserve his conscience, that is, his consciousness of what is essential in others and therefore in himself. In this context what we consider as will must belong to the individual self in pursuit of his conscience, and this is the only condition under which Harding recognizes what he calls 'the logic of the human will'.[17] Coleridge explains his idea of the two selves and the two wills in a language which he might well have used when he explained the difference between will and volition to Keats:

> As in the equation of the correlative I and Thou, one of the twin

constituents is to be taken as *plus* will, the other as *minus* will,
so it is here: and it is obvious that the reason or *super*-individual
of each man, whereby he is man, is the factor we are to take as
minus will; and that the individual will or personalizing principle
of free agency (arbitrement is Milton's word) is the factor marked
plus will;[18]

ɔut because this will 'is a factor in other moral *syntheses;* for exam-
ɔle, appetite *plus* personal will = sensuality; lust of power, *plus*
ɔersonal will = ambition . . .' it cannot form the specific character
ɔf the conscience; that depends on 'the other *synthesis,*' [LR IV
130–31] in which the free will is found in the other to whom we
ɔwn our allegiance, and in whom we find our true being, by the
subordination of our individual will, or volition, to that being. Our
conscience must exist prior to our involvement in any human
relationship, and become the ground on which we act towards
each other as separate individuals. To elevate relationship above
self-consciousness, human love above personal salvation, is not to
renounce the miserable and private self, but to deny the foundations upon which a relationship must be built. In Christ as the
Logos, Coleridge finds Reason at one with the absolute will; He
is therefore 'the eternal Humanity working in us',[19] and our very
conscience. The function of the conscience in every individual is
an imperative to do unto others what we would have them do
unto us, but pre-exists any particular act. In social relations, man's
self is modified by his consciousness of another, 'and there arise
impulses and objects from this *synthesis* of *alter et idem,* myself and
my neighbour,' and this is analogous with what takes place in the
conscience, but is not to be identified with it – for those impulses
are not necessarily the commands of Reason. Therefore, because
Reason is super-individual, and we are not restricted for our realization of it to any particular individual, and though our social
relations may lead us, 'while reason is the president', from the
lower to the higher forms of attachment, yet the conscience, creating in us that Person who unconditionally wills to obey the laws
of pure reason, existing separate to any actual relation, may declare
any given attachment contrary to the law of reason: when it so
acts, 'reason appears as the love of God; and its antagonist is the
attachment to individuals wherever it exists in diminution of, or
in competition with, the love which is reason' [LR IV 437].
  In 1818 Coleridge wrote in a letter:

To feel the full force of the Christian Religion, it is necessary,
for many tempers, that they should first be made to feel, experi-
mentally, the hollowness of human friendship, the presump-
tuous emptiness of human hopes. [CL IV 893]

In these last two statements lie the fruit of more than ten years
painful experience and continuous intellectual growth.

REASON, UNDERSTANDING AND THE PERSON OF CHRIST

Reason and Understanding[20]

What Coleridge believed to be the ground of our humanity and
our permanent being, he believed to exist equally in all men. It
was either wholly present or wholly absent, and as we have seen
this quality he called Reason. Without Reason we are no longer
human beings, and if we choose to suspend the activity of our
conscience 'in the inundations of the appetites, passions and
imaginations' making use of our free, phenomenal will in order
to abandon our free, noumenal will, then we will either rise into
devils or sink into beasts.[21] The incorporation of the truths of
Reason into the philosophical, the religious and the literary forms
of a culture is that which enables the progressive humanization of
a society, a state, a nation. But although Reason is either present
or not present in the individual, its activation in that individual,
as in the culture of his society, may be of various degrees. This is
because it is dependent on the Understanding for its expression
in the immediate world. Just as Reason may be regarded as the
organ of the super-sensuous and the infinite, so the Understanding is the organ of the sensuous and the finite, 'the faculty by
which we generalize and arrange the phenomena of perception'
[F I 156]. The formalization of the methods of the Understanding
is achieved in the study of logic. But, Coleridge goes on, *'real*
objects, the materials of *substantial* knowledge, must be furnished,
we might safely say *revealed*, to it by Organs of Sense'. These
organs are not, as Coleridge's language worryingly implies, the
faculties that permit us sense impression, but the singular Reason.
It is this organ that has 'the power of acquainting itself with
invisible realities or spiritual objects'.[22] But it is one of the chief
effects of man's fallen state that 'the Understanding and Exper-

ience may exist without Reason' – so that 'the mind of the flesh' usurps the life of the conscience, and the phenomenal denies the existence of the noumenal. The problem is exacerbated by the fact that 'Reason cannot exist without the Understanding; nor does it manifest itself but in and through the Understanding', and so it is quite possible that the life of the senses will keep the life of Reason submerged. It might be added that the Understanding begins to develop in man from the day he is born, but that we do not become aware of what Coleridge called Reason until late adolescence or early adulthood, when it will by its nature be felt to have pre-existed both awareness of it and the life the individual has so far had in the Understanding – an order of events that Plato recognized in his theory of Recollection, and which will always seem to speak of a disorder inherent in our being, of a Fall in 'the dark backward and abysm of time'.

The Ideas of Reason

Because Coleridge identifies Reason with the noumenal or permanent nature of man, he believes that what we seek in our love of another are the truths of Reason, the ideas that constitute our human nature, and this is why love, even in its commonest and most confused forms, is associated with the ideas and hopes of permanence. That within us which commands us to love is also that which commands us to seek the truly human being, 'the infant Christ' [CN II 2167] in the person we love, as Coleridge sought her essential self in Sara. And until that being is realized in our relationship, we must think that we are still more or less in the service of some species of desire rather than under the command of a truly charitable and reasonable love; but then whatever we discover in the discipline of love will be a truth of our permanent being – a truth of Reason.

But what are the truths or ideas of Reason? In one respect the answer is straightforward: a note of Coleridge's own from *On the Constitution of the Church and State* encapsulates what he says in various ways throughout his works. He believes that ideas are 'spiritual realities that can only be spiritually discerned' and that they constitute man's humanity:

For try to conceive a *man* without the ideas of God, eternity, freedom, will, absolute truth, of the good, the true, the beauti-

ful, the infinite. An *animal* endowed with a memory of appearances and of facts might remain. But the *man* will have vanished,
and you have instead a creature 'more subtile than any beast of
the field, upon the belly must it go and dust must it eat all the
days of its life.' [CS 47]

In the *Aids to Reflection* Coleridge calls these constitutive ideas 'the
peculia of Humanity . . . *congenera* of Mind and Will'.[23] But though
we can recognize these ideas as integral to our humanity, they do
not speak to us of a person: we might think of them as having
their absolute existence in God, rather than in God made flesh.
However, I think it is possible to discern in Coleridge's thinking
a second series of ideas which principally have to do with the
person of Jesus, rather than with God.

Coleridge frequently asserts that Reason cannot appear except
in the forms of the Understanding, that an idea cannot exist except
as a symbol, and that it must come forth from the moulds of the
Understanding in the form of a paradox. We can only express the
noumenal in the language of the phenomenal: this is necessarily
derived from circumstance, and is, as we shall see, historical in
character.

The relation between Reason and Understanding has parallels
with that between Reason and Religion. 'Reason first manifests
itself in man by the *tendency* to the comprehension of all as one'
[SM 60] (a phrase reminding us of the quest of the Conversation
poems) and thus seeks a one that is all. Religion, which begins
with the phenomenal self seeking a noumenal existence outside
but for itself, commands us to believe in a unique, eternal and
omnipotent being, separate from ourselves, who also *is* Reason.
Thus for Coleridge 'Reason and Religion differ only as a twofold
application of the same power' [SM 59]. However, the man in
whom Reason works unmodified by religion, by awareness of this
being separate from himself, will either lose 'the ONE in the striving after the INFINITE . . . or the INFINITE in the striving after the
ONE . . .' [SM 60]. Coleridge goes on to illustrate the connection
of this unmodified tendency with the fall of man:

The rational instinct . . . taken abstractedly and unbalanced, did
in itself, ('ye shall be as gods!' Gen. iii. 5.) and in its consequences, (the lusts of the flesh, the eye, and the understanding,
as in verse the sixth,) form the original temptation, through

which man fell: and in all ages has continued to originate the same, even from Adam, in whom we all fell, to the atheists who deified the human reason in the person of a harlot during the earlier period of the French revolution. [SM 61–2]

Religion prevents the Reason's tendency to self-deification because it presents the universal (Reason) as an ideal individual, at one with the God who is Reason, yet also in whom the forms of the human Understanding are perfected. What is truly universal is not found unconditionally in any mortal being: therefore the person aware of his Reason through his religion is able to see that what exists temporally and circumstantially in him has a real and permanent existence in a being outside him. But the person in whom Reason exists unmodified by Religion will regard himself as the final and perfect form for the existence of Reason, and thus deify all that he is, so giving in to 'the lusts of the flesh, the eye, and the understanding . . .'[24]

The object of religion is thus the ideas of Reason expressed in the forms of the Understanding. Coleridge says in his last published work, 'I would raise up my understanding to my reason, and find my Religion in the focus resulting from their convergence' [CS 171]. Ideally considered this focus is a person. Coleridge had discovered that our charitable loving of another human being was the medium by which God might act not only on us, but in us. Muirhead has also made it clear that Coleridge longed not just for a principle absolute and infinite in which to comprehend the unity of all things, but for a personal relationship with this power; he records this from the manuscript of the *Magnum Opus:* 'We may feel from and about a thing, an event, a quality, we can feel *toward* a Person only. The personal in me is the ground and condition of Religion, and the Personal alone is the object.'[25] To seek a principle, rather than to seek a person as the object of religion will, as we have seen, tend to an idolizing of Reason. Harding makes this point in respect of Coleridge's criticism of the work of two post-Kantians: 'In accusing Schelling and Fichte of "gross materialism", he was articulating the clear conception that religion . . . must germinate in the relation of a person to a person'.[26] One cannot attempt to enter directly into a personal relationship with the Absolute and Infinite without also materializing that power, as the irreligious man will sensualize his Reason. As it is only through the Understanding that Reason may be expressed, so it is only through Religion, or the rebinding of ourselves to a person both human and divine, that we may enter into relations with the Absolute and the Infinite. Coleridge always insisted that Christ as the Logos, or the Word, was the *human* Understanding – the Understanding enlightened by Reason. In Notebook 25 he writes:

> Contemplated in its eminence and absoluteness, Speech (Sermo, Verbum, Logos sensu infinito) denotes the essence of the filial Deity; but in its finite and derivative existence, it is the act, attributes, and in the most ancient languages, the name, of the *human* Understanding – i.e. the Understanding as distinct from Reason but not, as in inferior Natures, *contra*-distinguished therefrom. Divinely and in the fullness of Inspiration did the Evangelist affirm – In the beginning was *the Word:* and the Word, God of God, became the mediator between God and Man, and the Redeemer of Man. [N.25, p.175]

It was therefore only through Christ that Coleridge felt able to enter relations with God, thereby finding in his own psychology the truth of Christ's words, 'No man shall come to the Father except by me'.[27] As God is the substance of reality, so Christ as the Word is this reality expressed in the forms of the human Understanding, in ideas. In a marginal note on Jacob Boehme, Coleridge comments: 'In the Logos, or adequate Idea of the divine Being, all Ideas possible according to Wisdom, and Goodness . . . in the Son, I say, are contained all possible Ideas *eminenter*' [M I 573]. We have seen that on his way to Malta, Coleridge had located his Thought in the person of Sara Hutchinson, and that he found this person real chiefly in that she was an act of his conscience. Because the conscience is in essence the faculty by which we realize the 'infant Christ' in our souls, his comments on the Son are a logical development of this position. But though we may see the Word as the substance of all Thought, yet we are still in need of the discrete ideas that compose this whole – or else we will be little further forward than we were in the Conversation poems, when Coleridge presented us with an unmediated God of no distinct offices. A person can only exist under definite conditions, and if we are to know Christ as a person, we must know the conditional forms of his human existence: these forms, or ideas, will be both the life of God, or Reason, finitely expressed (and therefore symbols) and also the ideal organization of every human being.

Christ is the Word, mediating between the infinite and the finite, the absolute and the conditional. Coleridge's fullest statement on the nature of these ideas occurs in a note on Donne's sermons:

> . . . as the sacrament of the Eucharist is the epiphany for as many as receive it in faith, so the crucifixion, resurrection and ascension of Christ himself in the flesh, were the epiphanies, the sacramental acts and *phaenomena* of the *Deus patiens*, the visible words of the invisible Word that was in the beginning, symbols in time and historic fact of the redemptive functions, passions and procedures of the Lamb crucified from the foundation of the world; – the incarnation, cross, and passion, – in short, the whole life of Christ in the flesh, dwelling a man among men, being essential and substantive parts of the process, the total of which they represented; and on this account proper symbols of the acts and passions of the Christ dwelling in man, as the Spirit of truth, for as many as in faith have received him, in Seth and Abraham no less effectually than in John and Paul! For this is the true definition of a symbol, as distinguished from the thing, on the one hand, and from a mere metaphor, or conventional exponent of a thing, on the other.[28]

Here at last, we might say, are those ideas, or 'religious meanings' that Coleridge had first sought in Nature, and which he now finds in one Person, and as the being of every person.[29] This passage draws together several significant threads of thought. We see firstly that the particular forms of Christ's life are the life of the invisible made visible – Reason invested in the Understanding; secondly that these forms are phenomena, that is, conditional and therefore historic; thirdly that they are not the thing itself – the Lamb crucified from the beginning of the world – but symbols of that state and so not casually but essentially related to that condition, partaking in what they render intelligible; fourthly, these phenomena in a further or secondary sense are symbols of the true life of the spirit within us, a life the course of which is in its nature redemptive; fifthly, every man who receives the spirit of truth, receives thereby the spirit of Christ, whether or not he has lived in the Christian dispensation: he knows, as Job knew, that his redeemer lives.[30]

In the act of conscience by which he recognizes the infant Christ formed in his soul, a man permits in himself the beginning of a process of which the words annunciation, incarnation, crucifixion, resurrection and ascension are symbols actually participating in what they describe, the life of Christ on earth. Our communion with Christ is possible because his unique and historical life is the life of the spirit within every man. The doctrines of Christianity, Coleridge believed, 'all must converge to one point, and with them all the essential faculties and excellencies of the human being – so that Christ in the Man, and the Man in Christ, will be *one* in *one*–' [CN III 3803]. He had long thought 'that all the Dogmas of the Trinity and the Incarnation arose from Jesus asserting them of himself, as man in genere'.[31] The essential features of Christ's life are the stages of the redemptive process which rehumanizes our being, and this Coleridge again asserts forcefully in the 'Confessio Fidei': 'I believe . . . that his miraculous Birth, his agony, his Crucifixion, Death, Resurrection and Ascension, were all both Symbols of our Redemption (phenomena of the Noumenon) and necessary parts of the aweful process' [CN III 4005, f.5].[32] A symbol cannot be separated from the act or process it represents without ceasing to be a symbol. Reason is the organ of the spiritual in man, but the forms of the spiritual can only be disclosed through the Understanding. Such is God's relationship with Christ: the Logos has revealed to us in the flesh the essential forms of the spiritual life; it is a process, of which the key words are symbols, and as symbols they sustain ideas which cannot come forth from the mould of the understanding except as a pardox; or as Coleridge put it in Notebook 20, 'It follows from the essential character of ideas . . . that the terms of most frequent occurrence in theology, have a two-fold meaning' [N.20, p.54]. And in Notebook 36 he meditates at length on the two-foldness of the divine and timeless in the human forms of time, which

> emerged, as it were, from my perplexed thought, like the moon from a black cloud – and with it the thorough conviction that however unequal in intrinsic worth and dignity, each was the best possible . . . So do truths support each other – the two-fold character of Christ, the two-fold constituency of the Revelation, the two-fold Kingdom, the two-foldness of each of the sacraments . . . the two-fold character of the Scriptures, the two foldness of the Crucifixion of our Lord – these are the integral parts and materials of one harmonious system, each part distinct and interdependent. [N.36, pp.86–8]

The nature of this two-foldness is illuminated by a passage from *The Statesman's Manual*: 'In the Scriptures therefore both Facts and Persons must of necessity have a two-fold significance, a past and a future, a temporary and a perpetual, a particular and a universal application. They must be at once Portraits and Ideals' [LS 30]. And in the *Aids to Reflection* Coleridge makes it clear that this two-foldness is inherent in the process of redemption, and is the relation of the finite to the infinite:

> *God manifested in the flesh* is eternity in the forms of time. But eternity in relation to time is the absolute to the conditional, or the real to the apparent, and Redemption must partake of both; always perfected, for it is a *Fiat* of the Eternal; – Continuous, for it is a process in relation to man; the former alone objectively, and therefore universally, true. [AR 209, note][33]

The Primary Imagination

The power that binds the two aspects of a symbol, and the two parts of this system, into one whole is the imagination. It is actuated from within, from the well-head of Reason which is also the source of Religion, and it is a power which is constantly mediating between the free, invisible life, and the visible, confining form, between the energies of Reason and the forms of the Understanding. We have seen that Coleridge thought of Christ as the ideal union of Reason and Understanding, and therefore we must think of the imagination as a person-creating faculty: this will become more evident in a moment.

It is sometimes suggested that having struggled unsuccessfully to deduce 'the nature and the genesis of the imagination' from the distinctly human intelligence in the *Biographia*, and having described it as the power which enables the expression of Reason in the images of sense in *The Statesman's Manual*, Coleridge abandoned further thought on the subject. But various notes and marginal comments indicate that this was not the case: as late as 1829 he wrote, 'It is wonderful, how closely Reason and Imagination are connected, and Religion the union of the two' [F I 203,n]. His later notebooks also show the continuing importance he attached to the power, and that he continued to investigate the close links between the religious and the creative impulses. In Notebook 23 he asserts the necessity of the imagination in a man's religious life:

> But only as a man is capable of Ideas . . . and as far only as he is capable of an Ideal (practical product having its cause and impulse in *Ideas*, and its End, Aim and Object in the approximative realization of the same) is Man a Religious Being. But neither the one nor the other is possible except thro' the Imagination . . . neither, I say, are possible but by means of the Imagination, by force of which the Man
>   1. creates for himself, and for the use and furtherance of his *Thinking*, Representations or rather Presences, where experience can supply no more, but has already stopt payment.
>   2. feels wants (. . . desideria) and proposes to himself aims and ends that can be gratified and attained by nothing which Experience can offer or suggest; and to think and form the notion of a higher, purer Existence and a limitless Futurity.
>   [N.23, f.19.v]

The imagination is indeed expert beyond experience; it is that which constructs the 'inward Dream', or 'the notion of a higher, purer Existence' living in a heaven of 'limitless Futurity'. The proper function of the imagination is controlled not by the Understanding, but by Reason. And the man who refuses to admit Reason as a real power, 'the Alogist or Metapothecary', denies the reality of the educts of the imagination – turning, as the note goes on to say 'these presentiments, Desideria, and Aims', into 'mere Dreams and delusive phantoms'. What the imagination creates are not objects visible to the senses – not, it seems, the sensual matterish world of the *Biographia*'s primary imagination – but substantial Ideas which are true objects and real presences. These ideas are not, in the first instance, truths external to the mind, but truths of the mind, the power of Reason in the forms of the Understanding, the Word in words, the credal form of the infant Christ.[34] They are indeed the forms of the Logos, of the essentially human understanding, and in this respect the imagination works in a way analogous to that of the conscience, which creates the figure of Christ in our love of another. If we think of this process 'as a repetition in the finite mind of the eternal act of creation in the infinite I AM' [BLC I 304] I believe that we are nearer to the heart of Coleridge's thinking than if we consider the primary

nagination to be 'the living Power and prime Agent of all human
erception'. There is a contradiction at the very heart of this defi-
ition which points not towards the relation between Creation and
reator, but towards that between Son and Father. The creation of
1e world took place on one occasion, over a given time, and is
ot coeval with the existence of God: to describe creation as an
ternal act', and to place it *in* God, are theological blunders too
imple to ascribe to Coleridge. But the Son is co-eternal with the
ather, is eternally begotten, and since they are but one God, each
; 'in' the other. This is not so much a process of *creation* but rather
f *filiation*. The infinite I AM contemplates his Personality in the
on, and through an analogous act enabled by the imagination,
/e contemplate our distinct humanity in the invention of the ideas
1at constitute his Person.

In the *Biographia* Coleridge had hoped to show that by reflection
n his perceptions of nature a man could arrive at a form of self-
onsciousness which would enable him to realize that the forms
f nature were integral with the forms of his own mind. But he
iiled there as he had failed in the Conversation poems. The act
f imagination by which we create the ideas that constitute the
resence of a perfected being, the very forms of our proper
umanity, is the act which enables all men to realize their essential
nd otherwise latent being; it is a *primary* act without which we
annot be either religious or human. The secondary imagination
iffuses and dissipates the matter of experience so as to organize
according to these forms or ideas. It is the business of the
reative mind to unify the appearances of nature or the facts of
istory in the light of these ideas, in order to demonstrate either
1e reality of the world in which man lives or the work of pro-
idence in the processes of time. But this activity is not essential
) the humanization of the individual, and therefore may justly
e called secondary.

Subject and Object

Jonetheless, if these forms of the mind are not seen to bear any
elation to the world we find within ourselves, if what constitutes
ur experience is unspoken of in the language of our hearts, we
/ill, depending on the relative power of this experience and of
1e life we find within ourselves, either condemn the world as
nreal, or our inner life as a delusion. Coleridge realized this

potentially unbridgeable gulf between the world within and the
world without, but so sure was he, as a result of his meditations
of Will in conjunction with Reason as 'the ground of the Being
and the Cause of the Existence of the World' [N.26, f.36] that he
asserted that the reality of an external world depended wholly on
its obeying laws which are to be found as ideas in the mind
His long and complex note on the imagination in Notebook 2
recognizes the subjective origin of this power and continues:

> . . . but if subjective is yet universally subjective – Nay, farthe
> yet . . . if the Result be impregned and actualized by the Will
> which (as concentric with the absolute Will that is one with th
> universal Reason) is the source or index of all reality, and thu
> the *Objective* rise up, as a celestial Birth, in and from the universa
> Subject – O let it still be a mere Dream to Dreamers, an empt
> sound to the Blind, an apparition in the Limbo of modern Philo
> sophy . . . if only the souls of better mould, made to live in th
> courts of the Sun, could be called into the Valley of Vision, i
> only I could raise *them* . . . What a new Heaven and a new Eartl
> would begin to reveal itself – ah! mighty phantom, of which a
> their sensual reality is but the perverted Refraction! [N.23, f.20v

Only when we have established the idea, as Coleridge was bus
establishing 'a new Heaven' in the person of Christ, who is th
conjunction of the free Will and the absolute Reason, will th
object, 'a new Earth' rise up out of the chaos of immediate sen
sation into reality. And if the ideas of Christ's life are the trul
spiritual and human life within us, we will seek to find this lif
as an object, as something existing according to laws outside an
seemingly independently of us. It is my belief that Coleridge wa
never able to find an adequate object in Nature, firstly becaus
no satisfactory description of the 'germinal causes' or 'semina
principles' of Nature then existed, and secondly because the mer
appearances of Nature, detached from a knowledge of her laws
did not prove a sufficient substitute. However, Coleridge did dis
tinguish two aspects of Christianity, historical and spiritual, wha
he called 'The two-fold object of the Christian Dispensation – via
Christendom and *Inward Christianity*' [N.37, p.105], and as early a
his sojourn in Malta, he felt himself under pressure to discer
their relations:

O that this conviction [no Trinity, no God] may work upon me and in me/ and that my mind may be made up as to the character of Jesus, and of historical Christianity, as clearly as it is of the Logos or Spiritual Christianity – that I may be made to know either their especial and peculiar Union or their absolute disunion in any peculiar Sense. [CN II 2448; cf.N.26, f.51]

Christ is the subject, the permanent life of the mind and soul, and historical Christianity, which includes the life of Jesus, the object, or the forms of the mind expressed in time. In 1805 Coleridge was willing to admit that the two may not be fully co-ordinate or adequately reflective of each other. But in a later notebook, their interrelations seem established in his mind, and appear responsible for growth of the Christian Religion over the ages:

The two factors of the Christian Religion, the one indispensable to *faith*, and the other no less so to the faith of a *Christian* are: 1. The philosophy concerning Christ . . . 2. The History of Jesus Christ. The different ages of Christianity may be conveniently classed according to the due co-inherence of these, or the undue predominance of the one or the other. [N.21½, f.68v]

have tried to outline what Coleridge meant by 'the philosophy concerning Christ' in the foregoing pages: what he had in mind when he spoke of 'The History of Jesus Christ' is the subject of the penultimate chapter. It is sufficient for my immediate purposes if I have shown that Coleridge sought to generate the object out of his subject, and that this subject was always and only the person of Christ.

The Trinity[35]

Out of his method of developing a consciousness of the noumenal self, Coleridge had developed the essential forms of the Understanding; but this method also provides insights into Coleridge's apprehension of the Trinity, and into his ideas of personality and immortality. The language in which Coleridge describes the relations of the Trinity, is very similar to that which we have already heard him using of interpersonal relations. Thus he writes to Thomas Clarkson in 1806:

> God's Thoughts are all consummately adequate Ideas, which
> are all incomparably more *real* than what we call *Things*. God is
> the sole self-comprehending Being, i.e. he has an Idea of him
> self, and the Idea is consummately adequate, and superlatively
> real . . . This Idea therefore from all eternity co-existing with
> and yet filiated, by the absolute Being . . . is the same, as the
> Father in all things, but the impossible one, of self-origination
> He [Christ] is the substantial image of God, in whom the Father
> beholds well-pleased his whole being . . . [CL II 1175]

The idea that God has of himself is disclosed as a Person, and in
that Person he knows himself: Christ, we might say, is God's
means to self-consciousness; but by the very nature of God's per
fection, he cannot be other than God. He is thus, in Coleridge's
language, the consummately adequate idea of God, in whom the
Father finds his whole and perfect being.

It was on his way to Malta that Coleridge had discovered how
our idea of another may create what is truly self in us – and so
rise to self-consciousness. Just as Christ is the substantial image
of God, so Coleridge had felt that Sara was the embodiment of
his true self. In order to know himself, Coleridge sought for a self
outside himself, not himself, and yet so much more his sense of
Being than what he recognized as his phenomenal self. That is
as an intelligent creator of himself he sought, as he thinks God
has eternally begotten, the adequate idea of his being in a person
distinct from himself. And between the Creator and the begotten
Son, between Coleridge and his essential self, there is a recipro
cated bond of love, and this love constitutes a third being, the
synthesis as a consequence of Father as thesis and Son as antith
esis, which is neither, but separate and different from each. Coler
idge had had an experience that might be considered analogous
to this state of being, when he had once feared to talk, feared to
hear Sara talk, lest their speaking should break up the 'you-me
into you and me.[36] In its perfect state this third being is of a kind
with the Father and the Son, as Coleridge explains:

> But all the actions of the Deity are intensely real or substantial
> therefore the action of Love, by which the Father contemplate
> the Son, and the Son the Father, is equally real with the Father
> and the Son – and neither of these Three *can* be conceived *apart*

nor *confusedly* – so that the Idea of God involves that of a Tri-
unity; [CL II 1195–6]

It seems probable that Coleridge's understanding of the Trinity
was catalysed by his relationship with Sara Hutchinson, and so it
s of no surprise to find that the doctrine has an important place
n the 'Confessio Fidei', written at the height of the crisis of his
·elations with Wordsworth and Sara. In this he writes, very pre-
:isely, that it was 'in and thro' the Son that God created all things
ɔoth in Heaven and Earth [CN III 4005, f.6]. We have seen that
ıis own creativity and his ability to find a reality in the external
world, depended on his love for Sara, and the love active between
hem. The poet is only able to tame the chaos of perception
ɔecause he is a god in love, and has found an adequate idea of
ıimself in another person – the reality of whom is Christ. Through
hat Person he creates, or re-creates, the natural world in genuine
mitation of its original creator – a belief which has its origins at
east as far back as the verse-letter to Asra.
But there is one very important distinction between the divine
ınd human modes of interpersonal relations. This is elucidated in
ı letter of 1818; having asserted that the only possible mode of
:onceiving God both as infinite and personal is to think of the
nfinite God as *To Theion* and the personal God as *O Theos*, Coler-
dge goes on: 'and the contra distinction of God from all finite
Beings consists in God's having the *ground* of his existence in
ıimself, whereas all other Beings have their *ground* in another.
Therefore God alone is a self-comprehending Spirit; and in this
ıncommunicable *Adequate* idea of himself his Personality is
:ontained'.[37]
God is conscious of himself by means of his Son, by the eternal
ɔrocess of filiation; in this act of God's essential personality is
·evealed, and is perfectly co-ordinated with his absolute and eter-
ıal existence, with his immortality. This union is the ground of
he spiritual hopes of all human beings, for 'the mind can form
ıo higher conception of blessedness in employment, than to have
ı spiritual intuition of the union of the personality of God with
ıis infinity and omnipresence' [N.45, p.21]. However, human
ɔeings do not find the ground of their existence in themselves,
ɔut in another. From his youth it had been in Coleridge's nature
o find himself in his love of another, and as this instinct matured

it became his deliberate intention to realize his proper nature in
that of Christ as God. In Notebook 43 he wrote:

> For man ought to acknowledge no permanent *Self*, but God . . .
> to *exist in God* as the ground of his Being, his distinct *Personality*
> in proportion as he quells and *lays* the phantom Self of his
> *Nature* – i.e. the Ground, the Hades. [N.43, p.114]

And in his later years, this fact of our nature was a matter of bitter
personal experience to Coleridge. In 1831, he wrote:

> Alas! I implore the Light which is at the same time Life - . . .
> But I feel and find only the weakness, darkness, emptiness,
> hollowness, which are my Self – and therein my calamity and
> my sin, that I do find myself, instead of God and the Divine
> Man, one with God. [N.50, f.21]

Here Coleridge seems to be struggling with the difficulty which
beset Hopkins – of finding the activity within himself of that
Person whom he believed to be the life of his life.

In loving someone not themselves, human beings imitate the
divine act of filiation, and discover in the person whom they love
their noumenal or essential being, as God, in loving the Son,
discloses himself to himself. And similarly, as God finds his personality in his Son, so we find our true personality not in seclusion
from one another, not in our phenomenal qualities or accidental
uniqueness, but in that Being, perfected in Christ, that we discover
in our true and charitable loving of another person. In a *Magnum
Opus* manuscript Coleridge wrote: 'Granted that personality is an
ideal that progressive spirits are ever realizing in fuller degree, yet
it lives in the tension between Self and an Other beyond the self'
[Muirhead 229]. The more we approach that perfection where all
phenomenality is sloughed off, the more fully our Personality is
realized. So in the same manuscript we find: 'In reality personality
becomes more perfect in proportion as a man rises above the
negations and privations by which the finite is differentiated from
the Absolute, the human will from the divine, man from God'
[Ibid., 228.]

In another person we find the ground of our essential being,
and in our relationship with that person, our true personality. But
both are dependent upon our loving that person, and no act of

ove may occur without a simultaneous act of will. The act of love,
which is the integer of the Trinity, occurring analogously in us,
enables us to know in kind the condition of God's absolute being:
the more conscious we are of our true personality, the nearer we
are to participating in the divine life. Because all consciousness,
human and divine, depends upon an act of will, it follows that
whatever we know of immortality cannot be handed on from
person to person as are, say, the laws of physics; it is not a
knowledge possible in any informational way at all.

All knowledge worthy of the name, that is, that which is more
than mere statement of fact or recording of observation, had its
origins for Coleridge within the humanized heart. Equally all such
knowledge consists in the union of subject and object. But, as
Coleridge insists in Notebook 26 'the essence of self-consciousness
consists in the Distinction yet Identity of the Subject and Object,
Conscientis et Consciti' [f.46]. In order to become self-conscious,
a condition which is the ground of all knowledge, we must be
able to distinguish between subject and object – or in a more
familiar vocabulary, between self and other. Yet in order to obtain
knowledge these two states must be reunited. And because all
that is ultimately real, and all that may be known, resides in God,
Coleridge imagines that the Trinity is a subject-object relationship
in a permanent and eternal act by which the object discerns in
itself the ideas of the subject, and the subject evolves the laws of
the object: there is perfect distinction and perfect union, perfect
being united with perfect knowing.[38] But God is the sole self-
comprehender and consequently all human knowledge rests on a
union of a subject or self, with an object of not self. We have seen
that Coleridge found the sole reality of the other or not self in
Christ. The ideas that constitute his life are the objects of our self-
consciousness and the symbols of the life of the spirit in all and
each of us. In his love of Sara Hutchinson Coleridge had once
found a method of organizing his disparate perceptions into a
harmony that reflected the life he found within himself. His
thought had so matured that unless in his love of any particular
individual he could find Christ as the Word, mediating between
himself and his perceptions of nature, or the facts of history, all
perceptions would end in chaos, and all ideas as no more than
unreal notions. Only through the 'glory' that is Christ can we have

any hope of finding the life within us in the world without us
any hope of arriving at human knowledge.

Summary

If Coleridge had begun his poetical career in the early 1790s by
believing that the active world may reveal to the mind its essentia
organization, happy to think 'nihil in intellectu quod non prius ii
sensu', his imagination soon added, 'praeter ipsum intellectum'
That which was of the mind, but not first in the senses, he called
Reason, and we might characterize the rest of his career as the
attempt to learn how this immaterial and invisible power was
related to the Understanding, or the faculty which arranges our
sense perceptions and so gives us a being in time and place. His
search for the One, his attraction to the Vast and the Whole, are
symptoms of the emergence of Reason, but in the Conversation
poems there is no satisfactory relation between this and the sens
ible world, largely because the idea of the whole is seen to succeed
and to be consequent upon, but not to co-ordinate, sense impres
sions. However, in the Supernatural poems, the immediate i
not the poet's starting point, and we may think of his romanti
characters as substantiated by truths that the poet derives from
reflection on his own intellect and nature, as beings born of medi
tation rather than observation. It is characteristic of both the Mari
ner and Christabel that their nature is, or comes to be, disordered
so that their consciousness is based on sense and Understanding
rather than on Reason; and both also discover that they can only
cure themselves of their fallen condition by calling upon a 'sain
in heaven' to reactivate their will: they both require a being outside
themselves (who is outside time as well) and yet who is also a
function of their conscience, or their 'inward Dream', in order to
enable the re-orientation of Reason and Understanding.

By 1805, Coleridge had brought these discoveries to focus in hi
own life, and the problem he then faced can be put as a single
question: How can the person loved, the redeeming figure, be
known to have a reality independent of the senses, of the con
ditions of time and place, to correspond with that sense of immor
tality that rightly ordered love confers? Coleridge's answer wa
that our proper humanity is constituted of ideas which are per
fectly known and permanently existing only in God as Christ, bu
that he is the indwelling and substantial humanity of us all. Ou

true love of another is therefore the putting off of sense-based consciousness, and finding the figure of Christ in any one we love, and by doing this we find our proper self – that self which the conscience creates as the inward dream or saint in heaven. And as he is the substance of our humanity, Christ is all our human thought: therefore Coleridge gladly endorsed John Donne's, 'Blessed are they that inanimate all their knowledge, consummate all in Christ Jesus' [SM 70.n.]

Coleridge's idea of self or subject rested on his idea of Christ: knowledge is the union of subject and object, and the object cannot have a ground other that which it has in common with the subject. Thus Coleridge believed that the object would rise up out of the 'universal Subject', a 'new Earth' out of a 'new Heaven', and that a knowledge not so arising was partial and imperfect. As we go on to pursue Coleridge to the conclusion of his career we will see him beginning to treat the relationship between the individual self and the nation as that of subject and object, and find that his ideas of the constitution of the state, and of the progress of the nation in history, are both inanimated in his knowledge of Christ.

Part III
From Nature To The Nation

The proper Objects of Knowledge, and which may be regarded as the Poles of true Learning, are Nature and History – or Necessity and Freedom. [N.28 f. 12]

7

The Essential Self and the
Life of Nature

Life begins in detachment from Nature, and ends in union with
God. [LR IV 401]

THE BIOGRAPHIA: VOLUME I

The principle which is the turning point of all Coleridge's thought
in the first volume of the *Biographia* is the principle which has
informed all his thinking on the nature of the Trinity and of
interpersonal relations: that what arises from within a man is the
determinant of all reality. Only in self-consciousness, he says,
are 'object and subject, being and knowing . . . identical, each
involving, and supposing the other' [BLC I 273]. A few pages later
he again asserts 'that the act of self-consciousness is for *us* the
source and principle of all *our* possible knowledge [BLC I 284][1].

We have seen that out of his experience as a poet of the supernatural and his love of Sara Hutchinson Coleridge had found that
the most fitting object of the subjective self was a person, conceived by an act of conscience, and that the ultimate truth of
this act resided in Christ, the second person of the Trinity. Yet
surprisingly these hard-won insights seem to be entirely forgotten
when we come to the *Biographia* – so entirely forgotten that most
current critics advantaged, unlike Shawcross, with many of the
notebooks in print and all but two available for study, and with a
complete edition of the letters, are still tempted to write as if there
were no grounds for the case I have tried to sketch out.[2]

Therefore the question that arises is, what happened? I think
that the answer lies in seeing that instead of evolving an ideal
object of and for the mind from the groundwork of his deepest
experiences, and then through the mediation of this object gradu-

ally 'finding' the disciplines of philosophy, literature, history and theology – the process which he had so far intuitively followed and which he was to recommend as the method by which Christians should read their Bible[3] – the object in whose laws he had to discern the ideas of our being had been predetermined for him by his devotion to and admiration of Wordsworth's poetry: in relation to which any other object than nature is hardly conceivable.[4] But in all our dealings with Coleridge's thought from the Supernatural poems up to the present point, we have seen that nature has been what we might call an indirect object: that is, it has gained what life it has as a consequence of being viewed religiously, through the idea of another person. And in *The Statesman's Manual*, written immediately after the *Biographia* and published before it, Coleridge leaves us in no doubt that this is his understanding of the interaction of religion and nature:

> Religion is the sun whose warmth indeed swells, and stirs, and actuates the life of nature, but who at the same time beholds all the growth of life with a master-eye, makes all objects glorious on which he looks, and by that glory visible to others. [SM 48]

The verbal echoes of Coleridge's Brockenspectre experience aboard the Speedwell are surely no coincidence. The true and permanent life of nature can only be known through the charitable loving of another as our self – when we imitate the divine act of filiation. Nature has in no sense *made* any part of this love, and though on occasions it catalyzes a yearning in the poet's heart, that yearning is fundamentally for a human completion, as we saw in the Brockley Coomb poem. Coleridge's belief that nature is only made real through our love of another, first evident in the Harz Forest lines, and established in 'Dejection', has become a consistent part of his thinking.

In the *Biographia*, however, Coleridge attempts to make nature the direct object of knowledge, though it is considered as passive rather than active. The cause of this sudden radical shift of attention lies not only in his devotion to Schelling and other German nature philosophers, and in the pain attendant on his Trinitarian insights, but more directly – as a consequence of putting together his first collected poems – in a revival of interest in the most fruitful years of his own literary past, jointly with a revival in the long felt but never satisfactorily articulated sense of difference with Wordsworth over certain aspects of literary theory.[5]

The *Biographia* began as a preface to *Sybilline Leaves*, and was to have included a particular preface to 'The Ancient Mariner' on the supernatural in poetry – unfortunately never written. But it seems likely that a correspondence with Wordsworth had stimulated a rewriting of the original preface. Coleridge had been frankly disappointed by 'The Excursion', and news of this disappointment had passed via Lady Beaumont to the older poet – who demanded an explanation. The basis of Coleridge's criticism is that the poem fails in its presumed philosophical intentions:

> I supposed you first to have meditated the faculties of Man in the abstract, in their correspondence with his Sphere of action, and first in the Feeling, Touch, and Taste, then in the Eye, and last in the Ear, to have laid a solid and immoveable foundation for the Edifice by removing the sandy Sophisms of Locke, and the Mechanic Dogmatists, and demonstrating that the Senses were living developments of the Mind and Spirit in a much juster as well as a higher sense that the mind can be said to be formed by the Senses–. [CL IV 574–75]

Then he supposed Wordsworth would have gone on 'to have affirmed a Fall in some sense', illustrating this by reference to 'Fallen man contemplated in the different ages of the World', and so on to a scheme of redemption, concluding with 'a grand didactic swell on the necessary identity of a true Philosophy with true Religion . . .' From such a programme we might think that Coleridge had hoped that Wordsworth would produce sublime 'Religious Musings'; and though he had at least affirmed a disorder in one of his characters, he had not put this in an historical context, and most surely he had in no way affirmed the mind as sense-making. Indeed, it is the sensational influences of nature upon the Solitary that is to lead to his 'redemption', as it had to that of Peter Bell.

This dissatisfaction with Wordsworth's efforts may well have stimulated Coleridge to attempt in prose what he had hoped his friend would do for him in poetry.[6] It is coincident with a history of Coleridge's literary life and opinions because his own intellectual growth had moved from necessitarianism – in which the mind is the sum of its influences – to an idealism in which the mind gives significance and order to the world it beholds. In each system the imagination will be almost a different thing: in the first it will in some measure be stimulated by what it perceives, be acted on in order to react and so remove the film of selfish solicitude through which we view the world, and in the second it will find its power originating within the mind, and act on sense-presented material, shaping it by diffusion and dissipation to no end discernible from experience, but according to a scheme which the imagination itself holds before the mind as a series of 'presences'. And it is these 'presences' or ideas that are missing in the *Biographia*, as they were missing in the visions of the Conversation poems, ideas which were intimately associated with Coleridge's devotion to those people whom he felt constituted his inner life. The first system is a reviewing of the world, a cleansing of the doors of perception, but the second barely depends upon perception at all, and is rather a re-making of the world. Wordsworth, believing in the power of nature to act on the human heart, to reveal if not to make the mind, never fully emancipated himself from Hartley, and so as Coleridge felt as early as 1802, had a concept of the imagination at variance with the concept he came to hold. But, possibly because of his radical change of relations with the Wordsworth household in the intervening years, and because of his failure to capitalize on his private tribulations by producing the often mentioned *Logosophia*, Coleridge neglected the mediatory 'presence' or idea in the *Biographia*; seeking a direct relationship between mind and nature, believing still that nature was 'one mighty alphabet/ For infant minds', he shares one indissoluble prejudice with Wordsworth, that nature is the immediate object of knowledge. And in order to demonstrate this philosophically, Coleridge has to show that nature is directly involved with our self-consciousness. This fundamental and necessary presumption is the hallmark of the *Biographia*.

The Progress of Volume I

The intellectual biography of chapters V-IX is a consideration of the historical developments of the two poles of philosophy to which Coleridge had been alternately attracted in order to solve the problem of how the mind relates to the external world. Hartley had attempted to solve the problem of the existence of the percipient subject by supposing that one sense impression was likely to recall another, and that the human mind was produced by an immensely complicated interaction between external stimulus and associated recall. The process was entirely mechanical, and wholly dependent on our immediate perceptions. Coleridge reduces Hartley's argument to an amusing absurdity [7]:

Consider how immense must be the sphere of a total impression from the top of St. Paul's church; and how rapid and continuous the series of such total impressions. If therefore we suppose the absence of all interference of the will, reason, and judgement, one or other of two consequences must result. Either the ideas . . . will exactly imitate the order of the impression itself, which would be absolute *delirium*: or any one part of that impression might recall any other part, and . . . according to this hypothesis [this] disquisition . . . may as truly be said to be written by Saint Paul's church as by *me* . . . [BLC I 111–12, 118]

Extremes meet of course,[8] so we find that Priestley, another necessitarian, in order to explain thinking, 'stript matter of all its material properties; substituted spiritual powers; and when we expected to find a body, behold! we had nothing but its ghost! the apparition of a defunct substance!' [BLC I 136]. The result of Priestley's efforts was not a realization of the subject in the realm of matter, but because it stands upon the 'hypothesis of an external world exactly correspondent to those images or modifications of our own being, which alone (according to this system) we actually behold, is as thorough idealism as Berkeley's inasmuch as it equally . . . removes all reality and immediateness of perception, and places us in a dream world of phantoms and spectres, the inexplicable swarm and equivocal generation of motions in our own brains' [BLC I 137]. Having at the outset lost the percipient in the perceived, we are now lacking the perceived for the percipient. Knowledge is only possible when each is able to retain its integrity in relation to the other, while both are involved in a synthesis.

Clearly the problems that Coleridge had discovered in the materialism and idealism of his day were not going to be resolved by the methods derived from either system. Any attempt by the followers of one army to defend evident weaknesses were more likely to find them tumbling into the trenches of the enemy than establishing the high ground of unassailable truth. Thus there was the prospect that the intellectual camp followers would be restlessly marching from friend to foe and back again, permanently benighted, and that this would constitute a chapter in the history of modern philosophy – a living death indeed. But on to this battlefield in Coleridge's mind, there now marches a different kind of troop – the mystics, George Fox, Jacob Boehme and William Law, enabling Coleridge to see that a wholly different kind of strategy was possible: describing how these men made him conscious of a faculty which was possessed by his poetry, but which he did not possess in his thought, 'They contributed', he wrote, 'to keep alive the *heart* in the *head*; gave me an indistinct yet stirring and working presentiment, that all the products of the mere *reflective* faculty partook of DEATH, and were as the rattling twigs and sprays in winter, into which a sap was yet to be propelled from some root to which I had not penetrated . . .' [BLC I 152].[9] This is a graphic description of the distinction essential to Coleridge's thinking – that of Reason and Understanding. The materialists and the idealists, as Coleridge had so far met them, were chiefly men whose intellects had been made in that age of unrelieved understanding, the Age of Reason. They were all men who thought that thinking alone could solve the problems of philosophy, rather as it might be expected to solve a problem of mechanics. But Behmen, as Coleridge calls him, Fox and Law, much mocked by the very age against whose poisons they provided an antidote, instinctively realized that the discovery of truth required the co-operation of the *whole* man, of his moral and religious as well as of his rational nature: that is, they made Coleridge aware that the discovery and maintenance of truth depended not merely on intellectual ability, but, most importantly, on the will of man.

From Kant, Coleridge derived, at the very least, the nomenclature to distinguish Reason from Understanding.[10] But the mystics had given him a taste for what he found incomplete in Kant's works: for while his ethical system began with the assumed autonomy of the will, necessary to the activation of Reason, his speculative system began at the point of *reflection*, or natural consciousness. This division, which appears to make the Understanding the arbiter of speculative philosophy, and which he puts down to Kant having been in imminent danger of persecution from the King of Prussia,[11] Coleridge could not subscribe to, as it would have returned him to the battlefield from which he had just escaped: one of the main drives of the *Biographia* is to give speculative philosophy a groundwork in the will and conscience of man [BLC

I 154–55]. And it was from Fichte that Coleridge formally took the step for which the mystics had prepared him – to begin 'with an *act*, instead of a *thing* or *substance* . . .' [BLC I 158]. This decision finally released Coleridge from the 'adamantine logic' of his much admired Spinoza, and from the notion of the passivity of the mind and the activity of nature. Thomas McFarland believes that this separation precipitated the central and seemingly inevitable tragedy of Coleridge's life, his foundering before the two competing forms of existence, of self and of things, the resolution to which is still wanting.[12]

Having dismissed Fichte because his system degenerated into 'a crude egoismus' which condemned nature 'as lifeless, godless, and altogether unholy' [BLC I 159],[13] Coleridge finally settles on Schelling, in whom he first found 'a genial coincidence' with much that he had toiled out for himself, thus warning the reader of the plagiarisms that appear to follow. But in fact we have to wait some 70 pages before Schelling's nature philosophy is genially conflated with that of the author. By any standards this is a lengthy detour, and as often in Coleridge's divagations, it indicates the presence of unsolved problems.[14] We have seen that he had brought the history of his intellectual life to that point where, by virtue of the mystics, he had become aware of a power, as yet unnamed, superior to the mere reflective faculty which it was to illuminate. In the works of Kant he had found a systematic but imperfect treatment of these two powers.[15] The faculty that unites Reason and Understanding is the imagination, and Chapter X begins with an attempt to describe the nature and genesis of this faculty. But the attempt fizzles out before it is barely under way, and via the subject of pedantry the Reason-Understanding distinction is reintroduced in these its definite terms [BLC I 173 and n. 1]. It would now be reasonable to expect Coleridge to return to his treatment of the imagination, and to deal with the relations of Reason and Understanding formally, as he has graphically or poetically in the image of winter twigs awaiting their summer sap – an intuitive image of great precision.[16] But we enjoy no such treat. Instead, Coleridge remembers that to make this distinction had been one of the chief objects of *The Friend*, and rather than tackle the thorny problem of their relation, he prefers to remember the unrewarding struggle he had both to publish that journal and an earlier and hotter star – *The Watchman*. Having, by this progress, been brought back to the beginnings of his literary life, he sets out again on his intellectual travels, but traverses the same terrain again, though more rapidly, more sociably, more chronologically and with less philosophical reflection.[17] But he arrives in the company of the same man, Kant, at a place very similar to that to which we have already followed him. We have seen that in his experience, the appearance or recognition of Reason in and by man is the correspondent of a moral act, an act of will: the mystics had taught him that this higher power was not self-evident, as were the truths of logic or of the understanding. He now writes, 'I became convinced, that religion . . . must have a moral origin; so far at least, that the evidence of its doctrines could not, like the truths of abstract science, be wholly independent of the will' [BLC I 202–3]. What was true of the doctrines was also true of their Creator: belief in God is a moral act, for his existence is incapable of scientific verification.

So we see what a reading of *The Friend* and *The Statesman's Manual* has led us to expect – that Reason and Religion are two aspects of one power in Coleridge's mind, and that each can occupy the seat of consciousness in our being only through an act of will. But what is not yet clear, and what Coleridge has so far refused to treat, is the relation of Reason to the Understanding, or of the God believed in to the world perceived: two formulations of what is, in the *Biographia*, essentially one problem. In the Conversation poems Coleridge had hoped to discover religious meanings in the forms of nature, and now he is hoping to find that these 'appearances' or 'presences' are Reason-imbued constructs of the imagination, winter sprays filled with summer sap. There are indications that the loom of this problem was sweeping the skies beyond the horizon of Coleridge's consciousness: an idea, we have seen, is a truth of Reason in the forms of the Understanding, and is expressed as a symbol; this definition of an idea appears immediately after our first introduction to Kant, as a guide to the method by which his works must be read [BLC I 156–57]. A few pages later we are introduced to the imagination, or the power of maintaining an idea, through the word 'esemplastic' [BLC I 168]; and after stating that we can only come to a belief in God through an act of will, Coleridge recalls his philosophical belief in 'an infinite yet self-conscious Creator', and remembers that the 'admission of the logos, as *hypostasized*', that is, as the Person in whom God expresses the human ideas that are his image in us, and which are the primary objects of the imagination, 'in no respect

removed my doubts concerning the incarnation and the redemption by the cross' [BLC I 204–5]. But these potential discussions
which all, in one way or another, would have illuminated the
relations of Reason and Understanding, are here given up, and
never reopened elsewhere in the book.

Yet when in Chapter XII Coleridge seeks to answer the question
of how we become self or philosophically conscious, the trinitarian
model *ought* to have served him well. But he makes no further
reference to the Trinity; his planned 'Logosophia' is mentioned at
one crucial moment – just prior to the Theses which deduce the
principle of 'the absolute I AM' [BLC I 263, 283] – but has no
influence on the subsequent argument. To discuss the Trinity, and
particularly the relations between Father and Son, would have
inevitably involved discussion of the method by which we achieve
self-consciousness, and thus the appropriate object of knowledge:
for the only way of being sure that the object *is* a real object of
knowledge is to show that through it the subject rises to self-
consciousness. Such had been the course of Coleridge's relationship with Sara: in her he had found his permanent self, and
through her 'glory' he was able to conceive the unity of nature.
To introduce a discussion of the Trinity in depth would be but to
show that not a thing but a person is the means to self-consciousness, whether divine or human. Nature would then be relegated
to a secondary position, external to God's perfection. Since a philosophy of self as subject and nature as the unmediated object was
what Coleridge was mistakenly trying to construct, use of the
trinitarian model would have undermined the very foundations
not only of his building, but also those upon which Wordsworth
was trying to erect the first genuine philosophic poem' [BLC II
156].

Therefore, consciously or not, Coleridge excludes, as outside
the scope of the book, any further discussion of the Logos. His
whole bent is to show how, by an internalized act of will unrelated
to any other person, we can rise from natural to self-consciousness,
thereby establishing their interdependence. But Coleridge does
not proceed with this argument directly: because he has to find a
way of forgetting what he ought to have done, we are distracted
by another lengthy digression [BLC I 205–231]. On this occasion
he records his travels in Germany, gives us a potted history of
German literature, brings himself home to write for the *Morning
Post* on the grounds of principle alone, justifies his prose style,

and concludes Chapter X by defending the utility of scholarship. Chapter XI contains matters of considerable interest, particularly in relation to the growth of his idea of the clerisy, but it does not pick up what I believe ought to have been the main current in this stream of many other currents, eddies and whirlpools – the relation of self and other in the development of self-consciousness.

And so we are launched into the infamous Chapter XII, mastering which, according to Owen Barfield, we will be substantially seised of what Coleridge thought.[18] I think it is more accurate to say that we will master a confusion which plagued Coleridge for many years, and which Wordsworth employed as the staple of his poetry – the belief that the visible forms of nature and the forms of the mind are interchangeable. One thing is certain: the Logos and its significance is now well and truly forgotten. After a preamble on the necessity of humility before an author one cannot fully understand, Coleridge introduces a Reason-Understanding distinction not unlike that we first met with on page 152. Now, however, that 'higher ground' which is wanting is characterized as being the specific province of the philosophic consciousness, and only available to the individual by an act of will that begins from, but is not determined by, the products of natural consciousness. Coleridge's description of the relations between the two forms of consciousness is typically graphic:

> As the elder Romans distinguished their northern provinces into Cis-Alpine and Trans-Alpine, so may we divide all the objects of human knowledge into those on this side, and those on the other side of the spontaneous consciousness; citra et trans conscientiam communem. The latter is exclusively the domain of PURE philosophy, which is therefore properly entitled *transcendental*, in order to discriminate it at once, both from mere reflection and *re*-presentation on the one hand, and on the other from those flights of lawless speculation which abandoned by *all* distinct consciousness, because transgressing the bounds and purposes of our intellectual faculties, are justly condemned as *transcendent*. [BLC I 236–37]

It is worth emphasizing various points in respect of this passage. Firstly, the philosophic consciousness described here aimed to realize the truths of Reason by means of an act of will. But Coleridge is a little ambiguous as to who is capable of this act of will, and his remarks bear the stamp of unresolved conflicts.[19] Secondly, whatever else this act is, it is not an act of love, nor an act bearing any relation to any other person, and so the kind of self-consciousness Coleridge seeks here is divorced from the consciousness disclosed in the love of one's neighbour. Thirdly, though there is a continuity between the spontaneous and philosophic consciousness, the real nature of this community is lost in a string of muddled metaphors.[20] Lastly, though Reason or the philosophic consciousness is distinguished from both 'the products of the mere reflective faculty' which partake 'of DEATH', and from the Fancy or the power of re-presentation, yet the analogy suggests that the forms of the spontaneous consciousness are the forms of the Understanding – the sapless twigs of winter – and that finally it will be difficult to determine when they are and when they are not imbued with Reason.

After alighting on another remarkable image for the appearance of Reason in man – he compares it to the instinct which compels 'the chrysalis of the horned fly to leave room in its involucrum for antennae yet to come' [BLC I 242], thus distinguishing between the immediate and the potential, and again asserting that Reason, or the organs of spirit, will first appear in the moral being of man – Coleridge goes on to state what both analogies have assumed, and what he now asks the reader to accept as a temporary premise for the development of the argument: 'That the common consciousness itself will furnish proofs by its own direction, that it is connected with the master currents below the surface, I shall merely assume as a postulate pro tempore' [Ibid]. This is the fundamental presumption which informs the structure of the work. Coleridge begins with common consciousness and attempts to win his moral way up this stream into the mysterious land of philosophic consciousness, thereby proving that the former is substantiated by the latter and so validating his postulate. But in beginning with the objects of common perception and hoping that they will provide the forms of the Understanding (a process in effect reversed in the ten Theses) he has no model or analogy by which to steer his course – nothing which he might call 'The maysters of his long experiment'. When he abandoned any further consideration of the Trinity, he abandoned his hard-won model of how self relates to self-consciousness. As a guide in this treacherous terrain, Schelling is a poor and dangerous substitute. But he was the only possible guide to one who was determined to prove the knowability of the objects of immediate perception, simultaneously making them the forms of the Understanding. But following Schelling, Coleridge has very little success in elucidating the process by which we move from common perception to spiritual intuition. He emphasizes, as we would now expect, only the volitional aspect of the process:

> Now the inner sense has its direction determined for the greater part only by an act of freedom. One man's consciousness extends only to the pleasant or unpleasant sensations caused in him by external impressions; another enlarges his inner sense to a consciousness of forms and quantity; a third in addition to the image is conscious of the conception or the notion of a thing; a fourth attains to a notion of his notions – he reflects on his own reflections; and thus we may say without impropriety, that the one possesses more or less inner sense than the other. [BLC I 251]

This is really the only statement in the *Biographia* of how beginning in the Cis-Alpine plain of sense perception we may end up in the Trans-Alpine territory of Reason, or the inner sense. And it is hard to see how this process can produce any forms distinguishable from the mortified products of reflection - certainly if there are any, Coleridge never hints at what they are, and he has been forced to neglect a distinction he has just made: comparing a philosopher to a mathematician he states that

> The mathematician does not begin with a demonstrable proposition, but with an intuition, a practical idea.
> But here an important distinction presents itself. Philosophy is employed on objects of INNER SENSE . . . in philosophy the INNER SENSE cannot have its direction determined by any outward object. [BLC I 250]

This passage, and his translation of Plotinus on the next page – 'With me the act of contemplation makes the thing contemplated' – a reversal of the progress from common to philosophical consciousness – reminds us that Coleridge was quite accustomed to distinguishing between an object of inner sense, an idea, and an outward object of simple perception. But in his description of a man's development of his inner sense, Coleridge began with

sensation and sought to move inwards and upwards to the philosophic consciousness – an attempt parallel to that he had made in
the Conversation poems, and meeting here with an equal lack of
success.[21] Although the starting point, sensation or perception,
does not necessarily determine the direction of the free act, yet
the postulate he has assumed merely *pro tempore* has prevented
him from seeking an object which is primarily a mental object, or
idea. It is only in these objects, constitutive of a person, that a
man may know himself: so when, on the following page, Coleridge again asserts that the development of the true philosophic
consciousness is synonymous with spiritual growth, and gives up
any attempt to make out a systematic method of rising into this
consciousness, summing up the little he has said in a command,
the means to obey which is nowhere provided – 'The postulate of
philosophy and at the same time the test of philosophic capacity,
is no other than the heaven-descended KNOW THYSELF! . . . And
this at once practically and speculatively . . .' – this injunction
rings strangely in the ears of those who have listened to the poet
struggling bitterly towards self-knowledge through his love of Sara
Hutchinson, and who in the light of this experience discerned the
ground of all self-consciousness in love of one's neighbour, and
so in the ideas constituting the being of Christ.

It is because he has not properly distinguished between inner
objects or ideas, and the outer objects of sense perception that
Coleridge, prior to reuniting them in an act of knowing, is then
able to divide subject and object, synonymizing the former term
with 'self' or 'intelligence', and confining the latter term 'to its
passive and material sense, as comprising all the phaenomena by
which . . . existence is made known to us' and giving it the general
appellation, Nature [BLC I 254–56].[22] Coleridge's progress has so
far been unsatisfactory, but nothing I think is more so than this
unconsidered summary. The limitations he imposes on the words
'subjective' and 'objective' are deliberate fetters to prevent him
thinking about their meaning, and their relation to 'inness' and
'outness'. He has, in conformity to his predetermined end, so
reduced the terms that 'subjective' cannot refer to self as another,
and 'objective' means little more than *natura naturata*, the mere
appearances of nature.[23]

Coleridge proceeds by stating that if one begins with nature or
the object, then one must account for a coincident subject, and if
with self or subject then for a coincident object. Although he

believes that the highest perfection of natural philosophy 'would consist in the perfect spiritualization of all the laws of nature into laws of intuition and intellect' [BLC I 256], he chooses to begin from the subject, partly because he is not adequately equipped as a natural philosopher to work from object to subject (an historical condition yet to be superseded), and partly because the claim that there are things 'without us' is a presumption of which the other position, that I AM, is the ground. Then by working through ten theses, Coleridge deduces the mode of being of the SUM or I AM, of which he declares in Thesis VI,

> In this, and in this alone, object and subject, being and knowing are identical, each involving, and supposing the other. In other words, it is a subject which becomes a subject by the act of constructing itself objectively to itself; but which never is an object except for itself, and only so far as by the very same act it becomes a subject. It may be described therefore as a perpetual self-duplication of one and the same power into object and subject, which presuppose each other, and can only exist as antitheses.[BLC I 272–73]

We have seen that God is the sole self-comprehending spirit, and thus that, through his Son, he alone is capable of rendering himself self-conscious without relying on a being external to him. All mortals, Coleridge has clearly said, can only rise into self-consciousness through their love of another, a being outside themselves. What he says here of human consciousness he has previously ascribed uniquely to the Trinity. In Thesis VII he confirms his error:

> If then I know myself only through myself, it is contradictory to require any other predicate of self, but that of self-consciousness . . . [BLC I 276]

which implies a method to self-consciousness wholly at odds with his experience, a method which in Thesis IX he calls a 'primary ACT of self-duplication' [BLC I 281]. In order to rise to self-consciousness 'the spirit (originally the identity of object and subject) must in some sense dissolve this identity, in order to become conscious of it: fit alter et idem' [BLC I 279].[24] This is an excellent description of the relations of Father and Son in Coleridge's trini-

tarian model, but entirely neglects his belief that the individual
finds his free will in his love of another. This theme – of self-
consciousness achieved through a self-focussed act of will – per-
meates the theses: the conclusion to Thesis IX demonstrates clearly
not the significant differences we have seen between the divine
and human modes of arriving at self-consciousness, but their
essential similarity; the former is merely an absolute version of the
latter: 'We begin with the I KNOW MYSELF, in order to end with
the absolute I AM. We proceed from the SELF, in order to lose and
to find all self in GOD' [BLC I 283].

Since we are, in this system, but diminutive gods and goddesses, 'I am's', not the 'I AM', since Nature originated from God,
and in its development it is the ultimate object to God as the
ultimate subject,[25] so in its origins the life of nature is at one with
our potential self-consciousness: when this is undeveloped, when
we have not permitted the growth of the inner sense, our experience of nature 'is but vision nascent, not the cause of intelligence,
but intelligence itself revealed as an earlier power in the process
of self-construction' [BLC I 286]. What we find in nature we will
find in ourselves when we develop our self-consciousness – for
Nature is but a growth of God's self-consciousness, his separative
projection of himself. At this point it very much looks as though
Nature has replaced the Son in Coleridge's idea of God.[26] But he
does not permit himself any such sad meditations. Instead he
defines intelligence as a power 'with two opposite and counteract-
ing forces . . . in the one it tends to *objectize* itself, and in the other
to *know* itself in the object'. This is perfectly credible of the divine
intelligence, of the Father in relation to the Son, or of one human
being in relation to another, but not of either in respect to Nature.
The result is a conflation of the forms of the Understanding, of
the Logos, with the objects of common perception, and so mere
words supplant the Word.

Coleridge then asks us to assume that he has succeeded in
deducing the distinctly *human* intelligence. This given, he then
intends to deduce the imagination. He fails, of course, as he has
failed at all the most significant points in the development of his
argument. So instead of a deduction we have a declaration, that
famous declaration which considers the imagination as operative
on two levels – the perceptive and the creative. The production of
life consists in 'the existence, in the reconciling and the recurrence
of this contradiction between subject and object' and is the result

of God's self-consciousness. Our self-consciousness, here though
of as the same kind as that of God, differing only in degree, is
necessarily involved in an imitation of the same process; and as
we have seen, Coleridge presumed that the common conscious
ness was linked to the philosophic consciousness: therefore the
products of one are of the same kind as the products of the other,
or else there could be no communication between Cis- and Trans
Alpine territories of the mind. But the man in whom the powers
of Reason have awoken or been developed seeks to express its
particular truths in the objects of his perceptions, for he has gone
further up that stream first noticed at his feet than the man of
common consciousness. Therefore, though the two modes of
imagination supposedly differ only in degree and not in kind,
the man of secondary imagination, seeking to express his self
consciousness, cannot rest content with the order and arrange
ment of the products of the primary imagination – which we may
reasonably think partake of the inanimate cold world, the sole
form of consciousness of the 'loveless, ever-anxious crowd'. Thus
secondary imagination takes the products of the primary, but 'dis
solves, diffuses, dissipates, in order to recreate . . . at all events
it struggles to idealize and unify' [BLC I 304].[27] And this last
bathetic phrase demonstrates the irremediable difficulty of Coler
idge's formulation: how are the products of the primary imagin
ation practically distinguished from the educts of the secondary?
The failure of generations of able scholars to produce a cogent
answer to this question is embedded in Coleridge's mistaken
attempt to synthesize the appearances of nature with the forms of
the Understanding.[28]

Summary

Here the first volume of the *Biographia* ends, and in conclusion we
may rehearse the characteristic flaws of this piece of 'unformed
and immature' speculation.[29] Firstly, the predetermination of
nature as object precludes a real study of what is objective in
relation to the mind: here the word is limited to little more than
material sensation. Secondly, as a direct consequence of this, Col
eridge is unable to avoid entering God and Nature into a subject
object relationship; from all that he has said of this relationship
we realize that he must be unwilling to make this point fully
explicit, for it is the highway, if not the actual gate, to pantheism

n the *Opus Magnum* manuscript Coleridge writes that though Dichotomy, or the primary Division of the ground into Contraries s the necessary form of Reasoning' for any mind wishing 'to possess within itself the center of its' own system', yet he believes hat 'the inevitable result of all *consequent* Reasoning, in which the peculative intellect refuses to acknowledge a higher or deeper round than it can itself supply, is – and from Zeno the Eleatic to pinoza ever has been – Pantheism under one or other of its' nodes' [Op.M. II f.38]. Thirdly, in order to render self-consciousness continuous with the objects of perception, Coleridge has to bandon the Trinitarian God and the trinitarian model in relation o man – in each case making a sacrifice of persons to things which uns contrary to his nature and his development as I have so far raced it. There are two important corollaries to this: the first is hat because the object of potential knowledge is confused with ne means by which we become self-conscious, Coleridge is unable o make a proper definition of the forms of the mind,[30] and these ecome confused with the appearances of nature, and the result s that there are no ideas, eminenter or otherwise; the second orollary is that the moral act by which we are designed to become elf-conscious has no external relations, is but a narcissistic self-evelopment in which the free will is confused with personal olition. We have seen that well before 1810, Coleridge had felt it vas impossible to become self-conscious except, firstly, by loving nother person, and then the essential being in every person. Compared to this deeply social and humanizing method, that in ne *Biographia* almost bethings and dehumanizes the person who ursues it. I think it is no accident that Coleridge was convinced f Wordworth's incapacity to think of love as a separate element: e had not seen, nor felt, that the power of loving was one with the bility to rise into self-consciousness. Thus people in Wordworth's oetry become things, and such is the result of the very system hat Coleridge is here trying to advocate.

The construction of the first volume of the *Biographia* depended pon Coleridge's putting off his finest insights and most funda-nental beliefs. In the idea of the Trinity he had discovered a erfect model for the relation of noetic to logic, of Reason to the Understanding, of the absolute to the finite – a relation which not nly served as an analogy for the nature of human loving, but vhich may also be seen to provide a model for the structure of ociety, describing the means by which Christ is present amongst

us. 'No Trinity, no God', Coleridge had exclaimed in a notebook
[CN II 2448], and without the Trinity there is certainly no personal
God, no Redeemer, nothing but what might equally be called Fate
or Providence. Wordsworth had once shocked Crabb Robinson by
proclaiming that he had no need of a redeemer.[31] But this is the
consequence of his impersonal means of discovering his humanity,
of his refusal to countenance the doctrines of Christianity among
his 'few simple principles'.[32] Wordworth's proclaimed self-suf-
ficiency is the inevitable consequence of the system of philosophy
that Coleridge has attempted to delineate in this volume: not a
man knowing himself by the love of another, not a man discovering, as Coleridge had discovered, the insufficiency of the singular
and phenomenal self – his incapacity to *be* except through his
relations with others – but a man whole to himself hoping to enter
into a direct relationship with nature, a man whose powers of
Reason are not mediated by Religion, by the binding of his being
to that of another, but a man who thinks himself a miniaturized
version of the universal power. These are the consequences of
Coleridge's neglect of Trinitarian thinking, the consequences of
his hopeless search to prove that nature may be a direct object of
man's knowledge.

PHILOSOPHICAL PRACTICE AND PRACTICAL CRITICISM: THE BIOGRAPHIA VOL. II

Whether the theories of Volume I are realized in the practical
criticism of Volume II, whether or not there is an essential unity
in the work as a whole, are questions upon which critics have not
agreed an answer.[33] Although the principles of Chapters V-XII
were elucidated after he had written most of Volume II, and so
the carefully enunciated terms primary imagination, secondary
imagination, self-consciousness, and the distinctions and processes involved in them are not employed in the literary criticism,
yet I think it is an indication of the impracticability of his particular
distinction between primary and secondary imagination that Coleridge uses more familiar modes of thinking in this volume.

Perhaps his best practical definition of the relations between the
subjective and objective worlds of man and nature occur in the
Schellingian notebook essay of 1818, 'On Poesy or Art' – in which
he describes art as 'the mediatress between, and reconciler of

man and nature. It is, therefore, the power of humanizing nature, of infusing the thoughts and passions of man into everything which is the object of his contemplation' [BL II 253]. This implies that man and nature are independent and apparently unrelated worlds, and that the 'thoughts and passions of man', which supply the energy of the secondary imagination, are derived from a source quite separate from the world of nature – a view which Wordsworth could not have accepted without proviso. Thoughts and passions are taken as an adequate kind of self-consciousness, and the primary imagination – that 'repetition in the finite mind of the eternal act of creation in the infinite I AM' – which theoretically forms the basis of self-consciousness, seems to have no potential place. Art, though in reality a product, is here considered as more or less synonymous with what we must presume to be the secondary imagination – evident in a second definition: 'to make the external internal, the internal external, to make nature thought, and thought nature – this is the mystery of genius in the Fine Arts' [BL II 258]. In both extracts we see that Coleridge has presumed self-consciousness, by which the object is generated from the subject, and it is therefore difficult to believe that the mode of arriving at it, so carefully asseverated in Volume I, has any significance in relation to the final product.[34] We saw that Coleridge hoped to find the forms of the Understanding in the forms of nature. The practical problem was to distinguish between these as the products of common consciousness and the Reason-imbued philosophic consciousness. Here, instead of the generation of self-consciousness establishing a connection between the appearances of nature and the forms of the mind, so unifying religious meaning and natural form, nature has become merely external, and has ceased to be considered as an 'intelligence revealing itself as an earlier power in the process of self-construction'. The form for all imaginative activity is now to be derived solely from the *thoughts* and *passions* of man – a dangerous synonymization of two words which, in effect, he had struggled to desynonymize in order to rescue his love of Sara Hutchinson from the corrosions of time. These conflicting views each find their place in Coleridge's practical criticism.

If, for instance, one believes that nature may disclose 'The perfect image of a mighty mind', then the imitation of nature may be all that is ideally required of a poet. But to the reader such a passage may seem lacking any distinctive quality of feeling or thought, and little more interesting than the descriptive verse of Cowper or Thomson. Both Coleridge and Wordsworth, when seeking to illustrate the proper function of the imagination, alighted on poems or passages that are primarily descriptive, and that seem both idea-less and emotion-less to the modern reader. Coleridge, criticizing 'The Excursion' for paying too great an attention to detail – the work of Fancy – explains that,

> The poet should *paint* to the imagination, not to the fancy . . . Master-pieces of the former mode of poetic painting abound in the writings of Milton, ex.gr.

> The fig tree, not that kind for fruit renown'd,
> But such as at this day, to Indians known
> In Malabar or Decan, spreads her arms
> Branching so broad and long, that in the ground
> The bended twigs take root, and *daughters grow*
> *About the mother-tree, a pillar's shade*
> *High over-arched, and* ECHOING WALKS BETWEEN:
> *There of the Indian Herdsman shunning heat*
> *Shelters in cool, and tends his pasturing herds*
> *At loop holes cut through thickest shade*
> MILTON, P.L. 9 1100.

> This is *creation* rather than *painting*, or if painting, yet such, and with such co-presence of the whole picture flash'd at once upon the eye, as the sun paints in a camera obscura. [BLC II 127–28]

And though Coleridge has a particular point to make, (the 'latency' of all the senses in each) yet this is a passage which he thinks exemplifies the distinction between imagination and fancy. In his poems of the Imagination, Wordsworth includes 'Yew-Trees' and 'A Night-Piece', and Coleridge picks on the former as a prime example of the similarity of Wordsworth's genius to that of Milton. We can see that its descriptive mood is directly comparable to that of the passage praising the Indian fig-tree:

> But worthier still of note
> Are those fraternal four of Borrowdale,
> Joined in one solemn and capacious grove:
> Huge trunks! – and each particular trunk a growth

Of intertwisted fibres serpentine
Up-coiling, and inveterately convolved, -
Not uninformed with phantasy, and looks
That threaten the prophane; – a pillared shade,
Upon whose grassless floor of red-brown hue,
By sheddings from the pinal umbrage tinged
        Perennially . . .   ghostly shapes
May meet at noontide – [BLC II 152]

and the poem lumbers on into some very clumsy personifications. In neither of these two extracts, nor in 'A Night-Piece', do we feel that the poet has found an idea in the forms of nature: Wordsworth's personifications remind us of Coleridge's difficulties in finding a significance for his images in 'The Eolian Harp'. The vision is latent rather than nascent, and it is far from clear that it reflects any process of self-construction in the poet. In each case we are left 'to muse upon the solemn scene', thinking that though they contain much potentially interesting material, any of these poems could quickly degenerate into mere description, for no distinctly human thought arises out of, and no definite impressions have been impressed upon, these objects of nature.[35]

Simultaneously, the imagination put to work in this way becomes not a means of unfolding a progress, but a picture-making faculty, reducing all succession to an instant in the attempt to flash the whole at once upon the eye. It is thus not surprising that Coleridge discusses the arts of painting, sculpture and archi-tecture – which are essentially static, as the whole of each is comprehended in a single moment – in conjunction with music, poetry and drama, in which the whole evolves over a lapse of time, and is never wholly present or complete at any given moment [BL II 253–63]. As we have seen, his language implies that the fine arts supply poetry with a wholly adequate model of how the imagination should operate. This is the consequence of seeking the objects of one's being in the immediate objects of nature, which the senses inevitably present to the mind as a whole united in a single instant. The direct and unmediated contemplation of nature therefore tends to isolate an emotion or a thought from what preceeds and succeeds it, and so all genuine narrative is prevented. This as we have seen is the tendency of the Conver-sation poems, in which Coleridge tries to locate all human and natural life in the being of a non-personal God – who of course exists free of the idea of development or progression.

If on the one hand Coleridge thought that the forms of nature reflected the forms of the mind and imagination, on the other he believed that art was the product of man impressing his thoughts and feelings on nature. And if Wordsworth was a poet of the former kind for Coleridge, then Shakespeare is a poet of the latter kind, discussing whom in the *Biographia* he emphasizes not the presence of mind in the appearances of nature, but the modification of the images of nature by thoughts and passions, so rendering nature thought and thought nature. However, Coleridge's indiscriminate association of thought and passion, and his failure to refer any given thought or passion to a permanent or substantiating idea, allows him to delineate a theory of poetry with very evident weaknesses.

Having declared, in Chapter XV, that one of the proofs of original genius is the modifying of natural images, Coleridge makes a practical demonstration of his point. He takes these two lines of descriptive verse,

> Behold yon row of pines, that shorn and bow'd
> Bend from the sea-blast, seen at twilight eve.

and comments:

> But with the small alteration of rhythm, the same words would be equally in their place in a book of topography, or in a descriptive tour. The same image will rise into a semblance of poetry if thus conveyed:
>
> Yon row of bleak and visionary pines,
> By twilight-glimpse discerned, mark! how they flee
> From the fierce sea-blast, all their tresses wild
> Streaming before them. [BLC II 23]

We may think ourselves fortunate that Coleridge rarely applied his theory so flatly to his practice. He laughs at a young tradesman's 'No more will I endure love's pleasing pain/ Or round my *heart's leg* tie his galling chain' [BLC I 24], but his wanton anthropomorphizing is little better than the workman's mixed metaphors: both reduce the external world to the status of a toy

– to be played with for an hour, and then cast aside when one's heart is no longer in the game. However, Coleridge thinks of his lines as a model for the method by which Shakespeare wrote, and he turns to Sonnet 33 to substantiate his point:

> Full many a glorious morning have I seen
> *Flatter* the mountain tops with sovereign eye.

and though indeed the imagination, in part at least, is acting here 'by impressing the stamp of humanity, and of human feelings, on inanimate or mere natural objects . . .', yet in continuing to assert that this is the mark of Shakespeare's method, Coleridge hoists himself on his own petard: for both his theory, and the selected illustration, are little more than the projectionism that Owen Barfield objected to in I. A. Richards' interpretation.[36] The forms of nature either are co-existent with the products of self-reflection, or they are not, and if not, they cannot be adequate objects of knowledge, however much stamped upon, and therefore may not be employed as such in poetry, 'the blossom and the fragrancy of all human knowledge' [BLC II 26]. Poetry pursued according to this prescription of Coleridge's will quickly degenerate into a series of pathetic fallacies, and everything in nature, far from having a life of its own, will become a dreary phantom, substanceless and without reality except for that which it borrows temporarily from the mind. If Coleridge himself was liable to slip into statements which so fundamentally undermine an essential aspect of his proclaimed thought – that everything in nature has a life of its own, and that we are all one life – it is not surprising that his critics and commentators have had such difficulty in establishing an articulate embodiment of the skeletal theory.

But we may see that the cause of Coleridge's difficulty in producing a workable theory of poetry lies in his taking nature as the primary object, rather than as the secondary and dependent. He says of the two lines from Sonnet 33, that unaided 'by any previous excitement, they burst upon us with life and power' [BLC II 24]. This is a half truth that successfully obscures what is permanently true not only of this sonnet, but of most of the sequence: if we assent to Coleridge's words, we must forget 'the previous excitement' of the first 32 sonnets, and the simplest of facts that we derive from them. What inspired the poet was the condition of his relationship with his patron, and this is the poem's true object, for which the images are a metaphor and a description. *How* nature is described, *what* is seen, depended for Shakespeare, as we have seen it did most acutely for Coleridge, upon his love and knowledge of another person. This, ironically, is the purport of Sonnet 98, which he quotes in full on the next page, and which he associated with his love of Sara Hutchinson. In a notebook he confided that

> Every single thought, every image, every perception, was no sooner itself, than it became *you* by some wish that you saw it and felt it or had – or by some recollection that it suggested – some way or other it always became a symbol of you – I played with them, as with *your shadow* – as Shakespeare has so profoundly expressed it in his Sonnet – [CN III 3303]

The object of both poets' imagination, and the substance of their thought, is not nature, but that other person in whom they find their proper being: nature is the shadow, given substance by a person. The images of the world are not modified by ideas that correspond to the laws of nature, but by the ideas arising from the ebb and flow of the love that the poet feels. And if we think that Coleridge might claim that in this way Shakespeare has made a symbol of the images of nature, yet it seems to me that we must use the word loosely rather than rigorously. For if a symbol is to partake of the reality it renders intelligible [SM 30], once established we would expect to find a necessary and ineradicable connection between the chosen image and and the substantiating idea. But of course we do not. We do not find that the passion or thought expressed in the image reveals any law of nature, and therefore nature *per se* is not part of the reality which is rendered intelligible. It is not a symbol but a metaphor.

Critics have alighted on Coleridge's extracts from 'Venus and Adonis' because these and a few other quotations supply the rare occasions when we may test the truth of his theories on the pulse of poetry. These two lines,

> Look how a bright star shooteth from the sky!
> So glides he in the night from Venus' eye. [BLC II 25]

have borne the brunt of various attempts to demonstrate the symbol-making power of the imagination.[37] But the obvious criticism of these efforts is the requisite one: that the bright and rapid falling of a shooting star is in no *necessary* way connected with the fading of a lover from the beloved's sight. The passion felt as a consequence of the act or fact, and whatever idea may substantiate this passion, cannot be claimed to have found its unique correlative in the law governing the progress of a meteor. What we have is not a symbol, but a metaphor; not an essential but an arbitary connection, not a revelation of a law of nature, but only of Venus' emotional state. The lines are as rich and brilliant as Coleridge claims, and it is interesting that it is his commentators, rather than himself, who have taken them as evidence of the symbolizing power of the imagination.

What Coleridge makes too little of, and what we must think of as the heart of the poem, is the relationship between Venus and Adonis, the conflict of emotion between the two which determines the course of the action, and which supplies the energy of all the finest images and metaphors. For example, another of Coleridge's chosen passages, Venus' description of the hunted hare, is her attempt to prevent Adonis from the dangerous pursuit of the boar, 'Whose tushes never sheath'd, he whetteth still/ Like to a mortal butcher, bent to kill', and to turn him towards the safe pursuit of the smaller animal. Her long description is designed to whet his excitement by showing how clever a prey the hare is, how difficult to corner, and therefore how much pleasure may he had in the chasing of him. Whether she reads any of this back into her own pursuit of the timorous Adonis is less certain; but the hunting scenes are a major source of imagery in the poem, and arise out of its main theme – Venus' desire to court and capture the still-living Adonis.

Similarly, Coleridge's appreciation of one aspect of *King Lear* rests not to any significant degree on the progress of the play, on the course that Lear's disordered will, coupled with the filial ingratitude of Goneril and Reagan, put him to, but on the picture that is created by the union of Lear's feeling with the images of nature. Shakespeare

proved the indwelling in his mind of imagination, or the power by which one image or feeling is made to modify many others, and by a sort of fusion to force many into one – that which afterwards showed itself in such might and energy in 'Lear',

> where the deep anguish of a father spreads the feeling of ingrati-
> tude and cruelty over the very elements of heaven . . .
>
> [SC I 188; cf. LL I 81]

What Coleridge says here is only relevant to one scene, and imperfectly true of that: for Lear's tirade at the beginning of Act III has three distinguishable parts. In looking upon the fury of the storm, Lear at first would have it intensify itself to such degree not only so as to singe his white head, but also so as to destroy the world that has cast him out, the world 'That makes ingrateful man!' An interesting aspect of these lines, heightened in the next passage, is that Lear's desire for revenge upon his daughters is coupled with an instinct of self-destruction: this is not an aspect of Shakespeare's psychological insight that Coleridge is likely to have missed, but one from which his own theories have drawn him away. Secondly, Lear in fact sees no cruelty or maliciousness in the 'dreadful pudder' over his head: 'I tax you not, you ele-ments, with unkindness', he declares, quite contrary to Coleridge's reading; and though he subsequently calls them 'servile ministers' for apparently joining battle with his daughters against him, his third address, to the gods ruling these elements, makes them appear as the searchers out of truth, the divulgers of secret crimes. Lear's three distinct attitudes to the storm – as a destroyer of the world he has been rejected from, as a reluctant ally of his daugh-ters, and as a dreadful summoner to the seat of judgement – are all co-ordinated through our understanding of his relationship with his daughters: the first in his oft-expressed desire for revenge, the second in his reasonable paranoia in thinking all the world against him, and the third in believing that hid in the hearts of the likes of Goneril and Reagan there lies much undivulged evil. What Coleridge has failed fully to consider is that Lear's response is mediated by his disordered relationship with his daughters, and that the nature of this disorder is far more subtle than a sense of cruelty and ingratitude being spread over the heavens: in some measure Coleridge's reading tends to simplify and impoverish our understanding of Lear's speeches in the storm, and this is because he has not taken into account that the cause of Lear's passion is also its primary object, and governs the method by which he sees the world. This is the consequence of Coleridge's theoretical belief that poetry arises from the stamping of human emotions on the images of nature, and that nature is an object adequate to the subject constituted of thoughts and passions.

Imagination is the power that integrates subject and object, and unity for Coleridge when yoked to the belief that nature is a primary object, is not the process of purifying a passion so as to reveal its substantial idea, not the result of the progressive articulation of a living impulse arising from within, as it had been, say, for Milton in his portrayal of Samson, but, as the above quotation goes straight on to say, of the imagination

> . . . combining many circumstances into one moment of consciousness, [which] tends to produce that ultimate end of all human thought and feeling, unity, and thereby the reduction of the spirit to its principle and fountain, who is alone truly one.[38]

And this striking sentence about *King Lear* whirls us back to the Conversation poems, in which we have seen that the sense of unity Coleridge got from his various hill-top visions was also a sense of God's presence. It is certainly a remarkable thought that watching *King Lear* we may become conscious of God. But because he has attempted to give us the unity of the play instantaneously, and not in process, Coleridge has sought to present us with an un-Christianized God, a God of pure Reason unrevealed in human and finite form, with a principle and not a person, as he had also done in the Conversation poems and in the theories of Chapter XII.[39]

In a letter to Cottle criticizing his *Messiah*, Coleridge asserts that the 'common end of all *narrative*, nay, of *all*, Poems is to convert a *series* into a *Whole* . . . the snake with it's Tail in it's Mouth' [CL IV 545–57]. In this statement we see that he was sympathetic to the idea of unity in process, of a whole in which the beginning in some measure presupposes the end. Coleridge had found the essence of process, in human and spiritual terms, in the stages of Christ's life, and parallels between the symbols of Christian life and Lear's progress are possible. The origin of the drama lies clearly in the King's disordered will, in, as Coleridge lucidly puts it, 'Lear's eager wish to enjoy his daughter's violent professions, whilst the inveterate habits of sovereignty convert the wish into claim and positive right . . . [On] these facts, these passions, these moral verities . . . the whole drama is founded' [SC 329–30]. Lear has to become a new man, to restore himself to his humanity. He must put off the forms of thought and feeling which his tyrannical power has permitted to grow in him, and in order to do this he must, as Coleridge thought we all must, undergo a process which we can think of as analogous to that perfected by Christ. Lear's descent into madness, his rejection by the 'world', may be seen as an analogy of the crucifixion, his awakening, so wonderfully done by Shakespeare, as his resurrection into his better self, a new manhood which reveals his true, noble and generous nature. Authority for these analogies comes not only from A. C. Bradley and Kenneth Muir, but also from T. S. Eliot, who after tracing the messy business of divesting himself of the love of created beings in 'Ash-Wednesday', turned to a parallel awakening scene in *Pericles* as the basis of his resurrectional poem, 'Marina'.

And if we think of unity as achieved through process, not only may we think of the play as Bradley thought of it when he suggested that it could be entitled *The Redemption of King Lear*, but we may also see that there are aspects of the play imitative of that process which Christians believe has enabled the redemption of everyman. This is surely a much more satisfactory way of comprehending the religious significance of the work, than to suggest that Shakespeare's imagination is striving to create a static, instantaneous unity, the ultimate truth of which resides in a God holding no distinct offices, and disclosing no distinct ideas.[40]

We have seen that upon each occasion that Coleridge attempted to show that Shakespeare took nature as an object, what actually determined his vision was a relationship. Nature was never at the forefront of his mind, and though of course his sensitivity to the appearances of nature is evident in all he writes, it remains subservient to the 'form' or 'presence' established in the mind of the protagonist by his human relationships. But because his method of revealing the state of any particular relationship at any given moment depended upon the metaphorical use of nature, nature is often stamped upon with the impressions of human existence. However, those passions do not reveal any truths about or laws of nature herself, and nature therefore is a true symbol neither in Shakespeare's works, nor whenever it is taken as the primary object and confused with the forms of the mind.[41] In Coleridge's later thinking on the relations between ideas and nature, after he had restored the Trinity to its rightful place, we shall see that he gave the primacy to what he regarded as constitutive ideas, and that he sought to 'read' nature in their light.

FINAL ATTITUDES

Although Coleridge never ceased his Schellingian hope of finding in nature the forms and laws for the distinctively human ideas and processes, yet in later life his attitudes underwent a definite change. At its simplest, and earliest, it was a change of tense, from what we do find in nature, to what we may discover, as seen in these two comparable passages of 1795 and 1818: at 23 he wrote, 'The Omnipotent has unfolded to us the Volume of the World, that there we may read the Transcript of Himself' [LPR 94]; at 46, this revelation was still to come:

> Then will the other great Bible of God, the Book of Nature, become transparent to us, when we regard the forms of matter as words, as symbols, valuable only as being the expression, an unrolled yet a glorious fragment, of the Wisdom of the Supreme Being. [PL 367]

These extracts also reveal other differences: the phrase 'Transcript of Himself' suggests that God has fully revealed himself in nature, and may indeed be present in nature – sentiments not out of place in a pantheistic unitarian. The sentence from the *Philosophical Lectures* is much more circumspect: nature bears the same relation to God as the Bible – his work, but not Him – and reveals only a fragment of his real nature – opinions quite compatible with Trinitarian Christianity. This regress from the bold bad assertions of his youth is indicative of Coleridge's developments on other fronts. We have seen that in the *Biographia*, under the influence of his remembered past, Coleridge had attempted to derive man's self-consciousness from his immediate or common consciousness, in order to demonstrate the connection between the appearances of nature and the ideas that constitute our humanity. In *The Friend* however, an earlier work, but written with the help and care of Sara Hutchinson, there are hints that this is not a workable method:

> In order . . . to the recognition of himself in nature man must first learn to comprehend nature in himself, and its laws in the ground of his own existence. Then only can he reduce Phaenomena to Principles. [F I 511]

The emphasis is on man knowing himself before he seeks to 'find' himself in nature – to get a rod by which to measure nature. But as in the *Biographia*, Coleridge fails to adduce the method by which he must do this, and so these hints were not strong enough to prevent him stumbling on down the pantheistic path. Later, in a notebook entry preparative to the literary lecture of 1818, which Shawcross printed as the essay on 'Poesy or Art', this hint is more fully developed.

> He absents himself from her only in his own Spirit which has the same ground with Nature to learn her unspoken language . . . Not to acquire cold notions, lifeless technical rules, but living and life-producing Ideas, which contain their own evidence, and in the evidence the certainty that they are essentially one with germinal causes in Nature, his Consciousness being the focus and mirror of both. [CN III 4397, f.52]

The stress on acquiring ideas is important: it is in order to obtain these that a man must 'for a time abandon the external *real* . . .' [Ibid.] and this is tantamount to the admission that man cannot come to these ideas by meditation on nature, or by permitting its influence on him. He has to seek another way, which Coleridge does not specify either here or in *The Friend*. Ideas are the measuring rod by which we reduce phenomena to principles: without their mediation between us and nature, we will perceive nothing but discrete phenomena, or chaos – we will be incapable of reducing nature to order. The poet is a god of love who tames that chaos because he is a man who through his love has acquired self-knowledge in the form of life-producing ideas[42] – ideas which Coleridge claims are the informing principles of nature, the summer sap in the winter twigs, the truths of Reason in the forms of the Understanding.

But though the latter faculty may exist without Reason – for there is a human logos separable from the divine Logos – it will only do so in a way finally inconsistent with the truths of Reason: the lower form requires the higher for its proper function. So Coleridge asserted in his essay on the Church and State that 'In every living form, the conditions of its existence are to be sought for in that which is below it, the grounds of its intelligibility in that which is above it' [CS 183]. If we are to know nature, we cannot hope to achieve this end by the mere permission of her influence upon us. To make nature intelligible, we must bring to it that which we discern of ourselves, for we are 'above' nature, and therefore the grounds of its intelligibility. It is only by holding ideas before us as 'forms' or 'presences' that we can discern the coherency of the visible world. In the note which became the essay 'On Poesy or Art' Coleridge writes that 'the Idea which puts the form together cannot itself be the form, It is above the Form, and is its Essence . . .' [CN III 4397, f.53]. This is very true, but what bedevils both this note or essay and the earlier *Biographia* is the vagueness of the method by which we are supposed to come to this idea. Nature is still seen as a staircase by which man may ascend from common to philosophical consciousness by an act of will:

> In the objects of nature are presented, as in a mirror, all the possible elements, steps, and processes of intellect antecedent to consciousness, and therefore to the full development of the intelligential act; [BL II 257]

The objects of common consciousness are still confused with the educts of self-consciousness: it is not by ascending the steps of a process which is 'below' us, but by looking to the ideal of our nature – which is above us – that we become aware of the ideas by which we live. We seek our redemption in the Son, because he is the perfection of our being; nature finds her redemption in us, because we are that towards which she strives. Not to think and feel this, to find his religion not in Man, but in his experience of Nature, is the ground of Wordsworth's error, the cause of his failure to find a credible philosophy of nature, and of his failure to write 'the first and finest philosophical Poem . . .' [BLC II 156,n].

As Coleridge came more and more clearly to see that nature was incapable of revealing to man the ideas of his being or the forms of his intellect, so his experience of nature became less definite and more mysterious, more requiring something of him than saying anything to him. In 1816, looking from his study window he sees 'the flowery meadow . . . one of [nature's] most soothing chapters, in which there is no one character of guilt or anguish', and he goes on to compare the feeling this scene evokes in him with that of an infant asleep on its mother's breast. Of both he says

> The same tender and genial pleasure takes possession of me,
> and this pleasure is checked and drawn inward by the like
> aching melancholy, by the same whispered remonstrance, and
> made restless by a similar impulse of aspiration. It seems as if
> the soul said to herself: from this state hast *thou* fallen! such
> shouldst thou still become . . . what the plant is by an act not
> its own and unconsciously – *that* must thou *make* thyself to
> *become*! [SM 71]

Yearning, aspiration, longing, these are key words for our understanding of how Coleridge finally looked on nature. It is certain
that what he saw in the beauty of nature, perhaps in all beauty,
reminded him that he ought to become what he was not, that he
belonged to a world that he had not realized in himself. The
sentiments in the last sentence have close affinities with many in
the essay 'On Poesy or Art'. But it is interesting to note that in a
published copy of the *Lay Sermons*, he suggested that this sentence
should be entirely erased, because it was written when his views
of nature were imperfect. It is clear that what he was objecting to
was his proposal that nature supplies us with an image or a model
of the redeemed state: man cannot redeem himself by becoming
like nature, for it occupies a lower order of creation than man. To
erect himself into his true humanity, a man must aspire to that
which is above him, to the Son of God incarnate. The mystery is
that in finding his true nature in Christ, man is enabled to look
safely on nature, and there find Christ present too – as Hopkins,
his faith established, found him in the flight and fall of a hawk.
From the depths of what is otherwise death, or Hades, or Chaos,
there rises the reflex of a human face.

The notebooks offer further evidence of this progress in Coleridge. On occasions he attempts to come to the Logos beginning
with sense perception, by working, as Kathleen Coburn puts it,
'from "bottom" to "top" instead of (as one would have expected
of a Platonist) from "top" to "bottom" ' [CN II 3159,n]. This is
essentially the effort made in the *Biographia*, as well as in some
notebook entries in the Malta period. But another well-known
entry seems to offer a mid-way point between coming at the Logos
from nature, and coming at Nature through the Logos:

> In looking at the objects of Nature while I am thinking, as at
> yonder moon dim-glimmering thro' the dewy window-pane, I

seem rather to be seeking, as it were *asking*, a symbolical language for something within me that already and forever exists,
than observing anything new. Even when the latter is the case,
yet still I have always an obscure feeling as if that new phaen-
omenon were the dim awaking of a forgotten or hidden Truth
of my inner Nature/ It is still interesting as a Word, a Symbol!
It is *Logos*, the Creator! [and the Evolver!] [CN II 2546][43]

Thinking precedes observing, and so Nature is primarily a language, a means of expression for that which is permanent within
him, and which 'already and forever exists'. Nature has no significance or substance except that which it derives from the pre-
existing Logos, and even if Coleridge does observe something
new, the truth it awakes in the poet's inner nature pre-exists the
phenomenon. Coleridge wrote in *The Friend* that 'the senses and
their immediate objects [have] no true *value*, because no inherent
worth. They are *language*, in short: and taken independently of
their representative function, from *words* they become mere empty
sounds, and differ from *noise* only by exciting expectations which
they cannot gratify' [F I 440]. What truth nature has is derived
from the particular qualities of the human mind. Thus Coleridge
wrote in the *Aids*,

> . . . whatever things in visible nature *have* the character of
> Permanence, and endure amid continual flux unchanged like a
> Rainbow in a fast-flying shower, (ex.gr. Beauty, Order, Har-
> mony, Finality, Law,) are all akin to the *peculia* of Humanity,
> are *congenera* of Mind and Will, without which indeed they
> would not only exist in vain, as pictures for Moles, but actually
> not exist at all. [AR (1836) 347]

And just as we must employ these ideas to tame the chaos of our
sense perceptions, so God in the original creation made nature
out of chaos. In Notebook 43, Coleridge asserts that the spirit of
God breathed into Hades made Nature, and Nature then became
'a Materia Vocis, and then a Vox et Vocabulum, as the creaturely
correspondent to the Spiritus Energicus and the Verbum
informans . . .' [N. 43, p.94].[44]
But it is not simply a matter of utilizing a scheme – of applying
cold notions and lifeless technical terms. The ideas by which we
are to order our perceptions must rise up within us, living and

life-producing, as a consequence of an act of will by which we eradicate nature as the false ground of our being, and re-locate our self in the being of Christ as God. What we know of our life begins with the senses, but we learn that to lead a truly human life, a life guided by Reason, we must detach ourselves from nature and seek union with God; for man has no permanent self but God, and he will '*exist in God* as the ground of his being, his distinct *person*ality, in proportion as he quells and *lays* the phantom Self of his *Nature*, i.e. the Ground, the Hades' [N.43, p.114]. In striving to re-locate our being, sin is any act which returns us to our division from God, and 'makes us participant of the Hades', of a world without the informing Word [N.38, f.6v].

In all of us who have not, by deliberate and repeated acts, immured or destroyed our conscience, the hope of finding a permanent ground for our self, which will confer a reality on the world in which we live, is the base of all other hopes. In our love of another as ourselves, we seek our permanent self.[45] When we love in this charitable way, then we construct in ourselves that series of ideas which will make the world in which we live a real and substantial place. The act of conscience precedes its particular realization, and so if we find some beauty in the world it will be associated with a longing for the undiscovered person who will enable us to feel at one with what we behold. It is typical of Coleridge that he should recognize his past self in his mature thinking. In a late notebook entry, he recalls his sonnet on Brockley Coomb, with which I began my discussion of his poetry:

> My own Sonnet on Brockley Coomb ended with 'O were my Asra here!' expresses the universal feelings of minds loving or even pre-disposed to Love ('Lov'd ere I lov'd, I sought a form for Love') on the contemplation of a beautiful Landscape – a serene starry Heaven – or a sunset on the Sea-shore.
>
> [N.47, p.75]

The sonnet of course did not end as Coleridge records it here: he has, illustrating a trait noticed by Kathleen Coburn, substituted Asra for Sara, and associated Sara Hutchinson with an event that occurred before he met her. The beauty of what he saw at Brockley Coomb catalyzed in him a longing for that person who could give that and comparable scenes a substance and a reality. Had Asra been there, she would have been his Logos, his creator and evolver, as she had once been a shaft of light creating new fields in the moorland waste. This yearning for ideal human completion had prompted Coleridge on his longest journey, and he had come to see that this yearning finds it adequate object in those features of our humanity that are timeless and permanent, and which are fully and perfectly embodied only in Christ. And the 'outness', or substantial presence of Christ, Coleridge saw expressed in two ways: in history, where the doctrines derived from the stages of his life may be seen as ideas informing the growth of a nation; and in the state, where that yearning towards another as one's self, the basis of all social unity, may be modelled upon the moral qualities of his life.

8

The Idea of History

'By this I would imply, that Truth, narrative and past, is the Idol of Historians (who worship a dead thing) and Truth, operative and by effects continually alive, is the mistress of Poets, who hath not her existence in matter, but in reason.'
Sir William D'Avenant, quoted by Coleridge in CN III 3769.

Eternity is in love with the productions of time.
William Blake: Proverbs of Hell.

If by a sense of history we mean a fanciful union of past events with reliques and visibilia, then Coleridge had little or none, and despised its acquisition:

Of all men, I ever knew, Wordsworth himself not excepted, I have the faintest pleasure in things contingent and transitory . . . Nay, it goes to a disease in me – as I was gazing at a wall in Caernarvon Castle, I wished the Guide 50 miles off that was telling me, in this Chamber the Black Prince was born/ or whoever it was – /I am not certain, whether I should have seen with any Emotion the Mulberry Tree of Shakespeare.
[CN II 2026 f.6][1]

This is an early note, written at least 15 years before he arrived at what he thought of as his right understanding of nature. So he is here primarily concerned with freeing the appearances of things from the impositions and restrictions of thought, in order to allow 'the nameless silent Forms of Nature' to work on him in the hoped-for manner of the Conversation poems. But just as we saw that Coleridge found another poetic method by which he created the Supernatural poems, so in the course of this note we see him shifting his focus from the forms of nature to the men with whom those forms are traditionally associated. We are not quite certain

218

midway through whether it is man or nature that is regarded as transitory, whether the walls of Caernarvon Castle or the Black Prince. This is indicative of Coleridge's gradual modulation between his deliberate and his intuitive modes of thought. When, in the same note, he turns the light of his intelligence on the great men of the past, he says of them what he cannot say of nature: '. . . but a Shakespeare, a Milton, a Bruno, exist in the mind as *pure Action*, defecated of all that is material and passive. And the great moments, that formed them – it is hard and an impiety against a Voice within us, not to regard as predestined, and therefore things of Now and Forever and which were Always'. To associate this emotion with things of nature or reliquiary interest 'degrades this sacred Feeling; and is to it what stupid Superstition is to enthusiastic Religion, when a man makes a Pilgrimage to see a great man's Shin Bone found unmouldered in his Coffin' [Ibid.]. In August of the same year, 1804, he jotted down his belief that 'Childish minds alone, . . . can attach themselves to (so called) antiquities' [CN II 2167]. It is perhaps no accident that finding Sir Walter Scott his antithesis in this, for whom 'every old ruin, hill, river, or tree called up in his mind a host of historical or biographical associations', he also found that Scott's novels were the only ones he could read when he was ill. [TT 4 Aug. 1833]. The effortless association of contemporary modes of thinking and feeling with ancient characters, customs and places supplied some sort of analgesic to Coleridge's sufferings – took his mind off the physical pain without stimulating the pain of thought.

For quite unlike Sir Walter, and the Sunday sciolists of our own time, Coleridge neither regarded his senses as providing criteria for historical belief, nor used the information they provided to stimulate his imagination. His idea of history originated in the same act as that which enabled the Supernatural poems, a reflection by the mind upon its own acts in order to discover there the substance of all other form. The 'voice within us', or conscience, creates the idea of another person according to the precepts of constitutive Reason. Thus Shakespeare, Milton, Bruno and all persons who are to us substantial historical realities, are pure acts of our minds, as the Mariner was of Coleridge's creative mind, glorifications of our own being, and 'defecated of all that is material and passive', they might be seen as parts of a whole whose reality is eternal, founded in God, and given temporal incarnation by the epochs of divine providence. The germ of Coleridge's maturer speculations on the nature of history may be found in these phrases. The idea of history must be established, and derived from the nature of the human being, before we can determine historical realities. Unhappily men rush into talking about history before they have discovered the ideal truths of Reason in themselves. Thus their 'ideas' are sullied and imperfect: as Coleridge addresses his friend in the poem 'Reason' so might the muse of History address most of her exponents – in the words of Beatrice to Dante:

> tu stesso, ti fai grosso
> Col falso immaginar, si che non vedi
> Cio che vedresti, se l'avessi scosso. [PW I 487]

The worst forms of false imaginings create the superstition that allows the worship 'of cloutes and of bones', but the lesser forms permit both our enjoyment of Scott's novels and our admiration of the senseless motive-making and idealess abstractions of Gibbon and Hume.[2] A history not co-ordinate with the constitution of the mind of man, with Reason, was barely a history at all for Coleridge: the human mind is a refraction of the divine mind, in which all reality, and all the processes of time were subsumed. In fact Coleridge did outline three kinds of history: the narrative or chronicle; that which sought to establish a moral truth; and the philosophical [MC 146].[3] Only the last was of any interest to him:

> You must commence with the philosophic idea of the thing, the true nature of which you wish to find out and manifest . . . If you ask me how I can know that this idea – my own invention – is the truth, by which the phenomena of history are to be explained, I answer, in the same way exactly that you know your eyes were made to see with; and that is because you *do* see with them . . . in order to make your facts speak truth, you must know what the truth is which *ought* to be proved – the ideal truth, the truth which was consciously or unconsciously, strongly or weakly, wisely or blindly, intended at all times.
>
> [TT 14 April 1833][4]

Just as the State is much more the maker of man, than man the maker of the State, so Coleridge's idea of history is always and explicitly providential – a scheme in which each nation, and each epoch in each nation has its place. But the *story* was, he felt,

everywhere one and the same: 'Take from History its imper-
tinences and it differs from the Pilgrim's Progress only in the coincidence of Proper Names with those of the particular Time and
Country' [Egerton 2800, f. 169].[5] The substantiating reality of history is from God and of God: if Coleridge had in his youth hoped
to find in all the forms and presences of nature aspects of the
divine being, this hope is much more nearly realized in his later
life in his detailed study of history, particularly Hebrew history.
Because, for Coleridge, in God, knowing and being, thought and
action, subject and object, are perfectly united, it follows that the
course of providence is not related to God, as for Newton, Paley
and other Christian mechanists, as watch to watchmaker, but as
subject to object; that is, the course of providence is a revelation
of God's being, not just a roadway to heaven laid down by a
mysterious and unknown power, but that power manifesting its
nature in the development of individual and national lives. Thus
history is the revelation of a unique and perfect mind, and the
development of history is the gradual process of co-ordination
between the distinct powers of this mind.[6]

It is a fundamental tenet of Coleridge's that the nature of God's
being and the nature of the human intellect differ rather in degree
than in kind. We have seen that his interpretation of the doctrine
of the Trinity is also a model of human consciousness, and provides a model for that act which is the basis of human responsibility and human society. Coleridge's idea of history cannot be
considered apart from his insight into the nature and the faculties
of the human mind, for it is our only source of insight into the
divine mind, and present in each and every one of us, may be
regarded as a symbol of that mind and being in whom all time,
and therefore all history as a process of time, is eternally present.

Coleridge's lectures on the History of Philosophy are his attempt
to describe man's gradual revelation to himself of this mind: so in
the Prospectus he announces that his intention is to 'consider
Philosophy historically, as an essential part of the history of man,
and as if it were the striving of a single mind, under very different
periods of its own growth and development' [PL 67]. Historically
this single mind has been formed by a series of interrelated 'great
moments', or epochs, which have fostered its gradual revelation.
We have seen that Coleridge, by raising his Understanding up to
his Reason, hoped to find his religion in their common focus; and
that if the constitutive ideas of Reason are expressed through the

forms of the Understanding, the product, or educt, is in essence
the Person of Christ. In relation to this synthesis, faith is the
moral act through which the will activates the Reason, and the
imagination is the power which, subsequent to the act of faith,
enables us to behold the ideas or symbols which constitute the
spiritual order of Christ's life, and which are his life in us. All
these are the inward acts of the individual, the subject in search
of its proper being. But it is Coleridge's belief that these acts of the
individual conscience have occurred historically and objectively –
in nations, and over many centuries.[7] He thought he saw in the
progress of Classical European history a model for those operations of his own mind that he considered the foundation of his
Christianity.

In applying his scheme of the mind's chief faculties to classical
history, very broadly Coleridge regarded the Hebrews as the
nation of Reason, the Greeks as the nation of the Understanding,
and Christianity the historical consequence of their union in the
latter days of the Roman Empire. Thus in the Philosophical Lectures he spoke of the Hebrews and Greeks as 'imperfect halves
which, after a series of ages, each maturing and perfecting, are at
length to meet in some one point comprising the excellencies
of both' [PL 87]. Many of Coleridge's later works make passing
references to this scheme, and the essay on Aeschylus, and the
'Fly-catcher' series of notebooks, are concerned with validating it
in detail.[8]

If we begin with the Hebrews, we notice that Coleridge's primary concern is not with Reason itself, but with the fidelity of the
nation to Reason as exemplified in the living God. Thus he writes
in *The Friend*,

> In the childhood of the human race, its education commenced
> with the moral sense; the object proposed being such as the
> mind only could apprehend, and the principle of obedience
> being placed in the will. . . The aim was . . . to mature the truly
> human in human nature . . . of that in man, which of all known
> embodied creatures he alone possesses, the pure reason.
>
> [F I 500]

This general statement Coleridge renders particular as he progresses: 'And by what method was this done? First by the excitement of the idea of their Creator as a spirit, of an *idea* which they

were strictly forbidden to realize to themselves under any *image;* and secondly, by the injunction of obedience to the will of a super-sensual Being'. This reference to the story of the golden calf typifies the nature of the apostasy to which the Hebrews were constantly tempted, and from which their prophets were as constantly trying to refrain them.[9] One other feature of Coleridge's distinction is evident in this passage; we have seen him elsewhere in *The Friend* exclaim that 'Reason is our being', and that 'God is Reason': here he takes as one and the same the Hebrews' apprehension of Reason by an act of will, and their worship of their Creator as a spiritual being. This is as it should be, for 'the Bible differs from all the books of Greek philosophy . . . in a twofold manner. It doth not affirm a Divine Nature only, but a God: and not a God only, but the living God' [SM 33]. Coleridge gives further ground to this distinction in his essay on Aeschylus' *Prometheus Bound.* The Greeks, as did the Hebrews, held there to be an indeterminate Elohim antecedent to the matter of the world; but unlike the Hebrews, they considered this antecedent to be matter – a *natura deorum* in fact, in which a vague plurality adhered. This plurality is fleshed out in Jove, who 'est quodcunque vides', the very antithesis of the Hebrew God who revealed himself only occasionally and to select individuals, and who was entirely distinct from the world in which he manifested himself [LR II 350]. He was indeed to the Hebrews much less the God who made nature – in which they appeared to have taken little interest philosophically – and much more the God of the nation, their covenanted King, who was 'the *Jus divinum,* or direct Relation of the State to the Supreme Being' [SM 33].

Coleridge consistently represented the Fall of man as a disordered relation between the Reason and the Understanding – which we have seen as the informing energy of *The Ancient Mariner* and *Christabel* [Cf AR 249]. Both the Greeks and the Hebrews had a concept of this unaccountable fact, but each came at it from a different position [Cf. Shedd V 203–4]. For the Hebrews it appeared as any deviation from their allegiance to and worship of the living God, any attempt to express this idea in form or image. Their historical role was to mature the Reason through obedience to the will, so that eventually it could be properly expressed in the developed forms of the human understanding. Thus, uniquely, the Hebrews were a nation who, untempted, never allowed the information of their senses to provide criteria for their beliefs.[10] This act was the basis of their salvation as a nation; for those nations

> who determined to shape their convictions and deduce their knowledge from without by exclusive observation of outward and sensible things as the only realities, became . . . rapidly civilized! . . . They became the great masters of the AGREEABLE, which fraternized readily with cruelty and rapacity: these being . . . but alternate moods of the same sensual selfishness.
>
> [F I 502][11]

This is the historical consequence of the operation of the Understanding without the control and discipline of Reason, and its destructive and denationalizing tendency is the effect of man's fallen state. In the *Aids to Reflection* Coleridge gives a graphic account of the operation of the Understanding separated from Reason:

> In the temple-language of Egypt the Serpent was the Symbol of the Understanding in its twofold function: namely as the faculty of *means* to proximate or *medial* ends, . . . and opposed to the Practical Reason, as the Determinant of the *Ultimate* End; . . . without or in contra-vention to the Reason . . . this Understanding . . . becomes the *sophistic* Principle, the wily Tempter to Evil by counterfeit Good; the Pander and Advocate of the Passions and Appetites; ever in league with, and always first applying to, the *Desire*, and the inferior in Man, the *Woman* in our Humanity; and through the Desire, prevailing on the *Will* (the *Manhood, Virtus*) against the command of the Universal Reason, and against the Light of Reason in the *Will* itself.
>
> [AR 249; Cf. N.52, f.1]

The Understanding alone cannot prevent man from degrading his humanity by pursuing his appetites with consummate subtlety and arguments of a specious good. The ways of the Understanding are infinitely various, but Reason must tread a narrow path through a strait gate. The Hebrews, therefore, regarding all attempts to realize their faith in distinct forms a derogation of what they conceived to be a mystery, preferring, like Job, not to attribute effect to a cause beyond their comprehension, resisted the development of the Understanding, and so consequently never developed a philosophy distinguishable from, or a philosophy of, their religion.[12]

In all this the Greeks appear as the counterpart to the Hebrews; but they have their place in Coleridge's providential scheme, unlike other contemporary civilizations, because they heard and listened to the voice of Reason. Or more precisely, Coleridge found in Greek philosophy a tradition which, like that of his Platonic old England, was the true Greece, but yet in constant danger of being overwhelmed by the empiricists, materialists, subjective idealists, sceptics and pantheists of the day [PL 44]. This philosophical tradition came to Reason without the aid of revelation, thus affirming only a divine nature rather than a living God, but still managed to bring to an almost ideal perfection 'whatever could be educed by the mind out of its own essence, by attention to its own acts and laws of action, or as products of the same' [F I 505]. This indeed required a moral effort, for its antithesis, materialism, or 'the habit of looking so intensely at the external world with all the powers of heart fixed upon it, that at last the man . . . becomes a mere lover of self', arises out of 'a thorough coldness of the moral feeling' [PL 106–7]. It was a gigantic step for mankind, Coleridge declares, with more truth than heard in its lunar echo, when the ancient philosophers attempted to penetrate the origin of things by studying the operation of their own minds [PL 82–3]. And to Pythagoras he ascribes the honour of appearing 'to have been the first who sought in his own mind for the laws of the universe' [PL 106–7]. A page or so later he makes the moral basis of this giant step explicit when he writes that 'Pythagoras commenced philosophy in the faith of the human reason, revealed to himself by purity or moral character, the faith of that reason in its own dictates'.

Although no revelation was given to the Greeks, by an intellectual process analogous to the historical process that distinguished and united the Hebrews, Pythagoras and those following in his philosophical footsteps, notably Socrates and Plato, came to see its necessity. The will can never be an effect without ceasing to be will; it must, to retain its integrity, be its own cause, and so where not evident, cannot be deduced. The only proof of its effect and significance is therefore traditional and historic – this is how our ancestors have acted, and this is what they were, and therefore

to be of them we must act like them. We place our origin and that
of our ancestors in the Gods, and thus Pythagoras

> very wisely rested the whole upon a process of education, which
> in its first elements should be delivered from the Gods; in other
> words that it should be found in our nature, and from the
> constant tradition of our ancestors, guarding us against any
> doubt lest it should be a delusion in our minds that there was
> such a thing as virtue. [PL 119]

What is 'revealed' to the Greeks is therefore less the glory or
nature of God, and more the real nature of our humanity. This
emphasis upon tradition is typically Hebraic rather than Greek; in
general Coleridge thought that the Greeks rejected 'the traditions
of their ancestors and history . . . [and] followed the natural lead-
ings of the imagination or fancy governed by the law of association' [PL 92]. This, from Coleridge's point of view, is a recipe for
philosophical disaster, and we may think that it was into this
dough that his Greek philosophical heroes introduced their Hebraic leaven. It is clear, to paraphrase his own words, that in all
that makes Greeks Greeks for Coleridge, they are striving to be
Hebrews, to realize intellectually what the more primitive civilization took as the substance of their nation and their cultivation.
  The duality of the Greek civilization is also evident in their
religion. We have seen that for Coleridge religion begins with each
individual reverencing the invisible within themselves. Now the
main stream of Greek theology had no such origin: it began in
the senses, and was constructed rather by the fancy than the
imagination as we have used the word. Thus

> Wherever they saw motion, they supposed that in some way
> or other there was a vital or motive power . . . When they
> contemplated this motive power with regard to particular indi-
> viduals they called it soul, if with reference to anything which
> occupied a large importance and comprehended ·many souls,
> they would call it a God. But when they raised their sensuous
> imagination to the utmost and conceived the indefinite idea of
> an All, they carried on the same analogy, and the All was God.
>   [PL 92]

This of course was pantheism – at its highest – and polytheism in its decay. Despite the profusion of gods and goddesses, or because of it, and the presence of an All, an Omnipresence, Coleridge refused to countenance this as a religion.[13]

In its purest working the imagination dismisses the sensuous, and presents the truths of Reason in the form of ideas; it works independently of the senses, free of the immediate limitations of time and place, as Spenser's imagination had worked in the writing of *The Faery Queen*, and as Coleridge's had worked in the making of 'The Ancient Mariner', 'Christabel' and 'Kubla Khan'. The substance of these works is not evident to the senses, though finally expressed through them. This truth Coleridge had first related to national life when he was 23 or 24, in a poem which accurately reflects his life-long concern – 'The Destiny of Nations':

> For Fancy is the power
> That first unsensualizes the dark mind,
> Giving it new delights; and bids it swell
> With wild activity; and peopling air,
> By obscure fears of Beings invisible,
> Emancipates it from the grosser thrall
> Of the present impulse, teaching Self-control
> Till Superstition with unconscious hand
> Seat Reason on her throne. [PW I 134; Cf. ibid., 117][14]

His later views on the development of religion in a nation are but a maturation and a refinement of this: by fancy he will mean imagination, the person-creating faculty, and by Superstition the formal tenets of a rèligion revering the invisible nature of man. Thus Coleridge sought in the Greeks for evidence of a real religion – and found it in the existence of the Eleusinian and Samothracian mysteries. These, he thinks, were designed to counteract the popular mythology 'which afterwards the philosophers, without exception, opposed, considering it entirely destructive of all morality' [PL 90].[15] In Notebook 25 he is explicit about the religious nature of the mysteries; but for them he 'should scarcely concede the possession of a Religion to the Greeks' [N.25, p.55]. Indeed without them, he believes that there could have been no Greek culture as we know it:

The earliest Greeks took up the religious and lyrical poetry of the Hebrews; and the schools of the Prophets were, however

partially and imperfectly, represented by the mysteries . . . and
it was these schools, which prevented Polytheism from producing all its natural and barbarizing effects. The mysteries and
the mythical Hymns and Paeans shaped themselves gradually
into epic Poetry and History on the one hand, and into ethical
Tragedy and Philosophy on the other. [F I 503–4][16]

In his lecture on the Prometheus of Aeschylus in 1825, Coleridge
made a study of how the truths inherent in the mysteries were
reflected by the dramatist in this play. The mysteries, as would
any proper religion, inculcated a belief 'of a divine Providence, a
responsibility not confined to the Life present', and also tended
to excite 'a sense of Evil in the Heart of Man and a Hope . . . of
a Redeemer therefrom' [LR II 335]. These truths are dependent on
our recognition of the life of Reason within ourselves, and Coleridge considered not only the play but the myth from which it
originated 'as concerning the *genesis*, or birth of the *nous* or reason
in man' [Ibid.]. It is no accident of elocutary emphasis that italic-
ized 'genesis', for this most ancient of Greek myths 'is the very
same in subject matter with the earliest record of the Hebrews'
[Ibid.].[17]

We have seen that the Hebrews resisted the realization of the
truths of Reason in distinct images, and regarded any such act as
symbolic of man's fallen state. The Greeks, contemplating the
birth of Reason in a world of sense, controlled by its pantheon of
motives, came to a similar conclusion – that awareness of Reason
is simultaneously awareness of man's fallen state. 'The Prometheus is a philosophema [tautegorikon] – the tree of knowledge of
good and evil, – an allegory, a [propaideuma], though the noblest
and most pregnant of its kind' [LR II 336]. And with this play and
Apuleius' tale of Cupid and Psyche in mind, Coleridge wrote, 'In
the assertion of Original Sin, the Greek mythology rose and set'
[AR 285].[18]

The relations between Jove and Prometheus are a description of
the relations between Understanding and Reason, or more
specifically, Law and Idea [LR II 348]. Thus the fire, representing
'nous' in the allegory, is firstly 'superadded' to indicate that it is
no mere evolution of the animal basis, and did not grow out of
man's other faculties; it is 'stolen' to mark its difference in kind
from those faculties – its 'allogeneity' in Coleridge's words; it is a
spark, or as we might think, a catalyst, because it remains unmodi-

fied by what it modifies (the Understanding), retaining its integrity in all its expression. And it was stolen by a god to imply the homogeneity of the giver and the gift – God is Reason, and Reason is our being [LR II 352].

In order of experience, for the individual and for the race, we become aware of our senses and sense-impression before we become aware of the power of Reason or imagination. Thus in the Promethean myth, Jove is the ruling power, the impersonation of the law or nomos which is everywhere visible – the world as the designated dwelling of place of man. However, all good civilizations, like all good Platonists, realize that the mind is not a *tabula rasa*, but has within it a power of its own, a power that though it appears in the life of the race, as in each individual, subsequent to their experience of the immediate world and their own appetites, yet which as soon as it is felt is known to have pre-existed sense experience – as we know that the eye must pre-exist seeing.

Therefore Prometheus belongs to the race of gods preceding that of Jove; but because he realized that the power resided in this 'binder of reluctant powers, the coercer of and entrancer of free spirits under the fetters of shape, and mass, and passive mobility', he fought on his side in the war against the Titans. The ideas of Reason can have no expression except through the laws governing the Understanding, and any attempt by Reason to rule alone will lead to its overthrow and sensualization – as occurred in the French Revolution. But Reason must not capitulate to the Understanding, Idea must be continuously distinguished from Law as the producer from the product, as God is from the world he created. Prometheus, in this respect, is the 'impersonated representative of Idea, – or the same power as Jove, but contemplated as independent and not immersed in the product' [LR II 350]; yet contemplated as Nous or Idea, he is powerless, for all power, or productive energy, is in the Law. Thus the '*Nous* is bound to a rock, the immovable firmness of which is indissolubly connected with its barreness, its non productivity. Were it productive, it would be *Nomos*; but it is *Nous*, because it is not *Nomos*' [LR II 355]. In this powerless state, he is visited by the kindred deities: 'the most odious to the imprisoned and insulated *Nous*, is Hermes', who represents 'the eloquence of cupidity, the cajolement of power regnant' [LR II 356]. And in one of his remarkable leaps of imagination, Coleridge compares all the visiting deities to 'the pleasures of her own' with which 'Earth fills her lap' in order 'To make her foster-child, her inmate, Man/ Forget the glories he hath known/ And that imperial palace whence he came' – to all the sense impressions, we might say, that in other poems Wordsworth regarded as potentially revelatory.

Thus in the giving of Reason to man, the giver, who is also the gift, the Logos Philanthropos, the divine humanity, discovers his alienation from the nomos politikos, from the law, and the power regnant in Zeus or Nature. In this he discovers the fact, and the effects, though of course not the cause, of original sin. In his abstraction from sensation, Prometheus, as the pure Reason, is rendered joyless and uncreative. The poet some 25 years before, staring hopelessly from his study window in Keswick at the green light lingering in the West, had found himself in an exactly analogous position. Both the mythical figure and the poet are alienated from the nomos – from that place and those customs in which they are designated to maintain their being. Instead of law and idea, product and producer, being correlates and enjoying an incarnational relationship, they are contradicting each other so that the idea becomes powerless and the power idealess. Coleridge's 'coarse domestic life' has known 'No Hopes of its own vintage', and therefore he cannot express either joy or sorrow, because his own pasture or dwelling place, infected with his sin, cannot provide him with 'fair forms and living motions'. Sara, his heart within his heart, is fully integrated with her nomos, and therefore she may know that joy which is creative – which can only arise from the incorporation of the idea in the law. Coleridge, denied that place towards which his heart yearns, is thus permitted only 'abstruse Research', or the study of the disembodied Nous – and is simultaneously possessed of a gnawing grief, the smothering weight of which oppresses him as relentlessly as the vulture that fed daily on Prometheus' liver.

The solution to Coleridge's and to Prometheus' problem is the incarnation of idea in law; it is of no surprise that Coleridge felt that the Christian Incarnation was the vital and providential supplement to the idea of the Fall. And both in the myth and in the poet's life this new order of being is found in another person: in Alcides Liberator, in Sara Hutchinson. Both are types of a figure perfected in Christ; as we have seen, one of Coleridge's longest and hardest battles was to purify his act of conscience so that he loved Christ in all whom he loved.[19]

Neither Alcides nor Sara are the direct descendants of that panheism which Jupiter's relationship with Juno represents – 'the sacerdotal *cultus*, or religion of the state' – but of Io, or what Coleridge called 'the mundane religion' [LR II 358/351]. They are neither of them the creatures of the immediate and sense-made world, but of a religion separate and existing independently – rather as the Wordsworth household had its integrity apart from the integrity of the natural world, which its head found as the law of his own being. And it is only when the Reason is located in this form of nomos or law, that the natural world can in fact be known: Coleridge's exclamation at the end of this essay is redolent with the spirit of his Dejection ode: 'Nature, or Zeus as the [nomos en nomizomenois], knows herself only, can only come to a knowledge of herself, in man!' [LR II 358][20]

Thus both the Hebrews and the Greeks came to a realization of what Coleridge called 'the two great moments of the Christian Religion' – original sin and the necessity of a redemption from it Shedd I 300; Cf. Ibid. 290].[21] But although the Hebrews worshipped the God of pure Reason as a living and personal God, they failed to develop an understanding of their own history which would permit them to realize their redeemer – to develop a philosophy to welcome not a martial Messiah, but a spiritual Saviour[22]: in maintaining the purity of the idea, they risked idolizing it, and dressing it up in fantastic and wholly material notions, as in the French Revolution a courtesan was dressed up as Reason. The rest of the Greeks, though they neither knew of nor worshipped the living God, yet had a strong enough intuition of Reason to discern the proper nature of its relation with the life of the senses. From the union of these two cultures would arise a man, finding his 'nomos' in the life of his nation, yet one with the living God, representing the perfect union of idea and law, and therefore a redeemer. And Coleridge thought that Christ made his appearance on earth

> just at the time when the traditions of history and the oracles of the Jews had combined with the philosophy of the Grecians, and prepared the Jews themselves for understanding their own scriptures in a more spiritual light, and the Greeks to give their speculations, that were but shadows of thought before, a reality, in that which alone is properly real. [PL 111–12; cf. F I 504/506]

Thus he comments while reading Gibbon on Julian the Apostate:

'Had the Christians failed, a kind of Christianity would and must
have prevailed' [CN III 3818] and in a letter to Allsop he expresses
a variation of this scheme of Providence: 'The law of God and the
great principles of the Christian religion would have remained the
same had Christ never assumed humanity' [Allsop 47].

We have seen that Coleridge found Christ as a spiritual being
within him when, in an act of conscience, he expressed Reason
through the forms of the Understanding in a series of ideas. It is
through this act, by which we recognize the phenomenality of the
immediate self, and our true will residing in our love of another,
that we are able to transfigure our everyday relations with other
people, and find in them the living Christ. This is the method by
which the Christian community is created. But Coleridge sought
to objectify his insight further and found in history a process, the
development of which constitutes law, exactly analogous to that
which he discerned as idea in himself. Thus Christ is not only the
life of the spirit in each human being, but the life of history – that
life which the truly historical nations of ancient history were intent
on realizing, and in relation to which all other lives, individual or
national, were prefigurements or disfigurements. Therefore Christ's
incarnation was not just a phenomenon of history for Coleridge
but that without which all history would be meaningless:

> But for Christ, Christianity, Christendom, as centers of conver
> gence, I should utterly want the *historic* sense. Even as it is, I
> feel it very languid in all particular History. . . the objects seem
> to me so mean, so transient, as to degrade the agents.
> [N.51, f.19v][2]

History without the participation of the ideas of Reason is hardly
history at all, and is certainly not a matter of serious concern.

On the other hand, history is the process without which Chris
tianity cannot be objectified. Muirhead quotes from Ms.C.: 'Chris
tianity is a growth, a becoming, a progression . . . History there
fore, and history under the form of moral freedom, is that alone
in which the Idea of Christianity can be realized' [Muirhead 247].
Just as the individual, to activate the truths of Reason within him,
must, by a moral act, free himself from the tyranny of the senses,
so the idea thus arising cannot be realized as law except in those
nations where the moral freedom of the individual is not con

trained. What is a necessity of our inward and individual being can only be fully realized in the life of the nation. The close connection between ideas arising from the individual, and history as their objectification is often expressed in Coleridge's later note-books. He is complaining here of his want of health to write up his system – 'namely that the fundamental *Doctrines* of Christianity are *Ideas*, Truths having in themselves their own evidence . . . Truths that involve their *reality*, as Beings . . . that the Scheme is . . . true *historically* – the solution, the rationale, and the interpretative copula of the History of Mankind' [N.51, f.23v].

In history, rightly conceived, man finds himself, and therefore the study of history and the life of nations is a path to knowledge.[24] And the most profound question that all man's self-knowledge can lead him to ask is 'Do I need to be redeemed, and have I a redeemer?'[25] From the affirmative answer of every individual undistracted by the world's distractions, and from the historical affirmation given in their different ways by both the Greeks and the Hebrews, arise the redeeming figures of Sara, Alcides and Jesus, the embodiments and the perfection of our individual and national hopes. The life we wish to redeem we find within our-selves, and therefore our redeemer must act not only on us, but in us:

God became *Man*, that as Man he might act on and in Man. Is not this the Law throughout Nature? Can the Bird produce or act in the *Fish*, which he can act *on*, or on the Insect? Can the Man, as Man, act *in* the Horse, the Dog, the Sheep, on all [of] which he acts manifoldly? Whatever is of God is primarily *generative*. Redemption therefore is essentially *generative*. It is *Regeneration*, or the Eternal Generation of the Word.

[N.50, f.43-v][26]

We have seen that Coleridge thought that 'the Idea of Christian-ty' can only be realized in history. The Word is generated in us as idea, in history as law. Christ is the essential being in us all, and because his life is our life, Coleridge declares that 'The sum of my Belief is, that nothing happened to Jesus, which in and thro' him must not happen to every elect Believer' [N.39, f.21-v].

What did happen to Jesus? The rest of this chapter is an attempt to show Coleridge working out the elementary relations between

the life of Jesus and the life of the Hebrews prior to his incarnation.
His guiding thought, I believe, is that their history was a long
struggle to maintain the ideas which constitute his being, that his
life is the sum and substance of their history, and that which
their national life was ever seeking to realize in each individual
member.[27] It appears that Coleridge's study of the Old Testament
was dominated by his typological hope of finding in all the significant events and persons, the being of Christ, by his hope of
showing that the history of the Jews was in essence a history of
Christ: 'Who more convinced than I am – who more anxious to
impress the conviction on the minds of others – that the Law and
Prophets speak throughout of Christ?' [Shedd V 589].[28] This is not
only a quest to render the Old Testament a book of spiritual
insights for Christians, though it certainly includes this in its
scope, but it is also an examination of the ideal relations between
the life of the individual and the life of the nation. As the perfect
frame of man is the perfect frame of a state, so the nation – the
life of the state in time – expresses the perfectly realized life of
man. Coleridge's purpose in his later notebooks is to demonstrate
that the Hebrews, from their beginnings in Abraham, held, and
occasionally beheld, the idea of the human form divine, the Jeho-
vah-man, as the life and substance of their nation. This is an
idea which could only be fully revealed in the course of many
generations, but which would finally be realized in one person at
one particular moment in their history; and his life would indeed
in some measure be a rehearsal of the life of the nation, just as all
the previous significant events and characters had been prophetic
and typical of this single individual.[29] It is for reasons of this kind
that Coleridge believed that a form of Christianity would have
arisen had Jesus himself not been born and crucified among the
Jews: for his life is the *idea* of Jewish history, and thus the Hebraic
writings, in conjunction with Greek philosophy, would have inevitably produced something of the nature of Christianity.[30]

However, for the Christian faithful, he did live, and therefore
his life is the predetermining idea of the Old Testament, and
offers the only fully satisfactory method of its interpretation. The
Hebrews did not accept their own Saviour, and thus cannot be
trusted to read their own history aright: were Coleridge wishing
to convert Jews or Infidels by means of the Scriptures 'it should
be my *Boast*, that none but a Christian can understand them aright
For only the Christian reads them by the light of the same Spirit

by which they were first dictated' [N.38, f.14v]. That man alone who has faith in Christ has true insight into the providential history of the Hebrews.[31] Of course, this idea of history strained the traditional notion of the superiority of the New Testament to the Old – or rather disposed of it altogether – for they were different things. Coleridge did not think that Christ or the Apostles were contemplating the possibility of a new testament to make the old redundant. Christ himself spoke of coming to fulfil the law, not to abolish it, and he added but one commandment. Coleridge is therefore emphatic about the distinction between the two books:

> Speaking solely and exclusively in relation to *Scriptures* as Scriptures, I venture to affirm, that the best *Christian*-Scriptures, and of most edification for Christians of all classes and in all states and duties, are the Books of the Old Testament read and studied in the light of Christianity, and as having Christ and the Church in Christ as their both Subject and Object from Genesis to Malachi. [N.36, p.126][32]

The main object of those whose writings constitute the New Testament was not in any way to write a history, to discern the development of an idea in the life of a given people, but rather to bear witness to the fact that this idea had been realized, that the redeemer spoken of throughout Hebraic history had been made incarnate in a single individual: '. . . their object was to baptize into Christ the Law and the Prophets by the unfolding of their ultimate sense and purpose'. By discerning the relations between the life of Jesus and the redeemer spoken of in the Scriptures the New Testament writers were able 'to lay the sure foundations of historic Christianity, of Christ's mission in the Flesh as a *fact* of History – and on this fact to found the outward and visible Church' N.36, p.129].

If this is one aspect of the New Testament, there is another which seems to sit a little uneasily next to it in Coleridge's mind – the delineation of the essentially spiritual nature of Christ, and therefore the necessity of faith in Him prior to an examination of the acts accredited to Jesus. The inversion of this order, and the consequent materialization of spiritual truths, had been Paley's prime error. Coleridge infers from Acts XXIV 24–5, 'that the preaching of this great Apostle was chiefly directed to the unfolding, and defending the Religion contained in and flowing out of the Faith in Christ, rather than detailing of the extraordinary acts and incidents which accompanied our Lord's appearance in the Flesh' [N.38, f.12]. Perhaps Coleridge is aware that this statement is at least superficially inconsistent with that in the earlier notebook, for he tries to resolve the two in a way typical of his thinking, by asserting that the act of conscience, of faith, must precede our study of either Testament, that faith informs the facts, that 'even in the apostolic Age the credibility of History was not independent of the divinity of the Faith' [Ibid.][33]

Nonetheless, the New Testament primarily appeals to, and has its truth tested by, our subjective nature: 'The infallible Test of the Gospel Faith is that it appeals to all the constituents of our present Humanity, and brings them all to an equilibrium – to a Beauty of Holiness' [N.48, f.30v].[34] And though the perfect matching of the truths of human nature with Christian doctrine is a constant assertion of Coleridge's, yet 'the evolution of this idea in all the detail, commencing with an enumeration of our Powers . . . is indeed a desideratum' [Ibid.]. It is one that he never satisfied, and as far as I am aware it is one that, because current psychology is an empirical study, still remains to be satisfied.

Coleridge states in *The Friend* that Christianity is the idea, to which the Bible is law, and of which Christendom is the phenomenon [F I 506].[35] His study of the Old Testament was an attempt to show that Christ was the constitution of the nation, towards the realization of whom in a single individual their whole history was aimed.[36] In respect of this hope he believed that the second Person of the Trinity assumed humanity before being made incarnate: ' – if I am not mistaken some of the Greek Fathers considered the Lord's assumption of humanity as anterior to his incarnation' [N.44, f.62]. Whether fact or no, this supposition is essential to Coleridge's reading of the Old Testament. Commenting on *Numbers* IX 6–14, in which Moses requests guidance of the Lord concerning the keeping of the passover by men defiled, Coleridge presumably conscious that God is here not merely announcing the truths of Reason, but giving advice about their relation to the Understanding, remarks:

The Pentateuch can never be *rightly* estimated without keeping constantly in view, that it is not only God that communicate his will, but God *specially* present, God, the *Son of Man*.

[N.45, f.37]

Coleridge therefore insisted that the Jehovah of the Old Testament was not God the Father, but God the Son. In reference to
the Lord's commanding Jacob to return to the land of his fathers
(again a specific historical injunction, an intervention arising from
and applying to the Understanding), he wrote: 'I know few points
in Scripture, which it more concerns a Christian to bear in mind
than that Christ as the *Logos Theanthropos* was the Jehovah of the
Old Testament'. On the next page he laments that it is generally
forgotten, or even not known, 'that the Divinity, the Filial Godhead, was humanized before he was incarnate – i.e. manifested
himself *focally* (ut in foco) in an individual Man' [N.42, f.61-v].[37]

And in these late notebooks, Coleridge is evidently dissatisfied
with the traditional terminology that spoke of the three *persons* of
the Trinity. The three men who visit Abraham on the plains of
Mamre are not, in his opinion, 'an appropriate Symbol of this
great Idea'. That they have been taken as such is the result of a
confusion between the terms 'hypostasis' and 'person', between
the substantial nature of God and his distinctly human form. 'In
the Scripture Doctrine of the Trinity the Son alone is the *Person*
(the exegesis) of the Godhead' [N.42, f.41]. Whereas the Father is
invisible, ineffable, a God only Light, the Son is this being in the
form of humanity, the incomprehensible led out into comprehens-
ibility. In another notebook he speaks of the need 'to get rid of
that mischievous term, *Person* – and to confine the term to one
and its true sense, viz. that in which Christ is alone the *Person* of
the Father' [N.49, f.23v]. Just as our act of conscience, in which
will is perfectly co-ordinate with the ideas of Reason, creates a self
in whom we find our being perfected, so the Trinitarian God
renders himself a human person in Christ, and is only a person
in that he is human.

It is equally important to Coleridge's reading of the Bible that
Jehovah, the divine Man, was regarded by the Hebrews as the
king of their nation – and not just the adorable but mysterious
ground of national unity. In the course of a long note on *Numbers*
XXV, Coleridge wrote that he 'would again and again enforce the
necessity of bearing in Mind, that the Logos had willed to be
the Covenanted King of the Hebrew Nation – and tho' not yet
incarnate . . . He became Man, the (ideal) Man, before he became

a Man' [N.44, f.62].[38] God is only present to the Hebrews in this form, and failure to realize this will result in a failure to understand the relations between the nation and the individual, the people and their king. It is because he is human that he may guide the Hebrew nation, not merely in matters of principle, but in detailed matters of government, in which the Understanding, the human logos, must play its part.

As the king, God the Son is the symbolic unity of the nation, actually participating in what he enables. Coleridge asserts that 'the only possible unity of a Nation is Will = Reason' [N.42, f.62v], and we have seen that he thought that the essential element of Hebrew history was the disciplining of their will to the truths of Reason as manifested in the living God. 'Now Christ as the filial Godhead . . . is essentially and from everlasting was Will = Reason' [Ibid.]. In Christ, the king of the Hebrews, the ultimate end and aim of the nation is disclosed, that end which all individual citizens may realize in themselves by imitating their king, unconditionally willing the disclosure of the truths of Reason. In this same note, Coleridge develops the several functions of Christ as the Word. Having briefly stated that he is firstly 'the law of all Nature' and 'the *sub*stantial Humanity in and of Men', he reminds us that 'The Function must necessarily be manifested as a *Functionary*' – a manifestation that Coleridge had been unable to realize in respect to nature, and which in some measure was still a desideratum in respect to individual powers. But he is able to elaborate on 'the beautiful Harmony between the State and the Logos' who is

> the manifested yet visible King – the spiritual and the ideal, for the State is actual only in the Idea. The Idea is the Reality of the State, yea, *is* the State. The Word, as the begotten Word, is the personal *Idea* of God, one in the Many, the State is the impersonated idea of Man as Man – the Many as one. In order to be awakened to the sense of his personal individuality the Man must become a citizen – and as such a fraction – and this individuality in its outward exponent/ exclusive particularity, he sacrifices in order to contemplate and in the contemplation, *resume*, his integrity in the state.[39]

It is impossible for a man to be fully self-conscious – 'to be awakened to the sense of his personal individuality' – if he is no

a citizen: his sense of perfected other, which he really is, exists
for him not in his phenomenal self but in the State contemplated
as a whole. But this *idea* of himself is not alone sufficient; he wants
to see himself rise up in the state as a living man: and so he

> craves and seeks for a reproduction of his sensible
> Individuality . . . yet no longer as *his* but that of all – Now this
> is alike impossible *in* an Idea (for Ideas as such and simply as
> Ideas are necessarily universal–) or otherwise than as an Idea.
> The problem is solved in the term, *Symbol*, i.e. an Individual
> representative of the Universal. This then, to repeat my meaning
> – while we contemplate our integrity in the Idea, i.e. the State,
> we seek to behold our individuality in the Symbol – the Sover-
> eign of the State. [N.44, f.64v–65]

What we are, and what we seek to become, may only be realized
in relation to the life of the state. But because what we wish to
become is perfectly and properly human, we seek for a living
symbol of this condition – and find it in the King of the nation.
Of the Hebrew nation Christ is 'The *King* and *Head* of the State (a
state being the highest Product and epiphany of the Humanity)',
and as the King he symbolizes 'the immortality of the finite Person
in extenso, as the ever surviving Presence in the Successive' [N.44,
f.63].[40] Christ is both the ideal of human life, and that life extended
in time – from generation to generation of an historical nation.
The King is the person in whom every individual citizen is enabled
to find, in the present, the human form of the life of the state –
the human form of that which enables and realizes his being.[41]
The State or nation must be considered as existing as a kind of
person, 'in extenso', as Coleridge puts it. And because it is an
idea that is essentially person-making or realizing, it is also an
image of the noumenal self, the real self and not the phenomenal
self. In what was probably his last notebook Coleridge wrote that
'the true Philosophy is that the Self is in and by itself a phantom,
an ens non vere ens; but yet a non ens non prorsus non ens,
because it is capable of receiving true entity by *reflection* from the
Nation' [N.55, f.10]. The man who constructs his life in this way,
recognizing in the Symbol of the Nation simultaneously an image
of his very *Self* successively becomes a King and a King *indeed*
would in receiving his Homage inwardly perform the same, and
repeat it in his own soul as a homage to the great *Idea*, of which

Providence had made him the outward Word, the material exponent' [N.55, f.9v]. The idea of the nation is a person, and that idea is realized in Christ and symbolized in the King – who especially and providentially for the Hebrews *was* Christ.

Coleridge goes on to denounce the principles of modern Political Economy, because they proceed from notions of the false and phenomenal self, and pass onto an All, which is a mere Abstraction, and consequently are denationalizing in effect. That which constitutes the true loving of one human being by another, the finding in them of the real and noumenal self, is also that process by which a nation is created – a being which can only be fully realized in Christ and as Christ. In the same notebook he remarks, in relation to the Corn Laws, that the true lover of his country, is one who reveres his Nation 'as a living most real Individual' [f.8v].

Christ is the *majesty* of his people, in whom they find their individuality perfectly realized. The nation is the object of which Christ as Jesus is the subject – it is the law of which he is the idea, and the life of any properly historical nation is *his* life. Coleridge notes a verse from Isaiah – 'for the Lord hath redeemed Jacob, and *glorified himself in* Israel' [N.52, f.20]. The italics are his, and carry us back to his experience on board the Speedwell, and his then shocked discovery that what we find in others is ourself: the person sincerely loving another 'glorifies' the other, and is in return 'glorified' by them; each finds in the other a substantiation of their being – a being Coleridge came to see as inseparable from the being of Christ. But Christ himself, the One in the many, is not present only to separate individuals, nor only to that body of individuals who have proclaimed their faith in him, but also to the unity of being which constitutes the life of successive generations of a community – and which succession is, for Coleridge, also a progression, an evolution of man's humanity – and without consciousness of which a man cannot realize all that he potentially is. Christ is indeed 'glorified' in Israel, because Israel, faithful to him as her founding idea, finds the law of her history, her being in time, in the progress of his human life.

So Coleridge classified history into epochs, and associated these epochs with typical manifestations of the word.[42] Some of his classifications are very similar to those of Vico, whose *La Scienza Nuova* he had read in 1825, announcing that as a consequence he had experienced 'a revolution' in his thought [CL V 470]. But no revolution happens, in the world or in the mind, unless the wheel is already well weighted, and it has been part of my intention to show that Coleridge's growing dissatisfaction with nature as an object evoked an inversely proportional interest in history. When Vico's *'literary* history' came to Coleridge's attention it must have acted as a catalyst to much that he had already toiled out for himself.

Isaiah Berlin asserts that Vico was a dualist rather than a Monist.[43] But there is one entry in Notebook 20 which epitomizes many of the likely criticisms that Coleridge would have made of Vico. It is clear from this entry that Coleridge believes that Vico has not made a sufficient distinction between mind and body, or in the former's terminology, between Reason and Understanding: had Vico considered man's religious nature as that to which all else was subservient, he would not have committed the errors for which Coleridge here takes him to task. He is considering Vico's statement that self-love is the origin of society:

Hence the single savage is influenced solely by the principle of Self-preservation. He takes a woman, begets children, who remain with him. Habit, Appetite, the services of the Woman, gradually form a part of the confused reflection, or mental object, which he calls himself – and he then seeks the safety of his Family.

From families develop, in ascending order, neighbourhoods, tribes, towns and cities, the state, and finally the nation. Coleridge comments:

All this is true as far as conduct depends on the Understanding: the mistake consists in taking it, either as the adequate description of *Human Nature*, of the entire Man, on the one Hand, or as the ground and rule of Morality on the other. For the former it is too high, for the latter too low: for the former it is flattery, for the latter detraction. [N.20, p.33–4][44]

The implicit distinction between Church and State that Coleridge sought in all descriptions of man's development had no part to play in Vico's theory. The history of the Church is the creation of God, and therefore to Vico, whose chief epistemological principle was that we can only know what *we* create, it was not a valid

object of knowledge. How differently Coleridge viewed the matte
may be understood if we remember that he thought of the Hebrew
as the one true theocracy, that the whole history encompassed in
the Bible was a history of Christ, and that every state is striving
to become a Church, and thus to realize Christ.

Despite this criticism, there is much emphasis in the late note
books on historical patterns of development – from the individua
to the nation – that echo the Vichian scheme. When commenting
on Deuteronomy XV and XVI, Coleridge begins with, 'Ever more
and more do I find the truth and importance of my view, respect
ing the states thro' which Mankind must pass in order to actualize
and bring forth the full idea of Humanity', it appears that he ha
not acknowledged his debt to Vico. He goes on: '1 *Universal*
represented in the Individual . . . [Adam] was at once an Individ
ual and the kind – Homo publicus, a Universal Person and the
Redeemer (in the first Avatar, as it were) revealed himself corres
pondently'. Adam is a type of Christ because as an individual he
represents the Kind, what the Kind is potentially, though fallen
Christ presents this Kind realized in one individual.[45] Coleridge
continues: '2 the Races – Purification by destruction and the prep
aration for the Sloughing of the Morbid by destruction – Noah
and his 3 Sons – Second Avatar of Baptism, Repentance. See I
Epist, of Peter' [N.43, f.37v][46]

There is no reference in II Peter to Noah's experience as a type
of baptism, though it appears in other letters, for instance, I Peter
3, vv. 18–21. But Peter's argument is that God shall separate those
'walking after their own lusts' from those who have faith in Him
Noah's history forms an example of God performing this kind o
action. For Noah was 'a preacher of righteousness' and was thus
spared from the flood God brought in 'upon the world of the
ungodly' and upon their 'morbid' desires. Baptism, and this is the
imaginative leap made by the scheme of typology which so
appealed to Coleridge, is the separation of the individual from the
world of the senses, and of the wants and needs of the phenom
enal self, and his entry into 'another world that now is' – a world
ordered by faith in Christ whose emergence from the Jordan, and
the descent of the dove, is a re-enactment of Noah's escape from
the flood. This act of destruction over, and the old debased world
destroyed, God is at peace with the new race of men descending
from Noah. What happened to Noah can only be properly under-

stood, and its full significance demonstrated, in relation to the life of Christ.[47]

Vico's scheme, it is true, did not take into account the development of the races – for he did not begin with the idea of universal man, Homo publicus, but with a single man in a savage state. The next two stages in Coleridge's scheme, however – the appearance of the Family as represented by Abraham and the Patriarchs, and then the State or Nation as represented by Moses and the Law – are clearly parallel to that of Vico as Coleridge recorded it in Notebook 20.[48] What distinguishes the two schemes is that Coleridge sees each stage as representative of the life of man ideally conceived. What happened to Jesus must happen to every Christian on the road to redemption. Isaiah Berlin thinks that in a series of bold strokes, Vico's boldest was to have combined the Scholastic principle that we can only know what we create with 'history conceived as a collective social experience extended through time' [Berlin].[49] Coleridge assimilated this step and then developed it. For not only is his idea of history dependent upon a relationship between the life of the individual and the life of the nation, not only does he, like Vico, assume that they pursue analogous courses in which one is subject and the other object, and which therefore in synthesis is knowledge as 'verum', but he also thinks that this knowledge is *generative* – of Christ – and is therefore the substance and the realization of the process of redemption.

The 'prima facie vindictive and unchristianlike Injunction' of Deuteronomy XXV 17–19 was to Coleridge

but a fresh occasion for bearing in mind the distinction between *National* and *individual*, between the *successive* perpetuity of the Nation, and the proper immortality of the Person – and that the former was the specific object of the Mosaic Institutions, yet so as to make typical of and preparatory to, the latter, i.e. the truth in Christ. The purpose of this Injunction was to preserve an identity of consciousness (as it were) as of the Nation, analogous to that of the Individual. The Israelites in Jerusalem were to act and feel as if they themselves at a former period in their life had served in Egypt, marched and warred in the Wilderness. As the tiny suns in each of the myriad Dewdrops on bush or tree, the same image entire in each; so was the Nation to be in each individual Hebrew. [N.43, p.120ff; cf. n.49]

The great drama of the Bible is the struggle to recreate the unfallen Adam, to restore man to the immortality he lost when Adam fell. Coleridge's argument is that the historical events and persons 'made' under the pressure of this idea, purified from the distractions of the sense, prefigure the life of Jesus and partake of the nature of Christ. The objects created under the stimulus of the leading idea are manifestations of our essential humanity, but they are also of a distinct people in a distinct time, and form the consciousness of that people, a consciousness which constitutes the nation. These objects and manifestations are found fully present and ideally related in Jesus, who as a man is no more and no less than the perfect image of his nation, its whole history enclosed in a single dewdrop.[50] His life, the subject of the Gospel, is the fifth stage of Coleridge's universal history: Christ is 'The Universal individually, the Sun in the whole countless multitude of Drops, entire in each – The Gospel – ' [N.43, f.37v]. The idea of the whole exists objectively in the nation – for the nation is that one man eternally existing without corporality, the sun in the dewdrop, the man that has been, the man that will be, but except for one miraculous moment of history, not the man individually. So it is only in the nation that we can continuously behold our total and substantial being, the spiritual Christ in objective form.

His study of Deuteronomy, in Notebook 43, calls forth this idea more frequently from Coleridge than any other book of the Old Testament, and he is constantly seeking more inclusive expression for the relationship between Jehovah as King, the nation and its individual members. In his study of Chapter XXI 22–3, concerning the burying of a hanged man, he writes,

> Admirably too is this ordinance and the cause or reason assigned for it, fitted to keep alive in the Hebrew People the high privilege and implied command Ye are a holy People – a consecrated Nation. Ye are called, *all* to be Kings and Priests – for each of you is to contain in himself entirely the image of the Supreme King, of the everlasting High Priest. Your very land is to be a Temple, to be jealously kept pure from all profanation and defilement. [N.43, p.102][51]

As the individual strives to raise his Understanding to his Reason, so the State strives to be a Church – a condition more nearly realized in the Hebrew Commonwealth than in any other

nation in subsequent European history.[52] Each citizen in this theocracy is to find within himself 'entirely' the image of the Jehovah-
King and Everlasting Priest – that is, the Nation is to be the
completed image of King and Priest – the embodiment of their
being. The Mosaic code was designed as a nation-making Law,
'preparing indeed for the spiritual, but not itself such' [N.43,
p.109]. In relation to the life of the individual, the life of the nation
is extended in time, though representing the eternal and immortal
being of the covenanted king. Thus 'every past event was typical
and prophetic – and every present [event] required remembrance
of the Past for its right interpretation' [Ibid.].[53] At any one moment
the whole life of the nation was present in Jehovah (as we might
say that it is present in the Church in a modern nation) and when
its providential course had been completed in Jesus as Christ, the
nation, as found in the books of the Old Testament 'from Genesis
to Malachi' was the very life of God incarnate.[54]

As early as 1816 Coleridge had seen that the contents of the
Bible 'present to us the stream of time continuous as Life and a
Symbol of Eternity, inasmuch as the Past and the Future are virtually contained in the Present', with the prophetic and the historical
occupying interchangeable positions relative to the reader's place
in history, or analogously, in his reading [SM 29–30]. If a man
regards the antiquity of his nation with contempt, if he does
not thirst in the desert and march in the wilderness while safely
esconced behind the walls of Jerusalem, then he has no real being
in the present: for 'the indifference of the final fluxion of the Past,
and the initial Fluxion of the Future is Man's only NOW; and thus
by its perpetual and continual recurrence becomes for him the
image of the Eternal NOW' [N.51, f.4v–5]. This *now* is the life of the
nation in historial or prophetic form, and in which the individual
finds his proper being. To attempt to make a present of other
than the fluxion of the past and the future is to try to make the
phenomenal permanent: so Coleridge continues, 'Try to detach it,
to give it a substance of its own, and it becomes a phantom, a Lie,
a Life of Death, the image of the God of this world who was a
Liar from the beginning'.

In the life of the nation therefore we find, at the least, the
symbol of our immortality. This answers a question that Coleridge
once entitled The Great Problem: 'Why is there no mention of
individual consciousness surviving death in the Old Testament?'
[N.36, p.141]. It is not surprising that he recorded his answer in

Notebook 43: 'But the Law was *National* and civic – and the pro-
mise of Immortality, as explicitly announced, was to the Nation,
and successive' [N.43, p.62].[55] In the earlier entry, he compares
this succession to growth of the genuinely Catholic Church – as
befits a man who saw the Hebrew state as a form of Church, and
all nations striving towards churchhood.

We have seen that in Coleridge's epistemological theory, the
Old Testament is the object, the New the subject or that which
teaches subjective truths, and knowledge educed by their communion in the mind of the individual. When Christ was realized
as Jesus in Hebrew history, then the Law, the facts of history
found in the Mosaic records gained their true idea, and the idea,
the act of conscience which had maintained the unity of the nation
through many generations, was given objective reality. The
method by which this history was made is the method which
underlies all creativity. So the Bible is not for Coleridge, as it was
for Vico, atypical: it is rather the most perfect representative of a
process which must be evident in all historical nations – all nations
in which the religion is not confused or commingled with the
evidence of the senses, and which is institutionally distinguished
from the life organized as a result of sense perception and primary
needs. The ideal nature of Hebrew history Coleridge finds
reflected in the prophecies of Isaiah, where the nation is contemplated both actually and ideally almost simultaneously: 'Is there
not a *double sense*, the one an exterior shifting, and now contract-
ing, and the other steadfast, and unmoving, the *Idea* of the former.
Thus Israel-Judah. Do not these words sometimes express the
whole human Race, as contemplated under the *conditions* of
Redemption?' [N.52, f.19v].

The human race is striving to produce, or perhaps after Christ's
incarnation, to reproduce, the 'Shiloh, the Desire of Nations'.
What Hebraic history achieved subsequent history is in some
measure attempting to imitate.[56] In the 'Confessions of an Inquiring Spirit', Coleridge writes: 'The history of all historical nations
must in some sense be its history [that is, the history of Christian-
ity] – in other words, all history must be providential, and this a
providence, a preparation, and a looking forward to Christ' [Shedd
V 579]. All truly historical nations, the unity of which are founded
in God, have their life and being in Christ: they develop out of
faith in him, and they grow so that when their development is
complete, the nation as a historical entity will represent Christ's

being. And in that entity we will find that spiritual development necessary to our putting on our full humanity, our redemption and our immortality, existing in substantial form. The truth and the idea reside in Christ, are Christ; the law and the image reside in the nation – so long as the nation, or those who maintain the true idea of the nation while subjects of the state, continue to hold faith in Christ.

The main epochs of Hebrew history Coleridge found typical or prophetic of Christ. He did not attempt to work out a correlation between the history of any modern European nation and the essential stages of Christ's life, though of course he saw parallels between Biblical history and contemporary European events.[57] But the whole bent of his thought was to see the idea of man as the substance of the nation, and the realization of this idea in history as the evolution of the 'Now and Forever and which [was] Always' in the processes of time.

9

The Creation of the State

That man's Soul is not dear to himself, to whom the Souls of his Brethren are not dear. [F I 98]

SHAKESPEARIAN DRAMA AND THE CREATION OF SOCIETY

On 18 November 1811 Coleridge gave his first London lecture on Shakespeare, and the next day it was reported in *The Times*. The author of the article, Henry Crabb Robinson, attempted to characterize the import of the lecture given and those to follow: 'Unlike most professional critics on works of taste, his great object appears to be to exhibit in poetry the principles of moral wisdom, and the laws of our intellectual nature, which form the basis of social existence'.[1]

These are large claims, and the audience who heard Coleridge, their taste more or less formed by the canons of the 18th Century, might be forgiven for having regarded them as hyperboles more characteristic of the reputation of 'the wild and eccentric genius' than justified by his works, which had, at that date, been printed rather than published.[2] But Crabb Robinson knew his man, and it is my intention to show how accurate his inference was, and how we may indeed extract a model of society from Coleridge's meditations on Shakespeare.

We have seen that Coleridge thinks of the 'very and permanent self' as distinguishable from the investigating or meditating mind: the I is not the Thou, but yet the latter is the only means to self-knowledge that the former has. The act of conscience occurs prior to the assumption of duty or responsibility towards any particular individual, and is the regulator of our conduct once that responsibility has been assumed: it maintains the idea of the other person when that person is subject to, and possibly influenced by, wants incongruous with their 'human form divine'. As well as maintaining the idea of those we love, the conscience also determines how well our individual will coincides with the free or noumenal will, the will uninhibited by the mind of the flesh.

But if we are able to separate our act of conscience, by which we become conscious of ourselves as we become conscious of another, from our consciousness of any particular individual living or dead, it follows that instead of finding our sense of other in a person of our acquaintance, we may create an ideal or imaginary character, as Coleridge created the Mariner, in whom to find our being. This is the method by which, in its purest form, the Christian finds Christ, the lover the beloved, and, with due reservations to follow, the dramatists their characters. Allowing for a greater simplicity of vocabulary and expression suitable for a 'polite audience', this is the method, Coleridge asserts throughout his lectures, by which Shakespeare 'found' the classes of characters, the *genera* intensely individualized', that people his plays [SC 282]. These may be reduced to a few: and Biron, Mercutio and Benedick, for instance, Coleridge sees as all occupying one class; but each class, each type, is a creature of his meditation, born of inward observation by the poet from features of his own humanity, and not the product of merely external observation, which may produce a waxwork-like copy, but no living imitation.[3] In 1818 Coleridge expressed this notion succinctly: Shakespeare 'worked in the spirit of nature by evolving the germ from within by the imaginative power according to an idea' [SC 400]. We must, of course, distinguish between this ideal method in operation without other influences, and when working in combination with 'the mind of the flesh'. Very clearly, Shakespeare's classes of people are composed with these two minds interacting, and thus the characters he produces are not ideal in the sense that they represent human nature in its full perfection, but only in that they represent this nature acted on by distinct and universal passions – passions which are very often at odds with our proper being. It is in this combination that we find much that holds us in our reading of Shakespeare – the cause both of the vivid sensuousness of Venus and Adonis, and the passionate energy of Lear and Othello.

Coleridge not only asserts that Shakespeare's method was an analogy of his model of how we become conscious of our conscience, but illustrates how Shakespeare represented these same forces in his characters. In his two lectures on *Romeo and Juliet*,

Coleridge defended love 'as a passion in itself fit and appropriate to human nature' because 'it is a passion which it is impossible for any creature to feel, but a being endowed with reason, with moral sense . . .' [SC 106]. He insisted, as we have seen, that love was an act of the will, not something that man was subject to, and ridiculed 'the sickly nonsense of Sterne and his imitators . . . who maintained that it was an involuntary emotion' [SC 119]. This conjunction of Reason and will is exactly that which Coleridge believes creates our conscience and enables our faith – through which we find our permanent being in someone not ourselves. 'We may . . . conclude that there is placed within us some element . . . which is as peculiar to our moral nature as any other part can be conceived to be . . . name it, I will say for illustration, devotion, – name it friendship, or a sense of duty . . .' [SC 107]. This devotion to another, which Coleridge recognizes as the origin of indiscreet friendships formed by young men of genius who, thinking others stronger than themselves, want to see this ideal realized in their friend [SC 116–17], coupled with Romeo's strongly working passions, creates in him 'a desire of the whole being to be united to something, or some being, felt necessary to its completeness, by the most perfect means that nature permits, and reason dictates' [SC 95; cf. CN III 3514 and n]. This ideal being, because it originates in Romeo's conscience, pre-exists his knowledge of any person who might realize it. On these grounds Coleridge defends Shakespeare's picture of Romeo first falling in love with Rosaline: he impresses upon her all those ideas and feelings for which Juliet alone proves the true and adequate object – and in this he is typical of us all: 'Our own mind tells us, that in the first instance we merely yearned after an object, but in the last instance we know that we have found that object, that it corresponds with the idea we had previously formed' [SC 117].

Like 'Venus and Adonis', this play is dominated by the impetuous passions of youth, and if for no other reason, Romeo and Juliet's is thus 'a death-mark'd love'. Friar Laurence, the unheard voice of Reason in the play, refuses to leave the pair by themselves until 'Holy Church' has incorporated the two in one, so little control does he think they have over their own passions. He knows, like Coleridge, that man's Reason may be consumed by his passions: 'Two such opposéd kings encamp them still/ In man as well as herbs: grace and rude will'. His action, though, is but sowing straws in the wind, for rude will overmasters grace and seeks violent delights, which have 'violent ends/ And in their triumph die'.

Very similar forces are seen working to a very different end in the last of Shakespeare's plays – *the Tempest*. In the marriage of Romeo and Juliet, Friar Laurence had hoped to restore amity between the Montagues and the Capulets, and peace in the city. In the marriage of Ferdinand and Miranda, Prospero, like the Friar a white magician, employing natural forces to benign ends, and himself the very Reason ordering the drama, creates a symbol of the restoration of relations with Alonzo; and his own return to the city, whose proper rule he had neglected for the sake of his books, is a symbol of the restoration of right relations between Understanding and Reason. Miranda, who 'still dwells upon that which was most wanting to the completeness of her nature – these fellow creatures from whom she appeared banished' [SC 136], yearns for a neighbour. Her conscience is alive in the delicacy of her innocence, and so she has the power to suffer with those she saw suffer, whose very cry knocks against her heart. The idea of 'the noble creature' who will complete her being has been kept alive 'not in her memory, but in her imagination' [Ibid.] by the presence of her father – who embodies that quality she finds within herself – her Reason. Ferdinand's conscience is also evident in the grief he suffers when he supposes his father dead – 'Weeping again the king my father's wrack'; and though Prospero chides him for styling himself King of Naples, yet Ferdinand wishes with all his heart that he was not. So the origin of both Miranda's and Ferdinand's love lies in the respect that each feels they owe their fathers, their duty towards someone they have always seen as a being superior to themselves, and to whom their will is subject.

The music of the island allayed both the storm and Ferdinand's grief: on seeing Miranda, he presumes that Ariel's songs were hymns to her. This is appropriate, since his grief for his father could only be calmed by his finding a being more adapted to his own in order to complete his nature. On the same grounds, since he has forged his conscience from the conjunction of his Reason, the image of God within him, and his will, it is fitting that she should at first seem a goddess to him, and that to her he should seem 'A thing divine; for nothing natural/ I ever saw so noble'. Each senses the divinity in the other, and this sets the pattern of their wooing. The wittiness of Romeo and Juliet's sudden and unrestrained passion is almost entirely absent, and in its stead

each contemplates the other's loveliness and sanctity. Miranda
will not accept Prospero's assertions that Ferdinand is a spy, for
'There's nothing ill can dwell in such a temple', and remains
faithful to him despite her father's calumny. Of this Coleridge
wrote in admiration

> The whole courting scene . . . between the lovers is a master-
> piece; and the first dawn of disobedience in the mind of Miranda
> to the command of her father is very finely drawn, so as to seem
> the working of the Scriptural command, *Thou shalt leave father
> and mother*, &c O! with what, exquisite purity this scene is con-
> ceived and executed! [SC 280]

Prospero's harshness is a test of Miranda's fidelity, her fealty to
her own and newly discovered being, which she passes with flying
colours. Ferdinand is also tested: he draws on Prospero in the
spirit of wounded pride, like that which animated Mercutio and
Tybalt, when Prospero seeks to manacle his feet and neck together, and make him drink sea-water and eat fresh-brook mussels.
He is subdued, of course, by the magic rod of Reason, and then
voluntarily submits to be a hewer of wood and drawer of water
for the love he bears his oppressor's daughter. This love is charitable and undesiring – the subjugation of his senses to his love is
expressed in prison imagery: he would feel free,

> Might I but through my prison once a day
> Behold this maid: all corners else o' th' earth
> Let liberty make use of: space enough
> Have I in such a prison.

The exercise of will in relation to Reason is a necessity in the
courtship of Ferdinand and Miranda, to ensure their future happiness. Prospero leaves them to their devices, but with the dire
warning that if Ferdinand 'dost break her virgin-knot before/ All
sanctimonious ceremonies may/ With full and holy rites be minister'd', their marriage will not be blessed, but cursed. Under no
conditions must 'our worser genius' usurp that of Reason, and
this courtship is to prove that their awakened desires lead them
'not to sink the mind in the body, but to draw up the body to the
mind' [SC 97].
   In *The Tempest* it is Caliban who represents the effects of mind

sunk in the body, of having 'mere understanding without moral reason' [SC 142]. Caliban therefore finds his life in his senses, and not in his duty to another; so he has a 'repugnance to command', and though treated by Prospero with 'human care' nonetheless sought 'to violate/ The honour' of Miranda and to people the isle with Calibans. However, he is aware of Prospero's power, and so knows that he cannot escape fetching in fuel. But just as we are aware of our life in the senses before we are fully aware of the activity of Reason in us, so Caliban, in a significant conjunction of thoughts, says to Prospero:

> I must eat my dinner.
> This island's mine, by Sycorax my mother,
> Which thou tak'st from me [I ii 330–32]

It is in the nature of our senses to believe that they have a life of their own, and it is a condition of post-lapsarian man to be willing to believe that the Bower of Bliss, or the Island of the Lotus Eaters are places where our nature may find contentment. Caliban is perhaps expressing something of this kind, and also reminding Prospero that they are entered into a relationship, when he adds to the above: 'I am all the subjects that you have/ Which first was mine own king'. Therefore Caliban, who does not think that the 'Sounds and sweet airs' of the island have anything to do with him (in marked contrast to Ferdinand) will not or cannot recognize the role of Reason in his life, and so is a subject ripe for rebellion. When Stephano offers him a swig from his bottle, he offers him one of the greatest delights that a nature thus constituted can know. The sack to Caliban is 'celestial liquor' and he inquires of Stephano, 'Hast thou not dropped from heaven?' Caliban's hopes of repossessing the island are rekindled, and out of this grows the comic sub-plot to murder Prospero – upon which the sceptical Trinculo delivers the finest comment: 'They say there's but five upon this isle: we are three of them; if th'other two be brained like us, the state totters' [III ii 3.ff]. It is not intelligence that is chiefly in question here, for the plot to murder Prospero is founded upon the same kind of opportunism as that to murder Alonzo, and both are prevented through the agency of Ariel, but rather qualities of mind. Stephano and Caliban have no notion of the state independent of the suggestions of their senses, and both proposed king and potential subject are bound in allegiance by nothing more than a butt of sack. When the butt is empty, the state is moribund. Fortunately, there are more than five on the island, and several of them are not only better brained, but brained with Reason, by reference to which the individual is able to maintain the idea of the state independent of the senses. Prospero's deposition occured because he paid too little attention to matters temporal, to the instruments of power, but as the figure of Reason he is given the governance of the events that will enable his restoration, a restoration which will reconstitute a proper balance between the temporal and the ideal, between the Understanding and Reason.

Caliban and Ferdinand have in common the wish to enjoy Miranda. But whereas the one only wishes to gratify his senses, and does not seek the good of the chosen object, the other is devoted to her and seeks to cherish her being – that which is divine within her – and sees her as his proper self. Caliban's passion is essentially destructive, something from which no good can arise, but Ferdinand's love is constructive, and is potentially a symbol of the ordered state. This devotion to another, so important in Coleridge's theories as to how a state is made up, might be considered as one of the prime sources of motivation in Shakespeare's noble characters; wherever it occurs in a major figure, the progress of the play is towards restoration or reconstruction. Thus Hermione's love of Leontes eventually enables his recovery and their revival to each other; Cordelia's refusal to obliterate her father from her mind despite her banishment is co-ordinated with his return to sanity; and Pericles, Marina and Thaisa each act on the idea they have of one another, and are eventually restored to each other in body as well as spirit. Even a more complex character such as Hamlet acts in the light of his idea of his father, and questions his mother's behaviour in the light of the idea that he believes she ought to have had of her husband.

But where the idea of another person is not uppermost, even when the attachment is exclusive, the passion of the two people seems to be destructive rather than constructive. Coleridge greatly admired *Anthony and Cleopatra*, but believed that it 'should be perused in mental contrast with "Romeo and Juliet"; – as the love of passion and appetite opposed to the love of affection and instinct' [SC 316]. Cleopatra's love, he believes, 'springs out of the habitual craving of a licentious nature', though 'the sense of criminality in her passion is lessened by our insight into its depth and energy'. In that she does not seek the idea of Anthony, but only his physical presence, and can ask herself in his absence, 'Where think'st thou he is now? Stands he or sits he?/ Or does he walk, or is he on his horse?/ O happy horse, to bear the weight of Anthony!' she denies to him his nobler self as a soldier and a statesman. Her attraction for him is of the same kind, and so he consents to this limited view of himself, earning the scorn of such followers as Philo, who remarks,

> . . . when he is not Anthony,
> He comes too short of that great property
> Which still should go with Anthony. [I i 57–59]

The devotion that Anthony and Cleopatra have for each other is to the senses, rather than to 'that great property', the inward and invisible person. This is their mutual error and the cause of their destruction; but because it is a form of devotion, and because it is substantiated with an energy that is itself as rare as it is admirable, it is an error that evokes our sympathy rather than our condemnation, our respect rather than our revulsion.

But Shakesperian characters such as Macbeth, Richard III and Edmund, who either have no sense of devotion to another, or who act contrary to this mark of the conscience, find deeds to do from which our whole being withdraws: the epitome of this class is Iago. In her very interesting paper, 'Iago's Malignity Motivated',[4] E.S. Shaffer makes the distinction I have tried to draw in the previous chapters between the noumenal and the phenomenal selves, the self that loves and self-love:

> Coleridge argues that the self is indeed a kind of figment unless it is grounded in an idea of God which lends it reality. 'Self-love' in asserting its separate finite existence over against God precludes any such acceptance. Paradoxically, 'self-love', in separating the self from God, annihilates the self: for it is reduced to the disconnected and ephemeral passage of sense perceptions. [196–97]

Like many of Shakespeare's noblest characters, Othello is motivated by his devotion to another, and this devotion is the ground of all his significant actions throughout the play. Roderigo, suffering characteristically of Shakespeare's minor characters, a feeble imi-

tation of the passion that animates the hero, threatens to drown
himself because Desdemona will not love him. Iago's retort indicates how little he understands the emotion:

> . . . since I could distinguish between a benefit and an injury,
> I never found a man that knew how to love himself: ere I would
> say I would drown myself, for the love of a guinea-hen, I would
> change my humanity with a baboon. [I iii 312–316]

Because Iago has an enormous defect in his character, a want of
the sense of another as himself, the only self he knows is one
which is composed of appetites and desires, of all that is phenomenal and material. This self therefore has no foundation in the
permanent, seeks no final resting place, and to gratify its desires
is unhindered by any respect for lives not his: other people to Iago
may be causes, or means, or hindrances, but they are never the
bearers of his humanity. Coleridge describes him as having 'the
coolness of a pre-conceiving experimenter' [SC 384]; the coolness
derives not from his having designed an end or ends appropriate
to his acknowledged cause, but from his having thrown off 'all
restraint of conscience' [F I 120], and like the other 'mighty Hunters
of Mankind' from Nimrod to Napoleon, he combines 'Intermin-
ableness of Object with perfect Indifference of Means' [SM 65–6].
Iago's malignity therefore stems not from his wish to oust Cassio,
or to make use of Roderigo, but from the deep deficiency of his
character, his inability to conceive of self as other. In a person so
constituted there is no relation between motive and means, and
therefore to argue that the one is or is not proportionate to the
other is to loose one's bolt wide of the mark.[5] Reduced to its
unlikeliest example, my view is that Iago would as easily murder
someone who had done him out of sixpence as someone who had
made him a cuckold.

Iago is not motivated by a sense of real injustice, of wishing to
right wrongs that he has suffered; he acts agaodnst Roderigo, Cassio
and Othello without a properly formulated grievance, and so without a properly formulated purpose. It is in his nature to act – 'with
outward Restlessness and whirling Activity'; and in Coleridge's
description of lines 381–402 of Act I iii, as 'the motive-hunting of
motiveless malignity', the emphasis should be laid on the word
'malignity': for the ground of Iago's actions lies in his malignity –
which is one and the same with his inability to find himself in his

duty and devotion to Othello. The motive-hunting is, I am tempted to think, Shakespeare's puzzling to understand his own character rather than intrinsically Iago's. It is Iago's watchword that while 'trimm'd in forms, and visages of duty' he is one of those who 'Keep yet their hearts attending on themselves'. How deeply this sentiment affects his actions may be seen by comparing him to Kent, whose devotion to the insane and decrepit Lear is the ground of all his actions, and the mark by which he is known and loved.

Iago is an opportunist, and his skill is to combine the smallest of occasions into a tapestry of evidence by which eventually to ensare Othello. His sense of intellectual superiority is unmodified by any moral inhibition, and so he is able to exploit the weaknesses of others ruthlessly: Roderigo's gullible nature and his foolish devotion to Desdemona, Cassio's weaknesses in his cups and his open chivalry, are all grist to Iago's malicious mill.[6] But why should Othello be subject to his ancient's machinations? What is the flaw in his character that makes him a tragic character?

The two characteristics by which we recognize Othello are his successful soldiering for the Venetian state, which 'Cannot without safety cast him', and his love of Desdemona. Although we might wish to distinguish between what a man is and what he does, and although this distinction might reasonably be applied to Cassio, it would be wholly inappropriate to Othello. Desdemona fell in love with him 'for the dangers he had passed', and – married – sees

> Othello's visage in his mind,
> And to his honours, and his valiant parts
> Did I my soul and fortunes consecrate: [I iii 252–4]

She finds that his outward appearance – his visage, the honours awarded him by the state, and his valour are one with his mind, or inward being. If there is an Othello distinguishable from the man of arms, Desdemona does not recognize it, and it has no business in her love. Pleading to the Duke to be allowed to go with Othello to Cyprus, she asserts that if 'he go to the war,/ The rites for which I love him are bereft me'. His presence is the foundation of her love.

There is in this a sad parallel with Anthony and Cleopatra: neither could hold the other in their hearts except by means of their physical presence. Here Desdemona is saying very much the same thing: it is most unlikely that her love, as it has been presented to us, could survive Othello's loss of honour, or valour, or esteem in the eyes of the Venetian state. Desdemona is not credited with those qualities that we attribute, say, to Hermione. As Maud Bodkin has pointed out, when Iago describes Othello's successful wooing of Desdemona as 'bragging and telling her fantastical lies', he is correct in his implication of the kind of quality that underpins their love.[7]

If Desdemona loved Othello for the dangers he had passed, then he 'lov'd her that she did pity them'. Although Colereidge believed that 'Othello had no life but in Desdemona . . .' [SC 393], that she was his angel, a word of special significance to Coleridge as we have seen in respect of the guardian angels of the Mariner and Christabel, yet it seems to me that Othello's conception of his angel was primarily as a counterpart to his military and phenomenal self, and not as something essentially other and different from his own image of himself. Thus what attracts him to her is her sympathy with dangers passed, and not her revelation of a different kind of life; he calls her 'my fair warrior', a description only appropriate to her as a reflection of himself, and wholly inapt as a description of a person whose father thought that her blood blushed at its own motion. Her loveliness, her sympathy, but above all her presence is what makes up Desdemona to Othello: thus he says of her, 'Thou smell'st so sweet, that the sense aches at thee'; and as he is about to kill her, thinks of 'that whiter skin of hers than snow,/ And smooth, as monumental alabaster'; just before he brings himself to do the deed, he kisses her and comments, 'A balmy breath, that doth almost persuade/ Justice herself to break her sword'. Almost all his images of her are derived from the sensations of her presence and from her as a reflection of his military and phenomenal self: almost none are derived from Desdemona as an embodied idea, which has its permanence in the idea and not in the body. In 'Constancy to an Ideal Object', Coleridge sought to unite Thought as the one constant beyond the flux of nature, with a person, an embodied Good, and there find his home the true place of his being. This conception of a person is not within the compass of Othello's mind. About to extinguish the candle, he reflects on what it will mean to put out Desdemona's light:

If I quench thee, thou flaming minister,
I can thy former light restore,
Should I repent me; but once put out thine,
Thou cunning'st pattern of excelling nature,
I know not where is that Promethean heat
That can thy light relume: when I have pluck'd the rose,
I cannot give it vital growth again,
It must needs wither;

For Othello, Desdemona is almost wholly a thing of nature, and he knows nothing of her that might survive his taking of her life. Although he does say that he 'would not kill thy unprepared spirit . . . thy soul', this seems to be a thing of concern only to Desdemona, and not something with which he has had or will have any communication. Othello's rage at what he believes to be her infidelity is thus unmodified by any other kind of knowledge of her. Although Coleridge says rightly, and repeatedly, that Othello did not have a jealous nature, it is the horror of imagining her in another man's arms and bed which is always the focus of his passion.[8] Othello's too close a concentration on her bodily being is the cause of Desdemona's unmerited death.

His thoughts, after he has killed her, quickly return to himself and the military mask which she has loved. T.S. Eliot criticized Othello's last speech as an attempt to escape the reality of what he had done, as a cheering himself up, which he achieved by putting an aesthetic before a moral attitude[9]: an exact and interesting parallel to Coleridge's view that Iago's intellect dominated his sense of morality. But what Eliot has said of this last speech, I think true of Othello throughout the play – he has constantly failed to recognize the 'otherness' of self. Like Lear, and perhaps like many men of power, 'he hath ever but slenderly known himself'. And this was not changed by his love for Desdemona: for he loved her partly as an object to gratify his senses, and partly as no more than a female echo of himself the soldier. The fact that Desdemona lived for him chiefly in his senses, and that he never developed a distinct idea of her, separate from his phenomenal life, is what finally precipitated the tragedy. Without Iago, Desdemona might have lived, but the flaw in their love, which made Othello a tragic figure, would have remained.

Those major Shakespearian characters in whom the act of conscience is either prevented or imperfect, destroy both themselves and others; but where it is fully operative, they survive potentially destructive forces, and re-establish themselves in a new and more harmonious grouping. Coleridge believes that this act of conscience, by which we find ourselves in our neighbours, is the basis of society. Every noble mind thinks of itself as 'imperfect and insufficient, not as an animal only, but a moral being' [SC 95]. And out of this sense of imperfection develops what Coleridge variously calls devotion, friendship and a sense of duty [SC 107]. This is the moral basis of marriage, but necessarily not its sole cause: he clarifies his notion of man's relative standing in respect of heaven and earth prior to giving his definition of love:

> Considering myself and my fellow-men as a sort of link between heaven and earth, being composed of body and soul . . . yet united in one person, I conceive that there can be no correct definition of love which does not correspond with our being, and with that subordination of one part to another which constitutes our perfection. I would say therefore that –
>   'Love is a desire of the whole being to be united to some thing, or some being, felt necessary to its completeness, by the most perfect means that nature permits, and reason dictates.'
>   [SC 95][10]

The significant phrases of Coleridge's definition are 'nature permits' and 'reason dictates'. The moral hope or idea precedes and controls the natural or sensual union; if this order is maintained Coleridge sees marriage as a symbol of 'the grandest and most delightful of all promises . . . our marriage with the Redeemer of mankind' [SC 96–7]. In a marriage, each person is seeking in the other the 'infant Christ', and by so doing is seeking his or her true self. Although 'the word and its business may be carried on without marriage', it is only by means of this union that the essentially dehumanizing processes of thought and action inherent in trade and manufacturing may be rendered less brutal. Therefore 'without marriage, without exclusive attachment, there could be no human society; herds . . . there might be, but society there could not be' [SC 107]. Marriage, 'the knitting together of society by the tenderest, yet firmest ties, seems ordained to render [man] capable of maintaining his superiority over the brute creation' and thus man becomes 'as it were, a secondary creator of himself'.

[SC 96 Cf.CN III 3729]

From marriage 'arise the paternal, filial, brotherly and sisterly relations of life; and every state is but a family magnified' [SC 96]. Coleridge speaks on a very personal note of 'that delightful intercourse between father and child' which lies at the heart of family life [SC 107]. The serious aspect of this conversation is that the duties or acts of conscience are instilled in children by means of their relationships with their parents. Miranda finds the divinity in Ferdinand because of her filial allegiance to her father; his presence has given her the *idea* of another as herself, an idea which in her mind is conjoined with the idea of God, or a god, because her conscience, the union of her will and her reason as she finds it expressed in her father, has not been clouded by any wants for her phenomenal self.

As early as 1799, meditating on Poole's letter telling him of the death of his son Berkeley, Coleridge had written:

A Parent – in the strict and exclusive sense a *Parent*! to me it is a *fable* wholly without meaning except in the *moral* which it suggests – a fable, of which the Moral is God. [CL I 478]

In the rest of the letter Coleridge stresses his belief in the continuity of consciousness after the death of the body. What he seems to be saying is that as no parent is responsible for the consciousness of their child, so we are all in this sense children of God, and that in respect of this none of us are parents to each other. Thus at best human parenthood is a fable, or in Coleridge's mature vocabulary, a symbol, of which God is the permanent and death-less reality.

Coleridge revived the connection between God and parenthood in his later thinking. Muirhead, examining Opus Maximum Ms.B., quotes from a chapter entitled 'Of the Origin of the Idea of God'. In it he finds that the instinct that prophesies of religion is 'the impulse to respond to something beyond the self'.[11] This has its origin in the child learning that its first image of itself are the beings that it calls mother and father:

Why have men a faith in God? There is but one answer. The man and the man alone has a Father and a Mother (f.66) . . . Ere yet a conscious self exists the love begins, and the first love is love to another. The Babe ackowledges a self in the Mother's

form, years before it can recognize a self in its own. (f.65–6)
[VCL II ff.65 and 66; Happel 750]¹²

A father and a mother are fables, or symbols, the truth of which
is God. And this sense of another, in whom we find our being,
is developed in the relations of the siblings to each other. Just as
sons and daughters learn that their true wills are not their own
through the recognition of that of their parents, so love between
brothers and sisters prepares each for a successful marriage in a
slightly different way:

> By dividing the sisterly and fraternal affections from the conju-
> gal, we have . . . two loves, each of them as strong as any
> affection can be, or ought to be, consistently with the per-
> formance of our duty, and the love we should bear to our
> neighbour. Then by the former preceding the latter, the latter
> is rendered more pure, more even, and more constant: the wife
> has already learned the discipline of pure love in the character
> of a sister. [SC 110]

Thinking of the state as a family magnified, Coleridge adduces
'the beautiful gradations of attachment which distinguish human
nature: from sister to wife, from wife to child, to uncle, to cousin,
to one of our kin, to one of our blood, to our near neighbour, to
our county-man, and to our country-man'. This is a mature echo
of a thought he had had while lecturing in Bristol when he was
23 – against those who wanted 'free love' and the abolition of
exclusive attachment: 'The paternal and filial duties discipline the
Heart and prepare it for the love of all Mankind. The intensity of
private attachment encourages, not prevents, universal Benevolence' [LPR 46]. Out of the active conscience grow the conditions
by which all men may be united in society.¹³

'There is a religion in all deep love, but the love of a Mother is,
at your age, the veil of softer Light between the Heart and the
heavenly Father!' wrote Coleridge in 1821, tentatively enquiring
after Allsop's mother [CL V 180]. Certainly all the familial relations
that Coleridge has described prepare the individual to find his
being in his love of another, and so to recognize that it takes its
origin in what is given to all men by God as the ground of their
humanity, and partakes of his nature. The sketch that I have made
is ideal in the sense that it describes the various modes in which

the conscience may affect consciousness, and not the consequences of this mind interacting with the mind of the flesh. How
strong a force this last is, Coleridge knew well, but he saw that
the right method of dealing with it was not the impossible one of
rejection, but subjugation and subsumption. He pounces on the
error that human love and divine love are of a different kind in a
late notebook. In a novel by Henry Brooke the heroine addresses
her beloved: '. . . my dear, my sweet, my only enemy! You and
you only, Harry, stood between me and my God'. Such an attitude
has the tendency

> to keep up very false and debasing views of the Supreme
> Being . . . The Crown and Base, the Pinnacle and Foundation
> of a regenerate and truly Christian State of Mind . . . is to love
> God in all that we love, to love that only therefore in which we
> can at the same time love God. [N.47, p.5]

Coleridge goes on to find in a good and wise man an analogy of
the triune God who is eternally Good, Wise and True, as He is
the substance of all 'Life, Beauty, Love and Loveliness'. From the
idea of a triune God, Coleridge moves to the second person of the
Trinity, clearly excited by the development of his own thought:
'And what an accession does not this receive from the Idea of the
Son of God as the Son of Man, the indwelling ground and substance of our proper Humanity – the Idea of Christ, as the Divine
Humanity?

To love God in all that we love is to find Christ, our proper
humanity, in the heart of every human being. We have seen that
not until we enter a Christ-seeking relationship will we be able to
find out the true life of nature – which is *our* life, and which
therefore speaks of Christ, as all things rightly seen speak of
him. In an early effort to deduce the Logos from phenomenal
experience, Coleridge began with a memory of Malta:

> The sky, or rather say the Æther, at Malta, with the Sun appar-
> ently suspended in it, the Eye seeming to pierce beyond, and
> as it were, behind it – and below the aetherial Sea, so blue, a
> suffused oneness, the substantial Image, and fixed real Reflec-
> tion of the Sky . . . Logos ab Ente – at once the existent
> Reflexion, and the Reflex Act – at once actual and real and
> therefore, filiation not creation. [CN II 3159; cf. CN II 2346]

In his first series of lectures on Shakespeare, Coleridge wrote that the only true resemblance to a marriage, in which 'All the grand and sublime thoughts of an improved state of being dawn upon' man is 'the pure blue sky of heaven' [SC 112]. Taking these two passages together we may see the beginnings of a profound metaphor. The sea is 'the substantial Image, and fixed real Reflection of the Sky', just as in a marriage each partner finds his or her true being not in themselves, but in that substantial image of their being reflected in the other; this 'existent Reflexion' is simultaneously an act, the act of conscience, and reflex in that we are required to love our neighbour *as ourselves*. This process is analogous to that by which God has always had and will always have an adequate idea of himself. The sea and the sky, and the partners in a marriage, are not creating each other, but finding themselves in each other, making the real actual, and therefore involved in the process of filiation rather than creation. We might also think that there is a pun on the word 'Sun', which Coleridge plays with elsewhere.[14] The Son suspended in us is the light irradiating our otherwise darkened nature – a nature which we cannot realize until we find it reflected in the being of another, when we discover that that glory is our life and His life too.

A communion in Christ Coleridge regarded as the proper end of our social life. In a letter discussing the nature of the Trinity, he wrote:

> Man is truly altered by the co-existence of other men; his faculties cannot be developed in himself alone, and only by himself. Therefore the human race not by a bold metaphor, but in sublime reality, approach to, and might become one body whose Head is Christ (the Logos). [CL II 1197]

This is the ideal end of human society, from which it is constantly deviating under the influence of incongruous demands and exacerbated private wants. But it is the ground upon which Coleridge raised his idea of the Christian Church, and the source of his belief that, originating in the act of conscience, all properly constituted states were struggling to become a church.[15]

THE INDIVIDUAL AND THE STATE

We have seen how Coleridge's philosophical principles gave his
literary criticism a distinct form and purpose. As Shakespeare
found the world of his dramas originating from a principle within
himself, closely related to the act of conscience, which, in respect
of his characters, is constructive if operative, and destructive if
not, so it is characteristic of every human being to find the power
of loving not through the senses, as a consequence of the outward
appearance of the beloved, but through a feeling of moral
incompleteness; this is, essentially, a yearning for a neighbour in
whom to find one's proper humanity. This act of will constructs
the basic unit of society.

Self-knowledge, which we may distinguish from self-consciousness as the product of reflection on the acts of the latter,[16] and
man's instinctive search for another are the two co-ordinates in
The Friend from which Coleridge builds up his idea of the State.
But his undertaking is from the very first dependent on what
amounts to a severe intellectual task for the majority of his readers:
self-knowledge is not won passively: 'The primary facts essential
to the intelligibility of my principles I can prove to others only as
far as I can prevail on them to retire *into themselves* and make their
own minds the objects of their stedfast attention' [F I 21].[17] What
a man discovers if he makes the effort to examine his mind are
truths beyond the apprehension of the senses. But most people,
not conscious of these ideas as ideas, will instinctively and mistakenly attach them to some immediate and visible object. Coleridge had had an acute experience of this in his youth, and now
sees it as evidence of man's proper destiny and continuing error.
'The most imperious duty and the noblest task of genius' is to
restore the proper relationship between ideas and their objects [F
I 35].[18] This is the path to that true freedom where conscience
finds the ideas of Reason as her genuine objects. To illustrate this
'natural' perversion in man, Coleridge tells of the arrival of the
Queen of Prussia at Hardenberg House, and of the thrill that went
through the crowd as a result of the pomp and circumstance of
her arrival. Then, 'recovering from the first inevitable contagion
of sympathy', he describes his response to the scene:

O man! even nobler than thy circumstances! Spread but the mist
of obscure feeling over any form, and even a woman incapable

of blessing or of injury to thee shall be welcomed with the intensity of emotion adequate to the reception of the Redeemer of the World! [F I 36][19]

That this last phrase was not a hyperbole in Coleridge's mind is evident from a late notebook commentary on Numbers XXIII v. 21, which speaks of the longed-for Messiah, and which Coleridge calls 'a most sublime and pregnant text': ' "The Shout of a King" was among them – i.e. that shout which an expecting multitude send forth at the first sight of the Royal Chariot and Army beheld in the distance' [N.44, f.57v].

There is in man that which is stimulated into existence by the sense of obscurity and mystery. The final and proper object of this instinct is the hope of meeting with the Redeemer; but such is man's unwillingness to think about his own emotions and their origin, that he would rather fit them to any object of his *senses* than admit that their proper object is beyond such apprehension. Coleridge develops this theme further on in *The Friend*; he speaks of the duty of our habituating our intellect 'to clear, distinct, and adequate conceptions concerning all things that are the possible objects of clear conception' so that the deep feelings that have a necessary tendency to combine with ideas – 'ideas that are necessary to the moral perfection of the human being' – may be reserved 'for objects, which their very sublimity renders indefinite, no less than their indefiniteness renders them sublime: namely, . . . the Ideas of Being, Form, Life, the Reason, the Law of Conscience, Freedom, Immortality, God!' Coleridge reminds us that to connect these words, signifying immaterial and permanent things – the ideas of Reason – and the obscure emotions they evoke in us, with objects of the senses 'is profanation relatively to the heart, and superstition in the understanding' [F I 106].

What we must continue to hold in mind is Coleridge's demonstration that this mistaken adulation arises out of the rightly-working heart, for such a person is seeking his life in the life and appearance of a being outside him. The mistake in this case has been a too hurried going forth towards objects inadequate to those instincts or unconscious ideas; it is the act of the emotionally and intellectually immature. The effort Coleridge is asking his readers to make, or those who are tempted to feel as the crowd felt on seeing the Queen of Prussia, is an exact parallel to the effort he was at the time making to free himself from his devotion to

Wordsworth and Sara Hutchinson. To love the Redeemer in every person is good and fitting, but to love a man or a woman as a Redeemer is idolatry.

Coleridge's life-long effort to persuade his contemporaries of the validity and importance of his distinction between Reason and Understanding was in part motivated by his need to convince others that the mind may find objects which are not evident to the senses, and that these objects or ideas are constitutive of our humanity. Because the ideas of Reason are immaterial and invisible, it is only through the act of conscience that they can be realized.

The gift of Reason is that which distinguishes man from the animals – and not his more developed intelligence or understanding, which in kind, though not in degree, he shares with many of the lower orders of creation.[20] Reason is nowhere evident other than in man, and this belief prevented Coleridge from being a full-blown evolutionist; in his *Theory of Life* he did accept and utilize the idea of development of form from primitive to complex, and gave no credence to any absolute distinction between the life of stones, plants or animals. Reason is thus the divine spark that humanizes the animal man – 'the best and holiest gift of Heaven and bond of union with the Giver!' [F I 190]. It follows that this gift is given equally to all men, or else we would have to accept that God makes some men more human than others. Coleridge would not allow this and asserts that 'The primary powers of the Soul are in *all* men the same alike – these a principiis specie'. What distinguishes men are powers related to the Understanding such as 'Talent, Wit, Memory etc. a principiis individui' [CN II 3032].

Reason is therefore the source of the bond between man and man as human beings, and it is to the Reason that every leader of men must appeal if he is to create a human society, or achieve distinctly human ends. If we do not recognize this power of God within us, we will either, as individuals, sink into a state of bestiality, destroying our conscience by a determined and continuous ignoring of it, or worse, rise into tyrants, like Iago or Napoleon. Such men, without concern for the essential humanity of their fellow beings, treat them solely as instruments for their own ambition, ignoring what Coleridge thought of as the sacred distinction between things and persons, upon which all true State-wisdom depends. Since every human being is born with Reason, any being without it, whatever their external form, can only be a thing, and not a person. Only things can be used instrumentally; any proposed action that involves a person or people must accrue some benefit to them *as* people: they cannot be considered solely as means and not included as part of the final cause [F I 190].[21]

In contrast to the harassers and hunters of mankind, Coleridge's prime example of a governor of men was Sir Alexander Ball. He was able to weld a band of mutinous men into a contented crew, because he believed 'that no body of men can for any length of time be safely treated otherwise than as rational beings' [F I 540]. The men had allowed their calibanistic understandings to usurp their Reason, and though they had been treated with the greatest severity by their previous commander, this had merely changed the open violence 'into secret plots and conspiracies' [F I 169]. In order to re-establish Reason as the basis of his ship's community, Sir Alexander Ball instituted the rule of Law, which Coleridge calls an 'aweful power . . . acting on natures pre-figured to its influences'. How close this rule of Law is to Reason in Coleridge's mind is clear in the continuation of the passage:

> A Faculty was appealed to in the Offender's own being; a Faculty and a Presence, of which he had not been previously made aware – but it *answered* to the appeal! its real existence therefore could not be doubted, or its reply rendered inaudible! and the very struggle of the wilder passions to keep uppermost counter-acted its own purpose, by wasting in internal contest that energy, which before had acted in its entireness on external resistance or provocation . . . But who dares struggle with an *invisible* combatant? . . . – the more I strive to subdue it, the more I am compelled to think of it – and the more I think of it, the more do I find it to possess a reality out of myself, and not to be a phantom of my imagination; that all, but the most abandoned men, acknowledge its authority, and that the whole strength and majesty of my country are pledged to support it and yet that *for me* its power is the same with that of my own permanent Self, and that all the choice, which is permitted to me, consists in having it for my Guardian Angel or my avenging Fiend! This is the Spirit of LAW! [F I 171]

In enforcing the rule of Law, Sir Alexander Ball had re-asserted the ideal order by which every man must govern himself – for 'from [man's] creation the objects of his senses were to become

his subjects' [Ibid]. Each man knew that he must find his life in
the life of the ship; each looked to an order of existence outside
himself to which he was bound, but which also gave him his
being. This act was symbolic of that by which a state itself is
created out of a heterogeneous collection of people.[22] In his lectures on Shakespeare we have seen that Coleridge believed that
without that devotion to another as oneself which constitutes the
act of conscience, and is grounded in Reason, we may exist as a
herd, but not as a society. So part of his paean to Reason in *The
Friend* runs: 'To thee, who being one art the same in all, we owe
the privilege, that of all we can become one, a living *whole*! that
we have a COUNTRY!' [F I 191]

Any form of government which is not co-incident with the
Reason in man 'disennobles our nature, leagues itself with the
animal against the god-like . . . and fights against humanity'
[Ibid]. Therefore the principles of government, the means by
which heterogeneous individuals are made into a homogeneous
society, must be in harmony with the ideas of Reason. But this
does not mean that every government must be based solely and
absolutely on these ideas. For if we construct a society 'according
to archetypal ideas co-essential with the Reason' then 'as there is
but one system of Geometry, so according to this theory there can
be but one constitution and one system of legislation . . . What is
not *every where* necessary [will be] *no where* right' [F I 178]. Coleridge believes that by having stated what is in essence Rousseau's
system so forthrightly, he has thus demonstrated its absurdity.
He seeks to demonstrate the proper relation between Reason and
Understanding in construction of a constitution by reference to
that of the Israelites: the main office of a rightful government

> is to regulate the outward actions of particular bodies of men,
> according to particular circumstances . . . Can we hope better
> of constitutions formed by ourselves, than of that which was
> given by Almighty Wisdom itself? The laws of the Hebrew Com-
> monwealth, which flowed from the pure Reason remain and are
> immutable; but the regulations dictated by Prudence, though by
> the Divine prudence . . . have passed away; and while they
> lasted, were binding only for that one state, the particular cir-
> cumstances of which rendered them expedient. [F I 194–5]

Government is thus by the Understanding in co-incidence with ideas of Reason.[23] And just as the Understanding cannot usurp the Reason in the individual without a deterioration of moral character, one aspect of which we saw vividly portrayed in Christabel, so in political terms, a government of pure expedience, uncontrolled by reason, would lead to a rapid decline in the moral character of the nation. The order of proper government must of course first exist in the governors, an opinion of Coleridge's coincident with that of Berkeley: *'And whatever the world may opine he who hath not much meditated upon God, the Human Mind, and the Summum Bonum, may possibly make a thriving Earth-worm, but will most indubitably make a blundering Patriot and a sorry statesman'* [F 113]. In a notebook entry Coleridge wonders whether a nation of depraved individuals is a possibility: only, he thinks, 'under the condition of a previous religious Apostacy' [N.36, p.106–8] Religion is Reason in its practical form, and abandoned, he fears that the sexual instinct will dominate the individual, as it temporarily was to dominate Christabel. Under such conditions all true individuality is destroyed and the human species becomes 'but a repetition of the simple animal repeated indefinitely . . . Frightful perversion!' The truly human is lost as it bethings itself in its desires.

But though the ultimate ends of government must be co-incident with the ideas of Reason, its immediate purposes neither serve nor are ordered by them. Men first got together to protect their property, and this Coleridge consistently makes the basis of government.[24] The society created under the auspices of this immediate purpose is not an adequate reflection of man in his full humanity. The mere Understanding, unillumined by Reason, will tend to seek wrong ends, or find ends in what are properly only means. It may be argued therefore, that society of itself reflects the prepossessions of man in his unillumined and unredeemed state – and those who are guided by Reason will always do battle against the causes and effects of this condition. Man has a dual allegiance – on the one hand to seek to obey the dictates of his Reason in all their purity, and on the other to recognize his membership of a society composed of laws which give it its peculiar being. Prospero did not at first get this balance right, and consequently his power was usurped, and his Reason rendered impotent through his exile. This polarization of the individual and his allegiances is integral to Coleridge's thinking: that there is in man something not of this world, but vital to the regulation of his hopes and conduct here was one of his master thoughts, and is behind two further distinctions he makes in *The Friend*.[25]

While writing on libel, there is one maxim that he is tempted to seize as it passes across him. It is a very old truth,

> and yet if the fashion of action in apparent ignorance thereof be any presumption of its novelty, it ought to be new, or at least to have become so by courtesy of oblivion. It is this: that . . . Law and Religion should be kept distinct. THERE IS, strictly speaking, NO PROPER OPPOSITION BUT BETWEEN THE TWO POLAR FORCES OF ONE AND THE SAME POWER. I if I say then, that Law and Religion are natural *opposites* . . . let it not be interpreted, as if I had declared them to be *contraries*. [F I 94]

(The 'spirit of Law', or that which a man finds in and of himself and which Coleridge used of Sir Alexander Ball's command of his ship, is to be distinguished from 'Law' as used here, which refers to the regulations of the State.) Because Law and Religion are opposites and not contraries they are able to interact, and produce a condition, a synthesis, which represents the original power. Coleridge gives two examples, of how they should, and how they should not, interact. What the Law has made possible, that is, a creditor arresting a debtor, it does not necessarily command. Religion on the other hand, because all true Christians must regard their neighbour as their proper self, may positively command that the arrest is *not* made. Out of the constant opposition of these two forces, a third and different state arises which we call 'society'. And as long as these two forces are in a properly balanced opposition, society is healthy. But if one is usurped in the name of the other, as Religion usurped the aims of the Law in the Spanish Inquisition, then what belongs to the conscience of the individual is examined with the instruments of law, and imputed moral guilt is punished as a crime committed. On the other hand, Coleridge felt that the reverse was happening in his own day – and that no guilt was assignable unless a crime *had* been committed: a state of mind that allows us to make such commonplace statements as, 'I do no wrong unless I hurt somebody'.

In the 'Essays on Method' added to *The Friend* as a result of the rifaccimento, Coleridge makes a parallel distinction to that between Law and Religion:

As there are two wants connatural to man, so there are two
main directions of human activity, pervading, in modern times
the whole civilized world; and constituting and sustaining the
nationality which yet it is their tendency, and, more or less,
their *effect*, to transcend and moderate – Trade and Literature.
[F I 507]

The activity of trade, by which man satisfies his physical wants of
food, housing, clothing, and, in a civilized world, the multitude
of refinements that these bring with them, is enabled by his
considerable powers of understanding, and carried out under the
aegis of laws designed, in large part, to encourage, facilitate and
regulate this activity. Literature, on the other hand, as we have
seen in Coleridge's studies of Shakespeare, discovers the principles of its creation not in the laws of the land, but in the ideas
of Reason: it is therefore a reflection of man's spiritual needs and
contiguous with his Religion. And as one feature of society is the
balanced opposition of Religion and Law, so another is the proper
opposition of Trade and Literature. Yet both these may transcend
the national boundaries created by their interaction: trade because
its habits, customs and regulations must be adapted to the trading
patterns of other states; and literature, because it arises out of the
principles of human nature, will be of significance to all those men
and nations who wish to know more of themselves. Trade and
Literature are the two forces of one power, or one idea, which
Coleridge here calls the nationality: he uses this term more precisely in *On the Constitution of Church and State*, but in this instance
I take it to mean the social organization of a country or people. If
such a nation or state thinks of itself solely as a trading entity, it
ceases to be a whole, and becomes an aggregate of individuals
pursuing material needs, and subject to the sorcery of wealth. If
on the other hand a nation were to pursue none but literary or
religious ends, and took no care to preserve a local habitation
where to have its being, it would risk being usurped from within
or without, like Prospero, by those hungry for land and power. It
would not have the strength to defend itself from a material
aggressor, and would lose the title of nation.

It is my purpose to show that Coleridge's idea of the institutional
structure of the nation correspond with his idea of how human
beings are constituted – that the nation or state represents a type
of 'other' which is self. Although Coleridge was wary of the anal-

ogy by which he set some store – 'the problem is so complicated . . . as to render it nearly impossible to lay down rules for the formation of a state' – yet he wrote in *The Statesman's Manual* that the 'perfect frame of a man is the perfect frame of a state' [SM 62]. In a note on 'Richard II' he amplified this idea:

> Plato's Republic is like Bunyan's Town of Man-Soul, – a description of an individual, all of whose faculties are in proper subordination and interdependence; and this it is assumed may be the prototype of the state as one great individual. [SC 268]

The 'sophism' of Plato's *Republic* is that no individual is ever composed of merely one faculty, and therefore 'you could never get chiefs who were wholly reason, ministers who were wholly understanding, soldiers all wrath, labourers all concupiscence . . .' But Coleridge pursues his analogy on a more fundamental level. The faculties of Reason, Religion and the Will, he considers symbolic of a tri-unity which exists in the State as the Legislative, Executive and Ministerial powers respectively. Just as in the individual, Reason disjoined from Religion will deify all that the individual is, his understanding and his appetites, so Reason as Legislative power unmodified by Religion 'becomes mere visionariness in *intellect*, and indolence or hard-heartedness in *morals*'. It gives rise to the Jacobinism of the French revolution, 'which would sacrifice each to the shadowy idol of ALL', and is made up 'in part of despotism, and in part of abstract reason misapplied to objects that belong entirely to experience and understanding' [SM 63–4]. On the other hand, a Religion unenlightened by the universal truths of Reason, the executive separated from the legislative power, 'changes its being into Superstition, and . . . goes wandering at length with its pack of amulets, bead-rolls, periapts, fetisches and the like pedlary, on pilgrimages to Loretto, Mecca, or the temple of Jaggernaut, arm in arm with sensuality on one side and self-torture on the other'.

Reason and Religion, the Legislature and the Executive, may co-exist in the individual and the state respectively, only insofar as they are actuated by the Will or the 'sustaining, coercive and ministerial power . . . the officers of war and police in the ideal Republic of Plato' [SM 65]. Where it is 'co-adunated' with Reason and Religion, the Will appears in the individual as wisdom or love; but in separation from these it 'becomes satanic pride and rebellious self-idolatry in the relations of the spirit to itself, and remorseless despotism relatively to others' and gives birth to such harassers and hunters of mankind as Nimrod, Iago and Napoleon.

As we might expect, the last word that Coleridge considers in relation to Reason, Religion and the Will is Conscience. This is none of the three, 'but an *experience* (sui generis) of the coincidence of the human will with reason and religion' [SM 66]. We have seen that the act of conscience creates the ideas of our being in our love of another: the ideas of reason are united to the forms of being by an act of love. When the forms of the Understanding, or Religion, are enlightened by the ideas of Reason, a *person* is disclosed, a person simultaneously other and self. But a distinction of these powers, a recognition of their opposing qualities, is absolutely necessary before any kind of synthesis can take place. To maintain this distinction in the institutional life of the country had been Coleridge's purpose in opposing Religion and Law, Literature and Trade. I think we may also see this distinction of powers in Coleridge's final and conclusive distinction of Church and State.

THE CHURCH AND THE STATE

These are studied according to the *idea* of each, and as ideas are known by their ultimate aims, this supposes that each has a different aim or end. But before I attempt to distinguish these aims, it is worth bearing in mind that to each of these words Coleridge ascribed two meanings. Thus the Church on the one hand may refer to the National Church, which is not primarily a religious institution, and on the other to the Christian Church (a title with various synonyms which Coleridge uses to define its nature and function as closely as possible.) The State may either refer to the civil organization of the people, the body politic; or to that entity which is created from the resolution of the opposing forces of the National Church and the civil State, and which Coleridge sometimes but inconsistently calls the nation. It is the idea of the National Church and the idea of the civil State which I wish to elucidate first, before developing their relation to the Christian Church and to the Nation.

Although Coleridge seeks to define these words according to the idea, avoiding the inevitable defects of their historical realiz-

ation, in fact he moves, in John Colmer's words,[26] uneasily
between the two, and as one absorbs Coleridge's analysis, it is
clear that historical antecedents inform his thought quite as much
as ideal relations. His clearest distinction between the idea of a
state and the idea of a church occurs not in this essay but in a
notebook, where he writes,

> The proper object of a State is *Things*, the permanent *interests*
> that continue in the flux of its component Citizens, hence a
> distinction & if I might say so, a polarisation of ranks and orders
> is the very condition of its existence – while the proper Object
> of a Church is Persons, and no other than personal difference,
> intellectual and moral. The aim of the first, i.e. of a State is to
> preserve and defend the difference between the integral parts of
> its total Body, by establishing and watching over the differential
> grounds, & causes, and exponents of the difference – the aim
> of a Church utterly to do away even those personal differences,
> which it acknowledges, and of which it makes use – the com-
> paratively wise to equalise wisdom, the comparatively Good to
> diffuse the Good. [N44, f.75–6]

The distinction between Persons and Things informs all Coleridge's mature thinking, and as we have seen provides a principle
for the proper ends of government. Having established what we
might call the ideal distinction between Church and State, we can
now turn to the more historical analysis of Coleridge's last published work.

Taking the civil State first, how has the 'polarisation of ranks
and orders' been effected in 'every country of civilized men,
acknowledging the rights of property, and by . . . common laws
united into one people or nation'? [CS 24]. Coleridge's answer is
that 'the two . . . opposite interests of the state, under which all
other state interests are comprised, are those of PERMANENCE and
of PROGRESSION' [Ibid.].

The forms of permanence derive from the holding of land, and
Coleridge divides this class of citizen into two – Major and Minor
Barons, the latter also entitled Franklins. The acme of social progression being the possession of land, it is inevitable, in this
theory, that the forces of progression, or the manufacturing, mer-
cantile, distributive and professional classes have one ultimate
aim: 'To found a family, and to convert his wealth into land, are

twin thoughts, births of the same moment, in the mind of the opulent merchant, when he thinks of retiring from his labours' [CS 24–5]. The balance between these opposing interests is struck in the Houses of Parliament, with the Franklins and the representatives of progression in the lower House, and the Major Barons in the upper House.

That, very briefly, is Coleridge's understanding of the organization of the State, with its distinctions of wealth, rank and individual capacity. Set in opposition to it is the National Church, and its concern with persons rather than things. The object of this institution is 'to secure and improve that civilization, without which the nation could be neither permanent nor progressive' [CS 44]. Rightly managed, civilization is grounded in *'cultivation*, in the harmonious development of those qualities and faculties that characterise our *humanity'* [CS 43]. In these terms, the National Church is no church at all, and to illuminate his thinking Coleridge modifies the etymological significance of a Greek word: a church proper he defines as an 'ecclesia, the communion of such as are called out of the world' in order to pursue the particular ends of that communion [CS 45]. But the National Church, improperly styled a church, is an institution for which he coins the word *enclesia*, 'an order of men, chosen in and of the realm, and constituting an estate of that realm' [Ibid.].

That the National Church should have religious connotations is right and proper from Coleridge's point of view. There is an essential continuity between the cultivation of our humanity and our recognition of the truth of religious doctrines – especially those of Christianity – because both have their resting place in Reason, the supernatural and the God-like in us. The processes by which we may realize the ideas of Reason are at one and the same time the ways in which we develop our potential humanity, and a progress towards the recognition of self as other, the ultimate end of which is the finding of Christ. Nonetheless, Coleridge thought that it was both possible and necessary to distinguish between the process of cultivation, which will lead towards the understanding of religious truth, and the adoption of those truths by the free will. Therefore 'religion may be an indispensable ally, but is not the essential constitutive end' [CS 45] of the National Church. The relation between this church and the Church of Christ Coleridge called 'a blessed accident, a providential boon, a grace of God, a mighty and faithful friend' [CS 55], but insisted that the National Church is not an instrument by which the laws and aims of the Church of Christ are to be administered and promoted.

The officers of the National Church Coleridge entitled the Clerisy, in order to distinguish them from those with a specifically religious function – the Clergy. In effect the Clerisy is the body of learned people in the kingdom, and of course this body *includes* the Clergy. Although the functions of these two groups may ultimately be distinguished, yet in practice they work together 'in preserving, continuing and perfecting, the necessary sources and conditions of national civilization' [CS 53]. Because their functions are complementary, the 'two distinct functions do not necessarily imply or require two different functionaries. Nay, the perfection of each may require the union of both in the same person' [CS 57]. And Coleridge was profoundly disturbed by the prospect of their separation, with the consequent reduction, in John Colmer's words, 'of the National Church to the status of a sect' [CS 57].

How was the National Church to be maintained? Coleridge answered this question historically: 'it was . . . common to all the primitive races, that in taking possession of a new country, and in the division of the land into hereditable estates . . . a reserve should be made for the nation itself' [CS 35]. This is, of course, the tenth or tithe that the Hebrews gave to one of their tribes, the Levites. The English version of the system was, to Coleridge's concern, very much under pressure when he wrote, and was the subject of legislation in the General Registration Act of 1836, under the title 'The Commutation of Tithes'. Coleridge resisted the kind of political pressure that eventually brought this act into being, and though this might be cited as an example of his later reactionary attitudes, yet the failure to provide the National Church with an independent source of revenue has had substantial reverberations in our national life, the significance of which is perhaps more disturbing to us now than at any previous time. Coleridge's idea, as opposed to the outmoded practice of tithe-collection, may therefore still provide us with a method of understanding both the problem and the consequences of the proposed solutions.

In respect of the land under the control of a people or nation Coleridge entitled 'the sum total of these heritable portions' the Propriety; and the tenth reserved for the nation he termed the Nationalty [CS 35]. These two terms were, of course, in opposition, obeying Coleridge's belief in the universal law of polarity, and to describe the whole of which they composed the distinct powers he employed the term Commonwealth. Since this scheme essentially describes a division of land, it appears to relate solely to the forms of permanence within a nation, and the forces of progression seem to have no duties in respect of the nationality. However, before developing his idea of the Christian Church, Coleridge makes a brief recapitulation of his scheme. There he calls the possessions of both orders the Proprietage of the Realm [CS 108]. He then opposed the Nationalty to the Proprietage, as he had earlier opposed it to the Propriety, adding that he did so 'in the same antithesis and conjunction I use and understand the phrase CHURCH and STATE'. This leaves us with a choice of terms, but no clearer notion of what is due from the forces of progression in support of the Nationalty. It is possible that the ancient connection between land and church, in the form of tithes, going back to the reformations of Theodore in the 7th century was, even in the middle of the 19th century, so imbued in the English mind, that Coleridge had not realized that the basis of national wealth was rapidly shifting from agriculture to manufacturing, and therefore that his idea of Nationalty would have to be refounded.[27]

But this is a practical question, which need not be detrimental to the principle or idea. The main question is, What is the Nationalty to support? In discussing Henry VIII's misappropriations, Coleridge makes his answer clear: it has been

> consecrated [to the indwelling God], to the potential divinity in every man, which is the ground and condition of his *civil* existence, that without which a man can be neither free nor obliged, and by which alone, therefore, he is capable of being a free subject – a citizen. [CS 52]

The nationalty has been given to foster the powers of Reason in man, in order that these may combine with the powers of Understanding and so create a free citizen. Two pages later Coleridge sums up his opinions: 'The proper *object* and end of the National Church is civilization with freedom' [CS 54]. The next question is, How is this end to be achieved? Again, what Henry VIII ought to have done provides Coleridge with his answer: the Nationalty should have been distributed

in proportionate channels, to the maintenance, – 1, Of universities and the great schools of learning: 2, Of a pastor, presbyter or *parson* in every parish: 3, Of a school-master in every parish, who in due time, and under condition of a faithful performance of his arduous duties, should succeed to the pastorate; [CS 52–3]

Though it may be difficult for us now to accept that every diligent schoolmaster – and mistress – should see their hope and reward in the form of elevation to the clergy, this pattern of progression is entirely consistent with Coleridge's belief that the study or practice of the arts will lead towards religious belief: for what is essentially human in us, and is the object of such study, is *supernatural*, belonging to an order not available to sense.

Coleridge's scheme is not now practicable, but what we must constantly bear in mind when considering the permanent value of his thought, is the principle that underlies his propositions. In making the National Church an estate of the realm, opposed to the two other estates of Permanence and Progression, which combined to form the state in its more limited sense, Coleridge was keeping, in his day, and for us, taking, education out of the hands of the government.

It is, I suppose, a question as to whether the National Church has in fact ever existed. The term conveys a uniformity of function which is difficult to trace in the records of English history. On the other hand, it is equally clear that in all but the last hundred odd years (and Coleridge died a century and a half ago) the funding for arts, education and the church has come from sources that are independent of government. The question that we should ask ourselves in relation to Coleridge's idea is whether such a body as the National Church might be brought into existence, say, by taking the Arts Council and the Department of Education out of the hands of government, uniting these with the Church of England and representatives of other churches, so creating one body with a brief to educate rather than train, and with an inalienable source of income. Difficult though this would be to achieve, it might eradicate some of the deficiencies in our national life and educational aims that Coleridge foresaw.

Though there is much reasonable dissatisfaction with the management of education in this country, we are so accustomed to think of education as a government responsibility, that it comes as a novel and disquieting thought to many to suppose that it might be lodged in someone else's hands. Yet the cause of one of

our deepest worries is clearly defined in Coleridge's understanding of the role of the State: it is primarily concerned with Things
and not with Persons, with the material requirements of the various ranks and orders of society, and not with what unites person
to person, the God-given humanity which has its origin and its
field of action in distinction from nature and all natural needs.
However much it may seek to disguise its objectives (usually in
platitudes not so much truths bed-ridden in the dormitory of
government souls, as corpses frozen in the Whitehall mortuary) by
its very nature a government will be concerned with the training of
individuals in order to fulfill a perceived function in the economy
of the state, so making the trainees (and this is indeed a 'vile
phrase') 'useful members of society'. No one doubts the necessity
of acquiring a skill in order that they may find a job, and so support
themselves and their dependants. St Paul supported himself, at
least in some part of his life, by making fishing nets. But if the
import of his letters rested in the individual economic independence which he advocated, who (bar the Cabinet), would read
them now, and what would have become of Christianity? The
objection is not to the necessity which almost all admit, and which
it is the proper business of government to regulate, but to the
spectacle of the state seeming to determine the aim and end of
our peculiarly *human* and social life: criteria such as 'usefulness'
are essentially dehumanizing, as if a person were a thing to be
employed, discarded, or modified according to their utility.
Because the government is the only source of systematic action in
relation to education, and any debate must revolve around such
proposals as it deems fit to put forward, public thinking is necessarily dominated, if not controlled, by the notions that form the
ground of government action. Therefore it is inevitable that materi-
alistic and mechanical conceptions will command government
policy, and though this may be appropriate, say, in the regulation
of the economy, it is wholly inappropriate when we are seeking
ways of educing the potential human being in every person, fostering the seed of Reason that God has planted but has left us to
water; and this, the only real form of education, though it may
happen concurrently with a necessary training (Coleridge was one
of the first to make this distinction [CS 48 n.2]) is very likely to be
in some measure opposed to it, and therefore subversive of those
aims and objectives that unchecked the State will proclaim as the
right and adequate end of our existence: goals which are indeed

no goals at all, but mere shimmering mirages ever receding as we approach, hovering ahead of us in vacuous phrases such as 'the standard of living' (the definite article often replaced by a pronoun of possession, as if the impossible, the possession of this *ignis fatuus*, was the possession of *life*!). To all such false gods, before which the self is only the sum of one individual's needs, appetites, desires, interests, hopes, problems and so forth, a *thing* of sense with no before and after, yet demanding as a right that in a free society these needs should be met because such is the road to self-fulfilment, to all this, which leads to the dereliction of our humanity, education, as Coleridge understood the term, will always be opposed, because it teaches that there is no resting place in sense, appearance but no immediate reality, no foundation for life, that the laws of our humanity are ideas, or truth-powers, as Coleridge called them, which are in themselves free of time and place, and bring life to our lives when they order our apprehension of the world which we have been given to inhabit, and our relations with those with whom we share it. But how can this necessary opposition come forth from a state government, from the moulds of an institution that operates upon other and alien principles? It cannot, and Coleridge set the National Church in opposition to the State, in order that the larger State or Nation may have a properly ordered constitution.

Prophecy, as opposed to prediction, is the enunciation of an idea that yet awaits the circumstances of its realization [cf. CN III 3365]. In this sense Coleridge's writing on the Church of England has proved both prophetic and prescient. In a chapter of 'Regrets and Apprehensions' he outlines what he fears will happen as a consequence of the 'Spoliation of the Nationalty' – when the National Church, once believed to be an estate of the realm, is now distinguished from other existing churches 'by having its priesthood *endowed*, durante bene placito, by favour of the legislature – that is, of the majority, for the time being, of the two Houses of Parliament' [CS 61–3].

Coleridge's enumeration of the consequences of this spoliation of the National Church, is an indictment both of the condition of our society and of some of its objectives. Firstly, 'National Education (is) to be finally sundered from all religion' so as to become 'synonimous with Instruction' [CS 62]. The purpose of knowledge will thus be to give a person 'the power of doing what he wishes in order to obtain what he desires', and since all such knowledge is 'derived from the Senses', all subjects will be taught empirically, as 'the closer men are kept to the fountain head, the *knowinger* they must become'. By being separated from religion, education becomes reified, centred on things; and emphasizing man's control of and understanding of things, whether of nature or of his own construction, the individual's relation with his world becomes one of use: he seeks to satisfy either his own perceived needs, or those of the group of people to whom he belongs – society being too good a word for this form of collective existence. And it will be the tendency of a government system of so-called education to become dedicated to the satisfying of the various kinds of demand that this organization creates, with a concomitant tendency to channel its revenue to that end. This will inevitably restrict non-utilitarian research, and effectively make academic freedom, or the freedom to find, ennoble and enrich our humanity, a tag-phrase of little or no real value.

Secondly, the poor will be 'withdrawn from the discipline of the church'. The significance of this is a complex matter, involving the Poor Laws, from the allowances of which agricultural workers were for a time paid – the consequence of enclosure and the growth of large estates, and created by the 'new rich men' whose factories were made up 'of the wretchedness, disease and depravity of those who should constitute the strength of the nation' [CS 61–3]. Because of, on the one hand, what Coleridge called 'the disjunction of the Poor Laws from the Church' [CS 61 n.4], that is, the administration of the relief of poverty by a body other than the Church, and on the other the historical clinging of the Church to court and state since the Reformation, so allowing 'the hearts of the common people (to) be stolen from it [TT 8 Sept. 1830] the Church was to all intents failing to reach the majority of the population. By contrast, Coleridge felt that the Roman Catholic Church had always kept in touch with the people, and was therefore, in one respect, doing its proper job – mediating 'between the people and the government, between the poor and the rich' [Ibid.]. Any Anglican church-goer nowadays knows the burden of this inheritance: even the inner city parishes have a predominantly middle class congregation, unrepresentative of the local population. Large groups of people in our society, that have come into being since the Industrial Revolution, have never known the language of the Church, and this is in part due to the sundering of national education from all religion, and tacit encouragement by the state to see progress in life in terms of the quantity and quality of possessions; but it is equally true that the Church has never found a language with which to address these people – has never met them on the grounds of their experience.

The third consequence of the spoliation of the National Church, with the consequent lack of encouragement to see life as other than a series of material impulses, is the degeneration of the term *idea*, a state of affairs that despite his serious purpose, Coleridge has some fun with:

> Dr HOLOFERNES, in a lecture on metaphysics, delivered at one of the Mechanics' Institutions, explodes all *ideas* but those of sensation; and his friend, DEPUTY COSTARD, has no *idea* of a better flavored haunch of venison, than he dined off at the London Tavern last week. [CS 66]

Coleridge's heroes before the Restoration of 1660 were able to discourse on 'the IDEAS of Will, God, Freedom' [CS 64–5], on the idea of the beautiful and on the idea of the state and its relation with the individual; but subsequently all these great, Platonic ideas have been materialized by the philosophy of Locke and his followers, with the result that man is seen as an up-market ape,[28] whose natural rights and desires are placed above his duties and privileges as a citizen. And in this philosophy, just as things dominate the life of the ordinary person, so facts dominate the life of the intellectual: the supposition is entirely lost that ideas are not a generic abstraction from a number of facts or things (properly entitled conceptions) but are genuine and self-subsisting powers. Therefore facts uninterpreted by ideas are claimed as historical proofs, and take the place of ideas or principles in the life of the nation; state policy thus becomes a matter of material expedience, and not an attempt to guide the nation so that our political world becomes a reflection of our humanity. Thus 'the true historical feeling, the immortal life of an historical Nation, generation linked to generation by faith, freedom, heraldry, and ancestral fame (languish), and give place to the superstitions of wealth, and newspaper reputation' [CS 67, cf. F II 447].

What Coleridge here calls the 'despotism of finance in government and legislation', and the foolish equation of the health of the nation with the health of the economy, a perversion of the term common wealth from its original meaning of common weal or

well-being, is epitomized in our day by the frequent description
of this country as 'Great Britain plc' – half in jest perhaps, but too
near by half to the truth of common conception. The disease
Coleridge saw developing in his day rages amongst us with all
the appearance of life, but in reality the heat and energy thus
generated are but symptoms of the killing fever. Commenting on
Proverbs I 18–19, Coleridge wrote:

> Those engaged in making advantage of their neighbour, from
> the Thief to the Stock Jobber and a rapacious Attorney, lay wait
> for their own lives. 'So are the ways of every one that is greedy
> of Gain, which taketh away the life of the owners thereof.' O
> how is this verified in the present dedication of all ranks from
> cradle to coffin to the fiend Mammon, and the fiend-hag, Anx-
> iety! It has taken away the *Life* of England, and put a bustling
> drudging Death in its place. The men are corpses: while the
> Charnel-house, the dry Bones, are dancing and eddying like the
> fallen leaves with which the Gust of November strikes up a
> mockery of Life. [N.36, p.134]

If the true objects or ideas of man's moral and spiritual being are
rendered remote or incredible, and because no one can entirely
delude themselves into accepting their non-existence, or as Browning's Blougram points out, faith troubled by doubt can only be
exchanged for scepticism troubled by faith, then, like the controversy surrounding the sacrament, man will degrade the spiritual
into an image, and believe the image to possess spiritual powers:
it was in this frame of mind that the crowd watched the arrival of
the Queen of Prussia at Hardenberg House [F I 36], giving 'to the
spirit the attributes of the body, and . . . to the body the attributes
of the spirit' [PL 268], thus making an image real, and confounding
the notices of their senses with substantial and permanent truths.

To this degradation, and the associated getting and spending
by which we lay waste our lives, there is but one remedy, though
that remedy has several forms. Coleridge set down the formula in
the second of this two *Lay Sermons*: 'An excess in our attachment
to temporal and personal objects can be counteracted only by
a pre-occupation of the intellect and affections with permanent,
universal, and eternal truths' [LS 173]. Or in other words the only
preventative against the tyranny of the Understanding, which
results in 'Talents without genius: a swarm of clever, well-infor-

med men: an anarchy of minds, a despotism of maxims' [CS 67], is its integration with the ideas or truths of Reason. These truths or powers are continuous with the ultimate ends of human life, and enable us to contemplate our relations with the life which precedes and succeeds us, and which offers us a vision of freedom from some of the limitations of our mortality. And without a vision of this kind, we cannot be an historical people, only a succession of separate lives feeding upon the economy. Coleridge consequently set much store by the Proverb, 'Where there is no vision, the people perish' (Proverbs 29.18) and closely associated it with his distinction between Reason and Understanding [CS 58].

The truths of Reason, the powers of vision, are available to us in two principal ways – through the arts, and through religion. They have in common the presentation of the universal in terms of the particular or individual [SM 62], or in other words they present the ideas of Reason in the terms of the Understanding. This life is therefore the ground and source of the unity of the nation considered historically ('God is the unity of every nation' [CS 40]) and because Hebrew history is a model for all national histories, Coleridge believes that 'the morality which the state requires in its citizens for its own well-being and ideal immortality . . . can only exist for the people in the form of religion' [CS 69]. Though a sound, or Platonic, philosophy must form the basis of religious instruction, for a 'hunger-bitten and idea-less philosophy naturally produces a starveling and comfortless religion' [SM 30], the philosophy itself is neither available nor necessary to the majority of the population. Therefore Coleridge concludes that 'Religion, true or false, is and ever has been the centre of gravity in a realm, to which all other things must and will accommodate themselves' [CS 70].

THE IDEA OF THE CHRISTIAN CHURCH

If religion is the recognition that the supernatural in man is the ground and source of his humanity, and if religious practice is the loosening of his being from the shackles of sense, and rebinding it to the immaterial and invisible powers that he finds within himself, then the forms of and the methods to this common end are what distinguish one religion from another; and in respect of one's own beliefs, make one true and another false.

For Coleridge, Christianity was, of course, the one true religion, as it was true psychology and true philosophy, the other religions with which he was acquainted, chiefly Islam and Hinduism, being but partial refractions of its whole truth. But to talk about the Christian Church, especially the Christian Church in England, is not synonymous with talking about Christianity, and Coleridge distinguishes the two at the outset. The grandeur of his idea of Christianity is evident in the distinction: it is, he believes, 'the great redemptive process which began in the separation of light from Chaos . . . and has its end in the union of life with God' [CS 113]. But the Christian *Church*, which is primarily the earthly advocate of Christ's invisible and supernatural presence, and not a school of philosophy, Coleridge seeks to define only so as to distinguish it from the National Church.

Firstly, the Christian Church is not a 'state, kingdom, or realm of this world', nor an estate within any of these: 'but it is the appointed Opposite to them all *collectively* – the *sustaining, correcting, befriending* Opposite of the World!' [CS 114]. But he also believes that it acts as a focus for whatever is 'beneficient and humanizing in the aims, tendencies, and proper objects of the state' in order 'to radiate them back in a higher quality'; and he supposes that the Christian Church will complete and strengthen 'the edifice of the state . . . in the mere act of laying and securing its own foundations'. For these services, Coleridge continues, 'the Church of Christ asks of the state neither wages nor dignities. She asks only protection, and *to be let alone*'. And he asserts that the Christian Church asks nothing for its members that they are not already entitled to as citizens [CS 115–6].

If the first characteristic of the Christian Church is that it is not of this world, the second is that nonetheless it is a visible and public institution – 'visible and militant under Christ'. It is not a secret community, and has an existence that Coleridge calls 'objective', that is, it does not exist simply as a function of individual conscience, or as 'the kingdom of God which is *within*'. It is in fact 'a city built on a hill, and not to be hid' [CS 116].

The third characteristic Coleridge believes reconciles the first two. Whereas the National Church has the nationalty entrusted to its charge, and has a visible head and hierarchy, the Christian Church has neither, and so is marked by 'the utter preclusion of any local or personal centre of unity, of any single source of universal power' [CS 118]. It is therefore both visible and not of this world, and the absence even of a representative head should remind the observer both of Christ as the invisible head, and that every particular church is ideally the whole church, in perfect harmony with all other Christian Churches – centres everywhere and an absolute circumference nowhere.

And this leads directly to the Christian Church's fourth character – its universality of Catholicity. 'It is neither Anglican, Gallican, nor Roman, neither Latin nor Greek', and this is in direct contrast with the National Church of a country or state. Thus there is a Church of England, but it is the National Church, and is necessarily distinguished from the 'Catholic and Apostolic church *in* England' [CS 125].

These are the four distinguishing marks of the Christian Church, and I have outlined them before considering some of Coleridge's associated ideas, and some of the problems these now present to us.

Though Coleridge claims the Christian Church as an institution not of this world, and though he asserts that it claims nothing for its members that they do not already have a right to as citizens, yet because it is 'the appointed Opposite' to all States, Kingdoms, realms and estates, which collectively Coleridge calls 'the world', there arises the question of the Church's political rights. It is very unlikely that many States will thank the Church for opposing the 'inevitable evils and defects of the STATE, as a State', or give it unfettered opportunities for doing so [CS 115]. Even the British Constitution, upon which Coleridge modelled his argument, is very far from perfect in this respect. The shadow that hangs over all practical effects of government policy is the Prime Minister's final say in the appointment of bishops and arch-bishops: the frequent assertion by government that the effect of this or that policy is not within the scope of the Church, and that it should confine itself to spiritual matters, is effectively an attempt to prevent the Church speaking out against the evils of the state as a state. It is an attempt to shift the business of the church out of public life and into the private conscience, a reversal of the role that Coleridge believed right and fitting for both National and Christian churches. It seems to me a serious defect in our constitution, that the head of the civil state, the Prime Minister, should have the power to make the final choice of the senior officers of the Church of England, when as functionaries of both National and Christian churches, they are, in Coleridge's view, duty bound to countermand the gross idolatry of wealth, and the perverted idea of self that all materialism encourages. The right person to make such decisions in our present constitution is undoubtedly the Monarch, who as head of the nation, as opposed to the Prime Minister, the head of the civil state, looks to the good of the whole, the common wealth, rather than to the vulgar wealth.

But all this is small beer compared to the position of the Christian Church in a State avowedly atheistic. Since Coleridge believed that religion was the centre of gravity in a realm, and the Christian Church will complete and strengthen the edifice of the state as it lays its own foundations, he presumably had no conception of a State that did not make some obeisance, however feeble, towards religion. The opposition of the Church to the State, which meets with such a chilly response, even in a supposedly free and democratic society, is barely tolerable in a Communist constitution. In such a society the Church certainly won't receive wages and dignities from the state, nor is it likely 'to be let alone'. Merely in claiming its right to be, the Church is entering the political arena. But if, *de facto*, it does exist, what political rights might the Christian Church claim in an atheistic state? In the terms of Coleridge's idea, it might still be possible to say that what the Church demands for itself is no more than what its members have a right to demand as citizens – freedom of speech, free association, impartial justice, and so forth. In a one-party state the church is frequently the only voice to which the state will listen in respect of these rights. And it is certainly of significance in relation to Coleridge's vision that in a country such as Poland the Church is still more or less identified with the rights and hopes of the people; and that when Germany invaded Russia in 1941, Stalin, in order to mobilize as many people as possible, turned to the Church as the ultimate source of national unity.

THE CONSTITUTION OF THE NATION

Coleridge defined the Nation as the State in its larger sense – that is, as the whole of which the civil State and the National Church are the opposing parts [CS 31, 117]. But as we might expect, he also sought to define the constitution historically, as a unity in time. Thus he explains that a Constitution is an idea arising out of the idea of a state; . . . our whole history from Alfred onward demonstrates the continued influence of such an idea, or ultimate aim, on the minds of our fore-fathers, in their characters and functions as public men.

[CS 19]

Coleridge goes on to point out that a constitution is an idea, and that not only does it not have a correspondent material existence, but that it properly exists only as an idea or principle can, 'in the minds and consciences of the persons, whose duties it prescribes, and whose rights it determines' [Ibid.]. He concludes therefore that 'the constitution has real existence, and does not exist less in reality, because it both *is*, and *exists as*, an IDEA' [Ibid.].

Coleridge makes no attempt to define the distinct features of this idea; and he seems to place the Christian Church outside the pale of the constitution. These two facts may be reconciled. We have seen in the previous chapter that Coleridge's idea of Hebrew history, which he took as a model for all subsequent national histories, was essentially of a people whose destiny was both controlled and substantiated by the idea of a person, an idea that gradually unfolded in time, culminating in the incarnation of Christ, who represents the historical unity of his people. The idea that the Hebrews had was in itself unchanged by time, stood outside time, as the living and eternal God. In just the same way, the Christian Church, presenting itself as the visible symbol of Christ's invisible presence, and teaching the immutable truths of his being, stands outside the particular ways in which a state grows, but nonetheless in its relations with the National Church instructs the nation in the ideal forms of being.

The Christian Church has only a fortuitous existence in the life of the nation. Its union with the National Church is 'a blessed accident', and has not the guaranteed continuity of the latter. Though it is a visible institution, a city built on a hill and not to be hid, Coleridge states clearly in this essay that it has 'as such no nationalty entrusted to its charge' [CS 116–17]. The Christian Church is opposed to the world as presented in the union of National Church and State. But in his last notebooks, Coleridge became aware that the Christian Church was firstly 'the most efficient portion of the National Church', and secondly, as we should have supposed from his believing that the Nationalty had been consecrated to the potential divinity in every man, that the Christian Church had a right to the Nationalty 'which she can be deprived of . . . not without cruel wrong and calamity to the People, not without suicidal guilt of the Nation . . .' [N.52, f.8-v].

Coleridge believed that the intimate union of the Christian and the National churches was decaying. After observing that the Sacrament of the Church of England was no more than 'a visual metaphor for the mere purpose of reminding the partakers of a single event, the sensible Crucifixion of Jesus', he goes on: 'But this is a necessary consequence of a sterile National Church, instead of comprehending a *Christian* Church in its inmost concentric circles' [N.36, p.61]. He sees the National Church, 'almost the only remaining venerable symbol of our Nationality', in danger 'from the multitudinous eddy-pool and gulphs of self-interest', and the Clerisy no longer as officers of both the Christian and the National churches, but as being 'degraded into Stipendiaries of the Government' [N.50, f.36]. What he is witnessing are the first shadows of that long process in which all the functions of the National Church – education, relief of poverty, care of the sick and needy – will be secularized and metamorphosed into the Welfare State.[29] This is now our National Church, even our sole image of the nation, and is wholly divorced from the Christian Church. Coleridge, as he so often did, intuitively understood what was happening, and 'would fain blow a blast of Alarm'.

However, a partial remedy has been to allow the disease to run its course, and what Coleridge proposed has in some measure happened:

> I am far from certain, that a temporary separation from the State, by the abandonment of an irreligious, half-infidel, half-sectarian Parliament and Cabinet would not prove a gracious providence, a purification ending in a glorification of our Church.
>
> [N.52, f.8v]

The current Church of England, if weak in some respects, is certainly a purer institution in that existing governments are no longer required to pay lip-service to it. It is in a position, of which it has yet to take full advantage, to stand on the kind of non-party but political ground that Coleridge felt was one of its chief fields of action; it is capable of opposing the present evils of our constitution in which the Nation is more or less regarded as synonymous with the material interests of the State: one major consequence of which is that we are no longer truly a nation, but an aggregate of phenomenal individuals, an *All* which is 'a mere Ens imaginarium, a bare empty abstraction – the Goddess Multitudo in Numero', as opposed to a whole – 'a most living and life-giving Reality' [N.55, f.3v]. The Church of England has become more closely identified with the Christian Church, and the National Church, the civilizing force of the community, with the Welfare State. As at least the landed portion of the nationalty continues to support the Church of England, in effect the Christian Church has become more visible in the life of the country, even if the number of nominal Christians has declined. In some measure this solves a problem inherent in Coleridge's formulation: how a Christian Church could exist as 'an institution consisting of visible and public communities' without some form of financial support. But if it solves one problem, it introduces another: the Church of England now appears to be a kind of shell or holding company for the Christian Church, without influence on the National Church or the Welfare State, and therefore impotent in the cultivation of the people. The lack of distinct ideas, ultimate aims or purposes is only too apparent in the schemes of education purveyed today in our schools and universities.

In the National Church, Coleridge had in effect attempted to make an institution of the nation, and so to place the whole in one part. But the nation, we saw in *The Friend*, is neither in the institutions founded on the principles of Reason – Religion and Literature, nor in those founded in the Understanding – Law and Trade: together they constitute and sustain that nationality which separately it is their tendency to transcend. Reason expressed through the Understanding, Understanding disciplined in the light of Reason, this is the fundamental order by which a man must live and a nation must grow. The educt of this process is not a thing, an institution, but a vision first, and finally a person whose life is a series of ideas or symbols. To make the nation an institution is to make it a golden calf – or in our modern pantomimic state in which the true idea of the nation has been lost – the economic goose, that too many believe will one day lay the golden egg of perpetual prosperity.

THE CLERISY

The nation comes into being through the befriending opposition
of the Christian Church and the State – this world integrated with
'another world that now is', forming an historical entity, existing
as an idea in the minds and hearts of the people from the time of
Alfred to the present day. Though at first Coleridge made an
institution of the National Church, yet he came to see that the
nation was the original power or idea of which the Church and
the State were two forces. In this respect, and wittingly or unwittingly, T.S. Eliot follows Coleridge closely when he speaks of
culture as the incarnation of the religion of a people.[30] The clerisy,
in whom the synthesis primarily takes place, become the representatives of the nation. And so Coleridge thought of them. He comments on *Numbers* XVIII i:

> But in what sense could the Levites be supposed to *bear* the
> iniquity of the People? What is the primary sense of the Hebrew
> word? A grand and most instructive Moral politically I could
> deduce from it – regarding the Levites as the Representatives of
> a National Clerisy – viz. as they, so will the Nation be – they
> will be the index of the good and evil of the Community, and
> God will behold it in them as the responsible order, by omission
> or commission the main cause of the moral state of a People.
> [N.44, f.34-v]

The life of a nation is invested in, and is the responsibility of,
the clerisy. Both Coleridge and Eliot felt this responsibility in
themselves, and condemned what they saw as misgrowths in
national life. Richard Holmes, I think, is mistaken in contrasting
the clerisy as the redeemers of the nation with the creative artist,
or poet.[31] For poets do not belong to another order than the clerisy,
but as poetry is the flower of all human knowledge, so poets are
the clerisy in perfection.

The life of the nation is analogous to the ideal life of the individual. But institutionally the life of the nation is divided between
those who live, or attempt to live, by the principles of Reason, the
visible Church, and the community of the faithful as the ever-
present body of Christ, and those who live according to the Understanding, men of power and actuality. It is in the clerisy that these
two opposing forces find their resolution, and in whom we find

the living idea of the nation; we have seen that this idea is a person, divine in his full humanity, and therefore we would expect the clerisy as the representatives of the nation, also to be his representatives. Coleridge, in continuing the note above, came to that conclusion:

> As long as the Learned Order, the Appointed Ministers of the Word, remain faithful and zealous in their office, the occasional transgressions of the People will, be *stayed* on them . . . The process toward the appointed end is going on – and in this view the Levitical Order may safely be regarded as types and shadows of Christ, the everlasting High Priest.

It is one of the misfortunes of life in this country now that the principles underlying the operation of the civil state have infected the thinking of some groups within the clerisy, who, with other and more clearly human principles in mind, should oppose the state's detrimental effects. On the one hand, we have a kind of poetry which seems to originate wholly from observation, and to confine itself to the surface of life. The collocation of preciously-phrased images is taken as the poet's main task, and the reader is left to induce what meaning they can. So in one of its more absurd epiphanies, the sight of a butcher before his sausages reminds the poet of Brunel before his chains, and from this acci-dental association the poem takes its form – as if we might write poetry on the basis of Mendelian mutation, one in a million of any value to the species. But such a collocation is the basis for a poem today, and the substance of it a series of images, each the aimless echo of that preceding: they point to no end and reveal no life, either in the mind of the poet or in the world he observes. And Coleridge's criticism of Hartley's law of association is the adequate comment on this poetic method – any one object or impression may recall almost any other object or impression, and the result can only be 'absolute *delirium*'. There are other conse-quences of a principle of 'creativity' which dares not reach beyond the notices of sense. When Coleridge asserted that poetry should begin in meditation, not observation, he was firstly freeing the mind from the local, immediate and temporal, and secondly making room for that upsurge of power which is a thing in itself, and not an effect: he was making room for the mind not as a *tabula rasa* upon which the world writes, but as having a life of its own,

organizing the images of sense into a form which expresses the
mind's own truth. The relation of power to ideas is that of energy
to form. But poetry having this kind of origin is wholly without
credence today. It is as if having a notion of ideas only as generic
abstractions, and not as existing in themselves, those who write
poetry have ceased to believe in the inwardness of creativity,
confusing it with private feelings or personal emotion. Though
that risk remains, and indeed the more remote ideas become, the
greater the risk of confusing the merely private with the proper
power, making it almost impossible that one should come forth
without the other, to abandon the one because of the difficulty of
distinguishing it from the other, is to throw the baby out with the
bath-water. As a result two kinds of poetry predominate these
days: the most common, poems of delirium, in which the light of
specious sophistication picks out and plays with images from the
ever-varying surface of life, producing a merely banal account of
human existence; and rarer, and more interesting, poems of mania
– in which the inward obsession so dominates the mind that all
images and events are force-marched to one montonous drum-
beat. An undevout poet is mad, said Coleridge, and the madness
that characterizes today's poetry is the inability to behold 'a world
not this world' which might inform the images donated by our
senses.

That on the one hand. On the other, what Coleridge said of the
state of religion in his day is as true, if not truer, in ours: 'a simple
word characterizes the Religion of this Country, it is *idealess*, i.e.
no Religion. The Ideas that constitute Religion, neither exist *for*
the clergy nor *in* the Laity' [N.35, p.15]. Coleridge never minced
his words in asserting the relation of ideas to religion: 'A hunger-
bitten and idea-less philosophy naturally produces a starveling
and comfortless religion' [LS 30].

Coleridge took communion for the first time in 33 years on
Christmas Day, 1827, and acknowledging that he was coming into
the vineyard at the eleventh hour, added, 'Yet I humbly hope that
spiritually I have fed in the Flesh and Blood the strength and the
Life of the Son of God in his divine Humanity, during the latter
years' [N36 p60]. But clearly that experience of church-going was
not an entirely happy one, for it is on the very next page of the
notebook that he records that the Sacrament in the Church of
England is no more than 'a visual metaphor for the mere purpose
of reminding the partakers of a single event, the sensible cruci-

fixion of Jesus'. This division between private experience and public devotion is one which has grown wider in the Anglican Church since then, but it is of the same kind, and has the same remedy. And the remedy is to take ideas out of the realms of abstraction and into the realm of power. The effort that clergy and laity alike must make is to find how religious ideas are in themselves truth, and at one with human experience. And by religious ideas, I mean primarily the doctrines that define the life of Jesus Christ, and secondarily the dogmas which define the life of the Church. It is a major symptom of the disease we suffer that there are probably not three more unpopular words among church people today than 'doctrine', 'dogma' and 'idea', which are all claimed to reduce religion to theology, and life to the workings of the intellect. Because the division between idea and experience is so wide, it requires a moral, spiritual and intellectual Colossus to draw these two continents together. Coleridge was one such, and I return to one of his formative experiences to illustrate the relationship between a living idea and human experience: his witnessing of his own and the crowd's reaction to the arrival of the Queen of Prussia at Hardenberg House in 1799. After two hours waiting, the emotion of the crowd at the dramatic arrival of the avant-courier, galloping into the courtyard and cracking his whip, was so intense that Coleridge felt that they welcomed the innocuous Queen as they might have welcomed their redeemer. There, Coleridge felt, was the power of an idea at work. The willingness of the crowd to surrender their minds and hearts to a mere figure betokened a power or force in them seeking expression. But it was an idea by which they were possessed, and not an idea they had in their possession. And possessed, not possessing, they would have rather attached their emotions to any object of their senses than contemplate its proper origin and object. The right orientation, in the light of an idea, of emotions arising from commonplace events and attachments, to enable us to possess ideas, and free us from being possessed by them, so validating at once both the emotion and the idea, and making possible a genuine incarnation of the eternal in the forms of the temporal, must be the main task of those who preach to us. Coleridge put it another way when he said that he considered

> the disproportion of human passions to their ordinary objects among the strongest internal evidences of our future desti-

nation, and the attempt to restore them to their rightful claim-
ants, the most imperious duty and the noblest task of genius.
[F 1 35]

I would only add that it is the genius of our humanity that we
all have the power to understand this restoration. If the ideas are
not in the laity, it is not because the *power* of ideas is not in us: it
is because these ideas have not in themselves been appealed to,
nor seen as the means by which we may illuminate our experience.
(Another symptom of the disease we suffer is the tendency to
make individual experience the test of an idea, not vice-versa,
with the result that the common cause, and the cause of our
communion, is lost in the welter of private feeling.) Though now
the whole-heartedness of the crowd Coleridge stood amongst is
diminished in us by the current centring of life in the material
rights of the individual, one day perhaps even Anglicans will hear
the shout of a king amongst them, and private experience be at
one with public worship. Then those, like Coleridge, who feel
themselves to be Churchless Christians, exposed to a myriad of
temptations and bitterly wanting the aid of fellow-believers, will
find a blessing in the communion of the Redeemed [Cf. N.48,
f.41v–42].

And finally, if an idealess philosophy produces a comfortless
religion, of what kind is the comfort that a true religion provides?
To beings who experience passions disproportionate to their ordinary objects, 'Truth is self-restoration'. Why? Because 'that which
is the correlative of Truth, the existence of absolute Life, is [the]
only object which can attract toward it the whole depth and mass
of his fluctuating Being, and alone therefore can unite Calmness
with Elevation. But it must be Truth without alloy and unsophisti-
cated' [F 1 36–37].

The investiture of all that we call us and ours, whether things,
or people, or the institutions to which we belong, with the character of permanence, the tacit belief (too near the heart of our being
to be easily distinguished from it) that whom and what we love
will always *be*, the very difficulty of conceiving our not-being,
these are sufficient evidence that the permanent and the eternal
are the proper objects of man's attention. But the immediate investiture of the objects of sense with the idea of permanence is a form
of deception which a lifetime's experience may not remove, so
closely is the idea stitched into our consciousness. And the diffi-

culty of finding and staying our hearts upon those objects or ideas, the absoluteness of which, contemplated in abstraction from love or devotion, appear to reduce our deepest feelings to a shadow, means that frequently we come to one of two extremes – a disbelief in any life but this, or a disbelief that this is any life at all. And these extremes meet in their destruction of our distinctly human being, which, whatever else it is, is firstly a being in time, and secondly the only being we can have a knowledge of.

The consolation of religion then, as of philosophy, is this: that whereas we are continually tempted to focus our hopes of permanence in all that pertains to sense, and are therefore prey to the suffering and disappointment which the experience of mutability brings, religion, or at least the Christian religion, teaches that there is a person at one with absolute life, and that this person, whom sense cannot perceive, is the person making each of us what we are, and the person to whom we are always seeking to respond in others. But take away ideas, and the paradox always inherent in their expression, and we take away the very forms which enable us to confirm his presence amongst us, the very method to our communion as human beings. Without ideas not only can there be no religion and no philosophy, but there is little hope of a genuinely human society, and the aggregation of individuals collected under that term will be governed more and more by the principles that apply to things, and less and less by the principles that derive from, and enable the development of, our God-given humanity.

Conclusion

My conclusion is of course that Coleridge is a hero – and not a tragic hero, such as Thomas McFarland has made of him, looking squarely down the barrel of a gun, knowing all that he can do is die, unable to resolve the epistemological conflict that has no resolution, and which is everyman's tragedy, were everyman big enough to face it: and not of course a defeated hero, the marvelous poet who gave up poetry for metaphysics, turning his face to the wall (in this vignette played by Christian) and his back upon the vasty deep where we now sail, more or less rudderless. Rather I think of Coleridge as having a clear vision of where he would find his home, knowing that it would not be in this world (Charles Lamb spoke of him in his last days as having a kind of hunger for eternity) but at the same time profoundly aware that terrestrial charts can only be made by celestial observation; this life and that life not successive states, but the one permanent and the way of reading and giving vitality to the other – which is a language and form of expression. And for Coleridge, making the journey and making the charts were closely related activities: his was not the detached experiment with a religious or philosophical system, which Eliot believed the legitimate activity of a poet.

Whether he arrived at his destination we do not know, but such evidence as we have leads me to believe that what Coleridge proclaimed as truth he incorporated into his life. David Jasper speaks of the 'prayerful tone' of the late notebooks, and in them we find a profound consciousness of the person of Christ. As Coleridge lay dying, he asked to be allowed to be by himself, tended only by his nurse Harriet, so that he could bring his heart and mind into the presence of Christ. Can a man, who in his last hours willingly dispenses with the love and comfort of people dearest to him, in order to concentrate calmly upon a person intangible, invisible, who is thus willing to purify his motive on the ground of his beseeching, can such a man in any significant

298

sense be said to be defeated? I hear a sceptic mutter, 'Well, the old wizard kept up the fiction to the end, deluding both himself and others'. Perhaps, but in that perhaps lies all faith, all doubt. You pays your money and you takes your choice. Mine is that the mariner found his fairway home.

And what of the terrestrial charts that he has left us? To change the metaphor, they seem to be piles of huge but half-dressed stones, scattered across a vast, overgrown site, the plan lost, the purpose unknown, but indubitably magnificent beyond the reaches of our conception. That there is no building, all agree: I have tacitly argued that to see Coleridge's construction, it is perhaps wisest to arrange the individual works as though they themselves were the magnum opus – but to do this is only to make a plan, not to put up the building; the fragments of the Opus Magnum itself rehearse much that we already know of Coleridge's thinking from other sources, but do not seem to break new ground, interesting and corroborative though many passages are.

But there is another work, of which we have not even the smallest fragment, and only the barest of plans, which nonetheless seems as though it might have been the synthesis of all the main strands of Coleridge's thought – 'The Fall of Jerusalem'. In 1832, he said that he had 'schemed it at twenty-five; but alas! *venturum expectat*' [TT 28 April]. Earlier in his life, he believed that the poem had been first schemed when he was even younger; writing to Thomas Wedgwood, he says, 'I have since my twentieth year meditated an heroic poem on the Siege of Jerusalem by Titus – this is the Pride, and the Stronghold of my Hope. But I never think of it except in my best moods' [CL II 877]. And the best moods, as with the conditions necessary for the continuation of Christabel, no doubt became more and more infrequent. It is curious, though, that a work by which Coleridge set so much apparent store should feature so little as to be almost non-existent in his voluminous public and private writings. Coleridge was a communicative man, and it does not seem to us now that many of his significant thoughts passed away unrecorded. So can we trust Coleridge when he says that the work was to be 'the Pride, and the Stronghold' of his literary hope? Or is this not rather one of those vague literary ambitions that was nothing and came to nothing? It is a fact of human psychology that our deepest hopes often lie quiescent within us, so much so that our consciousness of them has no distinct form, and only in our 'best moments',

charged, say, by another man's genius, do we have the courage
to declare to ourselves (more rarely still to anyone else) what our
best hopes are, and what ends we seek. And though they are
largely unspoken, unthought of, these hopes work silently within
us, the original reason for being what we are, choosing to do
what we have done, but the motive lost in the long and weary
undertaking. Coleridge never did feel sufficiently unfettered, even
to return to the composition of the unfinished 'Christabel'. It is
not surprising then that the time never came when he was ready
to sit down to the construction of the epic for which all his
thoughts and studies were ultimately intended.

But how might 'The Fall of Jerusalem' fit into the scheme of
Coleridge's career as I have traced it? At the heart of his thinking
lies the distinction between Reason and Understanding, which
appertain respectively to 'another world that now is' and 'this
world'. The integration of these two, the timeless informing the
time-bound, enables the right ordering of human life and society:
without the ideas of Reason, the ideas of permanence, beauty,
truth, mercy, justice, freedom, harmony, love, we may have the
form of human beings, but there will be no humanity in us. The
presence of Reason prevents the Understanding from being limited to the notices of sense, to material facts and appetites, which
it would otherwise arrange to its convenience, calling the catalogue
knowledge. It is the Understanding, attentive to and disciplined
in the light of Reason, that creates the human being. In its ideal
state, this being is inseparable from the ideas of Reason, and
therefore, by way of example, when we look to or love another
person, their immortality or continued life is always our hope, if
not always our belief. Coleridge's point is that without these
hopes, without the belief that there is an ideal and permanent life
in all of us, we cannot have either a truly human or a truly social
existence. But how our life progresses in time has been modelled
for us by the interaction of Reason and the Understanding as
perfected in Christ. And in this respect Coleridge believed that
we should not regard Christ's life as a teaching, but as a series of
stages which exemplify the continuously changing relationship
between 'another world that now is' and 'this world'. Thus to take
a simple illustration applicable to us all, Christ's life began with
his annunciation to Mary, but it ended with his ascension from
her and from the world which had given him to her. In his childhood he was, like all children, materially dependent on his

parents; at the end of his life he declared that he was returning to his Father in heaven; in between are all the stages of that painful transposition from one state to the other: but at any one moment of this process he was never the less her son, and still remains her son in our consciousness. The Understanding could not of itself permit this reasoning. It would declare that the terms parent and child are descriptions of a biological or civil fact, which incurs, by force of nature or social regulation, a caring of one for the other, and which is terminated by death. It could not admit the paradox that we are seven, when there are only five of us to be seen, that a son or daughter is no less a son or daughter (or a brother or a sister) because they lie in the churchyard. Into the material fact Reason induces the idea, and this idea informs the human relations of parent and child, so that each looks upon the other not merely as a local and temporal presence, but as having the hope of a life beyond the limits of mortality.

Coleridge also felt that the doctrines or ideas of Christ's life were the major stages of Jewish national history; that is, they have an objectification which began with Abraham and ended with the destruction of the Temple, a process which I have outlined in Chapter 8. It is this process which seems to me to have clear associations with the planned epic. A poem requires two things – a story or mythology, and an idea or poetic impulse, a life within and a world without, and the resulting work is the union of power and form. Comparing his plan with that of Homer, Coleridge declared that as 'for the old mythology, *incredulus odi*; and yet there must be a mythology, or a *quasi*-mythology, for an epic poem. Here these would be the completion of the prophecies – the termination of the first revealed national religion under the violent assault of Paganism, itself the immediate forerunner and condition of the spread of a revealed mundane religion' [TT 28 April 1832].

'The Siege of Jerusalem' was to describe a unique moment in history – that moment when a national religion becomes a world (or at least European) religion. The story is to describe how the writings of the Hebrew prophets were fulfilled at one historical moment: but Coleridge was sure that this story was a prototype for all national histories. The moral failings and the destruction of the Israelites were foretold in their literature, and are unique, but

add only, that the History is the fulfilment, and that this History is the very Tap-root and Trunk of the Moral and therein of the physical and political *History* of the whole Planet – of all Human Progression, and I cannot conceive that any thoughtful mind, not perverted and rendered insensible by sophistry, should withstand the evidence. [N.43, p.31]

Well, almost all the historians I have met with seem to have withstood the evidence pretty well. But nonetheless I think that Coleridge's is a remarkable and even a workable plan. We have both the necessary 'mythology' – the prophecies – all pointing to one historical moment in which the poem is to be set, and the poetical impulse which sees the course of Jewish history, epitomised in Christ, as a paradigm for the progress of every human life: the inward and the outward have a common focus. There are difficulties, as Coleridge admitted, the chief being that an epic poem must have a personal interest: 'in the destruction of Jerusalem no genius or skill could possibly preserve the interest for the hero from being merged in the interest for the event' [TT 4 Sept. 1833]. As to whom the hero was to have been, Coleridge gives us no hint; and this is in itself another problem, since as Jesus he obviously could not have been present, and as Christ he could only have been present unseen.

However, that Christ's presence was in one way or another to have informed the poem there can be little doubt. In a notebook, and after repeated comparison of the Gospels, Coleridge wrote that 'the greater appears the necessity of connecting the assurance of St Paul respecting the ascension of Christ to the Throne of Divine Providence, as actually King and Lord, with the Jewish War and the Destruction of the City and Temple' [N.35 p.28]. That is, Christ's ascension from this life to the eternal is the idea that informs the destruction of the Jewish state, the historical fact; or, Christ's ascension is at one with the apotheosis of the Jews as a nation; and at the same time this fact of history initiates a repetition in the vulgar nations, which are on the verge of coming into existence, of the historical process which the Jews have undergone and which Christ perfected.

How closely the history of a modern European nation might be seen to parallel that which Coleridge ascribes to the Jews, no historian has to my knowledge tried to determine. But that, for instance, the terms annunciation and incarnation might provide appropriate ideas for describing the Anglo-Saxon and Medieval periods of English history respectively, is a scheme that has some attractions. If Coleridge believed that to know their history the Jews should, by force of imagination, march out of Egypt with Moses, build the Temple with David and Solomon, endure exile in Babylon with Ezekiel, and witness the fall of Jerusalem, and if this was in one way or another to constitute their 'epic', I see no reason why an Englishman should not cross the North Sea with Hengist and Horsa, listen to the preaching of Paulinus at the court of King Edwin, look darkly into the new future with Beowulf, ride to Canterbury with Chaucer's pilgrims, or to the perilous chapel with Gawain, be cast out of court and kingdom with King Lear, wander homeless with Wordsworth, and be called back into the garden by Eliot.

If any such scheme is possible, it has been made possible for us by Coleridge. The foundations he laid down may now be over-grown, but they are there, and only wanting our energy to make them visible. Coleridge's development, his giving up the writing of poetry himself, and his undertaking an arduous course of read-ing and research, is all part of a historical process necessary to the growth of poetry. His later work supplies us with a method of emancipation from mere intuition in respect of inspiration, from the incidental images of nature or myth or history in respect of form, and from our subservience, however disguised, to the ego-tistical sublime. For intuitions, Coleridge has given us ideas, for accidental illustration, providential history, and for the sublime self, the humanity of Christ.

Notes

PREFACE

1. LS 30.
2. Op. M. II, f.78.
3. *The Falklands War*, The Sunday Times Insight Team, (1982) 98.
4. Op. M. II, f.78.
5. CN II, 2598; SM 101.
6. *Hansard VI*, vol. 21, 640.
7. Ibid., 641.
8. *Complete Works*, ed. P.P.Howe (London: 1930–34) viii, 251.
9. *Debts of Honour* (1980) 37.
10. F I, 113.
11. N.3½, f.128.

CHAPTER 1: THE POETRY OF NATURE

1. Cf. *This For Remembrance*, Bernard Lord Coleridge, 58–60.
2. Cf. Brett and Jones, xix: 'Both of them were to observe what they considered to be "the two cardinal points of poetry . . ."'; CL I 142, to Cottle: 'We deem that the volumes offered to you are to a certain degree *one work, in kind tho' not in degree*, as an Ode is one work – and that our different poems are as stanzas, good relatively rather than absolutely . . .'
3. Cf. CL 1 631, to Humphry Davy: 'Christabel' is not included in the 1800 edition of the *Lyrical Ballads* because 'the poem was in direct opposition to the very purpose for which the *Lyrical Ballads* were published – viz – an experiment to see how far those passions, which alone give any value to extraordinary incidents, were capable of interesting, in and for themselves, in the incidents of common Life'. Where this leaves 'The Ancient Mariner' it is hard to see; how divided Coleridge's mind was on this topic is evident from his unfulfilled intention of writing a 'critical essay on the uses of the Supernatural in poetry' which was to have been prefixed to 'The Ancient Mariner' [BL 1 202].
4. Cf. WPW, 935; Abrams, *Tradition and Revolution in Romantic Literature*, 390–9, and Happel, 319; Abrams believes that Coleridge did not understand the 'revolutionary character' of Wordsworth's poetry, and Happel believes that Abrams does not understand Coleridge's notion of 'revolution'.
5. Cf. Moorman, 1, 349.
6. For further discussion of the nature and the differences of the shared enterprise, see S. M. Parrish, 'The Wordsworth-Coleridge Controversy'.
7. WPW, 23, 'Lines Left upon a Seat in a Yew-tree . . .

> Nor, that time,
> When nature had subdued him to herself,
> Would he forget those Beings to whose minds . . .
> The world, and human life, appeared a scene
> Of kindred loveliness.

8.   Cf. Brett and Jones, xxvii.
9.   'Coleridge and Wordsworth and the "Supernatural" ', 125–6. For *Spectator ab extra* see TT 21 July 1832 and 16 February 1833. What Kathleen Coburn says here is equally true of 'The Thorn'; and it is interesting that Wordsworth in his note to that poem in the edition of 1802–05, thought of his narrator as 'indolent', 'prone to superstition' and having a 'reasonable share of imagination' [WPW 1 512]. The interrelation of these qualities in Wordsworth's mind is significant; in the poem the 'supernatural' is the product of the narrator's superstition, and so it is easy to see why Coleridge was impatient with Wordsworth's 'matter-of-factness', his clinging to the palpable, and why Wordsworth was irritated at 'The Ancient Mariner's' improbability. Although Wordsworth classified 'Peter Bell' as a poem of imagination, S. M. Parrish thinks that 'Wordsworth "sweetened" and made endurable the theme of a curse [by making] the terrible "events" of 'The Thorn' not supernatural, or even real, but only products of the superstitious imagination'. ['The Wordsworth-Coleridge Controversy', 369.]
10.   This is not quite Wordsworth's view of the matter, however: 'Coleridge', he told Barron Field, 'was unable to project himself dramatically into his characters: having "always too much personal and domestic discontent" he could not "afford to suffer/ With those who he saw suffer . . . I gave him the subject of his Three Graves," Wordsworth continued, "but he made it too shocking and painful, and not sufficiently sweetened by any healing views. Not being able to dwell on or sanctify natural woes, he took to the supernatural, and hence his Antient Mariner and Christabel" '. [S. M. Parrish, ibid., quoting de Selincourt, *The Early Wordsworth*, 28n.]
11.   Cf. SC 84, 88.
12.   Cf. BLC II, 82–3; CL I, 493, to Thomas Poole: '. . . the mind *acts and plays a part*, itself the actor and the spectator at once!'

CHAPTER 2: THE CONVERSATION POEMS

1.   *The Religious Thought of Samuel Taylor Coleridge*, 25.
2.   The square brackets within the quotation contain Kathleen Coburn's translations of Coleridge's Latin and Greek.
3.   HCR I, 400.
4.   Cf. *Coleridge and the Pantheist Tradition*, 111, and *Romanticism and the Forms of Ruin*, 133–4: 'For tragedy and human existence are synonymous'.
5.   Coleridge goes on to say that Nature is sure to get the better of Lady Mind in the long run, thereby apparently reversing the order his mature thought is intent on demonstrating. But this letter was

inspired by the marvel of 'fire and water blending their souls for [his] propulsion' – that is, travel by steam-boat, yet his having no idea correspondent to this scientific development. He feels the grounds of the divorce between Lady Mind, or Philosophy, and the development of empirical thought – a divorce so absolute in our own time that few believe that the marriage ever happened, and even fewer that it ever might again. So Coleridge is not denying that mind and nature ought to be related as idea and law, but merely recording his growing sense of their separation. J. D. Boulger has written: 'A general observation from the entire set of marginalia on science might be that Coleridge could not shape the new science to an imaginative cosmos, and also could not be satisfied, and rightly so in retreating from it into an earlier and less scientific view'. ['Marginalia, Myth-Making and the Later Poetry', 313.] Cf. CN II, 2086, in which he describes his Malta journey as a 'wearisome fickle voyage, and no related Mind'.

6.   Cf. CL I, 588 for the notion that sense impressions create our being.
7.   First so entitled by G. M. Harper in 1925, who also included 'To William Wordsworth' and 'Dejection: An Ode'. Paul Magnuson ('The Dead Calm in the Conversation Poems', 53) points out that the other people addressed in these poems 'are centers of perception distinct from Coleridge himself'.
8.   If we take the Conversation and the Supernatural poems as two distinct kinds of poetry written by Coleridge, McFarland has identified a third, which he calls 'the hysterical sublime', and which is epitomized in such poems as 'Religious Musings' and 'France: an Ode'. He quotes from the former poem and says, 'There he sought to pile up tonal masses in the manner of Milton . . . but what he actually achieved was shrill turgidity' [RFR 242]. By and large I have to agree with McFarland's assessment, especially when Coleridge personifies abstractions; nonetheless, on occasion and without that particular artifice, Coleridge can manage a fine rhetoric not found elsewhere in his poetry. I particularly like lines 142–158 of 'Religious Musings' and lines 41–80 of 'Fears in Solitude'.
9.   Cf. McFarland's introduction to *Romanticism and the Forms of Ruin*, where he describes as 'diasparactive' that kind of experience in which our senses are subject to various, discrete and unrelated impressions. The essence of his argument is that our senses live in a phenomenal world – and that this constitutes our tragedy; many people, including poets of the deliberately visionless kind such as Philip Larkin, would find no cause to disagree with him. Only in the last chapter does McFarland consistently admit that our hearts do not – and that in this lies the solution to our otherwise delirious existence. The germ of this thinking is present in earlier pages – for instance, 'Without faith, in other words, diasparactive awareness would be horror' [RFR 44]. This is quite true and quite Coleridgean: the whole lies in the faith and not in the perception.
   'Pity', 'Brockley Coomb' and 'The Eolian Harp' were all originally published as 'Effusions': Paul Magnuson comments, 'As the word

effusion suggests, the lyrics were transitory expressions of emotion'. [' "The Eolian Harp" in Context', 5.]

10.   Cf. F I, 156, SM 59–62; cf. PW II, 1137 – on his reason for calling his *Poems on Various Subjects* (1796) 'Effusions' rather than 'Sonnets' – 'I might indeed have called the majority of them Sonnets – but they do not possess that *oneness* of thought which I deem indispensible (sic) in a Sonnet–' and two pages later he notes that the sonnet 'is limited to a *particular* number of lines, in order that the reader's mind having expected the close at the place in which he finds it, may rest satisfied; and that so the poem may acquire as it were, a *Totality*, – in a plainer phrase, may become a *Whole*'.
       Cf. N.50, f.31: 'for the Many comprehended in the One, and contemplated as one, is the character of all Truths, in that highest sense of the Word, in which, a Truth is contra-distinguished from a particular fact, incident or appearance.'

11.   HCR I, 400; cf BLC I, 158, CPI, 188–90, CL IV, 548.

12.   CL II, 864.

13.   Cf. CPI, 65, where John Beer traces the source of this imagery to Pope ('Windsor Forest' 19–20) and James Ridley's *Tales of the Genii* (1766, I, 70) and then says: 'But the more pervasive debt is to Milton's unfallen Adam and Eve in *Paradise Lost*, resting in a bower of flowers that include myrtle and jasmine and indulging to the full their innocent sensuousness'. It is worth noting that in this poem Coleridge thinks of himself as redeemed, and therefore believes in the innocence of his sensuality: the strength of his hope has temporarily mastered the facts of his experience – he had protested against Southey's moral press-ganging by asserting that to marry Sara Fricker would be but to use her as 'an instrument of low desire'.

14.   ' "The Eolian Harp" in Context', 6; cf. 7: 'The associations of these emblems come, not from their inherent nature, but from the signatures borrowed from tradition that the poet places upon the emblems; the whiteness of innocence, the myrtle's connection with Venus, and the eroticism of the evening star. Similarly the allusions to music in 'Effusion XXXV' ['The Eolian Harp'] contain a medley of various styles, dissociated as far as possible from an individual voice, and reminiscent of historical or period styles in classical and English literature'.

15.   That there are no distinct connections between the first verse paragraph and the second to line 25, it is not my intention to assert. Coleridge had not married Sara Fricker when he wrote the poem, and the images of courtship and prospective bliss are evident in both sections, though Paul Magnuson strains the credible limits of literary criticism in saying that 'In the hush of evening the harp "placed lengthwise in the clasping casement" becomes a symbol of sexual union'. ['The Dead Calm in the Conversation Poems', 55.] What I do assert is that the richness and variety of imagery is not substantiated by a unifying idea. To use McFarland's terminology, Coleridge's mind is working solely in the mimetic and not in the

meontic mode. Another link is made by K. M. Wheeler in a piece of observation that goes some way to redeeming her from her fall into the school of universal irony: 'Twilight is like the moment of perfect balance between the conscious and the unconscious mind . . . In this "trembling equipoise" or this "hovering on untam'd wing" between two opposite states, the conscious side of the mind is alerted to or discovers some external element to which it attends, while the imagination slips through the crevice of the twilight world and infuses that element with symbolic and mythical associations all its own'. [*The Creative Mind in Coleridge's Poetry*, 69.]

Paul Magnuson points out (' "The Eolian Harp" in Context', 8) that these lines were not satisfactory to Coleridge, either. 'In 1797 Coleridge tried to have an errata sheet printed with the instructions to "Scratch out these three lines – 'Where melodies . . . on untam'd wing' ".' Cf. CL I, 331 and PW I, 52, where in a note Coleridge describes these lines as 'intolerable stuff'.

16. Cf. Geoffrey Yarlott, *Coleridge and the Abyssinian Maid*, 96–7. He thinks that the later addition of lines 26–34 'clarified the amorphousness of the preceeding lines', but 'it wrecked the original structure completely, since for Coleridge to reject these thoughts as "unhallow'd" and "unregenerate" was mere nonsense'. There are perhaps two ways of answering objections of this kind. Firstly, by denying that there is anything essentially non-Christian in the interpolated passage: these and the original lines speak only of the harmony the poet senses between his inward life and that of nature (cf. HH, 77). What Coleridge rejects is the notion of lines 44–8, which suggest that the intellectual breeze is at once the soul of each object and the 'God of all'. Secondly, the desire to find 'Harmony' is but a sign of the awakening Reason (cf. SM, 60). Such an instinct is indeed an essential aspect of religious development, and is only antithetical to Christianity if it is not interpenetrated by what Coleridge called Religion, or the hope of 'finding' oneself in the love of another. It is my argument that his 'return' to the person of Sara is not mere form – for Sara had no delicate religious scruples – but an intuitive movement of his intellect which becomes the very ground of his Christianity.

17. Paul Magnuson (op.cit., 9) asks the same question in another way: 'Is the "intellectual breeze" a symbol as Coleridge defined it?' And he refers us to Douglas B. W. Wending, 'Two Modes of Apprehending Nature: A Gloss on the Coleridgean Symbol', PMLA, 87 (1972) 45–52, and K. M. Wheeler, *The Creative Mind in Coleridge's Poetry*, 81. And he comments on this passage in the poem: 'If it is philosophical speculation and symbolic, there must be an implied radical break in the rhetoric of the poem; the emblems and the similes in the first part of the poem must be discarded as at best capricious associations that have no relation to metaphysical speculation, even though their themes of idealized erotic love would seem to form a progress to spiritual love'.

18. T. S. Eliot, *The Complete Poems and Plays*, 184.

19. For a full analysis of the relationship between Keats and Coleridge in this matter, see Barbara Hardy, 'Keats, Coleridge and Negative Capability'. Cf. also K. M. Wheeler, op. cit., 75, on lines 23–5: ' "The Melodies . . . nor pause nor perch, hovering on untam'd wing" is Coleridge's (and Keats's) favourite characterization of the faculty of imagination, as hovering between or amongst possibilities'.
20. WPW, 481.
21. Cf. Paul Magnuson, op. cit., 16: 'The images, in the full satisfaction of desire, do not intend beyond themselves'.
22. Cf. Paul Magnuson, op. cit., 17: 'Having removed the figurative landscape of "Composed at Clevedon" [The Eolian Harp] Coleridge is left with a landscape that speaks a natural language. Yet that language is merely literal and inadequate to reflect a larger world'.
23. M. G. Cooke, 'The Manipulation of Space in Coleridge's Poetry', 182.
24. It is notable that well into his thirties, at least until he set sail for Malta, Coleridge felt that the experience of life depended upon rising above individual form: cf. CL II, 916 (January 1803), which describes a walk in a storm up Patterdale over Kirkstone and down into Grasmere: 'The farther I ascend from animated Nature, from men, and cattle, and the common birds of the woods, and fields, the greater becomes in me the Intensity of the feeling of Life . . . God is everywhere, I have exclaimed, and works everywhere; and where is there *room* for death? In these moments it has been my creed, that Death exists only because Ideas exist/ that Life is limitless Sensation . . . that Feelings die by flowing into the mould of the Intellect, and becoming Ideas; and that Ideas passing forth in action re-instate themselves again in the world of Life'. There is a paradox in this passage: the more Coleridge ascends from nature the more he senses that God is everywhere in nature. It might be argued that this ascent frees Coleridge of sense impression, and what he imagines as life, or God, is rather an emotion, a feeling of unity and harmony, than the result of immediate experience; and he is probably speaking of this emotion when he says, 'Life is limitless Sensation . . .' The reciprocal relation between Ideas and Feelings that emerges, despite an inauspicious beginning, implies that either may give rise to the other, and that a true idea and a true feeling are necessarily connected – a point of view we would expect of Coleridge.
25. WPW, 88; cf. CL I, 623–5, in which Coleridge describes Hartley as a child of Nature: '–he moves, he lives, he finds impulses from within and from without – he is the darling of the Sun and of the Breeze! Nature seems to bless him as a thing of her own! He looks at the clouds, the mountains, the living Beings of the earth, and vaults and jubilates!' The sad thing is, perhaps, that Coleridge's youthful ideas of fatherhood were transmitted all too successfully to his intelligent son. Consequently Hartley, despite the recognition

of his gifts, never did succeed in settling in society, and remained a wanderer all his life.

26. *Poems by Hartley Coleridge*, ed. E. L. Griggs, 3.
27. BL II, 255.
28. G. M. Harper's description of a characteristic action of these poems.
29. 'Coleridge's Conversation Poems', 289.
30. *Coleridge the Poet*, 66.
31. *Coleridge's Secret Ministry*, 221.
32. *Coleridge and the Abyssinian Maid*, 95.
33. *Samuel Taylor Coleridge*, 33. John Beer, in a paper entitled 'How far can we trust Coleridge?', given at the first Coleridge Summer Conference at Nether Stowey in 1988, reminded us that if we are tempted to criticize Coleridge for the 'drop in spirits' that many readers feel at the end of the poem, we should also ask ourselves how else we might expect the poem to end. John Beer then made an interesting connection between Coleridge's respect for the moral and social order conferred by the instituted Church, and Will Ladislaw's experience of Church-going in Chapter 47 of *Middlemarch*.
34. Cf. CL I, 192: 'Has not Dr Priestly forgotten that *Incomprehensibility* is as necessary an attribute of the First Cause, as Love, or Power, or Intelligence?'
35. Southey appears to have mocked Coleridge with his 'Meek Sister in the family of Christ' (CN I, 1815); Coleridge must have been miserably aware of the irony of these last two lines.
36. Cf. Happel, *Coleridge's Religious Imagination*, 36, quoting LPR, 203: 'Jesus reteaches humanity filial and paternal affection, by home-born Feeling, so that he may enter the ever-expanding circles of Love which allow individuals "to be absorbed in the love of God" '.
37. LPR, 46, cf. 170; CL I, 58, 86.
38. Cf. LPR, 244–8, on those, including William IV, who refused to countenance the abolition of the slave trade.
39. Happel, op. cit., 36, on Coleridge's view of Christ in LPR: 'The goal of his presence is to recall human beings to practical belief, to impress upon them the infinite power of God and the weakness and wretchedness of unassisted humanity'.
40. Cf. note 38.
41. Happel, 35, demonstrates that these lines are not what critics have often taken them to be – a posturing belied by his actions.
42. G. M. Harper's alternative title for the Conversation Poems.
43. Cf. note 7.
44. John Beer, in a marginal note on the typescript of this book, doubted that any irony had crept into his references to his wife so early in their marriage; but he refers us to RX 24.
45. Cf. Lamb's *Collected Letters*, I, 240–1.
46. Cf. K. M. Wheeler, op. cit., 132: '. . . a Christian conception of brotherly love and empathy is joined with a sweeping pantheistic conception of the "One Life" '.
47. Cf. Paul Magnuson, 'The Dead Calm in the Conversation Poems', 60: 'In this final prayerful hope for his son's growth Coleridge is

able to forget his own disappointment, but only through thinking of someone else's joy can he reach any of his own'. Magnuson reaches this conclusion: 'The central "I" cannot sustain an unqualified assertion of its own mystery of the "One Life". Only the mediation of other minds permits him to rise to unqualified assertion . . .' It is this kind of recognition that allows some critics to classify 'Dejection' as a Conversation Poem.

48. Yarlott, Ch.1, passim.

CHAPTER 3: THE SUPERNATURAL POEMS

1. Cf. CL IV, 597 – to Wordsworth: '. . . the senses [are] living developments of the Mind and Spirit in a much juster, as well as higher sense than the mind can be said to be formed by the senses.'
2. Yarlott, 83.
3. Ibid.
4. Cf. McFarland RFR, 86: Coleridge's influence 'accounts, I believe, for what seems to be a major contradiction in Wordsworth's expressed attitudes on a deeply important topic, that of the relation of the mind to the external world'. McFarland quotes the Prospectus to 'The Recluse':

How exquisitely the individual Mind
        . . . to the external World
Is fitted: – and how exquisitely too –
. . . The external World is fitted to the Mind.

McFarland comments: 'But in this fitting, Wordsworth's own instinctive understanding of the matter was that the mind passively fills itself from the greater reality of nature'.
5. Hazlitt, *Selected Essays*, 515; cf. MC, 386.
6. Coleridge's views on sleep may have some relevance here: 'In the paradisaical World, Sleep was voluntary and holy – a spiritual before God, in which the mind elevated by contemplation retired into pure intellect suspending all commerce with sensible objects and perceiving the present deity' [CN I 191].
7. Lamb, *Collected Letters*, I, 240.
8. Bearing in mind the theoretical basis of the *Lyrical Ballads*, the argument prefacing the poem in 1798 may have been there to reassure the reader of the 'reality' of the Mariner's journey. K. M. Wheeler, op. cit. 49, notes that the 'two features most distinctive in the 'Argument' are its specifications of geographical locations and its concern with time sequence: it seems to have no other function than to place the drama of the verse in a completely clear space/time grid'.
9. Op. cit., 724.
10. De Quincey, *Collected Writings*, II, 145.
11. John Beer, C. Vis., 134; cf. A. R. Jones, 'The Conversation and Other Poems', in *Writers and their Background*, 99.

12. Cf. CL I, 397 – this letter also states Coleridge's belief in original sin; CPI, 79 on N.35 f.36: Beer suggests that Baxter proposes that the dream may afford an occasion on which other principles are enabled to operate through one's own sensory apparatus.

13. Cf. McFarland, RFR, 225: in relation to Coleridge's metaphysics he points out that the three major poems are not overtly philosophical, 'but we must remember that these three poems were all more casual in their inception than we are accustomed to realize, and that Coleridge's esteem for them evolved during the passage of time and the praise of outside observers'. McFarland goes on to point out that Coleridge added the gloss in an attempt to give the poem more weight.

14. TT 6 July 1833: for Gillman's account see *The Life of Samuel Taylor Coleridge*, 301–2.

15. C. Vis., 167 These statements seem to be in conflict with much of what Beer says elsewhere about the poem: for instance, CPI, 148, 'Can we be sure that *any* of the events after the onset of the thirst agony have an "objective existence"?' CPI, 161, 'It is significant of the manner in which internal and external images blend in this poem that the "spring" in the Mariner's heart is followed by the longed-for rain'. On p.172 of CPI Beer sums up his view with reference to BL II, 257–8: 'Our discussion has shown the extent to which he tried to make "thought nature" in his poem'. That thought makes nature in the Supernatural poems, and not vice-versa, is the argument I am trying to develop, and for which Professor Beer has supplied me with much material. But are not these particular statements of his in opposition to his general, if earlier, thesis that meditation on the material universe, that is, subjecting oneself to sense impression, will enable man's spiritual quest?

16. Cf. Beer, CPI, 167, who believes that the cold of the polar regions stimulates the senses of the Mariner and crew, and the ice and snow 'counterfeit infinity': the Mariner's action in shooting the albatross 'cuts across the oppressiveness of the scene, transfixing the albatross into definite form'. But this is to forget that the worst of the voyage is over ('but not the boredom' – JB in a marginal note on this typescript) when the Mariner befriends the bird, and that the ice-pack is disappearing into the distance over the stern.

17. WPW, 481; cf. Beer, CPI, 164: he quotes from *Osorio* (PW II, 584 in CL I, 359) and then remarks: 'He has said enough, however, to give pause to any critic who would make him at this time too ready a believer in the power of nature to induce automatic moral benefits in man'.

18. Cf. CN II, 2090; the poem may have had its origins in Coleridge's ideas of original sin. A letter of early 1797 from Lamb (Marrs I, 97) indicates that Coleridge was planning a poem on the origin of evil; cf. CL I, 396, which discusses original sin and Augustinian theology. The interesting thing about 'The Ancient Mariner' is

that the one distinctly evil act, the shooting of the albatross, the quasi-murder of a Christian soul, appears to have no external impetus, no affective origin; like the will, it is without cause, and so free – it might be considered as an existential act. Cf. Jasper, *Coleridge as Poet and Religious Thinker*, 54.

19. K. M. Wheeler, op. cit., 42, believes that this commentary, added in 1815–16, ensures that 'both reader and poet must be understood as observers as well as makers . . . By destabilizing reality . . . [so] as to shatter the ordinary boundary between the two, the formal distinctions between mind and nature, external and internal, thought and thing, are questioned as real or illusory'. That this is the effect of the *verse*, I fully agree. But I believe, with McFarland, (RFR, 225) that the function of the gloss is precisely the opposite. Wordsworth (and Southey, cf. Jasper, op. cit., 52, quoting from *The Critical Review* XXIV, 1798, 197–204) had criticised the poem as having an insufficient basis in reality – in the palpable world. It is no accident that the gloss was added in 1815 when Coleridge was trying to show that all the Lyrical Ballads were of a kind. Both the earlier Argument and the later gloss serve the same purpose: to elucidate the action of the poem, and to attempt to give it a time and placeness which is necessarily absent from the verse itself because of its deliberate conflation of inward and outward worlds. Thus, for example, the gloss on lines 131–4, 'A Spirit had followed them . . .' with its apparently scholarly references to Josephus and Michael Psellus, is an attempt to remove the fanciful and fortuitous aspects of the appearance of the Polar spirit, which the extract from Burnet attempts more generally.

Dr Wheeler, op. cit., 52, observes rightly but infers wrongly: 'The two most characteristic elements of the gloss setting it apart from the verse are its geographical specifications and its technique of streamlining the narrative so that the sequence of events and their causal connections are made more clear'. This is spot on, but Dr Wheeler does not seem pleased with what she sees: 'The preoccupations in the gloss with time sequence, causality and spatial determinations seem contrary to the imaginative spirit explicitly free of the ordinary laws of time, space, and causality, both as exemplified in the verse's imaginative language, and as the imagination is described elsewhere by Coleridge'. Of course, we might say: who would expect the truths of poetry to be evident in the 'facts' of the gloss? The potential danger of this critical approach is realized a few pages later: '. . . the gloss intrudes with "Till a great sea-bird, called the Albatross . . ." "Sea-bird" directs attention to a literal, external animal, and then depletes the symbolic aspect . . .' Dr Wheeler would not have us think of the albatross as a bird at all, and this leads her, in Edward Kessler's words, 'to the absurd conclusion that the Mariner murdered a concept'. [*Coleridge's Metaphors of Being*, 48.]

Despite some revision to this passage, John Beer still thinks that I tend to read the poem as a single statement. That this is how I would like to read it, and how I think we should approach any poem presented as such, I happily admit. That the poem works equally well in all its parts, I am much less certain: Parts VI and VII do not seem to have the momentum of those preceding. The question then is, how true was Coleridge to the original spirit of the poem in his revisions; to what extent was he attempting to extract from the original a poem that was never there? To do justice to the question one must first of all admit that it is possible that a poet may have a clearer vision of the creative force behind a poem after, and some time after, its composition. He may come to possess the idea that once possessed him. If revision after the event is then allowable, what did Coleridge do to make 'The Rime . . .' a different poem? The answer is usually that he sought to Christianize it, to make it conform to beliefs becoming more and more important to him, but less and less so to subsequent intelligentsia. To answer this: firstly, it is possible that Coleridge's clearer vision of what he was trying to achieve, and a growing consciousness of the parameters of human life, may have gone hand in hand. There is an ebullience in the recorded origin and the deliberately medieval imagery of the poem that permitted the marvellous and the macabre for their own sake. My impression of Coleridge's revisions is that it is these wilful extravaganzas that he saw fit to remove. Secondly, and by far the most important, there is no evidence that Coleridge added anything to the specifically Christian paraphernalia of the poem (which, if significant, are few and far between anyhow) either in the gloss or in the text. His main act of revision has been to excise the medieval overlay, thereby freeing the poem from a distinct period or epoch. John Beer has pointed out that Coleridge's simple account of how 'Kubla Khan' was written, as recorded in a note attached to the Crewe manuscript, tallies closely in matter of fact with the more florid and diffuse account attached to the beginning of the published poem. If we can trust Coleridge in this controversial matter, can we not trust him in a matter much less revealing of his personal weaknesses? See n.33, Ch.2.

20. Cf. CPI, 29–40, and SM, 10: 'it was only to overthrow the usurpation exercised in and through the senses, that the senses were miraculously appealed to . . . The natural Sun is in this respect a symbol of the spiritual'. Cf. M I, 564, on Boehme, for a variant of this idea.

21. For a possible plan of continuation, in which Enos may play a significant part, see CN II, 2780 and note.

22. C. Vis. 173.

23. Cf. note 21.

24. The gloss attached to the two verses of lines 236–43 runs: 'He despiseth the creatures of the calm, And envieth that *they* should live and so many dead'. When we come to the stanza preceeding and preparing for the blessing of the watersnakes, the Mariner's

act is glossed: 'By the light of the Moon he beholdeth God's creatures of the great calm' [PW I, 198]. A connection is thus established between the 'slimy things', the 'creatures of the great calm' and the watersnakes – God's creatures. The inference is clear: they are the same animal variously conceived by the Mariner according to his state of mind, which is making what he sees and not being made by it. Cf. Abe Delson, 'The Symbolism of the Sun and Moon in *The Rime of the Ancient Mariner*'. He believes that in this poem 'Coleridge deliberately embodied a view of nature contrary to the one he was stating in more discursive poetry at the time . . .' and he comments on lines 272–81: 'There are verbal and visual parallels here to the imagery that appeared when the Mariner's ship was first stuck at the Line in Part II. The "slimy things" that "did crawl with legs" have become the beautiful watersnakes. The "green and blue and white" of the death fires have become the "blue, glossy green" and "shining white" of the tracks of the watersnakes, and the "reel and rout" of the death fires have become the pleasing "coils" of the snakes.' John Beer steers a middle and rather Wordsworthian course as to whether the reality is in the snakes or the Mariner's mind: '. . . the Mariner's response to the bright movements of the watersnakes can be seen to mirror the poet's delight at the play of energies in his own mind' [CPI, 179].

25. Cf. CPI, 168, and C. Vis., 158.
26. My assumption is, of course, that it is the Mariner's growth of consciousness that precipitates the events of the poem rather than vice-versa, and particularly in the latter part of the poem.
27. Shedd I, 268, M I, 684; cf. CN I, 209, 'Man knows God only by revelation from God – as we see the sun by his own Light'. F I, 105, 'Religion is the sun, whose warmth indeed swells, and stirs, and actuates the life of nature'.
28. Cf. Jasper, op. cit., 97, on SM, 6–7: 'It is the "habitual unreflectingness" of public religion which has led to its "spiritual slumber" '.
29. Cf. CN II, 2090.
30. Cf. Kessler, op. cit., 49: 'The Mariner's sin was what R. G. Collingwood called a "corruption of consciousness" and not some mistake to be corrected by a moral lesson' [*The Principles of Art*, 338].
31. Cf. CS, 171.
32. Cf. John Beer on 'Christabel': '. . . the attempt to represent redemption of evil by innocence was the rock on which the poem foundered . . .' [C. Vis., 197.]
33. Cf. Happel, 163: 'It was a method of clarifying the positive content of his own religious position'.
34. CPI, 114.
35. Cf. Wheeler, op. cit., 44: '–it is not to anyone that the Mariner tells his tale; he chooses his listeners instinctively, only those who

will be so deeply aroused by the tale as to be taught something "stunning" in its import'.

36. Coleridge does not seem to have brought his high view of marriage into this poem.
37. Some years ago, this was the conclusion of a *Punch* cartoon.
38. Kessler, op. cit. 48.
39. Cf. BLC I 111.
40. Nethercot, 55.
41. Gillman, 283.
42. C. Vis., 186–7.
43. CL IV, 917–18, and the whole of John Beer's article, 'Coleridge, Hazlitt, and "Christabel".' [*Review of English Studies*, New Series, Vol XXXVII, No. 145 (February 1986) 40–54.]
44. FQ I, i, 49.
45. Cf. Nethercot, 19.
46. Cf. CPI, 35–6, and Basler, 85–6.
47. TT, 321.
48. HH, 130; for two other interesting readings of the poem along this line, see the articles by Roy P. Basler and Jona Spatz.
49. Cf. F I, 189; CS, 15–16.
50. Cf. CN I, 658.
51. Cf. C. Vis., 191.
52. This disorientation might be connected, in Coleridge's mind with youthful fascination for the tale of a man compelled to seek for a pure virgin. To us the adjective verges on tautology, but his more discriminating mind discerns the potential disorder in which the fact is a symbol of a larger if not properly integrated whole. Cf. CL I, 347; E. E. Bostetter, 'Christabel': The Vision of Fear', 186; and p.51 of John Beer's article cited in note 43.
53. Cf. John Beer, op. cit., 50: that Coleridge wanted Geraldine to be seen as a *woman* is evident in two lines he inserted in Derwent's copy of the poem. He did so, John Beer believes, because it appeared to him that the theory that Geraldine was a man in disguise, which he attributed to Hazlitt, was gaining ground.
54. Gillman, 302.
55. In a letter outlining some 'local disagreements' with my reading of Coleridge's poetry, John Beer commented as follows on this paragraph: 'The argument that because it had been preceded by the projected 'Wanderings of Cain' and the finished *Ancient Mariner* this poem too must have a crime-committer as its centre does not seem to me at all strong: it is equally possible to argue that having in the *Mariner* drawn out one strand in the 'Wanderings', the one associated with Cain, Coleridge now wanted to develop the other – the one concerned with the innocent Enos and the victim Abel. I believe indeed the fact that Christabel's name is made up of 'Christ' and 'Abel' to be no accident'. I have modified the paragraph in the light of these comments, but I would still maintain that Christabel is the focus for that development of consciousness which is the stuff of the Supernatural poems, and

that she is not merely the agent in someone else's redemption; and that she is both innocent – that is, genuinely charitable – and the victim of Geraldine's awakening of her sexuality. The resolution of these originally conflicting forces is what I take to be the impetus of the unfinished poem.

56. This distinction between sense-based life and life derived from reverencing the invisible forms the basis of the chapter entitled 'Of the Origin of the Idea of God in the Mind of Man' in the Opus Magnum manuscript: 'Beyond the beasts, yea and above the nature of which they are the inmates, Man possesses love and faith and the sense of the permanent. As the connection and the intermedium of both he possesses reflection and foresight; in other words an understanding, which is therefore a human understanding . . . because it is irradiated by a higher power, the power namely, of seeking what it can nowhere behold . . . – the permanent, that which in the endless flux of sensible things can alone be known, and which is indeed in all, but exists to the reason alone, for it is Reason' [Op.M II ff.68–9].

57. Although Coleridge seems to have had ambiguous attitudes to his own mother, motherhood in general was a focus of his idealism. Cf. 'The Three Graves' – 'A mother is a mother still,/The holiest thing alive'. PW I, 277; CL II, 904–5, 'for the memory of a MOTHER – of all names the most awful, the most venerable, next to that of God!'; CL V, 180, and RFR, 114; and in the Opus Magnum manuscript, Coleridge wrote: 'As sure as ever the heart of man is made tender by the presence of a love that has no self, by a joy in the protection of the helpless, which is at once impulse, motive and reward, so surely is it elevated to the universal Parent. The child on the knee of its mother, and gazing upward to her countenance marks her eyes averted heavenward, while it feels the tender pressure of her embrace, and learns to pray in the mother's prayers and knows this alone – that they mean love and protection, and that they are elsewhere, and that the mother and itself are included in the same words, indeed are not there, nor the formal proposition; but the living truth is there, that which the mother is to her child, a someone unseen and yet ever present is to all'.

CHAPTER 4: KUBLA KHAN AND DEJECTION: AN ODE

1. Though Kathleen Wheeler is determined to make it more complex than it need be. She believes that Coleridge's preface is, like the gloss added to 'The Ancient Mariner', an ironic commentary on the poem. Thus, referring to the poet's three-hour sleep she writes: 'Coleridge may be ironizing by playing on the tradition that the Khan fell asleep and dreamt the plan of the palace to be built'. [*The Creative Mind in Coleridge's Poetry*, 23; cf. RX, 358. Cf. n.33, Ch.2.]

2. Cf. Wheeler, op. cit., 169, n.4: 'The Crewe Manuscript has only one major division, between lines 36 and 37; and though there are

various published divisions, even with these variations in mind, the reader usually senses a major division between the first 36 and the last 18 lines'.

3.   Cf.ibid., 27.
4.   *The Use of Poetry and The Use of Criticism*, 146.
5.   E. S. Shaffer, *'Kubla Khan' and the Fall of Jerusalem*, 18: 'Coleridge's notes suggest that "Kubla Khan" is based on his epic plan, and that his 'dreamwork' condensed the three Acts of the Apocalypse into the climactic moment of the First Act, when the Sixth Seal is opened'. If by 'notes' Shaffer means those on Eichhorn, she does not once quote here from the source that she says has formed her central thesis. It seems to me most unlikely that Coleridge himself ever considered this poem as a collapsed or condensed epic, and what is wanting at the outset of the argument is some glimpse of how the notes on Eichhorn follow a pattern of intellectual activity which runs more or less parallel to the progress of 'Kubla Khan'. But we are given neither those nor a close reading of the poem; and E. S. Shaffer is elsewhere given to magisterial statements the foundations for which she does not reveal to us: 'The shape of romantic poetry, indeed of poetry to the present day, begins to be visible as the eighteenth-century Biblical epic emerges into the lyrical ballad'. Op. cit., 62.
6.   Cf. Beer, C. Vis., 224, who thinks that this act of enclosure is nature-denying and symbolic of the Khan's lost innocence.
7.   Wheeler, op. cit., 33, thinks that 'the contrast between the Khan's architectural and landscaping gestures . . . and the natural, wild, and unencompassed scene of the "deep romantic chasm" . . . suggests the distinction between the secondary activities of art and culture . . . and the primary activities of perception'.
8.   Ibid., 34: 'The Khan measures and decrees and walls and girdles. He shuts out nature and imagination, and art degenerates'. A view shared by Yarlott (135/151) and Beer (C.Vis., 223–4). But why then does the awesome poet wish to *imitate* the Khan? (In a marginal note on the typescript of this book John Beer has written, 'He wishes to imitate the *ideal* action involved'. I find it difficult to determine an ideal action in the poem distinct from that recorded of the Khan.)
9.   It seems to me that the Khan is seen as the ideal creator, and that the poet is conscious of his unlikeness to this ideal figure. Cf. Wheeler, op. cit., 25 who thinks that 'the narrator is symbolically the imagination itself, or the ideal poet, the ideal creator, omniscient, mysterious and unknown'. This line of argument arises out of the mistaken assumption that the Khan's activities are opposed to the function of the imagination.
10. Cf. CN III, 4319, f.126; E. S. Shaffer, op. cit., 165.
11. Ibid., 106.
12. Cf. HH, 120–1.
13. Cf. E. Earle Ellis's commentary on the word 'abyss' in Luke 8.31: '**abyss** in Semetic cosmology is an abbreviated form of a mythopoeic

term, the 'watery deep', i.e., a vast cosmic sea under the earth. It symbolizes the chaos in opposition to which the world was fashioned (Gen. 1.2) and by which it is ever threatened. From this threat Jesus brings deliverance to man and to the whole created order (Rom. 8.19 ff.)'. *The Gospel of Luke*, The Century Bible, ed. E. Earle Ellis (London, 1966) p.131.

14. *Beowulf*, 11.82–3. Cf. what I take to be Robert F. Fleissner's not entirely serious article, *'Hwæt! Wê Gardêna*: "Kubla Khan" and Those Anglo-Saxon Words.' [*Wordsworth Circle*, Vol.5 (Winter 1974) pp.50–4.]

15. Cf. Graham Hough, *Selected Essays*, 86: 'It is not perhaps fanciful to suppose that Kubla, the all-powerful monarch who can create a palace and a garden by his mere decree, is the inspired poet-magician, who can similarly create his own world . . .'

16. Cf. Alice D. Snyder, 'The Manuscript of "Kubla Khan" ', TLS 2 August 1934, p.541.

17. *Paradise Lost*, IV, 280–4.

18. H. W. Piper, 'Mount Abora', 287.

19. Yarlott, op. cit., 60–4.

20. CN II, 3231; for the 'vital air' cf. Yarlott, Ch.2, passim.

21. For the true nature of prophecy, see CN III, 3365; cf. CN I, 94 and note.

22. The best general account of this poem is found in George Dekker's *Coleridge and the Literature of Sensibility*, which is marred only by his peculiar thesis that Coleridge developed the 'Letter' out of 'Dejection', and not vice-versa as is commonly and reasonably supposed.

23. McFarland, RFR, 29, seems to make the mistake of thinking that this is a Wordsworthian statement; he comments: 'Coleridge here speaks of "sublimity" as somehow co-ordinate with infinity and summons the natural phenomenology of rocks, waterfalls and mountains as exemplars'. McFarland then adduces a quotation from Wordsworth as a parallel: '. . . the rock and the Waterfall: these objects will be found to have exalted the mind to the highest state of sublimity . . . the absolute crown of the impression is infinity, which is a modification of unity'. In my opinion the opposing views expressed in each quotation are highlighted by the similarity of the subject matter.

24. McFarland, RFR, 88, gives examples of nature acting on the mind of man from Wordsworth's poetry, and then comments: 'To such a fundamental and pervasive acceptance of the passive relationship of mind to the activity of nature, Coleridge opposed himself absolutely'. Not absolutely, as the Conversation poems and McFarland's own comments on p.29 indicate, but I share McFarland's belief in principle. I am also glad to see that he confirms another opinion I have held since first reading 'To William Wordsworth' – that Coleridge's description of the theme of the Prelude

of moments awful
Now in thy inner life, and now abroad,

When power streamed from thee, and thy soul received
The light reflected, as a light bestowed

is actually a criticism of the power of Wordsworth attributes to
Nature, when it is rightly attributable only to him as a man – in
whom the mind is making the senses, and not the senses the mind.
        Cf. N.46, f.25v:

' "Fair as a Star when only one
        Is shining in the sky" – WW

– Now what is the beauty of a Star? Wherein consists, out of what
ground, arises the beauty of a serene starry Night? . . . Wherein
differs it from the . . . paper, I have thrown on the fire? Or the
Spark in the black Tinder Box? Assuredly we see the Star with the
spiritual Eye. The mind here transfers itself into the vision'.

25.   Cf. R. G. Collingwood, *An Autobiography*, 24–5.
26.   Cf. CL I, 381: 'The beings who know how to sympathize with me
        are my foliage'.
27.   Cf. CN II, 2623, 2624 and notes.
28.   The 'Letter to Asra' is printed in George Whalley's *Coleridge and
        Sara Hutchinson and the 'Asra' Poems*, 155–64.
29.   Yarlott, op. cit., 64.
30.   It is at this point that the 'Letter . . .' begins to lose its momentum,
        and to vacillate between Coleridge's love of Sara and the Words-
        worth household, and the state of his own 'house-hold Life'. His
        inability to resolve this conflict succinctly is a major reason why
        some critics prefer the poem in its published form.
31.   Cf. Dekker, op. cit., 103, who thinks of the harp as a 'metaphor
        for the poet himself, and that the dull sobbing draft of Stanza 1 is
        the figurative counterpart of the stifled, drowsy unimpassioned
        grief . . .' See also p.113.
32.   Cf CL I, 643.
33.   Dekker, op. cit., 103, believes that we must think of the harp as
        continuing to play while the poet is speaking.
34.   Dekker, 122, discovers that between Stanzas I and VII of the poem
        the poet has experienced a partial release, and comments: 'Unfortu-
        nately, it is by no means evident how this release was affected in
        the first place . . .' Had Dekker shown more interest in the verse
        letter he would have discovered that Coleridge experiences a partial
        release through his thinking on Sara Hutchinson; he turns again to
        the wind only when the imagined progress of his relationship with
        her has reached a desperate endpoint, for which the wind's frenzy
        is a metaphor.
35.   Cf. Kessler, 33; and CL II, 990: 'O God! when a man blesses the
        loud Scream of Agony that awakens him, night after night'.
36.   Robert Frost, *Selected Poems*, 158 (Harmondsworth: 1966).
37.   Cf. 11.208–15 and CL II, 669; there is something of Coleridge in the
        child that has lost its way.

38. Cf. N.46 f.21v – which might be taken as a profound comment on the change of direction at this point in the poem – from self to other: 'But as nothing finite can stand by itself, the disruption from the control of the moral Reason involves immersion in and a modification by, the Creaturely Will, the Life and the Mind of the Flesh. *Thus take the yearning to be beloved, the craving for sympathy*, in persons of active and constitutional sensibility: and trace this thro' the craving to become an object of sympathy, and in order to this to be at once an Object of Pity and of Admiration – *and then watch the day dreams*, that have perhaps been scared and frowned or scoffed away by the awaking conscience and the dawning Light of Reason, in order to detect the little tricks, and tricky imaginations, *by which the creaturely* will *subjectively* realizes for itself the sense of being beloved . . . It is therefore selfishness: that is the self is not only the starting-point *from*, but the Goal, to which the Soul is working during such moments . . . The whole procedure is there-fore anti-redemptive . . . It has the true mark of the Hades, contra-diction, falsehood . . .'

39. For 'mountain Birth', see Florence G. Marsh, *Notes and Queries*, 1955, pp.261–2, and Yarlott, 265.

40. Cf. *Logic*, 220: Coleridge, of course, does not believe in the literal power of the human mind to create something out of nothing.

41. On 'genial' see Jasper, 67–8.

42. For the image of eddying see Kessler, 15–37; and CN 1, 495/1589: 'River Greta near its fall into the Tees – shootings of water threads down the slope of the huge green stone. The whole Eddy-rose that blossom'd up against the stream in the scollop, by fits and starts, obstinate in resurrection – It is *the life* that we live'.

43. Cf. Dekker, 149, and Jasper, 65.

CHAPTER 5: THE GOD WITHIN

1. Cf. PW I, 125 and WPW, 195; for the influence of this mythology on the Romantics generally and Coleridge particularly, see Dekker, Ch. 1.

2. Cf. Helen Darbishire, *The Poet Wordsworth*, p. 90, writing apropos Coleridge's plan as outlined in CL IV, 571–6: 'This was what Word-sworth could not do. He had plenty of fertile ideas, but he had no constructive plan: it may be said without flippancy that in the event all that was accomplished of the great philosophical poem, apart from Book I and the magnificent Prospectus, was a Prelude to the main theme, and an Excursion from it'.

3. N. 23, f.20v.

4. Cf. Holmes, *Coleridge*, 34, and CL III, 489: 'If it could be said with as little *appearance* of profaness, as there is feeling or intention in my mind, I might affirm that I had been crucified, dead and buried, descended into *Hell*, and now, I humbly trust, rising again, tho' slowly and gradually'.

5. Among others, Kathleen Coburn has found echoes of the poem in

the following notebook entries: CN I, 1473, 1486; CN II, 1996, 2001, 2045, 2052, 2060, 2078, 2086, 2090, 2100, 2293, 2557, 2610, 2880, 2915.

6. Cf. CL II, 989–90, again to Southey.
7. CN II, 2091; cf. CN II, 2666.
8. Cf. CL II, 1084–5: 'What my Dream was, is not to tell'.
9. Cf. CN I, 1473 and n.
10. For a full consideration of the themes of crime, punishment and penitence in the early works of both poets, see C. J. Smith, 'Wordsworth, and Coleridge: The Growth of a Theme', and Douglas Angus, 'The Theme of Love and Guilt in Coleridge's Three Major Poems'.
11. Cf. N.43, p.69: 'The imperishability of Thought, and the perishability of the Consciousness, and the possible reviviscence of the latter by the former – these are the three aweful Facts of deepest interest for every Contemplative Man'.

    N.38, f.27v: 'The continued Flux and Repair of the Brain, and the imperishability of thoughts has always been a very impressive consideration with me. But above all, the deep sense of the need and necessity of a Redeemer, of a healthful Action to be set up in the distempered Being in order to the possibility of a recovery'.
12. *The Collected Poems of W. B. Yeats*, 295.
13. Cf. N.48, f.8: 'Lust can never be transubstantiated into Love – it is the lusting Man that gradually Depositing the bestial nature, into which he had fallen, under the subliming influences of Affection, Awe of Duty, and Sense of the Beautiful, is indeed transubstantiated (= born into) a *loving* Man'.
14. Cf. N.42, f.20v, on Genesis I 25, when Adam and Eve were naked but not ashamed: 'The mere *sensations* that accompany Lust, may exist, yet Love alone be the object of consciousness – It is only when these sensations are the direct object of consciousness, and desired for themselves, that Lust obtains a Being. It is no longer clothed and hidden in a loftier nature, and taken up into the Humanity, but the very fact of making itself naked comes to know its nakedness and be ashamed–'.
15. Cf. N.47, p.75, for the relations of Beauty, Love and 'Appetence'.
16. Cf. *Paradise Lost* V, 469–90, one of Coleridge's favourite passages.
17. Cf. N.49, f.41–2, and CL III, 304–5 on Wordsworth's idea of love.
18. Cf. Kessler 6: 'Being is the energy shining through phenomena, a movement toward that "ultimate Being" which cannot finally be realized in time and space. Perhaps his purest evocation of Being in poetry appeared in these "lines" . . .'
19. Yarlott, 47.
20. Cf. Prickett, *Wordsworth and Coleridge: The Poetry of Growth*, 24: 'The tone is pessimistic – even despairing'.
21. 'In the porch of Death' is an apt description of 'Limbo', PW I, 249; and it is worth noting that the 'old Man with steady look sublime' has lost his sight, and yet

He gazes still, his eyeless Face all Eye –
As 'twere an Organ full of silent Sight
His whole Face seemeth to rejoice in Light.

And so we learn that he is no inhabitant of Limbo, but seems to be rejoicing in the power of his inward eye, which is expressing itself in his countenance.

22. Cf. Happel, 216: 'Coleridge's dialectical method requires not only the ideal good or the ideal true as the objectives of human consciousness, but also a concrete good which "impersonates" the good and an individual truth which actualizes the true. It requires the idea of symbol . . . Symbol involves one's recognizing an individual or truth as the presence of the Good and the True'. Also ibid., 334: '. . . consciousness founds by its self-presentation, its self-mediation, the presence of the true, the good, and the beautiful'.

23. Kessler, 127, hopes 'to add to Prickett's meaningful discussion', but in fact what he has to say is very different from what Prickett has to say: my reading is much closer to that of Kessler, whose discussion occupies pp. 127–38; for Prickett's views, see op. cit., 22–45. for other refs. see CN I, 258, 430, 431; CN III, 3466; AR, 220; CL V, 266.

24. But little cause for Boulger's wholesale dismissal: *Coleridge as a Religious Thinker*, 210; cf. CN III, 4283.

25. Shakespeare's protean nature is also mentioned in CN II, 2396 and CN III, 3247.

26. Cf. the mirror image in the original version of 'Work without Hope', found in CL V, 416, where each becomes the means of viewing the infinite in the other.

27. That his moods were sometimes more negative is evident, for instance, CN III, 3796. But men are right in what they affirm, and wrong in what they deny.

CHAPTER 6: COLERIDGE'S CHRISTOLOGY

1. Harding, 155.
2. CN I, 1802; cf. CL IV, 893.
3. Harding, 155; N.26, f.53–4.
4. Cf. CL VI, 573.
5. Cf. N.41, f.145.
6. Harding, 150.
7. CN I, 1717, cf. CN II, 2058; Happel, 137, F II, 279. This conflation of Reason and the Will may be another cause of Kant considering, or Lovejoy considering on his behalf, that 'because evil is empirically ubiquitous, "All the noumenal egos, in short, are bad egos." And if the ego is noumenally bad, free will becomes once again impossible'. [E. S. Shaffer, 'Metaphysics of Culture: Kant and Coleridge's *Aids to Reflection*', 206]. I think Dr Shaffer would have solved some of the problems she raises in this essay more satisfactorily if she had incorporated Coleridge's short but intense 'Essay on Faith'.

8. Cf. Op. M. II, p.2: 'We may then without anticipation affirm that the identity of the absolute Will and the universal Reason is peculiar to the idea of God'. Cf. N.46, f.13v (1830): 'By the provision of transcendent Goodness God has permitted and enabled us to divide our personal Will from our corrupt and evil Nature'.
9. CN II, 3148; cf. CN II, 2712, 2860, 3148.
10. For the dating of this essay see CL V, 87 (1820) and note. Cf. N.37, f.5v–6 for a distinction between faith and belief.
11. ' "The Law . . . of Reason in the conscience [is] of far higher authority than the Light of Reason in the Understanding." Conscience precedes consciousness . . .' Happel, 733, quoting from N.26, f.40; cf N. 26, f.39v: 'This is the Corner-stone of *my* System, ethical, metaphysical and theological – the priority, namely, both in dignity and in order of generation of the Conscience to the Consciousness in Man. No I without a Thou: no Thou without a Law from *Him* to whom I and Thou stand in the same relation. Distinct self knowledge begins with sense of Duty to my Neighbor: and Duty felt *to*, and claimed from, my Equal, supposes and implies the Right of a Third, superior to both because imposing it on both.' And N. 23, f.32: '. . . since only by meeting with, so as to be resisted by, *another* does the Soul become a *Self*'.
12. Cf. Happel, 737, 'Conscience is the proper meaning of the will'.
13. For other comments on the nature of the conscience see CN III, 3281, 3562; CL III, 80 and 146.
14. 'Ultimately, this experience of a Thou, the "ought" of one's existence, is the experience of God.' [Happel, 742].
15. CN II, 2664; cf. F I, 112 and CN III, 3787.
16. LR IV, 433–4; cf. 431: '. . . as the identity or coinherence of the absolute will with the reason is the peculiar character of God . . . so is the synthesis of the individual will and the common reason . . . the required proper character of man'. Cf. Op.M. II, p.7.
17. Harding, 191.
18. LR IV, 430–31; cf. N2½, f.46v.: 'All Faith begins in a pre-disposition, analogous to instinct, in as much as the particular Will could not be awaked and realized into an actual volition but by an impulse and communication from the universal Will. This latter is the vital air which the particular Will breathes but which must have entered and erected the faculty [as the previous] and enabling condition of the first disposition to breathe, as well as the power of drawing Breath'.
19. Green, *Spiritual Philosophy*, II, 390; cf. Muirhead, 246.
20. The distinction between Reason and Understanding occurs throughout Coleridge's work: for a sample see F I, 154–61, 177, 190; SM, 59–62, AR (1825), 150 ff.
21. Cf. N. 18, f.167, Harding, 116.
22. AR, 347 (1836).
23. Ibid.
24. Cf. Hamilton, 124, for a comparable analysis of this passage.
25. Muirhead, 35.

26. Harding, 137.
27. But cf. AR, 272: awareness of Reason as God is the ground of the individual's coming to Christ.
28. Brinkley (ed.) *Coleridge on the Seventeenth Century*, 174–5.
29. E. S. Shaffer, *'Kubla Khan' and the Fall of Jerusalem*, 321 and n.: 'Coleridge agreed that the life of Christ must be regarded as doctrinal, not biographical'. Cf. N.30, ff. 29–29v; N.41, f.20–26, and f.41: '. . . it has long been the tendency of the Age to reduce the mission our Lord to a Teaching, a Revelation and to distract and draw off the attention from the truer and far more concerning view – that it was a *doing*, a series of redemptive acts realizing the doctrines long anticipated by faith. According to Paul the partriarchs held the same doctrinal faith as we, – they as Promises, we as Fulfilments'.
30. Cf. N.50, f.18v: 'I believe of all and for all – without the faith in the resurrection and the life the very grass under my feet would turn black before me'.
31. Cf. N.48, f.30v: 'The infallible Test of the Gospel Faith is that it appeals to all the constituents of our present Humanity, and Brings them all to an equilibrium – to a Beauty of Holiness. – The evolution of this idea in all the detail, commencing with an ennumeration of our Powers . . . is indeed a *desideratum*'.
32. Cf. LPR 160, and 235–6.
33. Cf. F I 316 and n.
34. Cf. Kessler, 11: 'Christ is man in the fullness of Being, neither a mere man more a mere metaphor, but a symbol that transcends all accident'.
35. The following short section on the Trinity is not designed to demonstrate the fullness of Coleridge's thought on this subject, but only to show how he co-ordinated and distinguished self and other in divine and human psychology respectively. David Jasper, the second of the book's three readers, wrote in his report that he needs 'to be convinced that Coleridge saw Christ as anything other than a symbol for Reason in man, and I suspect that he came to his later Trinitarian formula by a more philosophical route than Davidson suggests – by the dialectic triad, which was Coleridge's explanation in logical terms of the reconciliation of opposites'. My opinion is that the personal and the philosophical do not exclude each other in Coleridge's development. The late noteboks give me the strong impression of a man deeply engaged with the person of Christ. Cf. N.50, f.21, 28; N.48, f.42; N.45, f.19; N.44, f.44v; for his philosophical understanding of the subject, see Happel, Ch. 6, and Newsome, Appendices B and C, and CPT, Ch. IV.
36. CN III, 3705.
37. CL IV, 850; To Theion – the Divinity; O Theos – God, the Deity. (Liddell and Scott).
38. Cf. SM, 78 and n.; F I, 524; BL II, 216.

CHAPTER 7: THE PERMANENT SELF AND THE LIFE OF NATURE

1. Cf. Pym, 34, on Lessing's influence while Coleridge was in Germany; and N.47, p.20.
2. There are, however, several kinds of interpretation of the *Biographia* available to undecided readers – upon most of which Coleridge passed the prophetic comment: 'Any-mad-versions of an Author's meaning now a days pass for animadversions' [CN III 4124]. With impressive fairness Paul Hamilton, *Coleridge's Poetics*, 15, summarizes the opinion that it is an extended exercise in irony, a view exemplified in K. M. Wheeler's desire that we should approach the work as 'ironized, reductive readers'. His summary is just enough to invite our conviction, but a page or so later he writes: 'Coleridge mimes confusion and disruption so convincingly in his presentation that we seem in this case to have lost any criteria for distinguishing an incoherent text from one that demands an ironic reading . . . Over-ingenious sympathy for the broken argument of the *Biographia* condemns Coleridge's work to a sadly vicarious existence. We should accept that the absence at the centre of *Biographia* is a genuine hiatus in his thought, and not the mask worn by his supersubtle argument'. I agree. Coleridge was not a literary poseur, and would not have wasted his scarce energies in exhausting ironic gestures. My only dissatisfaction with Hamilton's commentary is that he does not probe the ground of this hiatus in sufficient depth.
3. Shedd V, 607; N.36, p.126; N.38, f.14.
4. Cf. BLC I, lxxvi. In discussing this text, Professor Beer said, 'The *Biographia* is all about 1798, and says nothing about subsequent experience'.
5. Cf. D. M. Fogel, 'A Compositional History of the BIOGRAPHIA LITERARIA'; BLC I, xcii.
6. Cf. TT, 21 July 1832.
7. Cf. CN III, 3708.
8. See also, F I, 110, 205, 529; CN I, 1725 and n.; CN II, 2066; CS, 96; AR (1825), 1.
9. Cf. Op. M., II, p. 36: Aristotle 'acknowledged the necessity of a principle deeper than science, more certain than demonstration; for that the very ground is groundless or self-grounded is, saith he, an identical proposition; from the indemonstrable flows the sap which circulates through every branch and spray of the demonstration'. Cf. Ibid, f.38, where Coleridge asserts that dichotomous reasoning always ends in pantheism.
10. Coleridge's debt to Kant is an involved matter. For some authoritative opinions see René Wellek, *Immanuel Kant in England*; G. N. G. Orsini, *Coleridge and German Idealism*; Thomas McFarland, CPT.
11. Cf. BLC I, 143.
12. Cf. CPI, 212, *Coleridge's Variety*, 164–5.
13. Cf. N.36, p.2: 'But observe that in my system *Object* is not, as in the Fichtean Idealism, the dead, the substanceless, the mere Idol,

but the absolutely free Productivity in the always perfect Product . . .'

14. Cf. N.28, f.29v: 'In short, Schelling's system and mine stand thus: in the latter there are God and Chaos: in the former an absolute somewhat, which is *alternately* both, the rapid leger de main shifting of which constitutes the delusive appearance of *Poles* . . .' But an alternative explanation for the digressiveness of this chapter is that it might be Coleridge's attempt to make the work more palatable to the 'reading public'.

15. But not of the relations between them; cf. Hamilton, 54.

16. Cf. F I, 523: 'From the indemonstrable flows the sap that circulates through every branch and spray of demonstration'.

17. See note 14.

18. Barfield, 242; McFarland does not have much time for Barfield's statement either – RFR, 309, and TT, 28 June 1834.

19. Cf. BLC I, 240–1; Coleridge asserts the absolute importance of achieving self-consciousness, but then asserts that it is an act only achievable by the few. Cf. BLC I, 236 and SM, 38.

20. BLC I, 239 and n. 1.

21. Cf. Op. M., I: in some ways this volume seems to be a rewriting of the philosophy of Volume I of the *Biographia*. Certainly there are passages which supply a comment on the inadequacy of its method: for instance: 'We are certain that the planetary mechanism contemplated mechanically and as inanimate cannot causatively explain life and organization; let us then examine whether we may not be more successful in reversing the order of priority, namely whether in life we may not find the conditions of universal organization and again in universal organization the conditions and the solution of mechanism – This is our present problem'. This Coleridge believes to be a more logical method because 'from mechanism to organization, i.e. from shape as the forma formata to form as the forma formans, there is no progression possible'. Therefore, we might add, from the common consciousness of things to consciousness of inner freedom, equally little progress is possible.

22. Cf. BLC I, lxxvi: 'Coleridge took for granted the opposition of the self ("spirit" or "self-consciousness") and of nature (the objective world)'. James Engel does not point out that this is perhaps a false or inadequate premise, and what he goes on to say is misleading, if not mistaken: 'The self *could* be an object, but only to itself in the original proposition, "I am" '. What Coleridge had learnt painfully in his love of Sara Hutchinson was that the self is only adequately objectified in its love of another, and the essential being of any such object is founded in Christ. Cf. N.56, p.20, the two ways of writing a history of Nature.

23. Cf. N.36 p.2 and p.40 for a more mature view of what constitutes an object.

24. Cf. SM, 95, CS, 84 and n.

25. PL, 407.

26.   Cf. Orsini, *Coleridge and German Idealism*, 215; Suther, *the Dark Night of Samuel Taylor Coleridge*, 169.

27.   Cf. Hamilton, 43: 'The primary imagination will account for the use of imagination in perception and knowledge; the workings of the secondary imagination will then explain the exertions of the poet's imagination in making poetry'. Although very few discussions of Coleridge's terminology actually get much further than this, yet if the matter was as pleasantly straightforward as Hamilton would have us believe, all the puzzling over what Coleridge actually meant would have been done with years ago. As I see it, what Hamilton's typical formulation does not explain is the place of the act of will enabling self-consciousness in either of the two modes of imaginative activity. If it is co-ordinate with the primary act, then perception is theoretically impossible without it – and this is clearly not the case; but if it is *not* co-ordinate with perception, why is perception considered an act of imagination at all? If, as initially seems more likely, the act of self-consciousness is related to the function of the secondary imagination, then in its effort to dissolve and dissipate, to idealize and unify, by what laws is it operating, and what is the structure of the unity that it is seeking to achieve? In other words, what has presented this power of the secondary imagination with its ultimate end? That the ultimate unity of all unities is God provides no immediately satisfactory answer, for Coleridge himself pointed out that an essential attribute of God as the first cause is incomprehensibility – which only a fading few take to be an attribute of poetry. The comprehensible form of God is his Son, the doctrines of whose life we may take as constitutive ideas. In my mind, these are the inventions of the primary imagination, and present the secondary imagination with the ultimate form of unity it is to create. Of the distinction between primary and secondary imagination, David Jasper, the second of the three readers of this book in typescript, pointed out that 'most critics (including Engels and Jackson Bate) see this as mirroring Coleridge's distinction between copy/imitation. They are wrong, and the primary imagination must be rescued as a creative faculty. (It's an important point.)' I agree; however, I do not think that simple perception is a creative act, nor that it should be taken as such: in my opinion, the creative aspect of the primary imagination is closely related to the act of conscience, as the next note attempts to explain.

28.   I suggest that there are *two* forms of the primary imagination: the conceptual which fits our involuntary sense impressions to preconceived notions or mental templates, so that objects may have a name, a place and a function to us – for instance, before we recognize a table we must have established in our minds the notion of a table; and the more fundamentally human power of, in Coleridge's language, *ideation*, which is the construction in our consciousness of those 'presences' which constitute our humanity, and which is implicit in every act of conscience, on every occasion that we find our self in our love of another person, and which is our

coming to truly human consciousness. The first form of primary imagination is a learnt response rather than a voluntary action; but the second is an act of the will, the centring of our self in our love and knowledge of another, and though enabled by the free will in one condition, may equally be disabled by the same will in another condition.

The secondary imagination is that which gives substance to the realities of self-consciousness by means of the forms of our perceptions – that power which establishes a relation between the phenomenal and apparently idea-less objects of outward sense, and the discovered objects, or ideas, of inner sense.

29. TT, 28 June 1834.
30. Cf. Happel, 211.
31. HCR I, 158, ed. E. J. Morley.
32. Unlocated.
33. Coleridge called it 'so immethodical a miscellany' [BLC I 88], and Leslie Stephen thought that it was 'put together with a pitchfork', (*Hours in a Library*, III 355). George Whalley ('The Integrity of the *Biographia Literaria*) and James Engel (BLC I, lxxiii) find a unity in the work. D. M. Fogel's 'The Compositional History of the BIOGRAPHIA LITERARIA' supplies most of the background necessary to establish one's own opinion.
34. That is, there is no essentially common ground between the knower and what is known, to achieve which had been the target of the act of self-consciousness in the philosophy of Volume I.
35. Cf. SC I, 215–6: Coleridge compares the variety of Shakespeare's mind with the aboreal variations Wordsworth presents here – that is, he introduces an *idea*.
36. Barfield, 218, n.19.
37. Cf. I. A. Richards, 82–4. For an excellent and Coleridgean definition of a symbol, see Dorothy Sayers' introduction to her translation of Dante's *The Divine Comedy*, Hell, pp.12–13 (Harmondsworth: 1949).
38. SC I, 188.
39. Hamilton, 181.
40. Cf. CN II, 24450, f.20v.
41. Cf. CN III, 4397, f.51: This entry demonstrates Coleridge's belief in the 'Wisdom in Nature' and the necessity of the creative mind to absent itself from nature to acquire 'living an life-producing Ideas', existing side by side.
42. Cf. N.35, p.60.
43. Cf. CN II 3026.
44. Cf. N.35, p.60: Coleridge feels 'the dread of prejudicing the minds of men against my views of the material and moral . . . Worlds as one *subject* comprehended in one scheme of redemption – and of particular Life beginning with detachment from Nature and to end in union with God – my view of Nature as the ens non vere ens, the opposite of God as the Spirit of Chaos, but made Nature by the *Word* thro' the super-induction of a tendency to supersede itself'.

45.		Cf. Kessler, 8.

CHAPTER 8: THE IDEA OF HISTORY

1.		Were it not for Christianity, Coleridge feels that he should 'utterly want the *historic* sense. Even as it is, I feel it very languid in all particular History . . .' (N.51, f.9). But in the same notebook a few pages earlier he wrote that a 'contemptuous disregard for Antiquity' is a sign of the moral deterioration in a people (f.4). These statements are easily reconciled if we bear in mind the distinction between sense-impression (or 'fact') and idea.

2.		Cf. N.34, f.3: 'I am persuaded that the Truth receives more and more serious injuries from motive-making, and other grave ways of Lying, by which actions the most independent are linked together by psychological and conjectural copula in our Voltaires, Hume, Gibbon, Robertson etc., than by the harmless conventional and well understood machinery of the Historic Epos in our ancient Historians'.

3.		Cf. Hamilton, 190: 'Eliciting a redemptive pattern from history is typical of Schelling, and leads to a scheme which seems unavoidably pantheistic, identifying God with his imminence in history'. The pantheism is avoided, in my opinion, because the subject-object relationship is developed in respect of the Son, and is external to the perfection of the Son's relationship with the Father.

4.		Cf. E. S. Shaffer, *'Kubla Khan' and the Fall of Jerusalem*, 45, 48; Cf. N. 41 f.3v, and TT, 31 July 1832.

5.		Cf. K. Coburne's introduction to the *Philosophical Lectures*, 42. Also N. 43, p.31: in which Coleridge asserts that the moral failings and the destruction of the Israelites is foretold in their literature, and is unique: but 'add only, that the History is the fulfilment, and that this History is the very Tap-root and Trunk of the Moral and therein of the physical and political *History* of the whole Planet – of all Human Progression, and I cannot conceive that any thoughtful mind, not perverted and rendered insensible by sophistry, should withstand the evidence'.

6.		This co-ordination is productive – of a person.

7.		Cf. TT, 3 Dec. 1831; N.20, p.55.

8.		Cf. E. S. Shaffer, op.cit., 36.

9.		Cf. N.43, p.49–51; CN III, 3581.

10.		Learning the distinction between Reason and Understanding was hard going for the Hebrews, and one lesson came from the false prophets whose prophecies were fulfilled. They were not on that ground to be followed, for 'if against an article of the *Faith* of the inward Revelation of the Reason and Conscience – the true yet criminal Prophet was to be put to death' and the witnesses were to infer 'that God had permitted this display to prove their fealty – in order to make them understand the difference between a *Belief* grounded on a deduction of the fallible Understanding from phænomena presented to the *Sense*, from the Faith in the eternal affirmations of the moral and universal Reason – which as applied to the determination of the free responsible Will become commands, categorical Duties, Ideas substantiated into *Laws* – I *am* the Lord thy God – thou *shalt* have no God but me–'.

11.   Cf. AR (1836), 249; PL, 110; N.20. p.47.
12.   Cf. N.52, f.1.
13.   Cf. Op. M.I., pp.48–51: Coleridge believes that wonder at the world will always lead to pantheism, and yet it is the common man's first apprehension of God. Contemporary pantheists make the same intellectual error as their ancient predecessors, and it is Wordsworth that he has in mind: 'But how often have I not observed men of ardent Minds in the early glow of self-thinking and the first supposed emancipation from the prejudices of the popular faith shrink from the use of the personal as spoken of the Deity and disposed in a more than Poetic interpretation to substitute for the living Jehovah, the Creator of the Heavens and the Earth,

> a sense sublime
> Of something far more deeply interfused,
> Whose dwelling is the light of setting suns,
> And the round ocean, and the living air,
> And the blue sky, and in the mind of man,
> A motion and a spirit, that impels
> All thinking things, all objects of all thought,
> And rolls through all things.

Many a Man, I speak not without knowledge, who lulled with these dreams and accustomed to interpret the Divine omnipresence in any sense than the alone safe and legitimate one, the presence namely of all things to God, has thought himself abundantly religious, yea! hallowing his Sabbath with the loftiest sort of devotion'.

14.   Orsini, 139; *The Watchman*, 132.
15.   Cf. N.36, p.126.
16.   Cf. E. S. Shaffer, op. cit., 135, 149–50, 152; N.23, ff. 44v–45; N.25, p.63: 'As it was the genius of poetic Greece in the earliest period to transform that which must be *thought* into a something that has happened (in the literal sense of the words) taken *place*, homeless truth into historic event; so in a later period [it] was the business of Philosophy and of the Mysteries (the nightly Penelope) to unravel the day work, and to reduce the mythic into *Laws*, sometimes openly, others at first in the veil of symbols'.
17.   Cf. N.36, p.104.
18.   Cf. BM Ms Egerton, 2800, f.49–49v.
19.   Cf. N.36, p.123.
20.   Cf. N.20, p.17.
21.   Cf. N.42, f.25.
22.   Cf. N.42, f.55; '. . . and woeful and verily judicial is the blindness

of the Jews who degrade the patriarchal Desire of Nations into a Jewish Napoleon'. Also N.36, p.65.

23. Cf. Shedd, I, 363.
24. Cf. N.25, p.103.
25. Cf. N.38, f.27v.
26. Cf. Happel, 205; LS, 176; N.25, p.55; CL V, 48.
27. Cf. N.42, f.59.
28. Cf. N.35, p.90; N.37, p.45; E. S. Shaffer, op. cit., 24–36.
29. Cf. N.21½, f.61; N.36, p.94; N.43, p.120–1.
30. Cf. N.20, p.55.
31. Cf. CL VI, 89.
32. Cf. N.23, f.82.
33. Cf. SM, 18.
34. Cf. N.35, p.50.
35. Cf. SM 55.
36. Cf. N.35, p.50.
37. Cf. N.50, f.28; N.47, p.78; *Genesis* XXXI, v. 3.
38. Cf. N.45, f.44v.
39. Cf. E. S. Shaffer, op. cit., 136.
40. Cf. Pym, 54–5, who believes that Maurice's similar opinion was derived from Thomas Erskine's *The Brazen Serpent* (1831). Maurice's words, that Christ is 'the Head and King of our Race', are closer to those of Coleridge than of Erskine.
41. Cf. N.44, f.65.
42. Cf. N.3½, f.104.
43. Isaiah Berlin, *Vico and Herder*, 14–15.
44. Cf. Ibid., 33; AR (1825), 240.
45. Cf. N.41, f.8: Adam was not only 'Man, but Mankind . . . The psychical Humanity was all in Adam, the spiritual Humanity all in Christ'.
46. Cf. N.37, p.70.
47. Jean Danielou, *From Shadows to Reality*, 79–82.
48. Cf. N.42, f.40; N.44, f.6.
49. Cf. N.42, f.39.
50. Cf. Cf. Shedd, V, 591.
51. Cf. N.44, f.29: 'The Priest was the representative of Jehova to the People, and of the People to Jehova – the Type of the God-Man, who as Jehova presented himself to Mankind, and as incarnate represented the perfected Man to the Father'. Also N.43, p.45–6; N.44, f.20.
52. Cf. N.44, f.75v.
53. Cf. N.37, p.45.
54. Cf. N.3½, f.128–9.
55. Cf. Pym, 83: 'The whole of the Bible, Coleridge wanted to argue, is what we might term an extension of the great 'symbol', the historical figure of the Incarnate Word'.
56. Cf. N.43, p.30–1; CL VI, 689 – the Biblical prophecies provide 'a magnificent Scheme of *History* a priori'.
57. For some details of these parallels, see S. V. Pradhan's article.

CHAPTER 9: THE CREATION OF THE STATE

1. SC, 42.
2. BLC I, 175 and note.
3. Cf. BLC I, 76 and note; II, 27 and note, 83–4 and notes, 212 and note.
4. The full title of which is: 'Iago's Malignity Motivated: Coleridge's Unpublished "Opus Magnum"'.
5. C. M. R. Ridley, *Othello* lxi (London: Methuen, 1968).
6. Cf. the comments of A. C. Bradley on pp.94–5 of Laurence Lerner's *Shakespeare's Tragedies* (Harmondsworth: Penguin, 1963).
7. Ibid., 103.
8. SC, 26, 381, 386, 393, 477, 530.
9. *Selected Essays*, 130.
10. N.60 considers these matters in more detail, and the relation between love and sexuality is again the question Coleridge seeks to answer.
11. Muirhead, 252.
12. The 'Opus Magnum' manuscript also reveals the close connection in Coleridge's mind of the ideas of Reason with two of the most significant terms describing human relationships. Discussing Reason gradually imbuing Understanding, he writes, 'It is true likewise that [it is] by this process that we are enabled gradually to see the reality of the higher, the reality of the objects of reason, I mean in and for itself, and finally to know that these are indeed and pre-eminently real. If you love not your earthly parents whom you see, by what means will you love your heavenly father who is invisible? – This is true, but it holds true so far only as the reason maintains its precedency, and as the objects of reason form the ultimate aim; and cases may arise in which the reason may declare – the reason I say as the representative of the supreme Will: "He that loveth father or mother better than me, is not worthy of me." . . . Here reason appears as *the love of God*, and its antagonist is earthly love or attachment to individuals, whenever it exists in diminution of, or in competition with, the love, which is one with reason'. [Op. M. II, 16.]
13. It would be interesting to know to what extent Coleridge's conversations on this topic influenced Wordsworth. There seem to be some connections: McFarland considers that R. J. Onorato's study of *The Prelude* 'has demonstrated quite conclusively that Wordsworth's enormous and idiosyncratic sensitivity to and valuation of natural objects arose from a projection of his relationship with his mother . . .' The consequences of his mother's early death, McFarland believes, is that 'the emotional sense of what Coleridge often called "alterity" was for Wordsworth displaced . . . into the forms of nature . . .' [RFR 148]. But Wordsworth did not consciously substitute nature for the family. McFarland believes that the 'family . . . was for Wordsworth the archetype of the ideal society and the centre of all that he held holy'; he goes on to quote Wordsworth

as recorded by Crabb Robinson: '. . . he did not expect or desire
from posterity any other fame than that which would be given him
for the way in which his poems exhibit man in his essentially
human character and relations – as child, parent, husband, the
qualities which are common to all men as opposed to those which
distinguish one man from another' [RFR 172]. Wordsworth as a
poet of the family is a strange notion to us; but in his own lifetime,
and before the publication of *The Prelude*, such a self-estimation
from the author of most of the *Lyrical Ballads* is not so wide of the
mark.

14. Cf. CN II, 2921.
15. Cf. N.44, f.65v. and 75–75v.
16. Cf. *Omniana*, No. 158, p.164; CN III, 3739; Happel, 92.
17. Cf. F I, 16–17, 25, 56, 150; F II, 150–1.
18. Cf. N.51, f.13v.
19. Cf. *Aids to Reflection* (1836), 34.
20. Cf. F II, 77–9.
21. Cf. Happel, 154, and F II, 125–6.
22. Cf. Cf. F II, 110–11; N.36, p.40.
23. Cf. Happel, 155 and F II, 130, 132, 139.
24. Cf. CS 82, F I, 199, 223; N.55, f.5 and N.49, f.12ᵛ.
25. Cf. F I, 441.
26. CS 57, n.2.
27. Cf. J. R. Green, *A Short History of the English People*, 4 Vols, (1892),
    I, 58, and F. M. Stenton, *Anglo-Saxon England* (Oxford 1947), 154–5.
28. Coleridge never accepted the idea that the *humanity* of human
    beings developed from the primates, but he was perfectly willing
    to accept that there was a physiological continuity. Cf. TL 33, 41–50.
29. Cf. Happel, 655: 'Coleridge is well aware of the human condition,
    and he portrays the concrete situation accurately for his own age,
    and with a certain amount of prescience for much of the remaining
    century. With the human context of education removed (the minis-
    try of the poor and education removed from the aegis of the
    National Church), education is redefined as informaton; and knowl-
    edge becomes simply the attainment of power . . . Popular ethics,
    divorced from reflection, emerges (sic) as a "digest of the criminal
    laws", and the population becomes mechanized "into engines for
    the rich", such that the public character, the national trust
    demanded of the owner of property, becomes simply spoliation.
    One is left with superstition of wealth and the reflective publicity
    of the newspaper'. Cf. CS 61–8.
30. T. S. Eliot, *Notes towards the Definition of Culture*, 28.
31. Holmes, 70.

Bibliography

PRIMARY SOURCES

Published Works

Aids to Relection, 1825, unless otherwise indicated
Anima Poetae, ed. E. H. Coleridge (1895)
Biographia Literaria, ed. J. Shawcross, 2 vols. (Oxford: 1907)
Biographia Literaria, (CC 7) ed. James Engell and W. Jackson Bate, 2 vols. (1983)
Coleridge's Miscellaneous Criticism, ed T. M. Raysor, (1936)
Coleridge's Lectures and Notes on Shakespeare and other English Poets, ed. T. Ashe (1883)
Coleridge on Logic and Learning, ed. Alice D. Snyder (New Haven: 1929)
Coleridge's Shakespeare Criticism, ed. T. M. Raysor, 2 vols. (1930)
Coleridge on the Seventeenth Century, ed. R. F. Brinkley (New York: 1955)
Collected Letters of Samuel Taylor Coleridge, ed. E. L. Griggs, 6 vols. (Oxford 1956–71)
The Complete Poetical Works of Samuel Taylor Coleridge, ed. E. H. Coleridge, 2 vols. (Oxford: 1912)
The Complete Works of Samuel Taylor Coleridge, ed. W. G. T. Shedd, 7 vols. (New York: 1853)
On the Constitution of the Church and State, (CC 10) ed. John Colmer (1976)
Essays on His Times, (CC 3) ed. David V. Erdmann, 3 vols. (1978)
The Friend, (CC 4) ed. Barbara E. Rooke, 2 vols. (1969)
Hints Towards the Formation of a More Comprehensive Theory of Life, ed. Seth B. Watson (1848)
Inquiring Spirit, a New Presentation of Coleridge from His Published and Unpublished Prose Writings, ed. Kathleen Coburn (1951)
Lay Sermons (CC 6) ed. R. J. White (1972)
Lectures 1795: on Politics and Religion, (CC 1) ed. Lewis Patton and Peter Mann (1971)
Lectures 1808–1819: On Literature (CC 5) ed., R. A. Foakes, 2 vols. (1987)
Letters, Conversation and Recollections of S. T. Coleridge, ed. T. Allsop (1864)
The Literary Remains of Samuel Taylor Coleridge, ed. H. N. Coleridge, 4 vols. (1836)
Logic, (CC 13) ed. J. R. de J. Jackson (1981)

335

Marginalia, (CC 12) ed. George Whalley, 5 vols., 2 published (1980-)
The Notebooks of Samuel Taylor Coleridge, ed. Kathleen Coburn, 3 vols. of text and 3 of notes published (Princeton and London: 1957-)
Notes on English Divines, ed. Derwent Coleridge, 2 vols. (1853)
Notes, Theological, Political and Miscellaneous, ed. Derwent Coleridge (1853)
The Philosophical Lectures of Samuel Taylor Coleridge, ed. Kathleen Coburn (1949)
The Poetical Works of Samuel Taylor Coleridge, ed. J. D. Campbell (1893)
Table Talk and Omniana, ed. T. Ashe (1888)
The Watchman, (CC 2) ed. Lewis Patton (1970)

Manuscripts:
Coleridge's Notebooks: Nos. 1–55, with the exception of No.29, which is in the Berg Collection in the New York Public Library, and Nos. 31 and 32, whereabouts unknown, are in the British Museum, Add. Mss. 47496–47550; Nos. 56, 59–63 and 65 are on Microfilm 48, in the Library of Reading University, which is a copy of Mss. in the possession of Victoria College Library, Toronto.
Egerton Mss. 2800 and 2801 are in the British Museum.
The three volumes of the 'Opus Maximum' manuscript are in the Victoria College Library, Toronto, and on microfilm at Reading University.

SECONDARY SOURCES

Works Cited

(i) *Books:*
Barfield, O., *What Coleridge Thought* (Oxford: 1972)
Beer, J. *Coleridge's Poetic Intelligence* (1977)
Beer, J., *Coleridge the Visionary* (1959)
Beer, J. (ed.), *Coleridge's Variety* (1974)
Berlin, I., *Vico and Herder* (1976)
Collingwood, R. G., *An Autobiography* (Oxford: 1939)
Danielou, J., *From Shadows to Reality*, trans. Dom Wulstan Hibberd (1960)
De Quincey, T., *Collected Writings* D. Masson (ed.), 14 vols. (1889–90)
Dekker, G., *Coleridge and the Literature of Sensibility* (1978)
Eliot, T. S., *The Complete Poems and Plays* (1969)
Eliot, T. S., *Notes towards the Definition of Culture* (1949)
Eliot, T. S., *Selected Essays* (1951)
Eliot, T. S., *The Use of Poetry and the Use of Criticism* (1933)
Everest, K., *Coleridge's Secret Ministry* (1971)
Gillman, J., *The Life of Samuel Taylor Coleridge* only 1 vol. (1838)
Green, J. H., *Spiritual Philosophy*, 2 vols. (1865)
Griggs, E. L. (ed.), *Poems by Hartley Coleridge* (Oxford: 1942)
Hamilton, P., *Coleridge's Poetics* (Oxford: 1983)
Happel, S., *Coleridge's Religious Imagination*, 3 vols. (Salzburg: 1983)

Harding, A. J., *Coleridge and the Idea of Love* (Cambridge: 1974)
Hartman, G. H. (ed.), *New Perspectives on Coleridge and Wordsworth* (Yale: 1971)
Hazlitt, W., *Selected Essays*, Geoffrey Keynes (ed.) (1930)
Holmes, R., *Coleridge* (Oxford: 1982)
Hough, G., *Selected Essays* (Cambridge: 1978)
House, H., *Coleridge: The Clark Lectures 1951–2* (1953)
Jasper, D., *Coleridge as Poet and Religious Thinker* (1985)
Kessler, E., *Coleridge's Metaphors of Being* (Princeton: 1979)
Lamb, C., *Collected Letters*, E. V. Lucas (ed.) 3 vols. (1935)
Lowes, J. L., *The Road to Xanadu* (1927)
McFarland, T., *Coleridge and the Pantheist Tradition* (Oxford: 1969)
McFarland, T., *Romanticism and the Forms of Ruin* (Princeton: 1981)
Moorman, M., *William Wordsworth: A Biography*, 2 vols. (Oxford: 1957)
Muirhead, J. H., *Coleridge as Philosopher* (1930)
Nethercot, A. N., *The Road to Tryermaine* (New York: 1939)
Newsome, D., *Two Classes of Men. Platonism and English Romantic Thought* (1974)
Onorato, R. J., *The Character of the Poet: Wordsworth in 'The Prelude'* (Princeton: 1971)
Orsini, G. N. G., *Coleridge and German Idealism* (Carbondale, Illinois: 1969)
Prickett, S., *Wordsworth and Coleridge: The Poetry of Growth* (Cambridge: 1970)
Pym, D., *The Religious Thought of Samuel Taylor Coleridge* (Smythe, Buckinghamshire: 1978)
Richards, I. A., *Coleridge on Imagination* (1934)
Robinson, H. C., *The Diary of Henry Crabb Robinson* T. Sadler (ed.), 3 vols. (1869)
Shaffer, E. S., *'Kubla Khan' and the Fall of Jerusalem* (Cambridge: 1975)
Stephen, L., *Hours in a Library*, 3 vols. (1892)
Warren, R. P., *Selected Essays* (New York: 1958)
Watson, G. G., *Coleridge the Poet* (1966)
Whalley, G., *Coleridge and Sara Hutchinson and the Asra Poems* (1955)
Wheeler, K. M., *The Creative Mind in Coleridge's Poetry* (1981)
Willey, B., *Samuel Taylor Coleridge* (1972)
Wordsworth, W., *The Poetical Works*, T. Hutchinson (ed.) (Oxford 1895)
Yarlott, G., *Coleridge and the Abyssinian Maid* (1971)
Yeats, W. B., *Collected Poems* (1933)

(ii)*Articles:*
Angus, D. 'The Theme of Love and Guilt in Coleridge's Three Major Poems', JEGP (59 1960) 658 ff.
Basler, R. P., '*Christabel*: A Study of its Sexual Theme', *Sewanee Review* 51 (Jan-March 1943) 73–95
Beer, J., 'Coleridge, Hazlitt, and "Christabel" ' *The Review of English Studies*, N. S. Vol. XXXVII, No. 145 (Feb. 1986) 40–54
Bostetter, E. E., '*Christabel*: The Vision of Fear', *the Philological Quarterly*, Vol.XXXVI (11 April 1957) 183–94

Boulger, J. D., 'Coleridge: Marginalia, Myth-Making and the Later Poetry', *Studies in Romanticism* vols. 11–12 (1972–3) 304–19

Coburn, K., 'Coleridge and Wordsworth and the "Supernatural" ', *University of Toronto Quarterly*, 25 (June 1956) 121–30

Cooke, M. G., 'The Manipulation of Space in Coleridge's Poetry', in *New Perspectives on Coleridge and Wordsworth* G. H. Hartmann (ed.), 165–94

Delson, A., 'The Symbolism of the Sun and Moon in *The Rime of the Ancient Mariner*', *Texas Studies in Language and Literature*, XV (1974), 707–20

Fogel, D. M., 'A Compositional History of the BIOGRAPHIA LITERARIA', *Studies in Bibliography*, XXX (1977), 219–94

Hardy, B., 'Keats, Coleridge and Negative Capability', *Notes and Queries*, 197 (July 1982), 299–301

Harper, G. M., 'Coleridge's Conversation Poems', *Quarterly Review*, 244 (April 1925), 284–298

Hayden, J. O., 'Coleridge's "Dejection: An Ode" ', *English Studies* (April 1971), 1–5

Lovejoy, A. O., 'Coleridge and Kant's Two Worlds', in *Essays in the History of Ideas* (Baltimore: 1948), 254–76

Magnuson, P. A., 'The Dead Calm in the Conversation Poems', *The Wordsworth Circle* (Spring 1972), 53–60

Magnuson, P. A., ' "The Eolian Harp" in Context', *Studies in Romanticism*, vol. 24 (1985), 3–20

Parrish, S. M., 'The Wordsworth-Coleridge Controversy', *PMLA* 73 (1958), 367–74

Piper, H. W., 'Mount Abora', *Notes and Queries*, 20 (August 1973) 286–89

Pradhan, S. V., 'The Historiographer of Reason: Coleridge's Philosophy of History', *Studies in Romanticism*, vol. 25 (1986) 39–62.

Read, H., 'Two Kinds of Poetry', *Agenda* 7 (Spring 1969), 34–40

Shaffer, E. S., 'Iago's Malignity Motivated: Coleridge's Unpublished "Opus Magnum" ', *Shakespeare Quarterly*, XIX No.3 (Summer 1968), 305–24

Shaffer, E. S., 'Metaphysics of Culture: Kant and Coleridge's *Aids to Reflection*', *Journal of the History of Ideas*, XXXI (April-June 1970), 199–218

Snyder, S., 'The Manuscript of "Kubla Khan" ', *TLS* (2 Aug. 1934), 541

Whalley, G., 'The Integrity of the *Biographia Literaria*', *Essays and Studies* (6 1953), 87–101

Works Consulted

(i) *Books*:
Abrams, M. H., *The Mirror and the Lamp* (New York: 1958)

Appleyard, J. A., *Coleridge's Philosophy of Literature* (Harvard and London: 1965)

Auerbach, E., *Mimesis: The Representation of Reality in Western Literature* (Princeton: 1953)

Bald, R. C., *Literary Friendships in the Age of Wordsworth* (1932)

Barth, J. R., *Coleridge and Christian Doctrine* (Harvard: 1969)

Barth, J. R., *The Symbolic Imagination* (Princeton: 1977)
Bate, W. J., *Coleridge* (London and New York: 1969)
Blunden, E. and Griggs, E. L. (eds.), *Coleridge Studies by Several Hands on the Hundredth Anniversary of his Death* (1934)
Boulger, J. D., *Coleridge as Religious Thinker* (Yale: 1961)
Brett, R. L., *Writers and their Background: S. T. Coleridge* (1971)
Calleo, D. P., *Coleridge and the Idea of the Modern State* (New Haven: 1966)
Chambers, E. K., *Coleridge* (Oxford: 1938)
Colmer, J. *Coleridge Critic of Society* (1959)
Collingwood, R. G., *The Idea of History* (Oxford: 1961)
Coulson, S. J., *Newman and the Common Tradition* (Oxford: 1970)
Croce, B., *The Philosophy of Giambattista Vico*, trans. R. G. Collingwood (1913).
Enscoe, G., *Eros and the Romantics* (The Hague and Paris: 1967)
Fruman, N., *Coleridge, the Damaged Archangel* (1972)
Haven, R., *Patterns of Consciousness* (Massachusetts: 1969)
Hayner, P. C., *Reason and Existence: Schelling's Philosophy of History* (Leiden: 1967)
Jackson, J. R. de J. (ed.), *Coleridge: the Critical Heritage* (1969)
Jackson, J. R. de J., *Method and Imagination in Coleridge's Criticism* (1969
Knights, B., *The Idea of the Clerisy in the Nineteenth Century* (1978)
Lukács, J., *Historical Consciousness* (New York: 1968)
Mill, J. S., *Mill on Bentham and Coleridge*, F. R. Leavis (ed.) (1950)
Preyer, R., *Bentham, Coleridge, and the Science of History* (Bochum-Langendreer: 1958)
Prickett, S., *Religion and Romanticism* (Cambridge: 1976)
Sanders, C. R., *Coleridge and the Broad Church Movement* (Durham, N. Carolina: 1942)
Suther, M. *The Dark Night of Samuel Taylor Coleridge* (New York: 1960)
Vico, G., *La Scienza Nuova* trans. T. G. Bergin and M. H. Fisch (Cornell: 1968)
Wheeler, C. M., *Sources, Processes and Methods in the Biographia Literaria* (Cambridge: 1980)
Wallace, C. M., *The Design of the Biographia Literaria* (1983)
White, R. J., *The Political Thought of Samuel Taylor Coleridge* (1938)
White, R. J. (ed.), *The Political Tracts of Wordsworth, Coleridge and Shelley* (1964)

(ii) *Articles:*
Chayes, I. H., 'Coleridge, Metempsychosis, and "Almost All the Followers of Fenelon" ', *Journal of English Literary History*, 25 (Dec. 1958), 290 315
Chayes, I. H., 'A Coleridgean Reading of *The Ancient Mariner*', *Studies in Romanticism*, IV (1965)
Chayes, I. H., ' "Kubla Khan" and the Creative Process', *Studies in Romanticism* VI (1966), 1–21
Colmer, J., 'Coleridge and the Life of Hope', *Studies in Romanticism*, vol. 11–12 (1972–3), 332–41

Gerard, A., 'Counterfeiting Infinity: 'The Eolian Harp' and the Growth of Coleridge's Mind', JEGP (LX No. 3 July 1961), 411–22

Gerard, A., 'The Systolic Rhythm: the Structure of Coleridge's Conversation Poems', *Essays in Criticism*, X (1960), 307–19

Harrex, S. C., 'Coleridge's Pleasure-Dome in "Kubla Khan" ', *Notes and Queries* (1966), 172–3

Haven, R., 'The Mariner in the Nineteenth Century', *Studies in Romanticism*, vols. 11–12 (1972–3), 360–74

Miller, C. W., 'Coleridge's Concept of Nature', *Journal of History of Ideas*, XXV (1964), 77–96

Mercer, D., 'The Symbolism of "Kubla Khan" ', *Journal of Aesthetic and Art Criticism* (12 1953), 44–65

Moorman, C., 'The Imagery of "Kubla Khan" ', *Notes and Queries* (Sept. 1959), 321–24

Patterson, C. I. Jr., 'The Daemonic in *Kubla Khan*: Toward an Interpretation', PMLA 89 (Oct. 1974), 1033–42

Raine, K., 'Traditional Symbolism in "Kubla Khan" ', *Sewanee Review*, 72 (1964), 626–42

Raysor, T. M., 'Coleridge and Asra', *Studies in Philology*, XXVI (July 1929), 305–24

Wellek, R., 'German and English Romanticism: A Confrontation', *Studies in Romanticism*, vol. 4 (1964), 35–56

Wells, C. A., 'Man and Nature: An Elucidation of Coleridge's rejection of Herder's Thought', JEGP (LI 1952), 314–25

Whalley, G., 'The Mariner and the Albatross', *University of Toronto Quarterly*, XVI No. 4 (July 1947), 381–98

Woodring, C., 'The Mariner's Return', *Studies in Romanticism*, Vols. 11–12 (1972–73), 375–80

Index

mistake of presuming God as
 object not act, 20
personal being of the Co-eternal
 Son of, xix
subsumed in the real name of,
 xiv
the other great Bible of God the
 Book of Nature, 211
the truly Beloved as symbol of,
 148
the world as transcript of
 Himself, 211
union of his personality with his
 infinity, 175
government, the basis of, 270
Gray, Thomas, 'Ode to Spring',
 143
guilt, 122–6, 271

Hampden, John, x
happiness, a fountain of
 intellectual activity, 130
harassers, and hunters of
 mankind, 268
Harding, A. J., 152, 165
Harper, G. M., 32, 88
Hartley, David, 186–7
Hazlitt, x; 49; cf. Coleridge, x–xii;
 C.'s verse obituary of, xi
Hebrews, all to be Kings and
 Priests, 244
history
all histories providential and
 Christ-seeking, 246
as an adequate object of
 knowledge, cf. Nature, 3, 4
as freedom, 181
classified by epochs, 240
facts as forms of historical proof,
 283
Hebraic and Hellenic h. uniting
 in Christ, 6, 222
Hebrew h. the prototype of all
 histories, 301–2
historians who worship a dead
 thing, 218
idea of history to be derived
 from our humanity, 220

meaningless without Christ and
 Christianity, 232
sense not the basis of historical
 judgement, 219
the revelation of mind, 221, 222
the story of history universal,
 221
three kinds of according to C.,
 220
Holmes, Richard, 292
Homer, 301
Hough, Graham, 7
House, Humphry, 46, 51, 77
human/humanity
a datum to be disclosed not
 invented, 47
best parts of human language
 derived from the mind, 45
Christ the eternal humanity
 working in us, 161
divine distinguished from the
 human, 151
divine h., Logos Philanthropos,
 alienated from law, 230
hollowness of human
 friendship, 162
ideas the peculia of our
 humanity, 164
one of the marks of, xv
real goodness of, xiv
revelation of our h. by the
 supernatural, 11–12
the proper end of our human
 relations, 34–5
the stages by which man realizes
 his humanity, 242–3
WW tracing in *LB* the primary
 laws of our nature, 11–12
Hume, David, 220
Hutchinson, Mary, 105
Hutchinson, Sara, 3, 4, 103, 105,
 230–1, 266–7: **Ch. 5 passim**
as C.'s God-bearing image, 150
as C.'s sense of Being, 174

idea
and effective image, 55
and mistaken objects, 265

their right relations and Prospero's return, 251, 254

their union creative of a symbol, 132

their union the object of religion, 165, 221

Trinity the model of their relations, 199

tyranny of the U. and the ideas of Reason, 284–5

united by imagination, 189

redeemer, 265–7; *see also* mediator, and angel, guardian

Christabel's redeemer, 82–6

clerisy as redeemers of the nation, 292

'Do I need to be redeemed, and have I a redeemer?', 233

need and necessity of a Redeemer, 321

redemption, 37

a blessing in the communion of the redeemed, 296

as the necessity arising from original sin, 231

basis of salvation of Hebrew nation, 223

C. has doubts about redemption by the cross, 190–1

Christianity the great redemptive process, 286

conditions of r. as represented by Israel-Judah, 246

craving for sympathy anti-redemptive, 153

guardian saint as enabling, 114

individual salvation C.'s prime concern, 152

influences of nature redemptive for Peter Bell, 185

life as a process of, 125–6

material and moral worlds under one scheme of r., 329

redemption essentially generative, 233, 243

the events of Jesus' life the path to r., 244

the focus of C's two kinds of poetry, 88

two-foldness of redemptive process, 168–9

relationships, 'Christabel' a network of, 73

religion

centre of gravity of a realm, 285

consolation of religion and philosophy, 297

defined as reverence of invisible substantiated by love, 152

enthusiastic Religion cf. stupid Superstition, 219

evidence of true Greek r. in the mysteries, 227

Greek mysteries, evil, and the hope of a redeemer, 227–8, 231

Greek religion began in the senses, 226

having a moral origin, 190

idealess in this country, 294

identified with true philosophy, 185

its likeness to Reason, 164, 276

law and religion, 271

religion and the arts channels for Reason, 285

religious meanings and the unity of life, **18–32**

the personal as the ground of religion, 165

the two great moments of Christian religion, 231

without reason changes itself into superstition, 273

repentance, 242

return, the r. of the Conversation Poems, **32–40**, 39, 43, 88

of the Mariner, 51

revelation, 225

revolution, The French, 231, 273

Richards, I. A., 205

Robinson, Henry Crabb, 18, 20, 200, 248

rottenness, pillared r. of the world, xi

Rousseau, J. J., 269

Russell, Bertrand, x

love, and the significance of symbols, 149
national history s. of inward life, 120
nature not a symbol but a metaphor, 206
representing the unity of life, 23–4
symbol and paradox, 168
symbols of primary imagination and the 'infant Christ', 5
symbol distinguished from metaphor, 167
the truly Beloved as s. of God, 148
sympathy, craving for, 153

Taylor, Jeremy, x, 60
Thomson, James, 202
thought, imperishability of, 321
tithes, 277
trade, and literature, 272
Trinity, The
a subject-object relationship, 177
and our indwelling humanity, 263
and the end of society, 264
as model of human consciousness, 221
as model for relations of Reason and Understanding, 199
C. dissatisfied with three Persons of the T. 237
dogma of the T. arose from Jesus himself, 168
no Trinity no God, 173
second Person of assumed humanity before incarnation, 236–7
the psychology of the Trinity, 173–7
unfollowed model of self-consciousness, 191, 193, 199
truth, distinguished from particular facts, 307
frozen in the Whitehall mortuary, 280

not bed-ridden in the dormitory of C.'s soul, 2
typology, 240, 242

Understanding, 162–3; *see also* Reason
and the Greeks, 222
Caliban as Understanding divorced from Reason, 252–4
existing without Reason, 162–3
forms of U. and the appearances of Nature, 197, 198
Greeks matured their U. by reflection, 6
ideas proceed from U. paradoxically, 164
organ of the sensuous and the finite, 162
powers of U. distinguish men, not Reason, 267
provides the possibility of experience, 4
serpent as the symbol of, 60–1, 81, 224
Sir Leoline judges only by means of, 75
unity
and sense perception, 20ff.
and the *Biographia*, 200
from the disparate perceptions of the Dejection Ode, 100–1
God the unity of every nation, 36, 285
God the absolute u. making all union possible, 132
of nature realized through love, 150
ultimate end of human thought, 209

Vico, Giambattista, *La Scienza Nuova*, 240–3, 246
denies knowability of Nature, cf. History, 3
vision, where there is no v., 285

Warren, Robert Penn, 51
Watson, George, 32